HOW WE WON THE RYDER CUP

Norman Dabell, a member of the Association of Golf Writers, has been covering golf since 1979. A former deputy editor of *Golf Illustrated*, once the oldest golf magazine in the world, he has been a freelance journalist and broadcaster since 1989. He was BBC Radio Five's golf reporter for ten years and currently writes for Reuters international news agency and the *Daily Telegraph*, and broadcasts for BBC Radio Ulster. His other books are: *How We Won the Open*; *Winning the Open, How We Did It*; *One Hand on the Claret Jug*; and *Natural Hazard*, an uproarious diary of his mishaps while working on the European Tour.

HOW WE WON THE RYDER CUP

The Caddies' Stories

NORMAN DABELL

FOREWORD BY **IAN WOOSNAM**

**Contributions from Bernhard Langer,
Sam Torrance, Bernard Gallacher
and Seve Ballesteros**

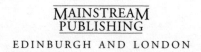

MAINSTREAM
PUBLISHING
EDINBURGH AND LONDON

This edition, 2006

First published in Great Britain in 1997 by
MAINSTREAM PUBLISHING COMPANY (EDINBURGH) LTD
7 Albany Street
Edinburgh EH1 3UG

ISBN 978 1 84596 167 1 (from January 2007)
ISBN 1 84596 167 6

Revised and updated, 1998, 2003, 2005

A catalogue record for this book is available from the British Library

Typeset in Stone Print
Printed in Great Britain by
William Clowes Ltd, Beccles, Suffolk

ACKNOWLEDGEMENTS

My eternal gratitude, as always, goes to that wonderful band of brothers, and a sister or two, the caddies, whose contributions have made this book possible. Thank you for your time and your patience. Thanks also to Ian, Bernhard, Sam, Mark, Seve, Bernard and Tony for your help.

CONTENTS

FOREWORD

BY IAN WOOSNAM

EUROPEAN CAPTAIN 2006

The team spirit in the European locker-room is what has carried us when we've been the underdogs, and it's carried us when we've been the favourites. I've now experienced it as a player and as a captain, and the great atmosphere between the lads has been so important. I'm not saying the Americans have not got on. It's just that we've always seemed to have the edge on that score. And the caddies, with their never-ending fund of jokes and anecdotes, just add to the spirit of things in the locker-room. That's priceless when you're under all the stress of the Ryder Cup.

But they're not just jokers. Over the years, we've had a string of first-class caddies who really know the golfing business. The experience of many of them has been absolutely vital in Ryder Cups. Not just yardages and reading lines, but saying the right thing at the right time, almost knowing what their player is thinking.

I've been lucky with my caddies. I had Phil Morbey, better known as Wobbly, of course, on the bag for many, many years, and we were great friends. It was hardly employer–employee. We had a great relationship. I can tell you, José Maria snapped him up when I decided I might not be playing so much and he would be best to move on to earn a better living. Now I've got the big white chief of the caddies, Martin Rowley. He was such a great help behind the scenes at the Ryder Cup.

FOREWORD

BY BERNHARD LANGER

EUROPEAN CAPTAIN 2004

Caddies are a very important part of the Ryder Cup. They can give a morale boost on the course and in the team room. It is important to keep players upbeat and happy. One of the caddies' jobs is to provide a positive outlook rather than a negative one. You will be what you think you are, so the caddies' input can prove vital.

In the early days, caddies sometimes felt they were second-class citizens, having to put up with poor hotels, poor food and poor travel. Now the caddies have everything pretty well catered for. Players don't play for money in the Ryder Cup and the caddies don't earn anything either, so they have to be taken care of very well, otherwise they may not be able to do a good job. Sometimes they have to walk five rounds in three days and that can be exhausting.

Most players have professional caddies. Very few have a different caddie each week, and that speaks for itself. Guys want someone they can trust, rely on, share things with and get advice from, whether it is concerning club selection or whatever. Some players don't want a lot from a caddie, don't ask which club, don't ask for the line of a putt; they just want someone to carry the bag, take care of their needs, be prepared and be on time. Others totally rely on the caddie and for them the caddie is all-important. We couldn't be there without a caddie. We wouldn't want to carry our own bags and without them something would be missing.

Under the unique pressure of the Ryder Cup, the caddie's input can be crucial. When the adrenalin is flowing, sometimes you don't think clearly. You can measure ten yards from a sprinkler-head and add it rather than subtract it, for instance, and suddenly you are 20 yards out. That's why a good caddie is needed. When you are down about your game, which is quite often, a positive caddie, instead of criticising you and making things worse, can lift you, remind you that you can play a bit and that you don't lose your swing in 20 minutes! A caddie can make you focus on your next shot, say something to get you into the present. That is when we play best – in the present, not in the past.

What I have felt is Europe's greatest asset in my eleven Ryder Cups, ten playing and one as captain, is the camaraderie, the friendships that are created and the closeness of everybody, the team, the wives and girlfriends – and the caddies.

FOREWORD

BY SAM TORRANCE

EUROPEAN CAPTAIN 2002

To get it right on a golf course you need to have a lot of things in your favour. You need a certain amount of talent for the game, of course, patience, determination, and not a small modicum of luck some of the time. Apart from the luck side of it, the other aspects are all in your own hands. But the difference between winning and losing can often be in someone else's hands, too – those of your caddie.

Just saying the right thing at the right time, building your confidence, or having the know-how to confirm what you might be thinking, even changing your mind occasionally – your caddie is your shoulder to lean on. Club selection is the player's responsibility, but you can't get that right every time unless you get the right advice . . . and definitely the right yardage. If you can get on with playing your best and leaving everything else to a reliable caddie, that's a load off your mind. They need to take all your moods and your tempers: if you've had a bad night, bad breakfast . . . they've got to put up with it. It's just another part of the job. If you are a full-time professional you actually spend more time with your caddie than you do with your wife! So the relationship between you is imperative, more so than the clubbing.

My caddie now is John Wilkie. John was best man at my wedding. I've known him for 30 years. He'd never caddied in his life before, but it seems to be working great – because we've got a good relationship.

I began my career with one of the best, Willie Aitchison, the man who helped Lee Trevino win two Open Championships and Roberto de Vicenzo another. Brian Dunlop was then by my side at that first momentous occasion for me at The Belfry, when we won the 1985 Ryder Cup, the first time the Americans had been beaten for 28 years. Then it was Malcolm Mason sharing with me more Ryder Cup triumphs and heartaches. Now it's John. Not a bad little quartet that, is it?

The most important thing of all, though, is that all my caddies were, and remain, great friends of mine.

The best feeling between a player and a caddie is when you win. The look on their faces . . . They're genuinely delighted for you – and they're looking forward to their 10 per cent!

Malcolm and John were my quartermasters and drivers at The Belfry to help us win the 2002 Ryder Cup. That is how much I valued their experience as part of a well-worked-out operation to beat the Americans. They were vital links in the chain of command, because winning the 2002 Ryder Cup was rather like a military operation. Nothing was left to chance.

It is very comforting, too, when you know you have old heads in the game like Pete Coleman and Andy Prodger on the bags of your two senior players. Monty might have been my rock on the course, but I know how much he valued the quiet words of Prodge in the heat of battle. And when you realise Pete has been with Bernhard through three decades, you know you not only have two masterful players to provide you with strength and experience at the top, but a pretty formidable four-man team. Then there was Billy Foster. Billy still looks a young lad, but he was taking part in his seventh Ryder Cup. You can't buy experience like that. It has to be earned, and Billy has earned it. He knows the team mentality and he's a cool man in a crisis, just what you want – a good team man with a stack of experience. He's only caddied for me once – when Malcolm was on his honeymoon – and I won the tournament with Billy. Malcolm didn't miss out, by the way. He and Billy both got a percentage.

The player and caddie are a team. With hindsight, one of the reasons, in fact the main reason, for our success at The Belfry was that we were a team. We pulled together when there were disappointments and drove home our advantage together when we were on top. There were no individuals, no one expecting preferential treatment, and no one left on his own to worry about anything. The European team was a unit and the caddies were part and parcel of that.

Our 2002 Ryder Cup caddies were fantastic. I tried to do what I could for them. They all had their own single rooms at The Belfry and a few other comforts, such as a cashmere sweater for the last day. I showed my appreciation by presenting each of them with commemorative yardage book holders, personalised to them from me. I regarded them as being just as important as the players.

FOREWORD

BY SEVERIANO BALLESTEROS

EUROPEAN CAPTAIN 1997

Severiano Ballesteros, a 'rake-rat' himself when he carried bags as a kid at his home club Pedrena, has employed more caddies than the Lyons Corner Shops. When it came to his captaincy in 1997 he found he had 13 enthusiastic carriers under his command, including his own bagman, Englishman Julian Phillips, nickname 'The Ferret'.

'Caddies play a vital part in any tournament and especially the Ryder Cup. They have all their normal duties and they are there to support their player, and give him encouragement and understanding when he needs it.

'There have been rumours that my relationships with caddies over the years have been bad, but it is not true. Sometimes characters clash, sometimes the player is not too happy, and then comes the parting of the ways. But I have always had respect for the worth of a caddie.

'Before the 1997 Ryder Cup I had a meeting with all the caddies and I impressed on each of them the need to make sure they kept cool and calm all week, because that way it brushes off on the player. The last thing you want is too much excitement.

'I think our caddies are fantastic, and that was a great help in winning at Valderrama.'

FOREWORD

BY BERNARD GALLACHER

EUROPEAN CAPTAIN 1991–95

I love the way caddies always say 'we' did this and 'we' did that. It sums up perfectly the very nature of the caddie–player relationship. How 'we' won the Ryder Cup. Indeed. And how 'they' lost it! That would probably be the caddies' philosophy. But, joking aside, golf is most certainly a game which nowadays demands two people out there doing their best – the caddie as well as the player. And that is particularly so in Ryder Cup matches.

There are 12 players and 12 caddies against America. They make up the team. Each one has a job to do and although it is the players who have to get the play right, it is vital that they have the right person alongside them while they assess every shot and every putt.

No other golf competition places more pressure on a player than the Ryder Cup, and having the correct advice and encouragement from the second person in the team can prove the difference between winning or losing their match – and, in many cases, the Cup itself.

When I first became captain at Kiawah Island in 1991, one or two of the players wanted to take their friends along on the bag. They were treating the match almost as a social occasion. I made them see the error of their ways and pointed out to them that, of all the weeks in the year, that was the one when they most needed their professional caddie. After all, the caddies have played a major part in the players getting into the Ryder Cup team in the first place. To most of them, it is the pinnacle of their careers. They want to beat the Americans as much as the players do and their enthusiasm for victory is infectious. They are so supportive.

I knew, for example, that I could always rely on a caddie for a straight answer when I had to weigh up how a player was playing in order to put the best pairs out. They wouldn't pull any punches on how their man was practising. They know the player almost as well as he knows himself.

Most players don't really like to change their caddies a lot because a regular caddie will know all their idiosyncrasies, their mannerisms, and how they prepare. The regular caddie will know if the player is a little bit jumpy on the first tee, and will know when they have to shut up. They know their man's moods.

Not all of the players and caddies are quite as in tune with one another as the team of Bernhard Langer and Peter Coleman, though. They were together for a long time. Peter is probably one of the best caddies in the world, and they did things to the very letter. Everything has to be spot-on and I know that, but I couldn't resist a chuckle at them while we were practising at Kiawah Island in '91.

Their course management was well renowned, even in practice rounds, and I was watching them going through their paces while playing with one of the inexperienced players that year, Colin Montgomerie. I used to put the first-timers in with players like Langer and Faldo in practice to help blood them.

They were going down the first hole and Peter and Bernhard were all set to measure up the yardages as they went along. Montgomerie and his caddie Kevin [Jasper Carrot] Laffey had already been out the day before and Peter shouted across the fairway to Kevin, 'How far is it from that water hydrant to the green?' Kevin shouted back, 'It's 173 yards.' Bernhard and Peter shouted back in unison, 'Is that from the front of the hydrant or the back of it?' We were talking about something like five or six inches in diameter! I'm not sure whether or not they were serious. But it wouldn't surprise me if they were. They are such professionals.

We have moved with the times to make sure that the Ryder Cup caddies are treated professionally as well. For the 1995 Ryder Cup, the committee decided that the caddies should travel with their players instead of making their own way. There were spare seats on Concorde, so everyone arrived at the same time. That got us off on the right foot straight away. We were all as one. I think the wonderful camaraderie that week within the European contingent was the single most contributory factor in bringing back the Ryder Cup from Oak Hill.

INTRODUCTION

Another resounding victory in 2004, this time at The K Club in Ireland, continued Europe's dominance of the Ryder Cup, making it a hat-trick of wins. The team was this time piloted by another of the great battlers in the biennial event, Ian Woosnam. The little Welshman had featured on winning teams four times, as well as in the 1989 halved match. He returned, at the helm, to follow in the footsteps of Tony Jacklin, Bernard Gallacher, Seve Ballesteros, Sam Torrance and Bernhard Langer, and lift Sam Ryder's trophy in triumph as a victorious captain.

Jacklin was the first in modern times to prise the trophy, instituted in 1927 by seed merchant Ryder, from America's grasp, six years after the team became Europe instead of just Great Britain and Ireland. He ended a 28-year stranglehold at The Belfry in 1985, which is where these Ryder Cup accounts begin.

In 1985, Torrance was the pivotal player, the emotional Scot who wept tears of joy as Europe at last delivered. Then, in 1987, against the odds, Europe broke new ground, winning for the first time on American soil. The Belfry provided the back-drop in 1989 for a first half in the match for 20 years. If that year was nail-biting, then it was the same two years later as another European wept at the end of a thrilling match at Kiawah Island. This time it was Langer shedding tears of despair as his side were beaten at the death. It was desperately close again in 1993 as Europe somehow snatched defeat from the jaws of victory. America did the same in 1995 as Gallacher's men hit back on a pulsating final day. The 1997 success by Europe was the first on the European mainland as Seve – and his buggy – rolled over the US in Spain. Vengeance was sweet for America two years later, after what will go down as an infamous, rather than famous, narrow defeat for Europe at Brookline. In the 2002 Ryder Cup, a match postponed because of the horrors of 9/11 the previous year, Torrance was at it again, weeping copiously with pride as his men won back the trophy. Then Langer, in 2004 at Oakland Hills, was at last able to blot out his worst moment in the Ryder Cup with his best, as Europe secured their record result, matching the 18½–9½ success of America's 'Dream Team' of 1981. Woosnam then moved things full circle. After being part of the side that ended America's domination of the Ryder Cup 21 years before, he led his Europeans to a second-successive 9-point demolition over their rivals from across the Atlantic.

Instead of talking to the players about all these victories and, nowadays, a few defeats, I have turned to the other 12-person teams – I say person because one of them is a woman – for tales from behind the ropes from those dramatic encounters since 1985.

Caddies always talk about how 'we' did this and 'we' did that. It is a loyal 'we'. The caddies have celebrated and suffered in these Ryder Cup clashes, frequently as much as their players. Some of the caddies in these chapters have served in five and six Ryder Cups, one of them in nine, so they know what they are talking about. Read now how 'we' won the Ryder Cup – and, occasionally, how 'we' lost it!

HOW WE WON THE RYDER CUP BACK

1985: A 28-YEAR WAIT IS OVER

THE BELFRY, 13–15 SEPTEMBER
EUROPE 16½ USA 11½

CAPTAINS: Tony Jacklin (Europe)
Lee Trevino (USA)

(European names first)

Foursomes (morning):
S. Ballesteros and M. Pinero (2 and 1) 1, C. Strange and M. O'Meara 0
B. Langer and N. Faldo 0, C. Peete and T. Kite (3 and 2) 1
A. Lyle and K. Brown 0, L. Wadkins and R. Floyd (4 and 3) 1
H. Clark and S. Torrance 0, C. Stadler and H. Sutton (3 and 2) 1

Fourballs (afternoon):
P. Way and I. Woosnam (1 hole) 1, F. Zoeller and H. Green 0
S. Ballesteros and M. Pinero (2 and 1) 1, A. North and P. Jacobsen 0
B. Langer and J.M. Canizares (half) ½, C. Stadler and H. Sutton (half) ½
S. Torrance and H. Clark 0, R. Floyd and L. Wadkins (1 hole) 1

Fourballs (morning):
S. Torrance and H. Clark (2 and 1) 1, T. Kite and A. North 0
P. Way and I. Woosnam. (4 and 3) 1, H. Green and F. Zoeller 0
S. Ballesteros and M. Pinero 0, M. O'Meara and L. Wadkins (3 and 2) 1
B. Langer and A. Lyle (half) ½, C. Stadler and C. Strange (half) ½

Foursomes (afternoon):
J.M. Canizares and J. Rivero (7 and 5) 1, T. Kite and C. Peete 0
S. Ballesteros and M. Pinero (5 and 4) 1, C. Stadler and H. Sutton 0
P. Way and I. Woosnam 0, C. Strange and P. Jacobsen (4 and 2) 1
B. Langer and K. Brown (3 and 2) 1, R. Floyd and L. Wadkins 0

Singles:
M. Pinero (3 and 1) 1, L. Wadkins 0
I. Woosnam 0, C. Stadler (2 and 1) 1
P. Way (2 holes) 1, R. Floyd 0
S. Ballesteros (half) ½, T. Kite (half) ½
A. Lyle (3 and 2) 1, P. Jacobsen 0
B. Langer (5 and 4) 1, H. Sutton 0
S. Torrance (1 hole) 1, A. North 0
H. Clark (1 hole) 1, M. O'Meara 0
J. Rivero 0, C. Peete (1 hole) 1
N. Faldo 0, H. Green (3 and 1) 1
J.M. Canizares (2 holes) 1, F. Zoeller 0
K. Brown 0, C. Strange (4 and 2) 1

THE CADDIES

DAVE MUSGROVE (SANDY LYLE 1985, 1987)

Nottinghamshire caddie, Dave Musgrove, learned his trade at Hollinwell, just across Sherwood Forest from his Kirkby-in-Ashfield home, first taking up a bag in 1955 at the age of 12.

In the 1976 French Open, Musgrove took over Seve Ballesteros's bag after his player, Vicente Fernandez, broke a finger, and that was the start of a four-year term with the Spanish maestro. After helping Seve win the famous 1979 'Car Park' Open, he switched to Sandy Lyle, carrying the bag to victory in the 1985 Open. After ten years' service with Lyle, the two parted company but, after a spell with 1993 US Open champion Lee Janzen, Musgrove and Lyle teamed up again. Musgrove declined when asked to carry Janzen's bag at the 1997 Ryder Cup, feeling it would be unfair to him and Janzen. His Ryder Cup-carrying career began when he caddied for Ken Brown in the 1977 encounter.

NICK DE PAUL (SEVERIANO BALLESTEROS 1985, 1987)

After starting his caddying career at the age of 30 in 1971, de Paul took over Ballesteros's bag in 1981. The Pennsylvanian caddie turned himself into a legend on both sides of the Atlantic for his unique method of practising. A former baseball player, de Paul used one of his old gloves to catch shots on the practice ground, even full-blooded drives. De Paul and Ballesteros's first hour came one year before their first Ryder Cup together – the Spaniard's epic Open Championship success at St Andrews in 1984. They ended their relationship as soon as the 1987 Ryder Cup finished.

PETE COLEMAN (BERNHARD LANGER
1985, 1989, 1991, 1993, 1995, 1997, 2002)

Pete Coleman's baptism of fire in Ryder Cups was alongside Tommy Horton in 1977 at Royal Lytham and the Surrey man has made an indelible mark on the Ryder Cup ever since with Bernhard Langer. Pioneer Coleman was the first caddie to gain a sponsor and the first to buy a Porsche with his winnings as he became the first celebrity bagman. A glittering array of talent has paraded alongside him, as he has tramped the fairways with the likes of Seve Ballesteros, Greg Norman and Nancy Lopez as well as Langer. The former assistant golf professional and railwayman who introduced the yardage measuring-wheel to the caddie circuit had two stints on Ballesteros's bag, in 1980 and 1983. Coleman rejoined Langer in 1985 to help the German to his first US Masters success. Another Augusta triumph followed in 1993 and the Coleman–Langer partnership endured for seven Ryder Cups.

ROY HOLLAND (NICK FALDO 1985)

West Midlander Roy Holland lived only a couple of par-fives away from The Belfry, so his call-up to take over Nick Faldo's bag at short notice for the 1985 Ryder Cup was a handy move. Holland's quiet, respectful demeanour was perfect for a Faldo going through the trials of a swing change in '85, and the Midlands caddie could also call upon previous Ryder Cup experience. He was with Brian Waites when the Nottinghamshire professional made his Ryder Cup debut at the age of 43 in the 1983 match at the PGA National course. Holland went on to accompany the prolific Tommy Horton to a succession of wins on the European Seniors Tour.

WARREN DARRELL (PAUL WAY 1985)

As a schoolboy Warren Darrell wanted to become a professional golfer, as did the friend he met at the Berkshire club where he occasionally caddied, Paul Way. Darrell followed up his ambition by taking a job in the pro shop on a YTS scheme at the Berkshire. After six months, Darrell realised he was not going to make the grade as a tour professional. So he went for the next-best thing and took on caddie duties for his friend, six months after Way joined the professional ranks in 1982. The pair, just out of their teens, featured alongside Seve Ballesteros in the 1983 Ryder Cup and went on to appear at The Belfry two years later, before Darrell left the caddying ranks.

TOM CULLEN (JOSÉ MARIA CANIZARES 1985, 1989)

It was rather fitting that a caddie nicknamed 'The Fireman' should carry the bag for a José. Tom Cullen did so successfully for three Ryder Cups, standing by José Maria Canizares in 1981 at Walton Heath before his memorable successes with the craggy-featured Spanish veteran in 1985 and 1989, both times at The Belfry. The two met in the mid-'70s, as Cullen explains: 'José had employed a local caddie who was a bit of a piss artist. He sacked him as soon as they walked off the range. He'd noticed me watching from the ropes and came up to me and asked if I'd like to see the golf closer up that week. If so, how would I like to caddie for him?'

BRIAN DUNLOP (SAM TORRANCE 1985, 1987)

Ayr man Brian Dunlop emigrated with his parents to Australia and renewed acqaintances with Sam Torrance to help him win the Australian PGA Championship. When Dunlop visited Britain for his brother's wedding in 1981, he decided to stay on and caddie full-time for Torrance. Torrance's Irish Open success clinched him his Ryder Cup place but their first taste of the match proved a bitter one in 1981, as Europe were hammered by, arguably, the best team ever assembled by the USA. Dunlop then stood by the side of Torrance when the triumphant winning putt went in at The Belfry in 1985, and the pair were together at Muirfield Village for the first victory on American soil. Soon after the 1987 success, Dunlop returned to Australia and his electrician's job.

THE ACTION

'So Sam then goes in with a nine-iron I handed him. Perfect. It pitched up and screwed back just before the big drop down off the tier. Then he holed the putt. History!'

The arrival of Tony Jacklin as Ryder Cup captain for the 1983 Ryder Cup at the PGA National course in America heralded a new dawn for Europe, who discovered that they might just be good enough to end America's quarter of a century of dominance. Europe found pride and confidence in a marginal defeat which went to the wire before they were pipped by just a point. A Lanny Wadkins chip for a half with José Maria Canizares was the key to victory in the end. It left American captain Jack Nicklaus kissing Wadkins's divot in relief and Jacklin determined not to let victory get away again.

Sandy Lyle's pithy bagman Dave Musgrove, who vividly remembered the last time the Americans had been toppled at Lindrick, just up the road from his Nottinghamshire home, was delighted when Jacklin took over. 'Jacklin was a winner, a big-occasion man, and he was perfect for the job. He wanted everything first class and he got it,' says Musgrove. This included insisting on the Europeans having their regular caddies accompany them to America on free flights.

Jacklin accepted the 1985 captaincy, where he would come up against the man who had denied him in the 1972 Open Championship, Lee Trevino. Trevino was a tough opponent – he called his team 'cry babies' when they complained about the partisan Belfry gallery's behaviour – but Jacklin proved tougher, especially with an on-course captain to rely on in Seve Ballesteros. Ballesteros again proved the inspiration, winning three of his four pairs matches with his 'alter ego', the quiet and unexcitable Manuel Pinero. They were the only ones to find success on the first morning but at the end of the first day Europe were only a point behind. This was thanks to a second win by the Spaniards, victory by the new partnership of Paul Way and Ian Woosnam, and a half through Bernhard Langer and José Maria Canizares.

Ballesteros was tireless, and his American caddie Nick de Paul had to do a manful job to keep up with the charismatic Spaniard. De Paul was used to the fiery Ballesteros, though, his temperament and his never-say-die spirit. He revelled in the way Ballesteros attacked the deadly tenth green, the watershed for both their first-day rounds. And de Paul cared not a jot whether he was being criticised for working in the 'enemy's' camp:

'It was curious to be American in the European team, but if things were said against me back home or if I was not popular with the American side, I wasn't aware of anything. I guess it was strange, but anybody who really knew me wouldn't have been surprised. I'd been caddying for Seve for a number of years and I wasn't going to give up the bag for patriotic reasons. It was my job.

'I knew The Belfry because we'd been there for a couple of tournaments. Seve was in great form that year and I'd been with him for several wins on the European Tour on our way to the Ryder Cup. So we were raring to go. I fully expected him to be playing with Rivero, but I guess Jacklin wasn't too impressed with Rivero's practising. We were out with Manuel Pinero instead.

'We got well in front early on against Curtis Strange and Mark O'Meara, four-up after six, but then we lost a couple of holes. Seve got us back by hitting the tenth green, though, and Strange and O'Meara just had too much to do from then on. It was a three-wood that did the trick in the morning at the tenth. Both times we had about 275 yards and Seve did it again in the afternoon fourballs, this time against Andy North and Peter Jacobsen. They were giving us a tough time until then, but Seve hit in to only 20 feet or so and that kind of knocked the stuffing out of the opponents, just like it had in the morning.'

The Bernhard Langer–Nick Faldo partnership had been highly successful in 1983, with three wins out of four. Jacklin could be forgiven for expecting the pair to be his main strength. Around this time, though, Faldo was deep in the throes of the major swing change with David Leadbetter that he would later reason helped him to win the 1987 Open Championship.

Faldo was far from comfortable still with his progress, but Jacklin, against the opinion of the pundits, decided to make Faldo one of his wild-cards. It was a gamble which never looked like coming off from the moment Faldo's erratic swing caused him trouble in the morning foursomes, while partnering Langer against Calvin Peete and Tom Kite. The big Englishman was unsurprised but so dismayed that he approached Jacklin and asked to be dropped. Jacklin acceded to Faldo's wishes. He did not appear again until the singles. Faldo did not make one solitary point. The pundits were proved correct.

His caddie had been brought in at the eleventh hour after Faldo had parted company with his latest bagman. His new man was Roy Holland, who lived close to The Belfry, an experienced caddie who had been with Brian Waites two years before in the West Palm Beach Ryder Cup:

'There was a lot of talk in the papers that Nick shouldn't be there because he was playing so badly. He was "dogging" it, as we caddies say, not hitting it very good and not playing well. Faldo wasn't expecting anything great and we were straight out in the first-day foursomes which isn't the best form of golf for anybody with a dodgy swing. You had to feel for Bernhard. He's a sort of "agony uncle" who seems to get lumbered with the problem players. They'd played well together at the PGA National, though, which I'd seen first hand, so we were ever hopeful it might work out.

'We were second match out and it was one of the most terrifying experiences of my life; hopefully controlled because I knew what I was doing. But it doesn't matter how long you've carried a bag and for whom. When the Union Jack and the Stars and Stripes are pulled up and you're ready to go, there are thousands of people around you and you're with Nick Faldo . . . I felt like I imagine a woman having her first baby must feel! It was a monumental experience. The guy's larger than life.

'He said to me, "I know you know your job, Roy, but I won't be asking you much. Just look after me, all the basic things, and see how we go." Well, that wasn't very well. We got into trouble on the third when he drove into a bunker and Langer couldn't get us out of the trouble. They battled well but Nick found the sand with his drive again on the ninth and they were two-down at the turn.

Whether it was getting to Bernhard or not I don't know, but he made a couple of mistakes as well and in the end we were well beaten.'

In 1985, Langer went to The Belfry as reigning US Masters champion. The dogged German came up trumps. His only defeat came in that opening foursomes partnering Faldo. From there the ice-cool Langer was untouchable. Part of the German's success is surely down to the man he had on the bag, Pete Coleman. The unassuming Coleman shrugs off the part he plays, but he was well aware of the part The Belfry gallery played in 1985, refuting the claims of such as Hal Sutton that week, that the crowd went over the top:

'There was a big crowd there wanting Europe to win. You can forgive them if they get a bit enthusiastic about the other team missing putts if it gives their team a chance to win. It's only human nature. The American gallery did just the same thing, perhaps worse, later on.

'There was a lot of support for us when we started on the first day with Nick but I'm afraid they were greatly disappointed because it just didn't work out. Nick was changing his swing and in the end he was just not hitting the ball well enough to be playing in foursomes.

'Things worked out better with Canizares in the afternoon and Bernhard found his real form. He hit two great shots in to less than four feet on ten and eleven for birdies and that gave us the cushion we needed, because it was a hard-earned half-point against Craig Stadler and Hal Sutton. It was an odd pairing for Bernhard with Canizares, that's why I think it worked. It was a new experience, but enjoyable. Bernhard can play with anybody, though.'

To offset reigning Open Champion Sandy Lyle and Langer's credentials, the American team had the US Open champion in Andy North and US PGA champion Hubert Green. Much of Europe's hopes rested on the broad shoulders of Lyle, the man who had carved a victory out of the rugged links of St George's only a few months before The Belfry showdown.

In the 1983 encounter, the partnership of Lyle and Ken Brown never got a chance to launch itself, Lyle being dropped after their opening defeat until the singles. Jacklin, however, decided to give it another try in the opening matches, despite Lyle's dislike of foursomes. It failed to work out again, as the pair lost heavily to Lanny Wadkins and Ray Floyd, on one occasion 'conned out of a hole', in the words of Lyle's caddie Musgrove:

'We're playing the third at The Belfry, into the wind on the first day. Ken Brown had the honour. He hit an iron. I thought it was a joke. My jaw dropped. We get up there and Lyle's got a three-wood to get on the green. That was pathetic. All they'd done was stand on the tee mumbling. It's 450 yards into the wind and I look round and Browny's got an iron in his hand. A joke.

'We get round to the eighth and Floyd snap-hooks it into the water. In America they've got these signals, like baseball. If it's OK, you get the arms wafted across the chest from outstretched, or a signal like a wide in cricket. If it's in the water, then you get the arm up and the thumb backwards telling you you're out of here.

'Well, with it being in England, the marshal was waving his arms to say it was in trouble, but it looked similar to the American signal saying it was OK. The fairway was bending into the water and rock hard and Floyd knew damn well it was in. But he said to Wadkins, "I think that ball's all right" – a load of rubbish because he knew it wasn't, never in a million years. It's Lyle's honour. And he takes the bait. He follows him in.

'He got conned by Floyd in the first place and by not wanting to go in the bunkers on the right in the second place. After that it was all over. The Americans didn't even have to play well.'

Matters were looking pretty dire for Europe by the time Sam Torrance and Howard Clark neared the closure of their match. Torrance's electrician caddie Brian Dunlop expected sparks to fly but had his own theory why the European pair finished up having a power-cut:

'The Europeans were fired up from the word go. Jacklin's pre-match speech had them glowing with pride and they never lost it. Trevino introduced his players and tried to prove their importance and class by how much money they'd won to show they were the better team. Well, Jacklin built up his players individually and then produced his master strokes at the end: "I give you Sandy Lyle, the Open Champion, Bernhard Langer, the Masters champion, Severiano Ballesteros, the best golfer in the world." Great psychology; a wonderful speech.

'Our first match was with Howard Clark and straight away, problems. Clarky is a great Ryder Cup player. As with his pal Jesse [Mark James], when it comes to golf, they've got a distinct dislike of the Yanks and it fires them up. But he's a nightmare to caddie for. And he hadn't got a proper caddie. It led to a lot of consulting, of course, and though I can't blame that for losing the first two matches, it obviously didn't help matters. I remember, too, having to tend the pin for Clarky all the time because his caddie, the Spalding rep Jim Trainor, had spikes on. That didn't go down well, and of course he couldn't do the yardages properly. Fair play to the guy. Clarky should never have employed him that week. But Clarky's Clarky.'

From 3–1 down, the fourballs finally kick-started Europe's victory drive. The players Jacklin announced as 'Little Woosie' and 'Way-Way' were the duo that cranked the starting-handle. Their opening-match nailbiter against Fuzzy Zoeller and Hubert Green paved the way to a two and a half to one and a half afternoon fightback which saw Europe catch up to within only a point of the Americans after the disappointments of the morning.

Jacklin had labelled Paul Way 'a cocky little bugger' when he took the Kent 20 year old – the second youngest to play a Ryder Cup at that time – on board for the 1983 event. However, Jacklin realised he might need someone with experience alongside him. Seve Ballesteros had been the Kent youngster's mentor of 1983. This time Jacklin chose the pugnacious Ian Woosnam to partner Way.

A few weeks before, Way had been struck down with tonsillitis and he confessed to being so weak when the team had been announced that he could hardly stand. But he gradually got his fitness back by working out and, come The Belfry, was ready for action, according to his caddie Warren Darrell:

'Paul's not the easiest person in golf to work for. It's a case of watch your head when the clubs start flying. He was very difficult in the early days and it always seemed to be, "It's the caddie's fault." But he's got a strong will and that showed itself again in 1985 playing with Woosie after a terrible time in the weeks before.

'Both Paul and I knew what the Ryder Cup was all about by 1985. My most vivid memory of the 1983 Ryder Cup was patting Seve on the back and saying "hard luck" and then seeing when he turned round that his eyes were full of tears. I was only 17 and suddenly it brought home to me the magnitude of the event and what it meant to players like Seve. Paul should have learned from the education Seve gave him that week. He led him round.

'I think everyone was expecting Paul to be paired with Seve again, but I think the pairing with Woosie proved just as good. They were like a couple of pocket-battleships, hitting the ball further than anyone all week.

'There were plenty of butterflies when Paul and Woosie were first off in the afternoon. Paul started off all right, but his golf deteriorated very rapidly. I'd been with Paul for the best part of five years. If I said it was a six-iron, he'd go with it. Then I'd take the consequences if I was wrong. I felt I knew when he was struggling. So I actually went up to Tony Jacklin and suggested he drop Paul for the second day, because he was playing that badly. But Tony stuck to his guns and put him back in.

'In a strange way, I think it helped. Paul was putting the world on Woosie's shoulders and Woosie came good because of it. Then Paul bucked up again. That was mainly because Paul enjoyed his week with Woosie so much. I felt Woosie brought a lot out of Paul, as much as Seve had done two years before. I think it was the first time, with Seve and Woosie, I'd ever witnessed Paul listen to anybody.'

Just one point separated the teams after the opening day. Jacklin decided to begin Saturday morning's fourballs with Torrance and Clark, despite the pair losing both their opening matches.

Torrance's caddie Dunlop hoped Clark had given his bagman a crash course in reading yardages and clubbing:

'I was giving Clarky yardage and all that kind of carry-on. Clarky holed some long putts when he and Sam did finally come off, though, on the Saturday morning. They beat Kite and North in their third match after Jacklin had decided to stick with the pairing. I tended the pin for Howard on the 11th and he holed the putt to keep things going.

'On the 15th, a three-tier green, he asked me the club. He had 84 yards to the front but 100 to the green, which made it 104 yards to the pin against a strong wind. I told him seven was too much so he went with an eight, hit the middle tier and spun right back down to the bottom. Wrong club. Howard not very happy. I'm supposed to be caddying for his partner! He just needed a wee cheat with an eight but he'd hit it too high.

'When he'd calmed down he asked me to hold the pin, because I'd brought him luck, he felt, on the 11th. The putt went in, a huge one. You've probably seen the scenes after it did. Clarky and Sam dancing around the green in those horrible yellow trousers. Then Clarky chipped in, or hit another big putt, on the 16th and it was as good as won.'

The match was tied up by the end of the second morning, through further splendid feats by Woosnam and Way, and at last that victory for Torrance and Clark. A halved match by Langer and Lyle with Craig Stadler and Curtis Strange, however, and a missed tiddler by Stadler, was to have resounding repercussions, as caddie Musgrove observes:

'Sandy was upset at being dropped the day before, but he couldn't have expected anything else. He sharpened up his swing in the afternoon instead, got his head working properly. And the next morning for the fourballs, they finally put him with Langer. It proved a turning-point for the Europeans. I couldn't understand why they didn't put him with Langer in the first place. It was obvious. Langer was going to do all the thinking. Lyle just had to hit the bleeding ball; don't worry about thinking! Him and Browny together, though? Never.

'Anyway, with Langer, they're two-down with two to play and it looked as though Sandy was still going to be on the losing side. But he was the only one who could get on the par-five green in two out of all of them. He did get on and holed a great putt all the way across the green for an eagle. Game on now. Anything can happen on the 18th at The Belfry. And it did. Langer was the only one with the bottle to make par and that won the hole, gave them a vital half.

'But Stadler should also have made a four, as we all know. He missed a tiddler, no more than 18 inches, maybe just less. That really was the key to us going on to win, I feel. I had a brilliant view of it and the ball never attempted to go in the hole. He had the putt to win the match so there was no question of it being given. But it never got near the hole. Straight after, Stadler turned and looked towards the lake. I thought he was going to throw himself in, so I thought I'd better get out of the road!'

Europe surged in front by completing a thrilling 3–1 whipping of the Americans in the afternoon foursomes. This was by dint of crushing successes by all four Spaniards in the European contingent. José Maria Canizares and wild-card José Rivero thrashed Tom Kite and Calvin Peete.

Featuring with Canizares was a Kent fireman who spoke little Spanish, but who had been on Canizares's bag at Walton Heath for the 1981 Ryder Cup demolition of the Europeans. Tom Cullen had not accompanied Canizares to Florida in 1983, when the Spaniard was held to the winning half by Lanny Wadkins, but Cullen knew how his man, 38 years old and the veteran of the European side, was determined to be on the winning team this time:

'A lot of people ask me how on earth I can communicate with José. Well, he doesn't speak English fluently and I certainly don't speak Spanish, but you'd be surprised how much English José actually does speak. He's a very private man, just a family man really, and doesn't talk a lot away from the golf course. But when we're out there he talks and I can understand his English no problem.

'During practice I think Jacklin always had in mind to have the Spaniards together, more for language, I suppose, than anything else. They were all good friends. But Rivero wasn't showing that well in practice and so Ballesteros and Pinero were put together and came off, so they were obviously going to be partners. We finished up with Bernhard Langer. I'm not sure it was a good pairing because Bernhard's a very strong character and José Maria's an extremely independent person, so they were never always going to agree on clubs. They didn't club each other much on the way round.

'They did enough to get a half out of Hal Sutton and Craig Stadler, though. And they don't come more determined than those two. José was the anchor man, though, and did his thing quietly, just backing Bernhard all the way and doing his bit. That worked fine when the Americans hit back. We did well to hold them to the half.

'It was an entirely different thing when we were paired with José Rivero for the Saturday foursomes. They were nattering all the way round because they had the same lingo, of course. They were both determined to win, loved the head-to-head feeling because they both like a bet on a game like that normally. They absolutely revelled in it and played some fantastic golf. Canizares sort of chaperoned Rivero, because it was his first Ryder Cup match, his debut. They were great friends off the course and knew each other's ways, knew how they might each be thinking when we came to a sticky situation. They read each other's putts and, really, Kite and Peete just didn't get a look-in.

'It was a slow start but the bounce forward for us came on the short seventh. Rivero hit the green and then Canizares holed this big putt across the green, actually going back over the fringe on the corner on his way to the hole. That gave them a real lift and you could tell they were going to be unstoppable after that. As we walked off I heard Tom Kite say to Calvin Peete, "Well, we really got our asses kicked, didn't we?" I just thought, "Yes, mate; you really did."'

Saturday evening saw the much-awaited singles draw revealed. Europe were desperate to extend their two-point advantage as soon as possible, to get on a roll.

Torrance's caddie Dunlop recalls how a certain Spaniard was delighted with his lot:

'I was grateful for the rest after three hard matches doing two caddies' jobs! I remember sitting at the players' table when Ken Brown holed the putt for him and Langer to beat Floyd and Wadkins. Seve gave this enormous growl, thumped the table and shot all the drinks up into the air.

'That put Europe two ahead and Seve was so fired up; we all were. Even Manuel Pinero, the quietest of men normally, was in aggressive mood. Sam told me that at the selection dinner, Pinero said, "I want Wadkins; I want Wadkins." The sheets came out and when the draw announced Pinero versus Wadkins, Manuel let out a roar nearly as loud as Seve's earlier on. He went off happy to his bed – and there was no way Lanny was going to beat him the next day.'

Already with a strong advantage, as a thrilling Sunday finale unfolded for the baying Belfry crowd, Pinero proved he was no paper tiger as he disposed of Wadkins in the opening match. Without doubt, early European successes lifted the spirits of those still out on the course and by the time Way came to the closing holes, Europe were definitely in the ascendancy. But that's when things started to go wrong, recalls caddie Darrell:

'I'm sure it was tiredness when Paul suddenly started to struggle again. He was paralysing Ray Floyd, playing golf the way Paul Way can play golf, hitting the middle of every fairway and holing some putts. Paul's putting that week was as good as I've ever seen it. He'd holed a couple of vital putts on the 18th in the pairs, one of them, I remember, a curving 15-footer to win a match. His putting was great and it was on the Sunday too. But then suddenly he started going backwards.

'The thinned sand-wedge he hit on the 16th, a fluffed chip and another fluffed chip showed he was going. You could see him giving the game to Floyd. It might have even gone that way if Floyd hadn't been forced to take a three-wood out of the bunker on 18 and dump it into the water. Paul was almost shaking in his boots. He was so twitched up and so nervous at that stage. He just couldn't hold the golf club. It's got to be a frightening position for anyone to be in because everyone – including the caddies – felt the pressure of knowing they could win the Ryder Cup at last. Every decision made, every club pulled out of the bag, could have meant the winning or losing of the Ryder Cup.

'And standing on the last tee and looking down the fairway you could see massive crowds. Behind us and alongside us, and behind the green, they were ten-deep. Absolutely incredible. I've caddied in Opens, and when you walk down the 18th the atmosphere makes the hairs on the back of your neck stand up, but this far outdid any Open.

'Paul was cringing in his boots on 18, because it's not exactly the easiest shot in golf. But while Floyd hit it across the water into the bunker, Paul happened to catch one slightly out of the toe, which gave it the perfect shape for the hole. It bent round the corner and found the middle of the fairway. Floyd then put it into the water and the pressure was lifted off Paul. But you had to bear in mind he'd played the last two or three holes like a 24-handicapper. He still had a difficult shot over the water. What he had to do was to get it on to the green. We chose a three-iron. He hit a straight shot. That's all I can say about it, semi-thin. His ball pitched just the other side of the water and took five bounces before it reached the back of the green.

'Remarkably, although Paul knew he was probably going to win the match, he was totally pissed off with the way he'd played the 18th, embarrassed for himself. That's the person he was. I just had to put my arm around him and tell him he'd done what needed to be done and forget about how it was done. I said, "Just walk across the water and take the applause."'

Before Woosnam capitulated late on to Stadler, Lyle was in command against Peter Jacobsen and Langer in total control against Sutton. The crowd demanded a Ballesteros victory.

Kite looked upon their encounter as a grudge match after Ballesteros had stirred up the American camp all week. And Kite seemed set to silence the gallery when he surged well in front of an off-colour Ballesteros and threatened to finish off the Spaniard out in the country, away from the brunt of his adoring fans. Ballesteros never knows when he is beaten, though. That just meant greater demands on caddie de Paul:

'I should have realised I was going to be in for a hard time with Seve next day when I saw the draw. For some reason Tom Kite, who I guess was their No. 1 player at that time, had it in for Seve. I think there was bad blood somewhere and Kite had said he wanted Seve. I don't know how he did it, but he actually picked Seve for the singles, so he must have had it in for him. Somehow the draw worked out just the way Kite wanted it. Seve didn't care who he played. He was going to be out there trying to win, whoever it was. I don't know what went on between him and Kite, but Seve has that way of rasping peoples' personalities, so I wasn't surprised that he and Kite were going into it like a little "head-to-head".

'Pretty well all the way to the stretch it was all Kite and I got a lot of flak from Seve, especially if I was out by half a club. That's the way he is. He's such an intense personality. A great player but intense. He wants everything to be perfect, and that's his way. He's a very difficult man to work with out on the course. I started to get a headache right from about the fourth when we bogeyed. Seve knew it was because he wasn't scoring well that Kite got on top. Kite was only level-par for nine and two-up and only one-under for thirteen and three-up.

'Seve was bunkered badly on thirteen to go three-down and steam was coming out of his ears by then. I was getting a lot of verbals. But then at last the mood changed even if my headache didn't. Seve stroked in an enormous putt on the 14th, nearly 40 feet, and his arms were pumping nearly as hard as my head! The crowd was enough to give you a headache. The noise was something else, and it was at quite a pitch when Seve holed a 15–20-footer on the next to pull it back to only one-down.

'We parred 16 – Seve had another chance for a birdie – and then he really went for it on the drive on 17. He told me he was going to cut the corner and he did, it was a fantastic drive under that kind of pressure. Only Seve . . . But then I had to go through it again when we overshot the green with a three-wood. The shot looked great, covering the flag all the way, but it got a bad kick through the green and he played a real bad chip back, even from the tough lie. Was I relieved when he sank the putt from about 12 feet to win the hole.

'The atmosphere was electric playing the last. I thought Kite was going to go in the water when he tried to cut a bit too much off but he outdrove us by easily 50 yards. Craig Stadler came running over to fire up Kite, I remember. He'd just won his singles against Ian Woosnam. And Trevino and Wadkins were there, all willing Kite to beat Seve. It would have meant so much to the American team to see the win go up for Kite. It was unthinkable to Seve, though.

'We hit a great four-iron from the semi to about 25 feet on the tier where the pin was but Tom was closer, about 15 feet. They both missed, but Seve hadn't lost – and that was mighty important, I guess, with the way things went on behind us. All I could do was think about getting out of here. I went straight into the bar and asked for aspirin. I was more wrung-out than for any match I can ever remember. I had to go into the locker-room and lie down on the benches for about an hour.'

Well before the Ballesteros versus Kite encounter, Langer had overwhelmed Sutton 5 and 4. It was a regal performance by Langer and his caddie Coleman felt a little lordly himself:

'Bernhard was one of the best players in the world in '85 and I knew it would be difficult for Sutton to live with him.

'Sutton didn't play that well anyway. Whether the crowds upset him, I don't know. But Bernhard was always in control without having to really raise his game and it was really all over after the first nine. We were five-up after twelve. We were out in the country after beating Sutton five and four so I had a long trek in. Then I spotted Lord Derby [president of the Professional Golfers Association], who'd been following our match on a buggy and asked him for a lift. He dropped me off at Bernhard's room and then took me all the way to my Porsche. I was home indoors by the time the final putt was sunk, watched it from the comfort of my own armchair.'

Lyle's defeat of Jacobsen put Europe on the brink, as Lyle's caddie Musgrove recounts:

'Lyle won 3 and 2, holing a good putt on 16. But he'd been out-of-bounds on the 13th. It's a short par-four, so Lyle goes for it. He hit it straight over the fence, cleared it by a mile. Good old Sandy. He was still three or four under-par by the time they finished, though, and I reckon theirs was the best match for quality. I was pleased Jacobsen played well. He's such a good bloke. He treats everybody the same. No edges, as we say in my part of the country.

'I went and sat in the bag-room to see how the overall picture was progressing. I could remember the last time we won, at Lindrick, so I was ever hopeful.'

Jacklin had had the quandary of where to play Faldo and decided to place him third-last out. There was little memorable about Faldo's singles. Even opponent Hubert Green, who had re-found glory by winning the US PGA Championship just weeks before the 1985 Belfry clash, was three-over by the time the match finished on the 17th. Green seemed perplexed by Faldo's poor play and put Faldo's caddie Roy Holland on the spot:

'Hubert's a bit of a head-banger, very eccentric on the course – his swing, the way he spoke and everything. He turned round to me and said, "Whatever are you doing caddying for this man?" I'm not sure whether he meant it in a derogatory way or not, but I decided to ignore it. I think he was a bit baffled as to why Nick wasn't playing well. He certainly had a lot of time for Faldo. When I went to him and declared the ball Nick was using after we'd made a ball change, he said, "You don't have to tell me anything. There are a couple of guys I would want to know exactly what ball they were playing, but not this guy. I never have to worry about how Nick plays the game. But I do wonder if he should have played at all."

'And it was true. Nick had a sort of apologetic manner all week. I think he was embarrassed with the way he played. He knew it was a team event and he felt he was letting team-mates down, I'm sure. It hurt him that he was in with 11 other guys and he couldn't give his best. They wanted him there because he was Nick Faldo. If it had been anybody else, he wouldn't have been picked.

'He never chucked the towel in against Green and fought right to the end. Not many people would have made it to the 17th with the problems he had. Nick's not a quitter. He just didn't enjoy it. It was a pretty awful stage in his career after all the success he'd had. It was a nightmare experience. The only thing he said to me when he was suffering out there was, "What do you think, Roy?" I didn't know what to say. What do you say to Nick Faldo?'

If a Faldo success proved unimportant in the end, then to Sam Torrance went the honour of bringing the Cup home. Torrance the people's hero, Torrance the ordinary bloke who liked a bet, a cigarette and a few pints, Torrance the nice guy. But also, Torrance the tough, the man from Largs who had learned the game at his pro father Bob's feet.

There could hardly have been a more popular player at The Belfry to commit the final act which ended 28 years of frustration in the Ryder Cup for those who had tried and failed to break the American grip. Alongside him was compatriot Dunlop:

'Sam will always be remembered as the player who sank the winning putt. Funnily enough, if Clarky had holed a four-footer on the 17th just behind us, he'd have been the man.

'It was a pretty funny day, bad weather, and Sam wasn't playing very well. Everything turned around for him on the 15th, though. He's two-down playing 15 and he's knocked it off the green into that sticky sort of longish grass. Andy North's knocked his six feet past in four. Sam then knocks it eight or ten feet past and I think, "Jesus Christ, this is over." Sam then holes his, North misses. One-down with three to play. Sam should have birdied 16, knocked it in to five or six feet, but missed it. Still one-down with two to play. Both of us anxious.

'At the 17th we knocked it up, second shot, in the left rough, but it was where the spectators had trodden down the grass, so we got a good lie. We knocked it on to the green. Birdie. All-square.

'By this time the crowds were almost hysterical, unbelievable. I'm churning. God knows how Sam feels. But he absolutely nails his drive down the last with a high draw. Perfect. Andy North knocks his into the water. Then he put it into the water again. So Sam then goes in with a nine-iron I handed him. He kidded me, "Is this enough club, youze?" Well, it pitched up and screwed back just before the big drop down off the tier. Perfect. No problems now. The nine-iron was just right. Then he holed the putt. History!

'The old arms came out and there was the emotion. Then he was completely engulfed; swamped. I couldn't get near him. It was a very special moment for him. Being a golfer myself it was a privilege to be involved in the moment. As well as Sam's finish, the most outstanding memory will always be of Seve. He inspired the whole team. We felt like celebrating forever.'

HOW WE KEPT THE RYDER CUP

1987: A MAIDEN VICTORY ON AMERICAN SOIL

MUIRFIELD VILLAGE, COLOMBUS, OHIO, 25–27 SEPTEMBER
USA 13 EUROPE 15

Captains: Jack Nicklaus (USA)
           Tony Jacklin (Europe)

(European names first)

Foursomes (morning):
S. Torrance and H. Clark 0, C. Strange and T. Kite (4 and 2) 1
K. Brown and B. Langer 0, H. Sutton and D. Pohl (2 and 1) 1
N. Faldo and I. Woosnam (2 holes) 1, L. Wadkins and L. Mize 0
S. Ballesteros and J.M. Olazábal (1 hole) 1, L. Nelson and P. Stewart 0

Fourballs (afternoon):
G. Brand Jnr and J. Rivero (3 and 2) 1, B. Crenshaw and S. Simpson 0
S. Lyle and B. Langer (1 hole) 1, A. Bean and M. Calcavecchia 0
N. Faldo and I. Woosnam (2 and 1) 1, H. Sutton and D. Pohl 0
S. Ballesteros and J.M. Olazábal (2 and 1) 1, C. Strange and T. Kite 0

Foursomes (morning):
J. Rivero and G. Brand Jnr 0, C. Strange and T. Kite (3 and 1) 1
N. Faldo and I. Woosnam (half) ½, H. Sutton and L. Mize (half) ½
S. Lyle and B. Langer (2 and 1) 1, L. Wadkins and L. Nelson 0
S. Ballesteros and J.M. Olazábal (1 hole) 1, B. Crenshaw and P. Stewart 0

Fourballs (afternoon):
N. Faldo and I. Woosnam (5 and 4) 1, C. Strange and T. Kite 0
E. Darcy and G. Brand Jnr 0, A. Bean and P. Stewart (3 and 2) 1
S. Ballesteros and J.M. Olazábal 0, H. Sutton and L. Mize (2 and 1) 1
S. Lyle and B. Langer (1 hole) 1, L. Wadkins and L. Nelson 0

Singles:
I. Woosnam 0, A. Bean (1 hole) 1
H. Clark (1 hole) 1, D. Pohl 0
S. Torrance (half) ½, L. Mize (half) ½
N. Faldo 0, M. Calcavecchia (1 hole) 1
J.M. Olazábal 0, P. Stewart (2 holes) 1
J. Rivero 0, S. Simpson (2 and 1) 1
S. Lyle 0, T. Kite (3 and 2) 1
E. Darcy (1 hole) 1, B. Crenshaw 0
B. Langer (half) ½, L. Nelson (half) ½
S. Ballesteros (2 and 1) 1, C. Strange 0
K. Brown 0, L. Wadkins (3 and 2) 1
G. Brand Jnr (half) ½, H. Sutton (half) ½

THE CADDIES

PHIL 'WOBBLY' MORBEY (IAN WOOSNAM 1987, 1989, 1991, 1993, 1995, 1997; JOSÉ MARIA OLAZÁBAL 2006)

The story goes that when Yorkshireman Phil Morbey went out on his first caddying assignment, his shoes fitted him so badly that he manipulated the bag in a sort of zig-zag fashion to compensate for his blisters. His wobbling gait earned him his sobriquet. 'Wobbly' quit his supermarket job in 1981. After at first declining the offer of Ian Woosnam's bag when in 1986 he was working for Howard Clark, Morbey moved to the Welshman's side a year later, with the Ryder Cup looming. Within a month Woosnam won the Lancôme Trophy, perfect preparation for their first Cup clash together at Muirfield Village. Their finest hour, apart from successful Ryder Cup matches, came when Woosnam clinched the 1991 US Masters title. After six Ryder Cups together, Morbey, on Woosnam's advice in 2001, left to carry for José Maria Olazábal.

ANDY PRODGER (NICK FALDO
1987, 1989; COLIN MONTGOMERIE 2002)

Diminutive Andy Prodger served two terms with Nick Faldo, his second stint by far the more outstanding one. The former golf professional first took the Faldo bag in 1980, but their real glory together came in 1987 and 1989. Londoner Prodger was with Faldo when he claimed the Open in 1987 at Muirfield and two years later when he edged out Scott Hoch for the US Masters title. The innocuous Prodger has, paradoxically, proved an arresting sight over the years. He was twice pulled in at Augusta for the heinous crime of not wearing an official badge. Then, as he relates in this chapter, he was gaoled after the 1987 Ryder Cup. Following the break up of his hugely successful partnership with Faldo, Prodger served several players for short periods. In 2002, by then 50, Prodger joined Europe's former seven-times No. 1 Colin Montgomerie.

SERGIO GOMEZ (JOSÉ MARIA OLAZÁBAL 1987)

Although Sergio Gomez was to become José Maria Olazábal's manager, at first their relationship was that of mentor and protégé. Gomez ran the Junior section at their club, Royal San Sebastian, and recognised the potential in the son of the club's greenkeeper in 1979 when Olazábal was 12 years old, after accompanying Olazábal during his formative years and then travelling with him as the young Spaniard carried all before him in the amateur ranks. Although Olazábal eventually took on Scot Dave Renwick to carry the bag professionally in 1986, Gomez still did the caddying duties in America and Japan. He thus featured in the historical Ryder Cup at Muirfield Village when the formidable partnership of Olazábal and Severiano Ballesteros was first fashioned. Soon after the 1987 clash, in January 1988, Gomez became Olazábal's professional manager.

BILLY FOSTER (GORDON BRAND JUNIOR 1987, 1989; SEVERIANO
BALLESTEROS 1991, 1993; DARREN CLARKE 1997, 1999, 2002, 2004, 2006)

Working as an apprentice joiner in his father's business, Yorkshireman Billy Foster fancied a more glamorous lifestyle and, aged eighteen, he took a six-week holiday with the aim of caddying at several events in Spain and Portugal. His father, who used to 'sack me three times a week anyway', gave him his blessing and 'packed me off with fifty quid and a bottle of brown sauce'. It led to a full-time career. Foster joined Gordon Brand Junior in 1986 and his caddying career really took off as Brand made the 1987 and 1989 Ryder Cup teams. Foster stayed with the successful Scot until 1991, when he got the call from Seve Ballesteros. The two were together for the Ryder Cups of 1991 and 1993. When Ballesteros's form spiralled downwards, Foster stuck with him but left, ironically, by the time Ballesteros had virtually sealed his 1995 Ryder Cup place. Foster appeared for a fifth Ryder Cup and with a third different master when he carried for Darren Clarke at Valderrama in 1997, and followed up with further appearances in 1999 and 2002 and, following a short break, 2004.

GUY TILSTON (EAMONN DARCY 1987)

You would swear you were seeing double if you happened upon a day on a European Tour event when Guy Tilston and brother Gary were on duty. They are the most identical of twins. Guy actually started work with Barry Lane, who practised at the Downshire course in Berkshire near the twins' school. But one day Guy could not make it. So Gary stood in – without Lane tumbling to the switch – and kept the job! Guy had caddied for Eamonn Darcy when the brothers used to carry bags as schoolboys at Sunningdale pro-ams, so the Irishman had no qualms about employing him for the 1987 season. It was a good move for both of them. Darcy won the Belgian Open – because, swears Tilston, he did a rain-dance in his room to ensure the tournament was curtailed to three rounds, helping the Irishman seal his 1987 Ryder Cup place.

THE ACTION

'Once Eamonn found out what Crenshaw had done, he was frightened. We both were. If we lost to a man with no putter, we'd never live it down.'

From the first encounter devised by Sam Ryder in 1927 at Worcester, Massachusetts, the Americans had proved invincible on home ground. In Muirfield Village, they had the course to continue their unbeaten run. Nothing could go wrong. After all, as their captain Jack Nicklaus pointed out, 'The other guys are good players, but they can't be talked about in the same breath as our 12.'

But the euphoria of 1985 remained with the European team. Captain Tony Jacklin declared before the 1987 showdown at Muirfield Village – the 'course that Jack built' as his own memorial – that his men feared no one. 'I've been coming to America for 20 years, and this is the first time I am really confident of winning,' announced Jacklin as he and the team disembarked from Concorde.

A vociferous visiting gallery roared them on to greater effect than the home supporters did on the first day. And Europe came up with three stunning partnerships: Nick Faldo and Ian Woosnam, Sandy Lyle and Bernhard Langer, and the brilliant new combination of Seve Ballesteros and 21-year-old debutant José Maria Olazábal, one of Jacklin's three 'picks'.

Faldo had not done himself justice in the previous Cup clash, his swing change with David Leadbetter taking its toll on his confidence. This Ryder Cup would be a different matter. The big Englishman came to Muirfield Village proudly holding the Open Championship title, his first major success. His swing change had been completed in time for him to lift the famous Auld Claret Jug in July – at the original Muirfield.

When the odd couple stood on the tee, Faldo and Woosnam's contrast in size proved a source of hilarity to the American gallery. Faldo's caddie Andy Prodger saw the European pair laugh last:

'I knew Nick had played so badly at The Belfry he had asked to be dropped after the first day. This time it was mighty different. He didn't play so well at the start of the opening foursomes, though, and I think he struggled more than Woosie really. But the signs were there with both of them and when I walked to the tenth tee I said out loud, "We're going to win this match." It was partly to try to gee things up a bit, although I did believe it as well. Nick said, "You're right, Andy. We are going to win this match."

'Then Nick really did start playing better. In foursomes it's not much good if one player's going well but his partner's not; you're going to get battered. Nick started hitting good shots, none better than the one he hit soon after agreeing that we were going to win. It was a brilliant shot in to the tenth, leaving Woosie with not much more than a tap-in. On that course, the tenth was a very tough hole to birdie and that gave us the inspiration to go on and win. When Nick starts to get the feeling he's got a chance to win, he goes into tunnel vision; every shot in his own mind has to be perfect. You could see the back-nine was a different ball-game. They were in a different gear.

'It was definitely a key to Europe winning. With Seve and Olazábal going well, our win meant the morning was halved. In the afternoon the team came out with all guns blazing. I'm not sure that would have been the case if we'd lost and it had been 3–1 down in the morning instead of 2–all.'

On Woosnam's bag was the former supermarket stacker Phil 'Wobbly' Morbey. The Sheffield bagman was pleased that the two Britons finally gelled:

'We killed them in the end. It just took nine holes to get used to playing together. We'd obviously played together in practice, but under Ryder Cup pressure, everything's different; different for the players and different for the caddies. Things going wrong can soon hit confidence and the putts weren't dropping for either of them going out. When they did start dropping, Woosie and Nick were unstoppable.

'I could tell how confident they were because I never got asked to read a line. The two of them together worked out the lines and they got them worked out brilliantly on the back-nine. Woosie was in a great mood when they finished and he told me before we went out in the afternoon that it was going to need a pretty good pair to stop him and Nick – or a pair with a lot of luck.'

The opponents for the afternoon fourball were Hal Sutton and Dan Pohl. Sutton was one of the players who had complained bitterly about the partisan behaviour of The Belfry gallery, to be one of those labelled a 'cry baby' by the 1985 US captain Lee Trevino.

America's self-appointed avenging angel Sutton and Ryder Cup rookie Pohl gave as good as they got for hole after hole as Faldo played it steady and Woosnam relished being released from the reins of foursomes, producing a splendid cut-and-thrust match. Not one hole was won out of the first ten before the absorbing struggle swung Europe's way, by virtue of the bravery – and fortune – of Woosnam, watched by his partner's caddie Prodger:

'On the 11th Woosie went for it with a wood, a risky shot with the creek running in front of the green. He knew he was flirting with danger. Nick and Ian discussed the shot but I think Woosie had already made up his mind and there wasn't much stopping him. It looked as though it was curtains for Woosie when the ball rattled into the branches of the overhanging tree but then suddenly out it came, and it landed pretty close. We made eagle and that turned it our way.'

One of the four amateur bagmen at Muirfield Village was José Maria Olazábal's mentor Sergio Gomez. Gomez, a family friend, had taken over the affairs of the gifted young Spaniard after spotting his talent while running their Royal San Sebastian Club junior section. Olazábal had joined the professional ranks, following a spectacular amateur career, to become rookie of the year in Europe after capturing two tour titles in his 1986 debut.

Neither Olazábal nor the partnership, nor Gomez, could have had a more difficult start. Their opposition was Larry Nelson and Payne Stewart. Nelson, 40 years old and the reigning US PGA champion from only a few weeks previously, was America's good-luck charm. His record was nine wins out of nine. And four of those victories had been against Ballesteros. Seve's bogey had to be laid. Gomez was fully aware of that. He was also aware that his young charge, who was to take him on professionally as his manager the following year, was going through a mini-crisis on the tee:

'At that time I caddied for José Maria in all the majors he played and every time he was overseas in the USA and Japan. Dave Renwick was his usual caddie, but he wanted me on the bag. The partnership with Seve was a natural one. Not only were they both Spaniards, but also Jacklin was inclined to put the most tender rookie with Seve.

'They could hardly have had a tougher start. It required a lot of thinking and discussion before they went out. They prepared very well. That's Seve. Nothing left to chance.

'Muirfield Village is a course where the four par-threes are even numbers and the four par-fives are odd numbers. Seve came to José Maria and said, "Listen, I'm going to be the one to tee off on the odd numbers because I'm longer with the driver than you are. That will make it easier for us for the par-fives. You are going to tee off on the even numbers because you are better with the irons than me. That will mean we will handle the par-threes better as well." That was the way Seve put it to José Maria, in confidence. It was a good thing to say and it definitely made José Maria feel comfortable, Seve involving him straight away in the plan of attack.

'The reason why José Maria wasn't hitting it as far as Seve was because he was using a two-wood off the tee. He came to the Ryder Cup definitely not at the peak of his driving power, and short on confidence with the driver altogether. So much so that he went to the pro's shop and bought himself a two-wood. He used that all week instead of the driver. Well, things worked out perfectly. It was a tight opening match but Seve's strategy worked fine.

'The afternoon fourball match was against Curtis Strange and Tom Kite and it got off to quite a start. On the first hole Seve missed the green on the left and had a tough chip. José Maria was on in two but with a very tricky long downhill putt. Seve said to José Maria, "You go first because your putt is not as easy as my chip." So José Maria putted up about two and a half feet past the hole. Seve then asked José Maria to putt out for the par, so José Maria asked Curtis if he could finish. Curtis refused, saying he might walk on his line when he stepped back. Strange was treated to one of Seve's most typical glares and then Seve said quite loudly, "Don't worry about it, José, because I'm going to hole my chip anyway." Of course, in went Seve's chip and he walked over to José Maria and said, "You can pick up your marker now, José, and don't worry, because Curtis isn't going to hole his putt anyway."

'But Curtis was trying to make some kind of mark on the match straight away – bearing in mind it was José Maria's first Ryder Cup and his age and all. I was tending the flag for that first putt by José Maria and Curtis walked over to me while José Maria was trying to putt and started to complain about how I was standing. I said, "Jesus, Curtis, what am I doing wrong? There's nothing wrong with how I'm tending the flag." Well, José Maria broke off and came over and said, "What's the matter, Curtis?" Curtis said, "Sergio's messing up the hole." It wasn't true, of course. I don't know what he was trying to prove. But it marked and soured the whole match. I can tell you, there were no "gimmes" in that match. It backfired on Curtis, though, because his behaviour just fired up Seve and José Maria even more. Seve holed a huge putt on the tenth to rub it in and by the time we got to the 17th he was already holding up José Maria's arm in a victory salute.'

Ballesteros was in his seventh year in tandem with the eccentric American caddie Nick de Paul, who put loyalty above patriotism. Clutching a bottle of the sponsors Johnnie Walker's golden liquid, which he dispensed into 12 glasses, the silvery-sideburned de Paul made his battle-cry, urging his fellow bagmen to 'whip these mother-f*****s' asses':

'I was anxious to let the rest of the caddies know exactly where my allegiances lay, so I got them all together after we flew in from the European Tour. That had been my home for the year. I was a European team caddie. The unified spirit between us all was fantastic. There was such a great feeling among us. And I think it spread through to the players, rather than the other way round. We were a good team and we knew we could win.

'Seve was his usual self, and couldn't wait to get at the American team. I knew we would play with José Maria Olazábal from the start. Seve always gets the rookies and their pairing was an absolute natural. All I had to do was try to keep up with my Spanish, because there was going to be a lot of it spoken. José's manager was on the bag and he's Spanish, so it was going to pay to know what they were all talking about. I'd learned my Spanish by answering Seve in his own language after he'd spoken to me in English. His English had come on leaps and bounds, better than my Spanish, in the years we'd been together.

'In the first match, Seve just took charge, coaxing José along, doing the yardages, reading the putts. He was just in charge. And his golf was formidable, as good as I'd seen him play, as good as the last round of the 1984 Open.'

The third telling European partnership was that of Lyle and Langer. After the all-Scots team of Lyle and Ken Brown had proved something of a shambles at The Belfry, Jacklin first tried Langer and Lyle with good result in 1985, and also matched Brown with Langer to satisfactory effect at The Belfry. Jacklin, therefore, had to toss up which one of the two, Lyle or Brown, should now partner Langer. When the combination of Brown and Langer lost out to Sutton and Pohl in the second match of the opening morning, it was logical for the captain to try out the German again with Lyle. As Lyle's astute caddie, the well-turned-out Dave Musgrove, had predicted, the partnership was made in heaven:

'The 1987 Ryder Cup was quite a landmark for the caddies. We got our air tickets and hotel rooms paid for and we got plenty of clothes: two pairs of quality trousers, three shirts to be worn as instructed, Glenmuir sweater, Footjoy shoes, socks and Pro-Quip waterproofs. Well, if you're representing your country – or in this case your continent – why shouldn't you be well turned out?

'Caddies getting privileges like proper air tickets instead of stand-bys or none at all stemmed from 1983. That's when good old Jimmy Cousins went to see Tony Jacklin, who was living in Jersey, and quietly said, "If you want the proper caddies out at the tournament, you've got to look after them." A few of the caddies from the ten of us travelling to Columbus were tempted when we got to New York for transfer. We had a chance to go on a later flight because the plane was overloaded. They said there was $250 dollars in it. When the lads found out that it was in TWA vouchers, they got back in their seats after scrambling over each other to get to the desk.

'The practice rounds when we got to Muirfield Village took ages to play. I can remember hanging around feeding the fish at halfway house while we waited to get back on the tee – golden carp, they were. Sandy knew the course. He'd finished sixth in the Memorial tournament there earlier in the year. He said: "The thing about this course is that you can remember every hole. Each hole stands out. With a lot of courses, the holes get lost from the memory eventually. Here there are no gimmicks. You stand on the tee and see what's to be done. The fairways are generous and all the trouble comes as you approach the green. Very fair." All the caddies thought Europe had a great chance. For years the Memorial tournament had been won by high scores and the area was prone to windy conditions. And it could be cold, suiting the Europeans more. In fact, we had a frost delay on the Saturday.

'Sandy was champing at the bit to play after not getting a game in the opening foursomes, although he never really expected to, because Tony knew he didn't care for the style of play very much. Langer and Sandy were an ideal combination. Sandy wants to get on with it; Bernhard wants to think about it. Langer speeded up a bit, Sandy slowed down a bit. Perfect. And they got on even better because they weren't trying to play the shots for one another.

'It was a bit of an up-and-down start for them. They were two-up very quickly against Mark Calcavecchia and Andy Bean. But it swung back their way and there was a four-shot swing in seven holes to put them two-up after 13. They were still one down after 15 when Sandy stepped in. He's never considered himself the greatest of putters but he liked the greens that week and he holed a big one on the 16th, about 25 feet for par, to keep us only one-down. I don't know whether it rattled the Americans, but they couldn't do better than bogey for the last two holes and we sneaked it.'

For the afternoon fourballs, after Europe had fought back to level the foursomes two-all, Jacklin decided to drop Clark and Torrance. Torrance's indifferent form in practice and in the first match was mainly down to his putting, his caddie Dunlop maintained. A suspect stroke which was causing a twitch was to lead to Torrance paving the way as the first European Tour player to switch to the long 'broomhandle' putter two years after the 1987 Ryder Cup:

'Jacklin had to go with the players who were playing well and when I walked off the ninth green in our foursomes match with Howard Clark, Jacklin collared me and said, "How are they going?" I said, "They're four-over and four-down," and I could see he was already tossing up the afternoon fourballs, even though we were first match out in the morning.

'Sam was really struggling with his putting and I feared for him. Clarky and Sam were itching to get out there again in the afternoon to make amends for losing but I don't know whether it would have worked. It was a terrible time for Sam with the putting and the next year was even worse. You only had to watch him in the singles at Muirfield Village on the last green, watch him putt and how bad the yips were. If Larry Mize hadn't gone into the water I don't know whether Sam would have made it in the two putts that he did, for the half. I guess it was no surprise when he didn't play again until the singles after losing that first match with Clarky.'

Rivero was paired with debutant Gordon Brand Junior. That was a surprise to Brand, who had heard through the grapevine that he would be playing alongside his experienced fellow Scot Torrance. It was also a surprise to Brand's caddie Billy Foster, also making his debut:

'Obviously you're nervous when you stand on the first tee with all the fans shouting, but once you get going it's like football. Once the whistle goes, you're OK. I'd been a bit apprehensive that Gordon might not get a game until the singles from the rumours that were going round, despite Gordon having a great season.

'I guess the nerves showed a bit for the opening hole. Gordon got into trouble in sand and José three-putted. Not the best of starts. But then they got better and better. They won that 3 and 2 and I think their win inspired the rest behind them. It was like a domino effect going through the matches and it was a fantastic afternoon for Europe.'

Europe thus completed a remarkable assault, whitewashing the Americans for the first time in a series. It left Europe two points to the good going into Saturday. The format had changed that year, so instead of play being reversed the next day, it was once again morning foursomes and afternoon fourballs. That could not put the Europeans off their stride.

Faldo's caddie Prodger believed his man became the linchpin for Europe's Saturday success:

'Nick was tremendously calm in the foursomes with Woosie against Sutton and Larry Mize, who I think were trying to whip up enthusiasm by the way they were whooping and hollering towards the end of the round. And it was a lot to do with Nick's coolness that they got a half out of the morning.

'You needed to be cool. Sutton was determined to get the American gallery going. He'd claimed the crowds had been against him in '85 and I think he might have wanted his gallery to be just as one-sided. He wanted the same thing to happen to the Europeans as had happened to him at The Belfry. The Muirfield Village crowd weren't that used to making lots of noise and earlier in the match especially, our 3,000 or so followers had been much more in evidence. Big Jack [Nicklaus] had even got cheerleaders in after the first day because the home crowd had been so subdued. For us, it was almost like being at home. So with Sutton whipping up the crowd and playing as though he wanted to win whatever, their half-point was hard-earned and very valuable.

'Against Tom Kite and Curtis Strange in the afternoon fourball, though, Nick really was at his best and Woosie played brilliantly as well. It was mind-boggling stuff – five birdies in five as they dovetailed superbly, and Kite and Strange certainly didn't play badly enough to be five-down after five and six-down after ten before losing five and four. The Americans were six-under through fourteen holes but Nick and Ian something like ten- or eleven-under. Kite and Strange were totally gobsmacked. Nick hit a lot of iron shots very close and a lot of confident putts. From conversation with him at the time, it was plain that the way the greens had been set up was backfiring on the Americans. They'd been cut ultra-quick in the hope that that would benefit the Americans, but in fact it helped the Europeans.

'Their putting strokes became better and better because of the quicker greens. Nick told me the speed of the greens was definitely helping him.

'So, what with the crowd being kept quiet through the way we were playing, and getting to terms with the very quick greens, it looked as though we were going to be in for a really big win.'

Stung by the previous afternoon's whitewash, which had taken the match to 6–2 in Europe's favour, and hurt by the lack of encouragement from the American gallery, Nicklaus decided something had to be done to whip up some support. He sought help from his players' wives and their friends, who became a group of Stars and Stripes pennant-waving cheerleaders to try to produce some razzmatazz and gee up his men. The band of 3,000 visiting fans soon gave as good as the cheerleaders were handing out, the chanted riposte being 'You've got the flags; we've got the players!'

The Lyle–Langer partnership continued for the second day and the European duo twice found themselves up against Wadkins and Nelson. Lyle's caddie Musgrove marvelled at partner Langer's meticulous attention to detail, but he was pretty sharp himself, too:

'Before the foursomes I said to Sandy and Bernhard: "What ball are you going to play?" I'd seen mistakes with balls happen before and of course it reared up again at Kiawah in 1991. Sandy played Dunlops and Bernhard with Titleist. They decided to play Langer's ball.

'After the foursomes, Sandy played the next two rounds with the balls Langer had rejected during our foursomes match. Every time we'd played a ball for a few shots, Langer would change it. So Sandy would pocket it. Sandy the Scotsman is determined to play a round with one ball, as he's done all his life, and Langer's reject balls weren't to be wasted!

'It was a crazy start. Nelson and Wadkins were on the green in two but it was a daft pin position and Nelson put their second putt – not the approach putt, mark you – off the green. We won with a bogey. The round proved a long old business but Bernhard was in charge of the thinking. He consulted my map of wind directions and speeds, calculated the wind direction on the first and worked out how the whole of the first nine holes would go. Then he checked it again to see if the wind had changed, checking it out with arrows I drew on the map. He's so thorough. The best example of that came in the foursomes at the 11th. He'd got Willy Hoffman on the bag, his coach, so I suppose he needed to consult with me over the yardages to make doubly sure. He said, "What have you got to the front, 227 or 228?" Well, I never give such precise yardages to Sandy, just 230 will do. So I said, "230." He said, "You mean 228 then?" He wouldn't give up two yards!

'Bernhard needn't have worried. It wasn't his shot anyway. He was just making sure. Sandy smashed a two-iron to a few inches, to leave Bernhard a tap-in eagle. A lot is said about John Daly's big-hitting, but at that time Sandy was longer. He could smash a two-iron miles – well, 228 yards, according to Langer, anyway – and hit the green. Wadkins admitted that Sandy's ironplay had killed them on the par-fives, and the 11th knocked the stuffing out of the Americans.'

Ballesteros and Olazábal made it three out of three for their partnership as they disposed of Crenshaw and Stewart narrowly in the foursomes, completing victory by one hole again. The all-important hole was the last, and it proved to be Olazábal's finest moment, as Gomez explains:

'José Maria hit a great tee-shot, but then somehow Seve got the second shot wrong and came up short. He couldn't believe it but it was in the bunker. José Maria then played a great bunker shot from a terrible position in the sand to about six feet. Stewart and Crenshaw had been in sand too, but they needed two putts from 15 feet for a bogey, so all Seve had to do was lag the putt for the bogey and the match win. I don't know how it happened, and nor did Seve, but somehow his putt went six or seven feet past the cup.

'At that moment, Nick de Paul, Seve's American caddie, slammed down the bag, turned to me and said in Spanish, "Why, oh why, does Seve have to be the aggressor?" And it was true. They only needed a five to win the match. Seve only needed to lay up the putt, but Seve is Seve and a half measure is never good enough for him. He wanted to win the match in style and tried to hole the putt. Well, José Maria made it and in the end played all the shots at the 18th. Seve knew, and there was even extra warmth in the victory hug for José Maria.'

For the Saturday afternoon fourballs, late because of early frost, Jacklin decided he had to double-guess Nicklaus. Wadkins and Nelson were dying to have a crack at Ballesteros. Nicklaus fully expected Ballesteros and Olazábal to be out last, as they had been for the first three matches. Jacklin, though, decided to switch Langer and Lyle to tail-end gunners. If Lyle's big-hitting had creased the mighty American partnership in the morning and Langer's studiousness had thwarted any home steamroller tactics, then that was going to be the case in the afternoon, too.

As Lyle's caddie Musgrove observed, it turned out to be a classic encounter that ended in the twilight:

'Everyone remembers Bernhard's chip-in on the tenth and the old legs going up in the air as he fell back into the bunker, but it was Sandy's eagle on the next hole which really killed Wadkins and Nelson, I can tell you. In fact, Wadkins admitted afterwards that Sandy's playing of the par-fives all day was what did them. Sandy hit a 3-iron over 230 yards at the long 15th for a second eagle and that put us three-up.

'Bernhard wasn't happy at the 15th and you could see a crack in his usual straight-faced looks when he got into all sorts of trouble. He was really angry with himself and did a lot of muttering and growling. That showed just what his pride's like, because he hadn't been out of a single hole all the round until then. He calmed down and he and Sandy blew a couple more kisses at each other after Sandy made the eagle, and I thought that would be it. But the Americans still hung on and won the next two holes, so that set up a fantastic finish. You could hardly see more than 50 yards in front of you but they wanted to finish off and not have to come back the next morning. It might have been dark but it didn't stop all four of them hitting great shots in on the 18th.

'You couldn't see properly but we judged Sandy's eight-iron in to be to about six feet and he turned round to Bernhard and said, "Get inside of that, then!" And he did. What we could see in the gloom was Jacklin and Angel Gallardo [one of the former Ryder Cup pros and a European Tour official who was helping with administration of the players] jumping up and down like demons alongside the 18th green. We gathered Bernhard had hit a bit close. When we got up there the hole was surrounded but Langer's ball was only about 18 inches from the cup. Nelson and Wadkins just walked over to it, shook their heads, and conceded. Langer's ball was picked up and handed to him and the scenes were fantastic. Everybody was really excited. What a finish!'

There had been only three defeats for Europe, including a surprise one for Ballesteros and Olazábal in the afternoon, but the visitors led 10½–5½.

Jacklin announced, 'I never thought I'd live to see golf the way it was played today. Pure, unadulterated inspiration' – and then set about how he was going to drive the nail home the next day in the singles.

His quandary was whether to play his strongest men at the top and go straight for the jugular or save his aces to the end. Jacklin decided that Nicklaus had no alternative than to try to earn points quickly in a bid to regain lost ground. So the European captain opted to put out some of his strongest players lower down in the final six.

As the home side struck back in a laudable rearguard action, there were worrying early setbacks that left the outcome still in the balance.

Ballesteros and Eamonn Darcy were the men to whom the pendulum of the 1987 Ryder Cup swung when the time came for victory or defeat.

Darcy was playing only his second match of the week when he came to his showdown. He still had to win a match after ten attempts in four Ryder Cups. With Woosnam, Faldo, Olazábal, Rivero and Lyle all facing defeat, Darcy and his caddie Guy Tilston, the first set of twins to make a Ryder Cup appearance, knew the Irishman had to break his duck in the Cup or all might be lost.

The singles which, everyone felt, finally broke the Americans' spirit was won by an Irishman with a unique swing, a flying elbow which might cause David Leadbetter to wake up screaming in the night. The point was wrested from Ben Crenshaw and victory was aided by a gentle tap of Crenshaw's putter:

'We'd spent the first one and a half days on the practice ground with Sam's dad Bob Torrance, who was teaching Darce how to hit the ball like the rest of the players. He had him swinging it without any flying elbow, without his legs moving around, completely orthodox. He hit the ball well. Bob had had a bet with the lads he could get Eamonn hitting the ball in an orthodox way and he managed it. Bob won his bet. Darce was hitting it just as the book tells you to, although it wasn't quite as good as Faldo's, which was what I think the original boast was! But that was never going to be any good out on the course. Darce couldn't get any feel that way. He's probably one of the best "feel" players in the world, so he had to go back to his own ways when he got out there.

'When we got on the tee, though, I was very nervous. I was quite young and singles was a bit different from having a partner. Eamonn's got a way of loading pressure on to his caddie. That's what I'm there for, so fair enough. But he's quite a difficult man to get on with. No disrespect to him, but it can be hard. You get rifled at you, "What club is it?" or "What's the yardage?" and he wants an answer straight away.

'I settled down when he hit two lovely shots at the first but then Crenshaw holed a huge putt, about 40 or 50 feet, to go one-up. Then Darce really got on a roll and he played some magnificent stuff, winning the fourth and fifth with birdies to go one-up. They both hit the sixth green in two – to around about 30 feet or so, but with Darce just outside Crenshaw. Eamonn got down in two putts, but Crenshaw, who's supposed to be the best putter in the world, three-putted for us to go two-up.

'Well, we walk on and Crenshaw stays on the green, hanging about practising the little putt he's missed. We go to the seventh tee, which is a par-five. Eamonn and I spent a few moments discussing the hole. Anyway, they both tee off, play their seconds and have 70-yard pitches. Darcy hit a really good shot to about four feet; Crenshaw fatted it into the front bunker, then knifed it over the green. He picks up Darce's ball as he walks past the green, and he's gone; conceded the hole. So there was no putting on that green. We're three-up.

'We walk up to the eighth tee. Crenshaw's there. Nicklaus is there. Crenshaw's going through his bag and putting across the tee. Darce and I didn't know what the hell was going on. When they saw us coming they quickly got themselves organised and by the time we got on to the tee they looked as though butter wouldn't melt in their mouths. I don't know whether Darce suspected anything, but all he said was, "I wonder what that was all about?"

'The eighth's a par-three and Eamonn was further away. He putted up to about four feet from a good way away. Crenshaw hits his putt with a one-iron! Darce said to me, "What the hell's going on?" We soon found out after Darce missed his putt to bogey and Crenshaw took two putts for par with his one-iron to get it back to only two-down. He'd given his putter a whack on the path after he'd three-putted the sixth – not like you see some of the guys whack it but enough. It was his old blade putter and it was because it was so old, it gave in; snapped right down near the neck, rendering it completely useless. It was done in anger, so he couldn't do anything about it.

'What a turn-up now. Darce three-putting with a putter and Crenshaw two-putting with a one-iron. He actually went through the bag, though, over the rest of the holes. He used a variety of clubs to putt with, either straight-faced or wedges. Long putts, the straightfaced clubs, and short ones, halfway up the ball with a sand-wedge. Once Eamonn found out what Crenshaw had done, he was frightened. In fact we both were. If we lost to a man with no putter, we'd never ever live it down. It put him – no, us – under a lot more pressure. Putting's bread and butter. How can Crenshaw win now?

'Crenshaw lost the ninth, not through his putter but because he went into trees and sand, so we go back three-up by the turn. Then Crenshaw three-putted the tenth after we'd gone in sand, lipping out with a one-iron and then missing the six-footer back with a sand-wedge. Darce then three-putted the par-three twelfth and that got to him a bit because Crenshaw managed to two-putt, and then at the 13th Ben stiffed it, hit it about six inches. He could have tapped in with anything. So Darce's suddenly only one-up.

'At the 14th they were both in good shape after hitting irons off the tee. It's a tough green to hit, although it's made for Darce, a nice little floated left-to-righter with an eight-iron. He pull-hooks it. Crenshaw's on but with a smelly putt, especially without a putter. Darcy plays a magic chip just down off the green, because the green's falling away and there's water three yards after the flag. Crenshaw somehow only takes two putts, though, so now it's all-square and Darce's worried. Europe's worried. We can see everybody out following us.

'On the 15th Darce was in places where we shouldn't have been and I did a lot of running around working out yardages from places I wouldn't normally have needed to go. But he got on to ten feet after being on the island and birdied. Crenshaw had gone through the green with his second, putted up to four feet for a birdie, but we were happy with the half.

'At the short 16th Crenshaw hits to only four feet and Eamonn's ball catches the bank on the green, which throws it off. He chips to six feet – and misses. So he has to concede the hole. That means he's now one-down for the first time since the first hole. Psychologically, that must have been a terrible blow and I guess it might have finished plenty of players, especially playing against a man with no putter and knowing what we knew from the scoreboard on how the team were now in trouble. We're bleeding. We were three-up only an hour or so ago. The guy's got no putter. It's a crunch match. We're hurting pretty bad and Darce must feel awful, but he's not showing it.

'On the 17th, Crenshaw misses the fairway right – not the place to miss it, because coming in there's a huge bunker left and trees to get over. Darce skies his drive. We've got a straightforward shot downwind off the right. I remember so well: 196 yards, 192 over the bunker on the right, let the wind take it over a bit of a valley. Crenshaw had to go over trees with only ten yards to land on.

'Darce comes over. "What club is it? What's the yardage?" I said, "Six-iron" and gave him it, telling him, "Get it in the air and it'll get there." I wasn't that confident about it, but I just knew five-iron was too much. What everyone had told me was that in this kind of situation they do get pumped up – with adrenalin – and hit it a bit further. If he rips it, he'll get it there. Five-iron big and you're history. I couldn't have asked him for a better strike but there was never a moment when I knew for sure it was making it over the bunker. It probably made it by six inches because we saw the sand fly up before – fantastic – it trickled up to about four feet. Such relief. Give him a wrong club and I'm in for it – not only from him but from all of Europe!

'Crenshaw went into the back bunker and could only make five even with one-putting, but we had a safe birdie. That was the big hole. We're back to all-square. At the last the pressure finally comes off a bit when Crenshaw hits into the water, takes penalty, and then hits into the bunker short for three; we are in the middle of the fairway. Well, pressure back on because Darce pulls his three-iron second shot into the same bunker as Crenshaw. He could have turned round and told me, "Not enough club," but he was man enough to say, "I pulled it."

'They pitch out, Crenshaw to about eight feet. Darce is about five feet but he's above the hole with a tough putt. Crenshaw chooses a one-iron and hits a swinging putt straight in. Darce's putt was never one you could go for. He had to hit it somewhere down the left side and try and get it dead weight and with luck it would go in. You were more likely to three-putt if you went for it. He hit it right in the middle of the cup. Magic! It brought tears to my eyes, tears of relief. The scenes then were frantic. People everywhere. I just raked the bunker. It would just have been so terrible if we'd lost to a man with no putter.'

Darcy's thrilling victory left Europe on the brink of retaining the Cup. Bernhard Langer's half soon after meant Europe could not lose.

Then Ballesteros provided the coup de grace. His caddie de Paul, the American who had hung his colours to Europe's mast, was there right at the very point when history was made, as his man holed the winning putt:

'We drew Curtis again in the singles and I thought, "Oh-oh; now we're in for a match." There was definitely some bad blood between Seve and Curtis, probably from the pairs match, and they were at each other right from the start. Perhaps it was because their respective camps had made out that each was the best player in the world at that time, I don't know. Whoever Seve played in a singles match, he seemed to get in a bit of a state, and kinda took it personally.

'There was a huge crowd following us and Seve hit Curtis hard straight away by chipping in from the bunker at the first. I'm sure it unsettled Strange because we got three-up on him quickly. We were three-up after ten and then Seve got mad because he hit into the water on the 11th. We were dallying a bit, sorting out what club and him thinking all the wrong things, of course, when Curtis hit. He went out of turn because we were away by about a yard or so. He was definitely out of turn but it didn't really matter – to anyone else but Seve, that is. Seve was mad and he wanted to penalise him and make him play it again. I had to talk him out of it. I told him I didn't think that would be a smart thing to do at all, if for nothing more than the tradition of the Ryder Cup. A little incident like that could upset the whole thing. I told him it wouldn't be gentlemanly.

'It took a lot of doing to make him reconsider. We lost the hole anyway. Seve was fuming and then he lost 13, so it was real tight now. But Seve settled down and took 14, he was so determined to win. Curtis couldn't stop him. We were two-up at 17, Seve hit it to 30 feet right in the heart of the green, two putts and it was over. The first win on American soil. Believe it or not, I was very happy – the only American at Muirfield Village who was!'

The European celebrations started, even though Brand Junior and caddie Foster were still out on the course. America could not get out of gaol but Foster and caddying pal Andy Prodger did that very thing:

'We kept looking at the scoreboards and I thought "sheeit", it might come down to us after all, right down to the death. You just couldn't keep proper track of it. Darcy's match was obviously important but then Ken Brown was beaten and there were only Seve and Gordon out on the course. We were one-up with two to play, right in the middle of the 17th fairway, and Seve holed his putt up ahead of us to beat Curtis Strange.

'Suddenly all hell broke loose; people dancing, people on the green. They're dancing around, singing, "We've won the Cup; we've won the Cup," and Gordon and I are standing in the middle of the 17th fairway. They're dancing on the green for ten minutes – and we can't play a shot. The champagne's popping and I'm in the middle of nowhere, feeling like a spare dick at a wedding! We stood there for 10 or 15 minutes but we had to carry on and finish the match. That was the frustrating thing. You just wanted to run up there and have a few beers, get stuck into the celebrations.

'Anyway, we lost the 17th to birdie and Gordon finished up giving Sutton a ten-foot putt on the last for a half. I was disappointed at him doing that. I wanted to win. But then I cheered up as I joined the party. It was fantastic. Champagne everywhere . . . Olazábal doing his dance . . . We had quite a few jars that night. Then home. We lost poor old Andy Prodger at the airport – and I was the cause of it really.'

Prodger takes up the story:

'We'd been given champagne and beer to drink on the way to Columbus Airport, and we were all very, very drunk. Eventually we end up at the connecting airport, Chicago, where Billy Foster got the pizzas in and we ended up having more beer. There was about a mile to walk to connect to our aeroplane and that meant going through security. Billy decided he was going to walk the wrong way through security. We're all carrying these nice little white holdalls we'd been given for the Ryder Cup and Billy gets called back. I said to one of the guards, "Yes, you want to be careful, because one of us might have a bomb in our bags." No sooner were the words out of my mouth than I was completely surrounded by security men. There was one guy who was particularly aggressive and I was frogmarched away to a room.

'Sergio Gomez and Roddy Carr [at that time Seve Ballesteros's business partner] tried to convince security that I'd just had a bit to drink and it was a joke. Security were never going to buy that, though, and the aggressive guy marched me away. I spent the rest of the night in a gaol in Chicago where the prison guards took delight in telling me I was going to enjoy my cell for the next 18 years. Eventually they let me out on bail at four o'clock in the morning, by which time, of course, I'd missed the flight home. For some reason I didn't have any trouble catching the corresponding flight the next night and they also accepted my original ticket, so I guess somebody had been working behind the scenes on my behalf. The trouble was, though, I was now down in the records as a criminal, a suspected saboteur! What was I going to do the next time I was in America? I'd only been let out on bail. And was I going to have to go back and answer the charge still?

'Well, as luck would have it, the man who ran Northwestern Golf, Nat Rosasco, was a good friend of mine. He was at the Dunhill Cup, which I had to go straight to. When he went home to America he got all the charges dropped. He's got a lot of clout in the States, for some reason. I even got my $100 bail back. Nick wasn't impressed when I got to St Andrews after my escapade. I'd missed a day's work.'

HOW WE HALVED THE RYDER CUP –
BUT KEPT IT

1989: ALL-SQUARE BUT THE CUP STAYS IN EUROPE

THE BELFRY, 22–24 SEPTEMBER
EUROPE 14 USA 14

CAPTAINS: Tony Jacklin (Europe)
Ray Floyd (USA)

(European names first)

Foursomes (morning):
N. Faldo and I. Woosnam. (half) ½, T. Kite and C. Strange (half) ½
H. Clark and M. James 0, L. Wadkins and P. Stewart (1 hole) 1
S. Ballesteros and J.M. Olazábal (half) ½, T. Watson and C. Beck (half) ½
B. Langer and R. Rafferty 0, M. Calcavecchia and K. Green (2 and 1) 1

Fourballs (afternoon):
S. Torrance and G. Brand Jnr (1 hole) 1, C. Strange and P. Azinger 0
H. Clark and M. James (3 and 2) 1, F. Couples and L. Wadkins 0
N. Faldo and I. Woosnam (2 holes) 1, M. Calcavecchia and M. McCumber 0
S. Ballesteros and J.M. Olazábal (6 and 5) 1, T. Watson and M. O'Meara 0

Foursomes (morning):
I. Woosnam and N. Faldo (3 and 2) 1, L. Wadkins and P. Stewart 0
G. Brand Jnr and S. Torrance 0, C. Beck and P. Azinger (4 and 3) 1
C. O'Connor Jnr and R. Rafferty 0, M. Calcavecchia and K. Green (3 and 2) 1
S. Ballesteros and J.M. Olazábal (1 hole) 1, T. Kite and C. Strange 0

Fourballs (afternoon):
N. Faldo and I. Woosnam 0, C. Beck and P. Azinger (2 and 1) 1
B. Langer and J.M. Canizares 0, T. Kite and M. McCumber (2 and 1) 1
H. Clark and M. James (1 hole) 1, P. Stewart and C. Strange 0
S. Ballesteros and J.M. Olazábal (4 and 2) 1, M. Calcavecchia and K. Green 0

Singles:
S. Ballesteros 0, P. Azinger (1 hole) 1
B. Langer 0, C. Beck (3 and 2) 1
J.M. Olazábal (1 hole) 1, P. Stewart 0
R. Rafferty (1 hole) 1, M. Calcavecchia 0
H. Clark 0, T. Kite (8 and 7) 1
M. James (3 and 2) 1, M. O'Meara 0
C. O'Connor Jnr (1 hole) 1, F. Couples 0
J.M. Canizares (1 hole) 1, K. Green 0
G. Brand Jnr 0, M. McCumber (1 hole) 1
S. Torrance 0, T. Watson (3 and 1) 1
N. Faldo 0, L. Wadkins (1 hole) 1
I. Woosnam 0, C. Strange (2 holes) 1

THE CADDIES

IAN WRIGHT (SEVERIANO BALLESTEROS 1989)

A former television engineer and insurance agent, Ian Wright rose to the top of the caddying tree when he accompanied Severiano Ballesteros to Open Championship victory in 1988 at Royal Lytham and St Anne's – in the very year he took over the unpredictable Spanish superstar's bag. In 1986 Wright was producing yardage books. Soon business flourished as all the top players used his charts, but there was one exception – Ballesteros. Instead, Wright got the Spaniard's bag. A mixture of Wright's placid temperament and Ballesteros's Latin blood seemed to work instantly. After moderate early success, Ballesteros surged back into the limelight after a quiet spell and capped his comeback with a stirring Open victory at Royal Lytham. A year later and Wright was at The Belfry for the Ryder Cup.

DAVE RENWICK (JOSÉ MARIA OLAZÁBAL
1989, 1991, 1993; LEE WESTWOOD 2002)

Rugged Scot Dave Renwick, a former North Sea and West Africa oilrig worker, was José Maria Olazábal's first serious caddie when the young San Sebastian pro took the European Tour by storm in his 1986 debut season. He was by the young Spaniard's side when Olazábal at last clinched the major he had threatened to take for some time, the 1994 US Masters. Within a month of Olazábal taking his first major title, however, the pair parted company. Following a long spell in America, including working for double-major champion Vijay Singh, Renwick moved back to Europe to take over Lee Westwood's bag. Thus Renwick provided yet another experienced ally in Sam Torrance's 2002 Belfry Brigade.

MALCOLM MASON (SAM TORRANCE 1989, 1991, 1993, 1995)

Lancashire caddie Malcolm Mason took up Sam Torrance's bag when the Largs professional was going through a desperate time with his putting and saw the affable Scot through a major change in his career. In early 1989 Torrance switched to the 'broomhandle' long putter soon after taking on Mason. They proved a deadly trio.

Mason began his caddying career in 1983 at Bolton Old Links for 'something to do' after becoming unemployed. In 1987 Mason took up the bag temporarily for Torrance and helped the Scot to three second places in Hawaii and Japan in only three weeks. When Mason and Howard Clark split up two years later and Torrance sought a new caddie, Mason was the first to be considered. The pair appeared in four Ryder Cups and when Torrance was captain in 2002, Mason was one of the Scot's 'quartermasters'.

JOHN GRAHAM (MARK JAMES 1989, 1991, 1993;
LEE WESTWOOD 2004, 2006)

Glasgow-born John 'Scotchie' Graham moved from his Maryhill home to London and his education there included golf. After working as a furniture-remover, Graham shifted his attention to the fairways in 1979 to take the bag of Sandy Lyle, who was launching his brilliant career. Lyle won the European Order of Merit with Graham on the bag. Graham built up a reputation as one of the best readers of a putt and after writing to Mark James for a job before the 1989 season, he was given a five-week trial period. During that time James won twice. Graham, who earned his sobriquet as a connoisseur of Scotch whisky, had five European Tour victories to go with three Ryder Cups with the droll Englishman. An 'on the wagon' Graham rejoined Lee Westwood in 2004.

STUART DRYDEN (RONAN RAFFERTY 1989; HOWARD CLARK 1995)

Dryden, born in England but brought up in Australia after his family emigrated when he was two years old, was on the point of retiring from the caddie business in 1989. Ronan Rafferty did not have a European Tour victory to his credit. Within a few months, Rafferty was a winner, Dryden was a happy caddie and the pair were on their way to sealing both a European No. 1 title for the Ulsterman and, naturally, following the success of the season, a Ryder Cup place. After his golden 1989 with Rafferty, Dryden gave up ideas of returning to the coal-mining industry for a while, but was again ready to drift off the caddie scene when he secured the bag of Howard Clark in time to go with the passionate Yorkshireman for a second Ryder Cup campaign.

FANNY SUNESSON (HOWARD CLARK 1989; NICK FALDO 1991, 1993, 1995, 1997)

Sunesson began her caddying career after watching the 1985 Scandinavian Enterprise Open. She moved on to the European Tour soon after, overcoming the pitfalls of having to spend her touring life in a traditionally male-only environment. After the disappointment of being dropped for the 1987 Ryder Cup by José Rivero, the Spaniard preferring to take his brother to Muirfield Village, Sunesson landed Howard Clark's bag and carried it at The Belfry in the 1989 tie. The following year she was approached by Faldo's coach David Leadbetter and asked to join up with his star pupil. Thus, at 22 years of age, Sunesson began a partnership with Faldo. Within months they won the 1990 US Masters and then the 1990 Open Championship. Sunesson accompanied Faldo to four major successes (also 1992 Open Championship and 1996 US Masters) and in four Ryder Cups.

MATTHEW BYRNE (CHRISTY O'CONNOR JUNIOR 1989)

One of four caddying brothers, Byrne grew up between the legendary Irish courses of Woodbrook and Bray. He began caddying at seven years old. Eldest brother Brian was the first to try out the European Tour, taking up a professional bag in 1987. Matthew soon followed. Tired of the humdrum life of a taxi-driver, he spent much of 1988 as a casual bagman on tour, working for anybody who wanted a caddie for a week or a fortnight. Then, at the year's finale, the Volvo Masters, Christy O'Connor Junior arrived without a caddie. Byrne took up the bag and helped his fellow Irishman to fifth place. It was to ensure him a job with the silver-haired veteran the following year and, with O'Connor's legendary two-iron, a place in golfing folklore.

THE ACTION

'He sort of looked side-on at me and I knew he was remembering his great shot at the hole before. He said with a big wink, "It's a two-iron, isn't it?"'

After two memorable victories, the huge home crowd at The Belfry prepared itself to witness a hat-trick of wins for Europe. It so nearly came off. As the American captain Ray Floyd said after an honourable but cliff-hanging draw which proved the equality of the two sides going into the match, 'First I didn't think there was any way we could lose, then I didn't think there was any way we could win.'

Floyd, given the job of reinvigorating America's flagging spirits after two defeats, added, 'In the end there was only one winner – that was the game of golf.' That was the perfect summary of the 1989 struggle. Floyd was referring to the last day's play, when The Belfry's notoriously difficult par-four 18th produced virtuoso performances from Kipling's twin impostors Triumph and Disaster.

If The Belfry had proved historical in 1985, it proved close to hysterical four years later. This Ryder Cup grandstand finish outdid even the maiden European victory in America in 1987. A 14–14 result was, arguably, a forseeable outcome when weighing up the strengths of both teams. America had in its ranks the reigning Open champion Mark Calcavecchia, the US Open winner Curtis Strange and the US PGA champion Payne Stewart. The European team could boast the US Masters champion in Nick Faldo. It had home advantage. And Europe also had the tried-and-tested men at the helm, captain Tony Jacklin and first-lieutenant Severiano Ballesteros.

It was an opulent-looking European 12 and their caddies that warmed up on the practice days. Each player sported over £5,000 worth of clothing and equipment courtesy of a number of manufacturers, as Jacklin's crusade to provide the best for his men reached dizzy heights. A huge tented village and media centre housing nearly 400 journalists showed how Ryder Cup fever had taken hold. More than 50 journalists came from America, and within the 200-million-strong worldwide television audience were millions of Americans watching live – proof that Ryder Cup fever had, at last, also gripped the United States.

The first ball that was struck on a grey, damp, Friday morning, was in error.

Ian Woosnam drove off in the mist, startling Tom Kite, who was in the midst of preparing to tee off himself, assuming tradition was being followed and the honour was going to the visiting team. However, Woosnam had taken the honour for Europe, as defending champions.

An initially uninspiring Woosnam and partner Faldo went on to halve the opener with Kite and Curtis Strange in what Faldo's caddie Andy Prodger felt would be a 'grudge match'. That was partly from two years before, and partly from Floyd's observation at the gala dinner that he was captaining the world's best dozen players:

'There wasn't quite the "gel" there'd been in 1987 with Nick and Woosie. You could tell there was a big difference in the rapport between them. Things weren't the same. They did well to be unbeaten for their first three matches. They were probably a bit tired when they lost the last match.

'Nick did have a special reason for beating a team led by Ray Floyd, though. Floyd was never a favourite of Nick's after the 1987 Open. On the very first hole at Muirfield, after Nick had taken a while to size up a shot, Floyd said, "I never thought you were ever going to hit that." It rankled with Nick and, I always felt, fired him up to win the Open that year. And there was a fair bit of needle between the two of them when they were paired together in the 1989 US Masters. [Faldo took particular delight in overcoming Floyd the following year in the Augusta playoff.]

'It's maybe no coincidence that Faldo has played well whenever Floyd has said the wrong thing and now to add to this was his gala dinner announcement proclaiming America to have the 12 best players in the world – in the year that Nick's the Masters champion!'

Europe did not make a full point in the morning. Ballesteros and José Maria Olazábal also had to settle for a half and America led 3–1.

Ballesteros's caddie Ian Wright admitted he had been on edge. Wright had accompanied the rejuvenated Spaniard to Open Championship victory at Royal Lytham and St Anne's the year before. But even with his successful year behind him, Wright was quaking in his trainers at the start and needed a soothing word from Ballesteros:

'For the first time since I began with Seve, my nerves were jangling when we set off in our match with Tom Watson and Chip Beck. At the second hole I worked my yardages out from the wrong sprinkler-head position and Dave Renwick, Ollie's caddie, had to come over and tell me to check because he thought I might have it wrong. I hastily redid my figures but it was too late to stop Seve noticing. I thought he'd be anxious and I was waiting for a stern lecture. Instead he said, "You're a little bit nervous, Ian?" I told him, "It's OK. I'll be all right now," and he said, "Right. Let's get going then," marching off without making any more of it. That calmed me down, because I deserved a right rollocking for making such a basic error as that.

'It was a real battle in the foursomes and we did well to get a half to go with Faldo and Woosie's half, or it would have been 4–0 down after the first morning. Ollie actually sank a great 20-footer on the 17th to get the half but the pair of them, typically, weren't satisfied with that and they were both very disappointed they hadn't beaten Watson and Beck.'

The home team came roaring back in the afternoon fourballs, though, with a narrow success for Sam Torrance and Gordon Brand Junior and resounding victories for Woosnam and Faldo, Howard Clark and Mark James, and, the most crushing of all, for Ballesteros and Olazábal.

With Torrance was his new caddie, Lancastrian Malcolm Mason, a man who had a few months earlier helped the Scot through a major putting change as his master launched the vogue in Europe for longhandled putters:

'Sam had really struggled at the beginning of 1989 with the short putter, suffering the "yips" like I'd never seen the like of anywhere, and his Ryder Cup chances looked pretty slim. He was striking it beautifully, but he could hit to three feet and then couldn't even touch the hole with his putt! I wanted to turn round and look away every time he had the putter in his hand. But he'd been in Florida and seen Orville Moody working with a long putter and thought it might work for him.

'It was quite difficult to get one made up. It took a lot of experimentation. For instance, he practised standing on top of his snooker table at home. Eventually he couldn't miss.

'Nobody on the European Tour had ever thought in a million years of using a long putter, so there was nobody to swap ideas with. He was under a lot of eagle eyes at the time. People said he couldn't do it. They said, "It wasn't cricket." In about six years he holes £3 million with his long putter! Sam had it with him on the first tee at The Belfry in '89 when I made my Cup debut – the most nervous moment I've ever had in golf. We won with Gordon Brand Junior in the afternoon fourballs on the first day and, ironically, it finished with a three-putt from Sam.

'We needed par on the last against Curtis Strange and Paul Azinger. Gordon was in a bunker and Sam right down the bottom tier on 18. Sam three-putted – in his early days the hardest putt to judge with the long putter was up a slope – but Gordon made one of the best up-and-downs from a bunker I've seen in my life to win us the point.'

It was far more cut-and-dried for Ballesteros's caddie Wright in that afternoon's fourballs:

'We drew Watson again in the fourball, this time with Mark O'Meara, and didn't we give them a roasting? We won the first five holes and from then on all we had to do was make sure we didn't get over-confident. Seve never lets up, though, and he wanted to win by the biggest margin he could, so when they made something of a fightback, he was the first to turn the screw again. I think he wanted to get it over as soon as possible so he could get out on the course and egg on the rest. On the 13th, for instance, there were two marshals standing on the apron of the green. When I gave Seve the driver I said to him, "You'd better watch the two blokes down there, the way you're hitting the ball." I said it jokingly, because we had well over 300 yards to the green. Seve was so pumped up that he hit his ball between the two of them. That finished the match six and five.

'The others were still well in the thick of their matches and I think when our win went up on the board it lifted everyone. I know it did the crowd. They cheered us all the way back to the locker-room, where Dave and I were able to get rid of the bags because Seve and Ollie [Olazábal] wanted to go out and give the rest of the lads support. We were able to watch the boys make it a clean sweep and that really got the crowds going berserk.'

Olazábal's regular caddie Dave Renwick was back on the bag for Ryder Cup duty. In 1987, Olazábal's manager Sergio Gomez had carried the Spaniard's bag. Scot Renwick's first Ryder Cup proved a red-letter week altogether. His man was never beaten in five matches:

'I was upset at losing the bag for 1987 at Muirfield Village and let it be known. But I just had to accept that José Maria had promised Sergio the job. I didn't like it, but had to take it.

'We had plenty of confidence from the pairs matches with Seve. They birdied 9 of the 13 holes to beat Tom Watson and Mark O'Meara, on the first day. The hole which stands out in the memory that afternoon against Watson and O'Meara was the tenth. Years ago, Seve had been the first one to really go for it, hitting the green 300 yards over the water. We could hit three-woods this time, because they'd moved the tee forward a little bit.

'I got a lot of satisfaction from José Maria hitting to just three or four feet, hitting the ball as near perfect as doesn't matter. Seve hit his to 20 feet. The opposition got into all sorts of trouble. Then Ollie didn't even have the chance to hole his, because Seve rolled in the 20-footer. That was almost it then. Watson and O'Meara didn't last much longer after that. Seve and Ollie were just magnificent.'

Another partnership to blossom was that of James and Clark. After a morning stutter in the foursomes, James's rugged Scots caddie John 'Scotchie' Graham was rather warmed by a fourball success over Fred Couples and Lanny Wadkins. That was because he'd had a run-in with Wadkins:

'It was really scary for my first Ryder Cup. On the afternoon of the first day on the 14th when we played Couples and Wadkins I went to get the flag out, not realising I was standing on Wadkins's line. There were so many markers around the hole because they'd all missed the green and chipped close. Wadkins snarls, "Get off my f***ing line, boy," and it made me jump so much that as I tried to get out of the way I started dancing on it in fright. Luckily for me, Couples made their par for a half before Wadkins needed to. Then, walking down the next fairway, Wadkins's caddie for the week, Tony Navarro, said, "Well, Scotchie, you'll always be able to say you danced all over Texas now!"'

So the second successive first-day afternoon whitewash by Europe gave them a 5–3 advantage. Honours were to stay even on the next day, with the home side keeping their two-point advantage for the singles.

There were hard-fought points by Europe to keep it that way. And as Ballesteros's caddie Wright reveals, a 'blood match' won:

'Very soon after we'd beaten them in all four matches on Friday night, Jacklin announced the foursomes pairings for the next day, and then we knew the opposition – Kite and Strange. Seve's like a bull with a red rag in front of him whenever he plays against the Yanks, but he's got a particular motivation with Kite. I don't know, but I understand Kite said something pretty bad about Seve once and the comments got back to him. Whenever Kite's name was mentioned, I could see the hackles rise. Strange and Seve aren't the best of pals on the course either, so I knew we were in for quite a match. There's no love lost between most of the Americans and Seve.

'As the morning wore on, as last match out we knew that we needed to win to keep Europe two in front. Seve and Ollie dovetailed really well because Kite and Strange never gave an inch. It all came down to the 18th. Seve and Kite both put their partners in the bunker on the last, so we were in for a tense finish. Strange had a pop at the photographers for clicking while he was trying to play and left Kite a difficult putt. Ollie just got on with it and splashed out to seven or eight feet. Kite missed his putt. Seve – and he was absolutely ecstatic when he did – got his. Strange was so upset he didn't even shake hands. I was astounded; not even a little dab of the hand to Seve. He just turned his back on him and marched off.

'It meant that Europe kept the two-point advantage going into the final fourball. We were out with Calcavecchia and Green and by looking at the scoreboard again it was plain to see the last two matches out, Clarky and Jesse [Howard Clark and Mark James] and us, were going to have to win to keep that two-point cushion for the singles. Well, we ended up watching Clarky and Jesse get their fantastic win because we'd finished by the 16th. It could have been a hole earlier but Seve's putt lipped out. Calcs [Calcavecchia] asked Seve if he was playing around with them!'

That Europe kept that two-point advantage for the singles was down to an exhilarating match that ended in near-twilight, the encounter between Clark and James and Payne Stewart and Curtis Strange. It was a match that first had the gallery hushed in apprehension and then lifting the rafters. As James's caddie Graham observed, it turned a grown man's legs to jelly:

'The Saturday afternoon against Stewart and Strange was the cruncher. It was frightening in the end. Before Howard sank the ten-footer for a birdie to win the 16th there was absolute stone silence from the crowd, which completely lined the whole hole. I was about ten feet from him, kneeling down, and I whispered quietly, "Nice and easy; nice and easy; nice and easy." He hit the putt and it went straight in. That got us back to level and the gallery went wild. They knew as well as we did that we were either going into the singles level or two-up.

'The whole Ryder Cup crowd was at the 17th, all the players, everybody. Howard sliced his drive into trees. Mark was in the left semi. Two world-class golfers, Payne Stewart [then US PGA champion] and Curtis Strange [reigning US Open champion] were in the middle of the fairway in the perfect position. Mark went first and hit a great three-wood which just caught up the fringe, 20 or 30 feet short of the flag. I don't think Stewart and Strange knew where it was. Because of the crowd's reaction, they thought it was quite close – closer than it was, really.

'Stewart carved his second way, way right and then Strange, who was so far up the fairway it was ridiculous, did the same. Pressure. It always comes down to pressure. They were both over in the little trees. They discussed their shots forever: walked back and forth, knocked it into the trap, didn't really get out of trouble. Jesse [James] didn't hit a particularly good chip, to about six feet short of the hole for his birdie chance. I gave him his line of "inside-left, or left-half of the hole". He made the putt. Afterwards he says, "I couldn't move any part of my body to try to line myself up. All I could do was hit the putter on line. My knees were shaking that much."

'On 18, Howard hit a tremendous drive and only needed something like a nine-iron, but Jesse was just in the trap. He then hit one of the best shots I've ever seen, a three-iron to fifteen feet. They were always going to make at least four and I just said to myself, "Gee whizz. We've got the point."'

That point was to prove crucial to Europe the next day as the 1989 Ryder Cup finale developed into a series of triumphs and disasters at one hole in particular, the formidable finish at The Belfry. Normally a backwater for ducks and coots, the 18th became an amphitheatre of victorious and vanquished gladiators.

If Europe were the white knights in shining armour to the partisan crowd and the Americans the dirty dozen, then Ballesteros was The Belfry gallery's Lancelot. After an unsuccessful skirmish with Paul Azinger, though, a mortally wounded Ballesteros was more Quixote than Lancelot.

Europe needed 5½ points to complete the hat-trick, but by the time Ballesteros and Azinger reached the turn, the scoreboard indicated they were down in nine matches. As Ballesteros's caddie Wright discloses, the bad feeling of the first nine holes did not get any better as their match came to a sensational conclusion:

'On the second hole Seve picked up the ball after firing it into the green about 12 to 15 feet from the flag, and was just going to throw it to me when he stopped and inspected it. He'd nicked the cover, ripped it a bit. He said "Change the ball?" to Zinger. Normally you'd expect a nod back but Zinger asked to look at it. He told Seve he didn't think the ball had gone, so Zinger said, "Let the referee decide."

'The referee – Andy McFee, who got all the awkward matches – was quite a way away, minding his own business down the bottom of the green, but Zinger threw him the ball. Andy caught it and said, "Not really." Seve grabbed it back – and holed the putt for a three.

'Zinger didn't like that and by the time we got to the tenth he was two-up and firing on all cylinders. Then we got a big stroke of luck. Seve should have been in trees on the tenth but his ball bounced out on to a bank and then on to the green. Zinger conceded and we won the next to get everything back. It was really ding-dong. Seve missed a three-footer on the 12th to go back one-down and then we had some unnecessary hassle. On the 13th tee Azinger's caddie stood next to the right tee block when Seve's about to tee off. It's a very narrow tee and you should really be standing off it and to one side. I'd done that myself. Seve wanted to tee up a bit to the right anyway.

'The caddie didn't move and he was obviously in Seve's way. So Seve said quietly – ever so politely, bearing in mind the way the match was and the pressure, and all – "Would you mind moving?" The caddie said, "Oh no." Whether that was no he wouldn't move or no he didn't mind, I don't know.

'He lifted the bag and then put it down in the same place, never moved an inch. I thought, "Hello, I'd better say something; it's up to me now," because I didn't want Seve getting into a heated argument with a caddie. So I said, "Come on, get out the way, Bill, man, there's no need for that." He shuffled about six inches, and that was no good.

'So in the end I just grabbed hold of him and moved him. A few words were exchanged, and although we weren't quite squaring up to each other, it was a nasty incident; a bit of unnecessary friction. It was all psychology and gamesmanship. When we walked away from the tee I said to Zinger's caddie, "What was that all about?" He just smiled. I took it to be a bit of a wind-up. Up ahead I could tell Seve and Zinger were having words. They were marching away quite briskly but it sounded as though Seve wanted to know why Azinger didn't ask his caddie to move away. I don't know whether he'd put him up to it or not. Paul's a great matchplayer!

'Zinger had a fantastic stroke of luck on 15 to go back one-up after Seve had got it back. His ball was going one hell of a rate when it whacked into the flag and dropped after he skinned one out of the top fringe. The ball would have run all the way off the top level if the flag hadn't got in the way. By the time we got to the 18th tee it was still one-up to Zinger but then he hooked his drive terribly into the trees left of the lake. Seve hit a solid shot but way right, on to a bank to the right of the fairway bunker. I thought, "We've got it now."

'I went straight to our ball and checked the yardage. Seve came over and we sorted out where the ball was and how it was sat: about 18 inches below his feet on a mound and about halfway down in the grass. Initially, he didn't get involved with Zinger's problems. I said to Seve, "Do you fancy a four?" He said, "No. I'm really happy with a three." We were all ready to go and then Seve glanced across because they were taking quite a time with the ruling for Zinger. All of a sudden Seve realised Andy McFee had gone right down the line of the trees on the left and it was then obvious where the drop was going to be.

'Seve started marching over there and my first thought was that I hoped he just kept calm. But then I thought about the drop more. Nobody, in all the years I'd been coming to The Belfry, had managed to get a drop where Azinger was getting it in the left trees. I've never known anybody to know exactly where the ball crossed in that position, even with marshals watching. There's no way you could tell how that ball had hooked off the tee. Previously, everyone else had had to drop back and behind the trees. I actually said to the spectators nearest to me that it had to be a drop back behind the trees.

'Seve started to shout that Azinger couldn't have the drop there. No way was it right. I just hoped he'd come back and not get too involved. But I felt he was right, knowing what I did about that hole. Eventually Seve came back and Azinger hit a wood over the water into the bunker, a great shot. I found out afterwards he'd dropped onto a path and had a great lie. But it was still a marvellous shot.

'In hindsight, I think Seve was greatly disturbed over where Azinger got his drop, and it probably affected him when he came to play his shot. It could have been a contributory factor to the very poor over-the-top swing he got on the ball – straight into the water. The way he'd been playing all week you'd have expected him, in those days, to cut it out the rough slightly, just cut it up a touch, even though his feet were below the ball. He could hold the ball up off a lie like that and you'd expect him to get it across the water without any trouble, somewhere near. If not on the green, at the worst to go into a bunker. He could have done that 95 times out of 100.

'As a caddie, it hadn't seemed a risky shot. I'd initially thought of a four-iron to get that bit more loft, taking into consideration a flying lie would get him the distance. But if he was holding it up, he'd got to go with what he was comfortable with. When he says he's happy, you don't question it. He went for me, but he was berating me because of his temper – for going into the water. He knew how bad a shot it was and how crucial it was. We then still had to get over the water and he growled at me, "Come on and get this yardage right. It'll be the first one you get right today." I was used to it. That was what I expected. He was angry, but then so was I. Then the decision was whether it was a nine or a pitching-wedge to get over. There was a light right-to-left breeze so we decided on a nine-iron to make sure we got on to tier the third level back, where the flag was. If we could actually hit behind the flag it would be perfect, giving us about six to eight yards to play with.

'He was a bit pumped up with adrenalin, hit a great shot over the flag, pitched on the bank and started to move back. I thought it would trickle back stone-dead but it stayed up there. Seve started chuntering again so I went off to pick up an imaginary divot – his own had gone into the water – to get out of his way. He was saying something like "I could have used a five-iron for that shot," so he was obviously still thinking about the first shot. I just wanted him to cross the bridge and get over there, and calm down until his anger had burnt out. That was my way with Seve.

'When he got up there he found his ball was about 25 feet on the top. It had only needed to move another foot and it would have been down the bank absolutely dead. Azinger pitched to about five feet. Seve then patrolled, prowled for minutes, then holed the putt down the hill. I was just glad the hole was in the way. He just looked at me and I shrugged my shoulders. I was thinking, if Paul holes his putt, I'm going to get out of the way. I could see my wife Lesley watching all this; I picked her out of the huge crowd at the 18th green. Well, Zinger holed it and Seve marched off. I could see the tears before he got off the green. He was choked. To lose it in those circumstances was too much to bear. Zinger can only go with what the referee rules, but to lose it after a decision which he thought was unfair was tough for Seve to take. With the bad swing and all, it was very hard for him.

'I took it badly, too. I felt we had to make at least a half in that first match, for team morale as well as the points. After getting into the locker-room, I picked up Seve's bag and threw it against the wall. Then I realised his Rolex watch was in the bag, the original white-gold one. To my relief it wasn't damaged. It triggered something off because I just sat there and I had a few tears as well. But then in came Seve. "Come on," he said. "We've got to get out there and support the team. We've still got a chance; it's a slim one, but we've still got a chance."'

That chance came in the form of Olazábal, Rafferty, O'Connor and Canizares. Olazábal's victory was achieved with the help of his doughty caddie Renwick, who was not slow in coming forward on the 17th:

'José Maria's singles was always going to be a tough one against Payne Stewart. Stewart was in great form, having won the US PGA and we expected a hard match.

'That's how it was. We were one-down with two to play. On the 17th [par-five] we were in light rough with the drive, not a great lie, with 230 to go.

'Ollie said to me, "What do you think? Should I lay up?" I said, "Hell, no. What's the point of laying up? You're one-down with two to play. Give it a go with the three-wood." He took the advice and got up to the green-edge, took two more for a birdie and won the hole. Obviously that lifted José Maria and had the opposite effect on Payne, but I don't know whether that contributed to Stewart going into the water on 18. We stood watching Payne trying to get out of the water near the edge. He put on his waterproofs and tried but he was getting nowhere.

'You don't really like to win like that but José Maria never said anything as we stood there. The crowd said it all with the "ooohs" and "aaahs" when Payne was swiping away. Nothing was said but José Maria knew he only had to hit it on to the green and the match was finished. We chose a three-iron, he hit it on to the green. Payne just walked over and shook his hand.'

The next pair to arrive at the 18th were Rafferty and Mark Calcavecchia. Rafferty, who would become European No. 1 that year, had not seemed mentally at his best, suffering a crisis of confidence, according to caddie Stuart Dryden. Rafferty, though, was to rise to the occasion in style:

'On the first day, Ronan hit the tee-shot off the first tee and said after it, "I cannot remember the swing; it was all over before it started. I'm just glad I made contact with the ball." He'd been worried in case he hit it into the tented village like he'd seen somebody else do before.

'The first match with Langer was probably a bit of a mismatch. It wasn't that they didn't get on, but I really don't think Ronan should have played anything but singles. Bernhard tried to help Ronan with second shots and so on, but I think he figured after five or six holes that they'd better go their separate ways.

'His second match had been another strange pairing. With Christy they played quite nicely from tee to green, but when they got on the green it was just diabolical. At least Ronan played and got a feeling of what a Ryder Cup match was like. It maybe would have backfired if he'd just been thrown into the singles.'

'He was pretty apprehensive about it all. As well as he was playing, the thought of the Ryder Cup was, maybe, a little overwhelming for him. He wanted to be involved in it, but I think nerves were quite a big factor for him. I knew that when he got in contention in tournaments he was quite nervous. It was funny, because then I felt he wanted to talk and we got into some pretty good conversations under pressure. He always had this cool exterior. I think he was churning inside when the heat was on.

'It all came out on the Saturday night, when Tony Jacklin had to have a little pep-talk. Ronan's confidence must have been low after playing in those two matches. I think Tony did well. He must have said some good things. Ronan came out and probably felt a little better about himself.

'We're drawn against Calcavecchia, the Open champion. Obviously Calcavecchia must be full of confidence.

'There wasn't anything in it until the tenth and he said to me, "Shall I go for it?" I said, "Well, your wedge play is pretty sharp. Let's just knock it down there." Ronan hit a good seven-iron but Calcavecchia hit a great three-wood right in the middle of the green and took the hole.

'They stayed pretty well together and it all came down to the 17th and 18th. On the 17th, Calcavecchia blew it straight over the corner, a great tee-shot. Ronan hit it too straight and through the fairway, so we've got to lay up. Calcavecchia hits it into the greenside bunker and looks as though he's going to make birdie.

'I pace out 180 yards and I was thinking six-iron, but when I got back for the normal conversation and said "What have we got?", he said, "Four-iron." I was totally bamboozled by that. So I had to have a think about this. If I come at him with a six-iron, it's going to totally confuse him. So I look at the yardage book and I see this area eight yards behind the flag. If I suggest a five-iron, he's not going to be confused. He's going to go along with that and the worst thing that can happen is that he gets on the back fringe, this eight yards behind.

'So I say, "I think it's a five-iron, plenty of club, and you can commit yourself with it." He hits a nice shot with the five-iron – and actually finishes on the back fringe, about nine yards from the pin. He walks up to his ball and says, "Jeez, I don't really know what I was thinking there. That four-iron was in the hot-dog stand!"

'Calcavecchia doesn't play a good bunker shot, gets it out to ten feet. Ronan rolls it down close, gets given it; Mark misses. So they now step out on to the 18th tee all-square and Ronan's got the honour. When we get on to the tee there isn't a marshal in sight. "Strange," we say. But we automatically think it's all right to go. Ronan said to me, just before teeing off, "This is what it's all about, what all those hours of practice are all about." He stood up and nailed it, hitting the perfect drive. The split-second the ball had pitched, marshals flocked out from everywhere. Everybody had been over looking at Payne Stewart, who was trying to slash it out of the water. There'd been a mistake, because at least one marshal should have stayed in position to look after the next match coming on the tee – ours.

'I think that was where the match was probably won, because then we had to hold fire. And for Mark to stand on the tee for what seemed like eternity to him would have done him in. He knows that his opponent is in the middle of the fairway and it's not a particularly easy driving hole. When the time did come for him to drive, he just skied it. It was a sky, no two ways about it. It came off the top of the club and was never going anywhere near clearing the water, and it just plopped straight in the middle. So we wander down to our ball, I pace out the yardage and we've got a perfect four-iron. We look back and Mark's dropping his ball on the island. My thoughts were that he'd just pitch it down in front of ours and make us hit a shot to the green. Anything can happen at that stage, thin it, hit it into the water as well, anything.

'Calcavecchia pulls the cover off a three-wood. I thought if he hits his absolute best, he can probably get it just past halfway over the water. I don't know whether he'd tried to calculate how far he had, but there was no way he could get it to dry land. He hit it solid – right into the middle of the water. Ronan was getting a bit flappy at this stage, not really knowing what was going to happen, and he said to me, "Am I going to have to hit the shot now?" Mark pulled his glove off, about-turned, and walked smartly over the bridge.

'So Ronan says, "What's happening now?" I said, "He's going to come over now and he's going to shake your hand and congratulate you. And you're going to win your first Ryder Cup point." Ronan says, "What? I don't have to hit the shot?" I said, "No. All you're going to have to do is pick your ball up. Don't pick it up until he comes over and actually says he's conceded, though."

'That's exactly what happened. After, Ronan says, "What would it have been?" I told him not to worry about it because it was history now but that I'd have said a four-iron. He said, "Well, I don't know. I think it would have been a three-iron, just to make sure I got over."'

Before Rafferty played his part in the halved match, Clark was crushed by Tom Kite. With Clark was Fanny Sunesson, who got her Cup chance after being dropped by José Rivero in 1987 at Muirfield Village.

Sunesson had already shared in two victories with Clark and James, the second dramatic one helping Europe go into the singles two points up, instead of being all-square. She had to be philosophical in singles defeat:

'José Rivero took one of his brothers to the 1987 Ryder Cup and I should have been there. I was very, very, very – extremely – upset about it. I left him the week after. So it was great to be in this time, and my Ryder Cup debut was exciting more than worrying – because I was a woman caddying. But the fact I was the only female didn't make me more determined. I was a caddie, as opposed to being female or male. It was my job. It wasn't as if I hadn't caddied before and the boys have always treated me nicely, so the Ryder Cup was no different. There's a great team spirit in Ryder Cups and we all got on really well together, and helped each other out.

'The week just went by so quickly – the fantastic finish by Howard and Mark on the Saturday obviously made such a difference on how we started the singles, and it was great to be a part of it. You felt that match rather made the whole point of the Ryder Cup, why we were out there.

'Howard was unlucky in the singles against Tom Kite – unlucky, that is, to have come up against Kite in the draw. Nobody could have lived with Kite that day. He was awesome. I think he was something like six-under for the first nine and eight-under after eleven. Unbelievable. And Howard was a couple over, so that exaggerated it. It seemed like Kite was making birdie every hole, hitting shots in to five feet, four feet, all the time. Howard played all right and took it well. If he'd been eight-over and someone level-par and he'd lost, then he'd have been upset, but he knew there wasn't a lot he could do about it.'

James, though, continued his success into the singles as he overcame Mark O'Meara. James's victory acted as a great morale-booster for the Europeans and the crowd, as caddie Graham observed:

'Jesse played so good it was scary. On the sixth he hit his second shot twenty feet past the flag and he asked me for the line. The green looks as though it goes from front to back and left to right, so we are going back up the hill. I said, "Outside-left and up the hill." He hit it right in the middle and said, "Great read." That gave me a lot of confidence and he obviously had plenty too, because on the way down the next fairway he said, "Scotchie, there's no way he can beat me." He was right. He just "flagged-it" all day.'

It was Christy O'Connor Junior's second Ryder Cup. He played his first in 1975, when he lost two pairs matches and never got picked for the singles. Disappointed at missing out on the 1985 Ryder Cup, O'Connor was chosen at the last minute for this one because Sandy Lyle had declined Jacklin's offer of a wild-card. The man from Galway, whose similarly named uncle had graced the competition years before, was determined to justify his wild-card.

He was, therefore, outraged on the morning of the singles when he read in one of the Sunday newspapers that his selection had been a big mistake, and that he was not worthy of his place. That newspaper article was to prove O'Connor's driving force. Then a two-iron handed by caddie Matthew Byrne provided what has become a legendary outcome:

'I didn't know much about Christy's selection because in the week he was chosen I was in Holland with my brother Brian, who was in hospital on a life-support machine after a car accident. I got to hear about Christy playing when I arrived to caddie for someone else at the first tournament following selection, the Swiss Open, which he wasn't playing in. We caddies arrived late, about three in the morning, and we had to sleep in the lobby of our hotel because there were no beds until the next day.

'I was dozing when Edinburgh Jimmy [Rae] came in and told somebody the Ryder Cup team. I heard him say Christy was selected and I thought, "This is a wind-up." We'd all been trying to get each other's chairs to sleep on and I thought he was trying to get me up and out of my chair because I had the best seat in the lobby. Then the next morning an elderly couple whom I half-recognised came in and they came over to congratulate me as Christy's caddie – in the Ryder Cup. Then I believed.

'With me being away with Brian in Holland, I hadn't worked with Junior for three weeks. I saw him for the first time the week after Switzerland, but it didn't dawn on me to ask if I'd be on the bag at the Ryder Cup. I just assumed I would be. We played a practice round with Des Smyth – it was the European Open at Walton Heath – and Christy mentioned while we were going round that he had had hundreds of letters from home offering to carry the bag in the Ryder Cup. Des turned round to him and said, "Matt's your lucky man. I tell you, when he's on the bag your luck changes. Now you're selected for the Ryder Cup, he's got to be your man."

'Christy hadn't played in the Ryder Cup for years and he'd never won a point, so I think by putting Junior and Ronan out together to warm them up for the singles, Jacklin risked losing one point to try to win two the next day. At the time I thought it was wrong but in hindsight it was a brilliant decision. Whether their poor foursomes display, mainly the greens, would have affected them for the singles I don't know, but Christy was fired up before we had our usual 40 minutes' warm-up, hit a few putts and went out to the first tee.

'He was so angry when he read something in one of the papers which said he didn't deserve his place, or something like that.

'Seve had had a few encouraging words with him at breakfast – I was there – telling Junior, "You're here because you deserve to be and you don't have to even think about whether you are worthy of a place. You're here on your own merits, so go out and win." When Junior got to the tee and met Freddie Couples, I could sense the determination in him. At the first he stood up, ripped it down the middle, took a wedge to 20 feet – in. Birdie. He was one-up for the third with Fred in trouble but then Couples hit an unbelievable seven-iron to ten feet and won the hole. We lost to par on the fifth to go one-down. We decided that was as far down as we could afford to go, knowing Freddie. So Junior started playing safe, cagey. Junior had the feeling that Couples thought it was going to be easy and he said to me, "If I can just keep with him down the stretch, the last three or four holes, I can get him."

'Junior holed a monster putt on the ninth to get back to all-square. That was just what we'd aimed for – not to be anything worse than one-down by the turn. We were better than that. But then we lost the tenth to a birdie. I knew in my heart and soul that driver wasn't the club. They'd moved the tee forward and it was only 210 to the front to what's not an enormous green. The pin was only on at about ten yards. He said, "Do I go for it?" I said, "You've got to. This guy's going to hit it easily. If we get on, then the pressure's on him." He wanted the driver to cut it in about 230 yards. With a cut that would have been fine, but it was too much club and he found the back bunker in an impossible lie. Couples hit the green and made a two-putt birdie, so we were back one-down.

'As we were walking down the 11th I said to him, "Stick with this guy; don't give him anything." He looked up at the scoreboard and said, "Ah sure; will you look at the team?" I think we were down in ten matches. It looked as though we were being killed. He then said, "My job is to win my match. That's what I'm going to do." It was the way he said it. Sometimes you can see it in players when they are so hungry to win. Such a determination. They're not going to be beaten. That showed at the 14th after Couples had holed a "side-winder", a 25-footer with about a five-foot break. Pressure then on us, but Junior knocked in his six-footer to keep only one-down.

'The 16th was the big hole. I'd got lucky with a perfect number for 110 yards into a crosswind. Junior cut a wedge and almost pitched into the hole, stopping three feet away. Couples two-putted, so here was the big chance. It was a really, really tricky little putt, the three-footer, a lot of break on it. Junior asked me what I thought the line was, saying, "It's left-centre, isn't it?" I knew it was a lot more, left-edge rather than left-centre. But the bottle was beginning to go, my legs were shaking and all I could say was, "It's more than left-centre, just inside." I was really starting to go. The putt just sneaked in on the right-edge and we won with a birdie.

'On the 17th I'm pleading inside, "Just go for it. We've got two holes to play, let's try and win it. A half will be OK but just go for it and try for the win." I turned round and didn't dare look at him. I gave him the wind direction – downwind, left to right – and pulled out the driver – still without looking at him. I said to him, still without looking, "When you're ready. Just keep it nice and smooth."

'He hits a fantastic drive, cuts the corner and we've got nothing in at all. Well, 250 yards left, but straight downwind. Couples didn't cut enough off but he's still all right. For the second shot, Junior says, "What do you think?" I thought two-iron because the pin was well back, 24 yards back on a huge green. This was the first time the two-iron came out the bag. He hit it so well and so far, it actually travelled 280 yards, just off the back edge. I couldn't believe he'd hit it that far. He told me, "That felt just great." He'd hit it so well it had gone even better than I'd planned. Couples just missed the green, chipped up to eight feet. Christy had a chip first downhill and then uphill, didn't kick off the downhill enough and just died on the uphill, eight feet short. They both missed their putts.

'Jacklin came over to Junior on 18 and said, "Anywhere on the fairway." Junior hits a cracking drive 270 yards in the dead-centre of the fairway. When we get down there, Couples has hit the ball 60 yards further than I could even dream a player could hit it. There's a tree left as you look down the 18th fairway. What you have to do is hit it right of the tree with a little draw. Couples had hit it 20 yards left of the tree. Fading! I thought it was impossible he could carry it that far. I made it 300 yards' carry.

'It was dead-centre of the fairway and I just couldn't believe it. I was gutted. But Junior was dead calm and said, "What have we got, mate?" I said, "We've got 172 to the green, 209 to the flag and it's uphill into the wind." He sort of looked side-on at me and I knew he was remembering his great shot into the green at the hole before and what he'd used. I didn't need to offer any advice. He said with a big wink, "It's two-iron, isn't it?" I pulled it and stepped back dry-mouthed. The nerves were so tight. Off we go.

'He hit this incredible shot. The ball's trying to draw, trying to fade, trying to do everything, but it keeps going straight at the flag – almost in slow motion.

I'm saying, "Be up, pitch in the right place; carry the water; don't be too long. Don't go right." The ball got so many instructions that I don't think it knew where it was going and it tried to get into the hole to get out of the way. It ran up to five feet. Christy was ecstatic. If Junior hadn't hit that shot, then I think Couples would have made a birdie. From where he stood, with the green being tiered and well underneath eye-level, it looked like a tap-in.

'The minute Couples hit his shot he knew he was after making a balls of it, blocking it straight-right. He let go of the club and shouted something in anguish like, "What have I done?" We marched straight off and I crouched to watch him chip on. It was a good chip but his ball trickled just past Junior's marker. I looked across and we knew he just had to make this. I knew, though, that he'd been playing cagey all the way round, nearly always lagging his putts and hoping he was doing enough to finish it before the end. I said to myself, "There's no way he's going to make this."

'Junior came over to me, and for the first time he looked nervous. He said, "Do you think I can make this one? What do you see? Is it . . . ?" He was talking too quickly, really nervous. I said, "Listen. It makes no odds what happens, you are definitely going to make that putt." I had to be a bit aggressive with him. Then I swung round and added, "It makes no odds because you're not going to have to make the putt anyway. He f***ing won't!"

'I think to myself, "What in God's name are you saying?" But, sure enough, Couples misses the putt. He walks straight up and picks up Junior's marker. Christy was just mesmerised and stood there like a statue for a few moments, drained and a bit dumbfounded until it hit him. Then there was just chaos. Players jumped all over him, his wife is there and there is such emotion. Such emotion in fact that I forgot to put the pin back in. I didn't know where the bag or the pin was, I was so disorientated. A referee had to come over to me and said, "Excuse me, but could you replace the flag? José Maria Canizares wants to play his shot!"

'I'll never forget what Junior said later on when we were all celebrating in the team lounge, with Christy and Chris de Burgh singing and Sam Torrance pulling the pints. He slapped his arm round my shoulders and said, "This man is the best caddie you'll ever meet under pressure and it's a lot to do with him that I did what I did today." I was a proud man.'

There was no prouder man in all of Spain or Europe, as José Maria Canizares became the one who ensured the Cup stayed his side of the Atlantic. When his caddie Tom Cullen saw the length of the putt they were faced with to first try and make at least a half by not three-putting, he agonised over the craggy Spaniard's ability to even see the hole:

'José Maria had done tremendously well to stay with Ken Green because he was a tough opponent right from the first shot. We'd got three holes behind but José clawed everything back by the time we got to the 18th tee with three birdies. On 18 I could see the pin was in the middle tier of the three, and I told him what the line in and distance was. He said to me, "We've got to get this club right because of where the flag is. If it's too long I'm in trouble, and I'd better not be short either." We decided on a five-iron but he tugged it a bit and it pitched just off the green, hit a hard bit of ground and shot up the back of the green just to the side. That upset him because if he'd hit the green it would have been close to the flag.

'Now we've got big problems. Not many people knew it but José had terrible eyesight. He really needed two sets of glasses out there – one pair to drive with, because he could never see a ball in the air once it had gone a certain distance off the tee, and another pair for the greens. His problem was cataracts in the eyes and he needed an operation to put it right. I was worried he couldn't even see the hole, let alone the line of the putt. But José's very independent when he's putting and it wasn't very often he'd ask me to read the putts. I didn't have a lot to do with this one. He hit a fantastic putt down to only about four feet, the pace just taking it wide.

'I just shook my head in admiration because I swear he wouldn't have been able to see the hole that well from where he was. He must have been all of 50, maybe even 60, feet away. If he could get it that close, I now felt he wouldn't miss the four-footer. Green had missed one just a bit longer and three-putted to bogey, so this one was to keep the Ryder Cup. I went to the side of the green and got ready to leap in the air. I didn't have to wait long.'

Also watching Canizares hole the putt which made sure the Ryder Cup stayed in Europe were Brand Junior and caddie Foster. They wondered, with a shot to the last green to come, whether they could make the decisive half a point:

'Gordon holed a six-footer on the 17th to bring it back level against Mark McCumber and hit a great tee-shot on the 18th. We walked over the bridge and Graham Heindrich, a caddie mate who was working for television, came up to me and said, "If you look up, Canizares has got this to win and keep the Cup."

'I was obviously engrossed in our game and didn't know what was happening up ahead, but when he said that I looked up to see Canizares hole. I shouted out, "You beauty!" It was just like '87 when Seve holed out in front of us to win the Cup when we'd still got to finish. You just wanted to run up and join in the celebrations. But I had to come down to earth quickly because we hadn't won yet.

'So then I'm thinking it's the ideal scenario: Gordon getting the half that's going to win the Cup again. We've got a four-iron to the green. This is going to be it at last. He tugged it a bit and the ball kicked into the bunker. O'Meara hit to 50 feet on the bottom tier and two-putted. Gordon played a poor bunker shot to about 15 feet and missed the putt. I was gutted but thought, "Not to worry because the lads behind will do the job."'

Regrettably for Europe, they did not. Second to fall of the four left searching for the half-point was Torrance, the player who had sealed Europe's thrilling success the last time the Cup was played at The Belfry. Torrance became an angry man this time, as caddie Mason reports:

'Tom Watson was going through a bad time with his putting and Sam suggested earlier on in the week that he ought to give the broomhandle a go. Tom scorned the idea. He said he'd sooner retire.

'After eleven holes, Sam was three-down. Watson had holed everything. Sam must have got inside him six times on the front nine. We were hitting good putts but the ball just wouldn't go in the hole. At the 12th Sam came out of the bunker to two feet and I thought it would be given. Watson said to Sam, "I should probably give you that, but I think I'll test you." Whether Watson wanted to see if the long putter would stand the test or not, I don't know. Tom holed a ten-footer to win the hole anyway. But it was the worst thing he could have done to Sam.

'On the next tee I don't think I've ever seen Sam as angry in my life. He hit nearly 300 yards on the 13th and he was using an old wooden wood, not metal. He was wound up so much. We were only 50 yards off the green and he chipped to three feet and won the hole. He birdied the next as well, to win that.

'Sam was steaming but twice good putts failed to drop on 15 and 16 and so this is it, two-down with two to play. On 17 Sam lipped out, and you could see Watson's relief when he had two putts for the match. His caddie said to me, "If Sam had holed, there was no way Tom would have won the last because he was rocking." He knew what he'd said to Sam on the 12th was wrong and he was feeling the pressure. If Watson had had to go down the last, I think we'd have had the half-point.'

Europe's hard-luck stories continued to the end as they failed to capture the half-point. Caddie Prodger explains Faldo's defeat to Lanny Wadkins:

'Nick decided to hit a three-wood off the tee on the last, and hit it straight at the bunkers. Then he pulled it ever so slightly and it went into the water. That was it. It seemed somebody had to hit it in the water every time a match came to the last – and the big finger came down on Nick.'

That just left Woosnam to nail down the victory against Curtis Strange. It didn't work out for him either. Caddie Morbey relates a similar finish to O'Connor's a little while before, but this time with the boot on the other foot:

'The turning-point came at the 15th. We were just off the green, lying one-up. We holed it from off the green and I gave it the "10–0". I'm up in the air and he can't believe it's gone in. But then I'm aghast because Strange has followed us in.

'With never getting a singles point, the pressure mounts up every time and I felt it. I thought if we could have gone two-up there, with two to play, he'd have done well to have beaten us. Then Curtis birdies 16, 17 and 18. Suddenly we've lost – from nowhere. Woosie never did anything wrong. Strange hit a two-iron to eight feet on the last and we couldn't do anything to stop him. He'd had four birdies over the last four holes.'

HOW WE LOST THE RYDER CUP

1991: A 'WAR ON THE SHORE'

KIAWAH ISLAND, SOUTH CAROLINA, 27–29 SEPTEMBER
USA 14½ EUROPE 13½

CAPTAINS: Dave Stockton (USA)
Bernard Gallacher (Europe)

(European names first)

Foursomes (morning):
S. Ballesteros and J.M. Olazábal (2 and 1) 1, P. Azinger and C. Beck 0
B. Langer and M. James 0, R. Floyd and F. Couples (2 and 1) 1
D. Gilford and C. Montgomerie 0, L. Wadkins and H. Irwin (4 and 2) 1
N. Faldo and I. Woosnam 0, P. Stewart and M. Calcavecchia (1 hole) 1

Fourballs (afternoon):
S. Torrance and D. Feherty (half) ½, L. Wadkins and M. O'Meara (half) ½
S. Ballesteros and J.M. Olazábal (2 and 1) 1, P. Azinger and C. Beck 0
S. Richardson and M. James (5 and 4) 1, C. Pavin and M. Calcavecchia 0
N. Faldo and I. Woosnam 0, R. Floyd and F. Couples (5 and 3) 1

Foursomes (morning):
S. Torrance and D. Feherty 0, H. Irwin and L. Wadkins (4 and 2) 1
M. James and S. Richardson 0, M. Calcavecchia and P. Stewart (1 hole) 1
N. Faldo and D. Gilford. 0, P. Azinger and M. O'Meara (7 and 6) 1
S. Ballesteros and J.M. Olazábal (3 and 2) 1, F. Couples and R. Floyd 0

81

Fourballs (afternoon):
I. Woosnam and P. Broadhurst (2 and 1) 1, P. Azinger and H. Irwin 0
B. Langer and C. Montgomerie (3 and 1) 1, S. Pate and C. Pavin 0
M. James and S. Richardson (3 and 1) 1, L. Wadkins and W. Levi, 0
S. Ballesteros and J.M. Olazábal (half) ½, F. Couples and P. Stewart (half) ½

Singles:
N. Faldo (2 holes) 1, R. Floyd 0
D. Feherty (2 and 1) 1, P. Stewart 0
C. Montgomerie (half) ½, M. Calcavecchia (half) ½
J.M. Olazábal 0, P. Azinger (2 holes) 1
S. Richardson 0, C. Pavin (2 and 1) 1
S. Ballesteros (3 and 2) 1, W. Levi 0
I. Woosnam 0, C. Beck (3 and 1) 1
P. Broadhurst (3 and 1) 1, M. O'Meara 0
S. Torrance 0, F. Couples (3 and 2) 1
M. James 0, L. Wadkins (3 and 2) 1
B. Langer (half) ½, H. Irwin (half) ½
D. Gilford (half) ½, S. Pate (half) ½ (match not played)

THE CADDIES

MARTIN GRAY (DAVID GILFORD 1991; THOMAS BJØRN 1997)

The Lindrick club in Nottinghamshire, scene of the 1957 Ryder Cup triumph over America, helped introduce Gray to caddying and took him, subsequently, alongside David Gilford at Kiawah Island. Having obtained a government grant to launch his career in 1989, Gray became one of those rare caddies who have won first time out when Gilford clinched the 1991 English Open at The Belfry to earn his Ryder Cup billet. Gilford had already arranged for fellow professional golfer Glenn Ralph to caddie for him at South Carolina but a few quiet words from European captain Bernard Gallacher, and Gray was installed. In 1997, after a spell with Seve Ballesteros, he carried for Dane Thomas Bjørn to help Ballesteros lift the Ryder Cup at Valderrama.

Another one from the Selby club in Yorkshire to hit the road, in 1980 Wooler left school with no job, so he jumped at the chance when his new club professional David Jagger invited him to accompany him to the Irish Open at Portmarnock. In the third round they played with Greg Norman. Jagger outplayed the Great White Shark. 'After we finished the round, I went to shake Greg's hand,' says Wooler, 'but he just looked down his nose and turned his back on me. I vowed I'd get him back. A few years later when I was with David Feherty we played with Norman again. He had a great day and was full of the joys of spring on the last. He then walked over to me to shake hands – and I just looked the other way and walked off the green.' Wooler accompanied Ken Brown to the 1983 Ryder Cup at the PGA National. A second Ryder Cup trip to the USA came after he took up the bag for Feherty eight years later.

LEE ADELLY (STEVE RICHARDSON 1991)

The Steven Richardson–Lee Adelly duo was one of a handful of partnerships over the years on the European Tour forged between friends and clubmates. Adelly gave Richardson basketball lessons and English amateur international Richardson repaid the compliment by bringing down Adelly's handicap at their club, Lee-on-the-Solent in Hampshire. Richardson helped out in Adelly's painting and decorating business, so when Richardson joined the touring pro ranks, it was a logical move for Adelly to follow him. In 1991 two early victories ensured a Ryder Cup place, astonishingly, by the spring. A fiery individual, Adelly once served a tour suspension after breaking a South African caddie's jaw in a fight.

'TURNBERRY GEORGE' SPRUNT (PAUL BROADHURST 1991)

At the tender age of 13, George Sprunt followed in the footsteps of his grandfather, the original 'Turnberry', who not only caddied but carried out starter and ranger duties at the Open venue. Having befriended Paul Broadhurst's caddie Bill 'Yorkie' Brown, Sprunt inherited the midlander's bag after Brown was killed in a car accident on the way to a tournament in 1989. A victory at Hoylake in the 1991 Pro-Celebrity event and then a thrilling runner-up spot in the German Open that year, took the pair to Kiawah Island. Girvan man Sprunt then retired to run the European Tour's 'Caddie Shack'. Tragically, he was returning from his final event of 1996, the Volvo Masters, when he, too, died in a road accident.

THE ACTION

'If he could have played it over again, he might have hit it a little bit harder. The spike mark was the sad part of it all, though.'

The final putt on the final hole. It could not have been closer. It signalled victory for America over a mammoth and often tortuous 7,240-yard course which had brought its combatants from both sides to tears long before Bernhard Langer wept for Europe. After two defeats and a losing draw, Sam Ryder's Cup was back in an American showcase.

However, the St Albans seedsman would have been bewildered and ashamed that his venture had arrived at such a pass as to be called the 'War on the Shore'. Three terms without success, and the memory of The Belfry's partisan gallery, left the home crowd baying for victory. America's team, stung by past defeats and whipped up to a frenzy of passion for the Stars and Stripes by media hyperbole, were determined to win. Regrettably, it seemed, at any cost.

Europe, with a new captain and five rookies in the side, might have collapsed under the early pressure, leaving no last-day, last-hole, last-putt drama. But under the leadership of the upright Bernard Gallacher and inspired by the on-course tenacity of Severiano Ballesteros, they helped take the match to its breathtaking zenith.

Gallacher had taken over from the highly successful Tony Jacklin after serving as vice-captain. He was the ideal man to follow in the footsteps of a captain who had taken Europe to two victories and a tie in three successive campaigns. For America, the 1970 and 1976 US PGA champion Dave Stockton was a relatively surprising choice to try to stop the rot.

Early sabre-rattling and exchanges between the two captains was to turn into something a little more sinister. An unsavoury altercation in the opening foursomes seemed to set the tone on the early part of the week. Soon, a 'Desert Storm' cap was jammed on the head of the pugnacious little Corey Pavin as a golf war broke out.

Ballesteros's confrontation with Azinger in the 1989 Ryder Cup had refused to lie down. Now they were drawn together again. Seve's caddie Billy Foster prepared for fireworks:

'Kiawah Island was something else. And it all happened on the first morning. Seve was right on top of his game, leading the money list in a year when he won more in the world than anybody else. But Azinger and Beck were playing fantastic golf that year too, so I knew we were in for a match.

'The Americans got off to a great start and they were two-up after seven when José Maria comes over and says, "I'm sure it's happened twice now; they've swapped balls. That hole they were playing a 100 compression when they finished, but when they were downwind, they played a 90 compression ball." [Ryder Cup rules stated that a player must use the same compression ball throughout a match, and that also applied to foursome-play.] Well, when Azinger and Beck played the eighth, Seve and Ollie kept an eye on things and saw they'd done the same again – 90 compression and then 100 compression. So Seve told one of the European players following our game, "Go and get Bernard Gallacher. I need to speak to him."

'They'd just teed off at the ninth, with Seve and José two-down, when Gallacher turned up but we had to get on with it. They told Bernard on the ninth fairway what they thought had been happening. Zinger had just holed a great putt on the ninth green to win the hole and go three-up. The crowd were going mental, screaming "USA, USA, USA," and Zinger, after punching the air, was leading them with his arms waving up and down, shouting "USA, USA, USA," going a bit mental himself. I looked at Seve and a glare of steel came into his eyes. He whispered, "You sonofabitch." His fuse was lit good and proper.

'When we got to the tenth tee there was chaos – European officials, US officials, television cameras. This is when the row really kicked off. It was all happening. At that time, José was the one doing all the spouting-off, saying, "You played a 100 compression here and a 90 compression there; you did this on the fourth, that on the seventh; you've been changing the ball." Zinger was arguing back, saying they hadn't changed the ball, and the argument went on for about 20 minutes altogether. But after ten minutes, Zinger started to change his tune, saying, "Well, maybe we did change the ball here and there, I'm not sure." Zinger kept saying, "We weren't cheating," and Seve told him, "Paul, nobody's accusing you of cheating – just breaking the rules. That's a bit of a different thing."

'Once he found out, though, that there was nothing anyone could do about it once the hole has finished and the pin gone in, Zinger backed down, knowing they were going to be three-up. If they'd been called in the middle of the hole, Seve and José could have done something about it. Once they finished the hole, it was all over. So then Zinger said, "Oh yes, we did do that, but we didn't realise it was illegal." We had to get on with it and as soon as the ruling came about I said to the lads we'd got to forget it and put it behind us.

'We restarted and Zinger walked past me, saying almost under his breath and sort of sneering, "Nice try!" Well, the horns came out then on Seve and Ollie. Seve was absolutely seething but you could see he was in control – and so was José Maria. Seve said, "That's it. We'll see how they play with the right balls now." He was on fire. We shot something like five-under-par on the back-nine. From being three-down, they won five holes out of the next eight. I thought it would be the best golf I'd ever see, bearing in mind the circumstances.'

Olazábal's caddie Dave Renwick gives his view of the controversy: 'Ollie was sure the balls were being switched around but, of course, he couldn't go and inspect them and it wasn't until he was absolutely sure and had it confirmed by Seve that they called in Bernard Gallacher.

'A lot of people said that the incident affected Zinger and Chipper but it wasn't the case. It was the way Ollie and Seve played on the back-nine. They were awesome. The greens were rock solid and it was really difficult to get anywhere near the pins because they were nearly always tucked away in tough places, probably to try to give the Americans that little extra edge. Seve and Ollie just fired straight at the pins on the backside and never gave Azinger and Beck a look-in after the turn.'

As the rest of the European team reeled under an opening onslaught by the Americans and slumped 3–1 down in the morning, Ballesteros and Olazábal saw it as their duty to get their team-mates into winning mode. The luck of the draw pitched Ballesteros and Olazábal again into battle with Azinger and Beck.

By now the Americans had put in a complaint of their own, upset at Ballesteros continually clearing his throat. Beck, who had admitted to being affected most by it in the morning, and Azinger accused Ballesteros of coughing during their swings. An American official monitored the throat-clearing at his men's behest and reported that he thought it excessive and often ill-timed. So Azinger complained to Gallacher, but could not convince the European captain it was deliberate. That meant the afternoon fourballs was never going to be full of bonhomie, as Foster recalls:

'There was no love lost between the two pairs that week. Not a lot of chat went on in the afternoon between the teams on the first tee. We heard there'd been complaints about Seve clearing his throat during the matches. He does it all the while, it's a habit he's had for years. He most definitely does not cough during players' swings. That's utter rubbish and just sour grapes if anybody said so. Seve plays the game hard but he doesn't need to do things like that. In the afternoon he just wanted to get stuck in and "kick their asses" again, he said. And they did.'

Backing the Spaniards in the afternoon, there was a demolition of Corey Pavin and Mark Calcavecchia by Mark James and Steve Richardson to mark the burly Richardson's Ryder Cup debut. Sharing in the glory was caddie Lee Adelly:

'We were told we'd be travelling out to the island by minibus so, as you do, we had a few beers – some of the caddies eight or twelve beers. Then when we got there they drove us to this car-lot and told us to take our pick – one car each. Well, some of the caddies couldn't walk, let alone drive, so we ended up taking only four cars instead of twelve.

'It was a big experience for me, going as Steve's friend as well as being his caddie, but the rest of the caddies were great with me. I'm not one of these guys that goes out on the course and checks over every ridge and pin placement. I just read the yardage chart and that's it. But if some of the guys who did take it that far went out and found something that wasn't quite right, they came and told us. There was great teamwork. I had the easy ride. Some caddies were really nervous. Martin Gray told me he had stomach cramps and pains all the first day, but I just said to myself, "I'm not playing, so I've no need to be nervous."

'Steve practised badly, but he often does. He can practise poorly and then turn it on in the tournament. Mr Gallacher didn't know this and thought if he was no good in practice, how was he going to be any good in the match? So Steve didn't get picked for the first foursomes.

'I don't know whether Mark James said anything, perhaps that he fancied playing with Steve because of his strength and his hitting ability, but Steve got a game in the afternoon fourballs. Mark was great. We worked as a team. Jesse did his yardages and I did our yardages and we checked each other's so we didn't make a mistake. In the five and four opening win against Pavin and Calcavecchia, Steve started a bit dodgily and Jesse was just solid, down the middle on the green, made three or four pars on his own. Steve relaxed because of Jesse's steady play and then on the sixth he hit a big drive but then went into a bunker with his six-iron. He then holed the bunker shot for an eagle and that really settled him down. They just cruised round after that.'

While James provided the experience for rookie Richardson, his caddie John 'Scotchie' Graham could also call upon past Ryder Cup outings, having been part of the winning team two years before at The Belfry:

'The War on the Shore. It was really scary, but the best Ryder Cup you'll ever be in. Langer and Jesse had played well enough to beat Floyd and Couples, but they didn't get the breaks and then Mark and Steve hit it off well together. When we walked down the tenth with Steve, he could see all his family and friends lining the fairway and the crowd chanted, "Rico, Rico, Rico." I don't know how it made him feel but it made me feel determined I was going to do everything I could to help us win. And I'm caddying for Jesse!'

Also on the first afternoon, Sam Torrance and David Feherty, one of the European Tour's most renowned and enduring friendships, were delighted to capture a half off Lanny Wadkins and Mark O'Meara in the fourballs. Ken Brown's 1983 caddie Rod Wooler returned to Ryder Cup duty to carry the bag for the former opera-singing Ulsterman with the quickest one-liners in golf:

'David and Sam were just inseparable and played together in practice every day. We played Seve and Olazábal and Sam opened his mouth and suggested playing for money. It cost them about two hundred quid. Feherts said of Kiawah Island, which is a Pete Dye course, "Dye and Nicklaus are like landscapers on acid." But he played it well in his first match for real, played fantastic golf to let him and Sam claw it back. They were three-down after nine holes but Feherts played fantastic golf. He hit a great little five-wood to three feet on the 14th to get them back to only one-down.

'But his big moment came on the last. We were one-down going to 18 and David hit to eight feet to set up a chance to win the hole and halve the match. The crowd was electric but Feherts handled it brilliantly. Sam helped him line up the putt and in it went. Very brave.'

For Faldo and Woosnam, the reigning US Masters champion, the difference of a putt going in or not shaded the result of their opening match as they went down narrowly by one hole to the reigning US Open champion Payne Stewart and Mark Calcavecchia. But that was the last time they looked anything like winning as a pair. After a comprehensive defeat in the afternoon the Faldo–Woosnam partnership was over, probably forever.

Caddie Morbey found the 'little-and-large' combination firing on less than all cylinders as they embarked on quite an unnerving week:

'There we were, stuck out in the middle of the Atlantic, the opponents in army hats – it was a bit naughty. The fans were terrible that week. For our first match, we had a tough one against Stewart and Calcavecchia. I know afterwards the papers said Nick and Woosie didn't try that week, but that was absolute rubbish. The Ryder Cup's the Ryder Cup and if anybody thinks they weren't trying then they don't know the players like the caddies do. They were both playing poorly and they didn't blend together. They were obviously both hoping to build on the first two Ryder Cups in which they played together and were the top team, but it didn't turn out that way. Faldo's a very difficult man to play with and if you're not on the same wavelength as him you're lost. They just got the mix wrong. Woosie would recommend he hit that club but then Nick hit something different – and vice versa. They did not play well as a team.

'It was close in the foursomes and we could have won it just as easily as we lost it. Calcavecchia chipped in on 16 to make it two-up to the Americans from pretty well nowhere. Then the Yanks messed up the 17th – Stewart went into the water – but we could only halve the last. But they struggled in the afternoon against Floyd and Couples as soon as Woosie missed a short one on the 11th and Faldo fluffed a chip. Afterwards, Woosie told me that he wasn't confident of playing in the foursomes again and told Bernard so, mainly because he wasn't driving the ball that well.'

Europe were again rocked back on their heels in the Saturday foursomes. First to go down were Torrance and Feherty. The second match, though, was much tighter and if it had been a boxing match, James and Richardson would have lost on a split decision. Richardson's caddie Adelly took the boxing analogy even further:

'It was all pretty close in the foursomes and we were all-square at the 16th. Calcavecchia, whom we drew again, hit his third shot into a sand-dune on the right, a waste bunker. He was near a fence but it was a lateral-hazard as well, so with it being inside a red line, he couldn't get a free drop away from the fence. The Americans said they'd wait and get a referee anyway. I said, "It's no big deal, it's inside a red hazard line, there's no free drop, let's get going." Payne Stewart's caddie said to me, "Why don't you f*** off. Leave it to the ref." I said, "No. You f*** off, I'm staying. I'm just as much involved as anybody." Then Mark came over and said, "Lee, leave." So I strolled off.

'They were told there was no free drop and Steve then hit a perfect three-wood for Jesse's pitch. It looked a funny pin position so I walked up and had a look. Jesse said, "What do you think?" and I advised him not to go for the pin because if he went big there was no shot. After asking me, though, he did go for it and the ball stopped on the top ledge. Steve ran this big putt down the ledge, slightly heavy-handed, four feet by, and Jesse missed it. The Americans up-and-downed it from the dunes for a six, so it was a half that should have been a win for us. They also halved 17, so all-square still.

'On the 17th, Stewart's caddie's still having a go at me but I'm too busy trying to help us win the match, which is at a critical stage with just one hole in it. But on the 18th he was still being aggressive and I finally snapped. I said to him, "If you don't shut up I'm going to drill you. I don't care whether it's Ryder Cup, in America, whatever or wherever, if you don't shut up you're going to be on your ass." That did shut him up this time.

'At the 18th, Jesse drove into a waste bunker. Steve hit a brilliant shot to about a yard short of the green. I was hoping Jesse would put it really close. He played a brilliant putt, right around the slope, a big right-to-left break, to about four and a half feet. Steve went for the putt and didn't even hit the hole. Sad, because we lost the match on that putt.'

A new partnership was tried out in the Saturday foursomes, that of the highly experienced Faldo and rookie David Gilford. When the two Englishmen were slaughtered 7 and 6 by Azinger and Mark O'Meara, the British press lambasted Faldo. They criticised him for leaving Gilford to fend for himself and for failing to strike up any rapport with the softly spoken first-timer, who had lost in his opening match with fellow rookie Colin Montgomerie. Caddie Sunesson believes Faldo was maligned and misunderstood. She was also disgusted with some of the behaviour at the formidable venue:

'Getting Nick's bag was a dream come true and we had a marvellous year, but he wasn't in good form at the start of the week at Kiawah Island. It was always going to be a tough week. Some were looking upon it as a kind of war. That was totally out of order. Corey Pavin wearing a "Desert Storm" cap was a disgrace and very upsetting. It's only a golf game and I guess he forgot that people were dying out there in the real war. It was taking the mickey out of them and their families. I thought it was in very bad taste. Maybe he did not see it that way and thought that he was just supporting America but I don't think he should have acted the way he did.

'It was a hard week. Work-wise it was tough, walking up and down all those sand-dunes. I didn't like the course. I don't have trouble carrying a bag because

I'm a woman – it was hard for all the caddies, hard physical work. At the end of the day, you just had nothing left at all. You wanted nothing more than a hot drink and bed, and a good night's sleep.

'When we started, the crowds made it like a war feeling. They were awful. The behaviour was often bad, shouting and not a good atmosphere.

'Things just didn't work out this time with Ian Woosnam. It was quite close in the morning match on the first day. Mark Calcavecchia's chip-in on the 16th was really the key to who won that one. But it wasn't good in the afternoon and so the next day we were put out with David Gilford. He's very quiet.

'The main thing was, though, that the two of them just did not know each other at all. Well, they certainly hardly knew each other. I think Nick had talked to him once, or we'd played with him once. I don't think that was the right situation to put them in. David's a good player and Nick's a good player but that doesn't mean they are immediately going to be good players together. They did not know each other and so of course they didn't do much social talking to each other. When they needed to talk over the golf, they did. There was no ignoring of David. They just came up against opponents who were playing well and they lost just like anybody could have lost.'

Gilford's caddie Martin Gray, who needed Gallacher to step in and make sure he even made the trip, saw things in a similar light to Sunesson:

'David had already arranged with Glenn Ralph to caddie for him. There was a furore because Ralphy was a PGA professional player and it was felt that he shouldn't be caddying in a Ryder Cup. I just kept out of it. In the end Bernard Gallacher took him to one side and put him right on it. They wondered, for instance, where Ralphy was going to base himself – in the caddie-shack or with the players? Would the caddies welcome him, not being one of them, if he did decide to go with them? He's a grand bloke, Ralphy, but I think Gilly got a lot of stick from all sides, definitely from some of the caddies, and after Bernard had taken him to one side, David asked me at the Epson Grand Prix, a couple of weeks before the Ryder Cup, if I'd like to go to Kiawah Island.

'I was desperate to do a good job then, and I was really, really nervous. So I decided to glean as much as I could from the experienced caddies, falling in with the way they did the yardages and so on. In practice we generally played with Broadie and in practice David was unbelievable. I don't think he missed a fairway over the three practice days. We played against Seve and Olazábal one day and I think Ballesteros was quite impressed because David was so straight. That was his strength. His weakness was always his chipping.

'I guess Seve must have said something to Gallacher because he was put in straight away with Monty, two rookies together. They made a few mistakes coming down the stretch because they'd come back from a bad start when they were both very, very nervous. Monty wasn't in the same class in those days. They were like lambs to the slaughter, a bad pairing I thought, two rookies together. Then they split Faldo and Woosie up and David and Faldo got hammered.

'There was a lot of bad press about Faldo blanking Gilford but it didn't really come over like that on the course. Gilly's a nightmare to try and get into – quiet as a mouse – and Faldo's not really an extrovert. David was certainly not in awe of Faldo. He's got plenty of self-belief and knew his strengths. It was just one of those days when the Americans clicked. Everything they did was bang-on. Everything Gilford and Faldo did just wouldn't come off. There is no truth in the stories that say Faldo deliberately ignored David. He would be marching 30 or 40 yards in front of me, Fanny and Gilly, and it was difficult to keep up with him, but once they got up over their balls he'd come across, ask what yardage he'd got, discuss clubs with David. He lined him up on the greens. They talked OK. They were both trying their nuts off but it was just one of those things. Nothing happened. But Faldo being who he was and is, he got a load of flak.'

While Europe crumbled around them, Ballesteros and Olazábal were not to be denied and their 3 and 2 success over Ray Floyd and Fred Couples provided the launch-pad to an exhilarating afternoon for Europe as the visitors bounced back to win the fourballs 3½–½ and square the match 8–8.

That undefeated afternoon for Europe included victories for more rookie–veteran partnerships as Gallacher juggled to find a successful formula. Woosnam and Paul Broadhurst led the way with a scintillating success over the determined Paul Azinger and Hale Irwin.

Broadhurst's caddie was the thoughtful Scot, 'Turnberry George' Sprunt. Despite his player being one of Europe's men in form, 'Turnberry' had quite a wait before he could go through his paces:

'Paul got to Kiawah Island through guts. He went into the Ryder Cup with a lot of confidence but he didn't really practise very well, to be fair to Bernard Gallacher, who didn't pick him until the Saturday. Bernard was there to see who was swinging it well. Broadie's got a very individual swing, too, and it didn't look at its best. On the evidence of the practice rounds, Gallacher wouldn't chance him.

'Then when Paul did play, he was the one who shone out of him and Woosnam in the fourballs. They both played very well from tee to green but Woosie missed a few putts whilst Broadie made them. In fact Broadie ended up lining up the putts for Woosie – on his Ryder Cup debut! Broadie holed one from 60 feet, with two breaks, left to right and right to left, on 13 before we turned into the wind. That proved the turning-point in the match. The match was all over on 17. First time out and he's won. It was a relief for me as well. You don't have as much pressure as the player but you want desperately to do the right things. By the time you play your second Ryder Cup match, it isn't quite so difficult.'

Another new partnership to prevail was that of Langer and Montgomerie, with victory over Steve Pate and Pavin 2 and 1. There had been conjecture all week over whether Pate would be fit to play, having suffered heavy bruising to hips and ribs on the Wednesday on his way to the official welcoming banquet, when his car collided with another team car.

James and Richardson then hit back against Wayne Levi and Wadkins. James's caddie John Graham was delighted to get one back at Wadkins – and Wadkins' daughter:

'I must have a thing with Lanny Wadkins, because in 1989 I'd trodden on his line and had him growl at me and this time I had trouble with his family. We were playing the 16th, par-five. Jesse's hit his third in, a nine-iron, right on the flag. I could hear Lanny Wadkins's daughter nearby saying, "Go in the bunker." Jesse's ball pitched nicely on the hill but then screwed back and ran down the hill – into the trap. I thought, "You bitch!"

'I wanted to get back at her on the next hole because we halved when a win would have made it a 3 and 2 victory for us. On 17, the short hole across the water, the crowd behind the green were just like a football match, with flags waving and so on. Richardson hit first, a nice big crafty hook, like he does, to about 25 feet past the flag. Somebody in the crowd yelled, "He swings it like a duck!" That got a glare from all of us, but then Jesse also hit the green. Wadkins then hit it left and Levi in the water, so we're feeling good. As we walked up I thought I'd get near Lanny Wadkins's daughter. I found her and just stared at her with a big grin. I let her know, "That's got you back." Then I went to the European section and said, "Give us more!" They did and so did we. Our win meant we'd won the first three matches in the afternoon to level it.'

Could it be a whitewash for Europe again? It all rested on the last match – Ballesteros and Olazábal against Couples and Stewart. After all the previous day's incident, subterfuge and suspense, caddie Foster watched a memorable encounter:

'It was the finest display of Ryder Cup fours you'll ever see. It was nip-and-tuck all the way. At the 15th, we're one-down. Couples has duck-hooked off the tee; Stewart, Olazábal and Seve were down the middle. Couples could only move it 100 yards and had a 100-yard bunker shot for his third. Olazábal and Seve are on the green. Seve's hit a great shot to 15 feet. Stewart's hooked into bushes. Now we're looking good.

'Couples goes into the greenside bunker for three and Stewart's up in the bushes, thrashing away and breaking branches. Seve's going absolutely mad, shouting, "Somebody get an official; do something about this." So eventually a referee goes over there and disqualifies Stewart for snapping branches everywhere. He's out of the hole.

'Seve's played two world-beater shots to 15 feet and Olazábal's on the green, Couples is in sand. This has got to be all-square. Couples, though, comes out of the bunker from 30 yards short of the green – and holes his bunker shot. As his ball's coming out, I'm saying, "You can f*** off doing that!" I looked at Seve and his chin bounced off his toes. Couples walks on to the green with his arms out, giving it 10–0. The crowd are going absolutely wild because they're certain they've got the half. But I could see that look come over Seve.

'Olazábal misses his long putt and now it's Seve's turn. He bins it and we win the hole with a birdie. Seve doesn't go through any dramatics. I'm the one who screams out, "Get in, you beauty." He just stands in front of the crowd with his hands on his hips for a second or two, then he looks at Couples. Just a few moments ago Fred and the crowd have been going crackers. Now Seve's broken his heart. Then, from the 16th, all you could hear was roaring from the European section of the crowd, wives, girlfriends and the rest of the team not playing included. The Europeans were chanting and singing. Their camaraderie was fantastic, magnificent. From 600 yards away you could hear them in full voice. The nearer you got the louder it got, banners waving . . .

'We halved 16 and on the short 17th Stewart and Couples both hit bad tee-shots; Olazábal's hit a two-iron to six feet, flagged it, great shot. The European crowd were going frantic. Considering this was our fourth game in two days and we were walking around in more or less two foot of sand all the time, our bodies were absolutely knackered. But I'll never forget walking down that hole. The crowds were chanting and singing and I was lifted. My body must have really been ready to drop – but I was floating. I couldn't feel the bag.

'Couples, though, from short left and behind a dune, hit the green and holed out from about ten feet; great shot and great par. Ollie missed his birdie, though. We're last match out, and at the last. It's dark. All you can see are the silhouettes of Seve and Ollie with an orange background. We're in trouble. The Americans have made safe pars, tapping in, but Seve's hit to 15 feet for three after going in the bunker. Olazábal's seven feet short after a much weaker putt up.

'Seve being Seve, and having all his experience, he took the responsibility away from José and said, "You go first, José; no problem. I'll hole mine for definite, so you knock yours in first." Seve didn't want to miss his and give Ollie the ultimate pressure of having to hole his seven-footer. José holed it and it was probably the loudest cheer I've ever shouted in my career. The crowd was delirious, yet you could hardly see them.'

So Europe entered the singles all-square with 11 matches to try to keep the Cup, 11 because of the withdrawal of Pate. Stockton had risked playing him in the pairs, so he could first of all test out the extent of the injury under match conditions and then get match-practice before his singles. After playing in the losing fourballs with Pavin against Langer and Montgomerie, however, Pate decided he was not fit enough to play. This was a mystery to Langer, who said, 'I saw the bruises he had around his stomach and hips, but he seemed to play all right against us and it didn't seem to affect his movements or his swing. In fact I think he played better than Corey Pavin.'

With the draw already made, Ballesteros was down to meet Pate in the singles. Gallacher used his option of withdrawing the player he had entered into the dreaded envelope, should any opponent be unfit to play. Instead of Ballesteros being pulled out, the Spaniard was switched to play Wayne Levi. This meant that the enveloped player, Gilford, was the unlucky man. Earning an automatic half was no consolation to Gilford, nor his caddie Gray:

'We were gutted. The "Grand Señor" swapped with us and took Levi. Gilly was looking forward to the singles to try and get a bit of self-respect back. He fancied playing on his own – more his style – and was determined to get a point. He wanted to prove he was good enough to be out there on merit. Levi, too, was playing terribly and David fancied beating him. He was their weak man, so it was a brilliant draw for Gilly.

'The worst of it was that we had no idea the night before that Gilly's name was in the envelope. We all thought Pate would play anyway. Gilly only got to hear about his name in the envelope on the morning when Bernard came and told him. It must have been a dreadful shock, and he was absolutely gutted. He disappeared and hid away, with no opportunity to put the record straight. I didn't see him until the matches were under way in the afternoon. I'll never forget the look in his eye as he stood holding an empty envelope and a slip of paper.'

Faldo, first away, had every reason to search for that little bit extra in his game that had been painfully missing in his three losing pairs matches. He was up against his old adversary Floyd. As far as the 1991 Ryder Cup went, Floyd was one-up. Faldo sought revenge, knew caddie Sunesson, even if her player's previous day's absence had caused further bad press back home:

'The papers gave Nick a bad time, complaining that he didn't come out and support the other players. That was ridiculous. He was practising. Practising and practising. I should know. His game was not in the best of shape and we needed to practise. He was doing that for his team. It was a hard afternoon's work and it paid off in the end when he beat Floyd by two holes. It was a different Nick out there. And that was all down to the work he had put in when he was supposed to be ignoring his team. After he'd beaten Floyd we had plenty of chance then to go out and support the team.'

Feherty then put Europe in the driving seat by beating Payne Stewart, as caddie Rod Wooler reveals, with a little help from his friends:

'All week David was hitting the ball fantastically well but struggling with the pace on the greens, struggling with his putting in general. He had his sports psychologist Alan Fine over for the week and we practised the putting for hours each night. His great mate Sam [Torrance] helped out, too. By the time we got to finish on the Saturday night, Dave had got it right and he turned round to me and said, "No matter who we've got, I'll kill them." I just looked at the ground and hoped. We got Payne Stewart, and that, I thought, was perfect. David had played against Payne in the Kirin Cup and beaten him.

'We got a couple up early. You remember the good clubs you give and on the fourth after he'd gone into the dunes, he wanted to hit four-iron. But I reminded him it was always longer out of the sandy stuff. He hit a three-iron in to ten feet and won the hole. I got a pat on the back and David took control. We were three-up on the back-nine and Payne holed a big one to stay in the game. On seventeen we were two-up. Monty's behind us in danger of losing; Faldo's in front with just about the beating of Floyd. Bernard Gallacher's dashing about, knowing just how important our match is.

'You could tell the frustration was building in Feherts, waiting and waiting on that 17th tee. It's a tough hole, a par-three, and a lot of matches finished there that week. When we can go, it's 250 yards into the wind. We knew it was going to be a one-iron, a one-and-a-half-iron, really. But all we had to do was hit the green. Then the match was virtually over, because of the toughness of actually doing that on 17. The tension of waiting, though, put my heart in my mouth. It's what Ryder Cups are all about, I suppose.

'Stewart went first, took his time, came up short. With all the waiting it must have been 20 minutes we were stood on the tee before David hit his one-iron – right into the heart of the green. Stewart pitched long so I said to David, "Just lag her up, boss." He did and it was all over. I could let my emotions out at last. I punched the air. I'd been terrified at times.'

Directly behind, Montgomerie looked defeated. Four-down with four to play. His opponent Calcavecchia, however, inexplicably then collapsed. Montgomerie won all the last four holes for a half, Calcavecchia finishing triple-bogey, bogey, triple-bogey, bogey. The 1989 Open champion dissolved, too, into tears.

Europe kept its two-point advantage. That was reduced to one when Olazábal allowed Azinger revenge for his pairs defeats.

Next match up was Richardson's with Pavin. Could the Hampshire combination of Richardson and his sparring-partner Adelly prevail in the face of histrionics by his opponent and a near-hysterical home crowd?

'I wasn't nervous at all, never once all week in fact. I'd been caddying for two years and I was confident of picking the right clubs out now I was on my own. The greens were pretty tough to read but you could always get them on the right side. If we hit one close we could give it a lot of attention but often they were long ones, 30–40 feet, and we weren't going to hole many of them anyway. At the Ryder Cup I read a lot of greens. Steve tended to under-borrow. Against Pavin, though, we just got outputted. Corey would be eight feet, Steve eight and a half. Steve would miss, Corey would get it. Corey was the best player in America that year.

'Pavin got his nose in front and started giving it all the Desert Storm rubbish, wearing the camouflauge cap and all. He was inciting the crowd, punching the air – a pain in the ass. It niggled Steve terribly and I don't think he'll ever forgive him. It was more than just gamesmanship. There was no need for it because theirs was a superbly competitive match anyway. When Pavin was two-up after seven he was really going for it with the gallery, punching the air every few minutes.

'As we got past the turn I looked up at the board and said to Steve, "I don't want to pressurise you, but if you lose your game, we're going to lose the Ryder Cup, it's that close." He said, "Oh thanks, Lee. There's no pressure on me then?" I said, "Well, you've got to know, you're a man." To his great credit, Steve got it back to only one after the 13th, which was definitely one for the memory.

'The officials had said to the wives and girlfriends not to go ahead of play in case something happened, like if they kicked a ball or something. It could be deemed bad sportsmanship or something, even if it was an accident. If the caddie goes ahead and he gets hit it's two shots, but not if it hits the girls. Anyway, Steve hit his second after a big drive, a four-iron, purposely at the bank on the left, the dune, above the green. It's only got to come off there and it's stiff. Pavin's wife was up ahead close to the green on this dune, in fact only five yards from the flag. The ball came towards her and she panicked, stumbled down the sand-dune and scoured a footprint about eight or ten inches deep. Our ball was about a third of the way down her footprint. It stayed up there instead of falling down close to the flag as we'd intended. It's waste bunker, so it's tough luck. She was in tears, because she knew she shouldn't have been there. I felt sorry for her, because she was so upset.

'Steve managed to scramble it out of this hole after Pavin had mucked up his approach. We made par. Pavin bogeyed it. So we're back to one-down. But Steve missed the green going for it on the short 14th. Pavin deliberately laid up short, confident in his ability to chip the ball close. He did that and went back two-up. It all came to a head on the 17th, the one Pavin has made a legend with his leaping out of the bunker and charging down the green.

'Before we played the 17th, which was probably the toughest hole on the course the way it came into play all the while, Bernard Gallacher came out to see Steve. He said to him, "It's a one-iron for you, Steve." Steve told him he hadn't got a one-iron, so Bernard said, "Well, you'll have to hit a three-wood then." He didn't know Steve that well at that stage, not realising what a big-hitter he was. Steve said, "No, I'll have to hit a three-iron." We'd already decided it. He hit the three-iron, a great shot but a little big, about 20 feet away from the flag. Pavin, being one of the shorter hitters, especially into the wind, chose a three-wood and it plugged in the face of the bunker on the left side. He went for the safe shot, playing percentages because he's two-up.

'Pavin was on the slope and he only had to get it out because then it had to

96

go close the way the ball would run. It was like a railway track coming out. It could go a yard either side. Splash! As soon as he hit the ball he dived out of the bunker and chased his ball down, shouting and punching the air, urging it on and on to the hole. If it had been a couple of years later I'd have thrown him in the lake. I'd only been on tour a year and I was a bit more of a gentleman at that stage.

'He got it up and down, give him his due, and Steve rolled up, couldn't get the birdie. I was so annoyed I packed everything up and went back to the villa for a particular reason. I just knew if I saw Payne Stewart's caddie, the guy I'd had trouble with earlier, and he said something smarmy, I'd have decked him. I didn't want to do that.'

Ballesteros's 3 and 2 victory over Levi gave Europe hope still. Ballesteros was in murderous mood, to the amusement and discomfort of caddie Foster:

'Everybody thought it was going to be a turnover. Seve's on his game, Levi's playing rubbish. But on strokeplay, Levi could have had the second-best score that day. Seve played fantastic, really on his game.

'At the 13th there was quite a stir. Levi's rolled it up to two feet. Seve's putting his ball down and Levi says, "I'll finish." Well, you can't do that in matchplay; you've got to mark. Seve goes absolutely ballistic. "This sonofabitch is crazy. What is he doing? You can't do this. Call an official." Levi knew he was in a match then. If he didn't before.

'I'll never forget going down the 16th fairway. He was anticipating the kill, just like the matador he is. He's about ten feet off the floor, almost mental, worked up to a pitch, and he snarled, "Billy, I'm going to kill this sonofabitch; I'm going to kill him, going to kill him!" I'm hoping he is and I'm feeling the same but I've got to try and get him to show a little bit of decorum, so I say, "Seve, Seve, relax, tranquillo, tranquillo, mate. Just do the job." I'm having to pull him back and say "Don't worry, you've got him." He's fantastic, Seve. He gives it his all. He settled down and did the job.'

Immediately, Ballesteros's point was wiped out, though, as Woosnam succumbed to Chip Beck, who lived up to his name with a chip-in eagle at the 11th after the little Welshman had fought back from being two-down early on. That drew the teams level again. Who would crack next – and would it be at the 17th, where golfing ghouls from both sets of supporters fringed the lake awaiting the next mishap? Indeed it would finish at the 17th, this time Ryder Cup newcomer Paul Broadhurst prevailing as he and ailing caddie George Sprunt made it two out of two:

'The night before the singles I was not well at all and the doctor gave me a pill as I tried desperately to get fit to be with Paul the next day. I did try to force something down and I was in the official dining-room with Malcolm Mason, Sam Torrance's caddie, when Mark O'Meara's caddie Donny came in. He was wringing his hands and full of the joys of spring. Malc said to him, "What's making you so happy?" He said, "The draw's out and we've drawn Broadhurst, just the man we wanted. We should have an easy game." Malcolm said to him, "Well, it might not be that easy, you know." He just carried on crowing, "Yes, it will, man; easy." He had no idea who I was, of course. I just put my knife and fork down and walked out. I wasn't angry, but I just didn't feel like getting involved in any scene. I shook his hand on the first tee the next day, but that was because he offered his. I certainly wouldn't have offered mine first. But I was determined we were going to win.

'Broadie knew he was up against it because O'Meara was a very good player. I'd done my geography homework, though, and I thought Paul would be favourite. The course is very long and it has nine holes which are really into the wind, which would be left to right and needing a solid right-to-left shot. Paul's a great drawer of the ball and O'Meara's a fader. I felt O'Meara would struggle into the wind – it was around 35mph – and it wouldn't be a problem for us. O'Meara wouldn't be able to get up on some of the long par-fours and Paul would with his strong draw. I told Paul that. I said, "Remember when we come to these holes, we've got the advantage." It worked out exactly like that.

'Coming in, though, I thought it wouldn't. O'Meara hit a one-iron into the wind on to the 220-yard 14th green, only just on, when I didn't think he had a club in the bag to get there. We went in the left bunker. O'Meara runs it down to a foot after we'd come out of the bunker to 20 feet. We were two-up so I said to Broadie before the putt, "We should be thinking of closing the match down now. Let's have this one." He holed it. A very, very important putt.

'Then I thought we should win 16 but again O'Meara hung on. We hit driver, three-wood, seven-iron, to show how long it was playing. O'Meara nearly got up, but he's in the greenside trap in three. The trap's so steep it's impossible to see over it and I'm thinking again that it's all over. He played to a foot below the hole and we missed a difficult one coming down. Unbelievable. O'Meara's hung on again.

'I say to Paul, "Whatever he's done, he cannot get over the water at the 17th." Paul says, "Don't be sure about that." I said, "I'm telling you. This is our trump card. He's definitely not got a club in the bag that can clear the water and stay on the green." He didn't. He had two attempts. We were in the trap with a two-iron under the wind but OK. O'Meara's third shot was right into the teeth of the wind and he fell about a yard or so short. It was all over.

'Later on, when Bernard Gallacher said that if any mistakes were made, one of them was that Paul Broadhurst should have played earlier. But I don't think it was Gallacher's fault because if you had seen somebody practising as badly as Paul had done, you wouldn't have played him earlier. But Paul's at his best when he's playing for someone else. He will not let people down.'

Torrance's defeat by Couples and victory by Wadkins over James left Europe in debit by a point.

So it all came down to Langer and Irwin. The huge crowd gathered and waited at the closing holes. It was like a soccer cup-final crowd watching *Gunfight at the OK Corral*, with Langer and his caddie Coleman in the corral:

'Everybody was going frantic and it was just a din, with people shouting things – sometimes not good things, but sometimes encouragement. The Americans were obviously trying to put us down but the outnumbered Europeans did an unbelievable job to keep us up. We thought if we could hold Irwin until past the 13th we'd have the advantage playing the last five holes because they were all into the left-to-right wind. Irwin was about 20 yards shorter than Bernhard and if we were struggling with the wind then he surely must be too.

'We were only one-down after 13 but we got it wrong at 14, the par-three. His four-iron covered the flag all the way but the wind got at it just a little bit too much and his ball spun back down the hill. It wasn't such a good chip and he three-putted as well. He was very angry with himself because he knew that he would have chipped it close nine times out of ten for his three and Irwin had taken four.

'As I know perhaps better than most, Bernhard's never beaten at that kind of stage. And he was thinking of the team; I remember that from the little bit we did get the chance to talk. He was just fantastic, taking the pressure like I don't think many players in the world could. The whole finale was something that you'd normally read in a thriller. This time, though, it was real life. It was the most exciting Ryder Cup finish there'd ever been and I reckon it ensured there will be Ryder Cups for the next 20 or 30 years when people look back and remember the excitement. They'll hope there might be plenty more finishes like that.

'You've got to give Bernhard credit for it. The tension must have been incredible – in fact, I know it was from his facial expressions and mannerisms when we discussed things. After Hale bogeyed the 15th, Bernhard made a fantastic up-and-down from the deep bunker on the 16th, holing from eight feet to keep it to only one-down. The tension was unbearable for me, so goodness knows what it was like for him. At the 17th he knew again it was make-or-break. We hit one-iron and Hale hit three-wood. Bernhard just missed the green pin-high-left and now we had problems because he then had two slopes to get over. Hale was nearer, with only one slope to worry him. We studied it and Bernhard got it to within six feet: a good putt, but would it be enough?

'At this stage it's desperate. One good putt from Irwin and the whole shooting-match is over. Hale had sunk some great putts as well, putting much better than Bernhard, and had holed a couple of 15-footers and a couple of 12-footers, so I was tempted to close my eyes. You could have heard a pin drop. But nerves must have been really getting to Hale because it went a good eight feet past – and he missed the one back. It was a marvellous putt from Bernhard. To sink that six-footer to get the match back to level was about the bravest thing I've ever seen in golf. At that point I thought we were going to win because Hale was definitely struggling. Who wouldn't have been? Bernhard had enough spirit to keep it going, because his putting was very suspect, by holing those great putts on 16 and 17 to bring the match down to 18. Everybody should remember that. The finish wouldn't have been a finish if he hadn't done that.

'On the 18th we got a good drive away straight down the middle but Irwin did not hit his at all well. His normal cut-shot didn't cut back and it turned into a pull. Where it was heading, it would have been in the sand-dunes. That would have made it unplayable, the way the crowd had walked through those dunes. As far wide as it was going, it definitely looked as though it was going to be in a far worse position than it finished up. We couldn't actually see whether it was kicked back out, whether it just hit all those hundreds of spectators, or what. They all rushed forward and blanketed out our view. When we got down there, Hale's ball was somehow on the fairway.

'Bernhard had hit a good 30 yards longer and we had a three-iron in after Hale hit a three-wood close to the green. More pressure. We only just missed the green by about two feet and when Hale stubbed his chip about 25–30 feet short I thought the Europeans in the crowd were going to explode. The Americans were very quiet at that point. There was quite a mound in the way of Bernhard's shot so he decided on the putter. I thought it was going in. But it just missed the cup and ran about six feet past. It seemed to pick up speed right at the very end because I thought it was stone-dead, the weight, and so did everybody until it kept on rolling. It was into the grain and into the wind, but it just kept rolling.

'Then Hale putts up and leaves a putt of about two and a half feet. Bernhard gives it. Whether he should have or not, that's Bernhard. Hale was shaking so much at that stage. He'd played the 18th like a ten-handicapper. The way Irwin was going, it was a big putt to give. But Bernhard played it to the true spirit of the Ryder Cup. You shouldn't win on somebody else's mistake. It would have been sad for Hale if he'd had to play it and had missed it. Great for Europe, but Bernhard wasn't about to give him the chance.

'Anyway, Bernhard's left with an easy putt to read; an easy putt, normally, to hole. It was a left-edge putt but right in line with the left edge, about a foot from the hole, was this big spike mark which stood up quite high. So he said to me, "Do you see that?" and I said, "Yes. You can't help but see it. Just hit it inside and hit it hard." He hit inside – but he just didn't hit it hard. That was the difference. If he could have played it over again, he might have hit it a little bit harder because if he'd missed the return it would have still been the same result. But Bernhard's a lag-putter. Most of his putts you have to read to drop at dead weight. That was something you could never have done with that putt because it would never have got through the spike mark. Sometimes spike marks don't affect the ball. In the player's mind it is always going to affect it. Especially to keep the Ryder Cup.

'The spike mark was the sad part of it all. It could even have been one of our own players. It decided it.'

HOW WE LOST THE RYDER CUP AGAIN

1993: DEFEAT COMES HARD FOR EUROPE

THE BELFRY, 24–26 SEPTEMBER
EUROPE 13 USA 15

CAPTAINS: Bernard Gallacher (Europe)
Tom Watson (USA)

(European names first)

Foursomes (morning):
S. Torrance and M. James 0, L. Wadkins and C. Pavin (4 and 3) 1
I. Woosnam and B. Langer (7 and 5) 1, P. Azinger and P. Stewart 0
S. Ballesteros and J.M. Olazábal 0, T. Kite and D. Love III (2 and 1) 1
N. Faldo and C. Montgomerie (4 and 3) 1, R. Floyd and F. Couples 0

Fourballs (afternoon):
I. Woosnam and P. Baker (1 hole) 1, J. Gallagher Jnr and L. Janzen 0
B. Langer and B. Lane 0, L. Wadkins and C. Pavin (4 and 2) 1
N. Faldo and C. Montgomerie (half) ½, P. Azinger and F. Couples (half) ½
S. Ballesteros and J.M. Olazábal (4 and 3) 1, D. Love III and T. Kite 0

Foursomes (morning):
N. Faldo and C. Montgomerie (3 and 2) 1, L. Wadkins and C. Pavin 0
B. Langer and I. Woosnam (2 and 1) 1, F. Couples and P. Azinger 0
P. Baker and B. Lane 0, R. Floyd and P. Stewart (3 and 2) 1
S. Ballesteros and J.M. Olazábal (2 and 1) 1, D. Love III and T. Kite 0

Fourballs (afternoon):

N. Faldo and C. Montgomerie 0, J. Cook and C. Beck (2 holes) 1

M. James and C. Rocca 0, C. Pavin and J. Gallagher Jnr (5 and 4) 1

I. Woosnam and P. Baker (6 and 5) 1, F. Couples and P. Azinger 0

J.M. Olazábal and J. Haeggman 0, R. Floyd and P. Stewart (2 and 1) 1

Singles:

I. Woosnam (half) ½, F. Couples (half) ½

B. Lane 0, C. Beck (1 hole) 1

C. Montgomerie (1 hole) 1, L. Janzen 0

P. Baker (2 holes) 1, C. Pavin 0

J. Haeggman (1 hole) 1, J. Cook 0

M. James 0, P. Stewart (3 and 2) 1

C. Rocca 0, D. Love III (1 hole) 1

S. Ballesteros 0, J. Gallagher Jnr (3 and 2) 1

J.M. Olazábal 0, R. Floyd (2 holes) 1

B. Langer 0, T. Kite (5 and 3) 1

N. Faldo (half) ½, P. Azinger (half) ½

S. Torrance (half) ½, L. Wadkins (half) ½ (Match not played)

THE CADDIES

ALASTAIR McLEAN (COLIN MONTGOMERIE 1993, 1995, 1997, 1999, 2004, 2006)

Modern history graduate Alastair McLean was paid the highest of compliments by Colin Montgomerie when he was handed a ticket home on Concorde in 1994. Montgomerie had just lost a playoff with Ernie Els for the US Open title. He said to McLean, 'Here you are. We've both had a tough week. Let's travel home in comfort. We deserve it.' After graduation in 1984 and 18 months without a job, but with his handicap down to one, McLean hit the road, eventually nearly helping Denis Durnian to a Ryder Cup place. After they parted company in 1991, and following a short stint with Mark Mouland, McLean teamed up with Montgomerie to help him become European No. 1 seven times. The pair split for over two years but came together for the 2004 match.

The other half of the Tilston identical twins (see Chapter Two), Gary was born six minutes later than brother Guy and appeared six years later in a Ryder Cup encounter. While Guy can count a victory at Muirfield Village in 1987 with Eamonn Darcy, Gary was left with the crushing disappointment of The Belfry in 1993 with Barry Lane. At 12 years old, he began caddying with Guy at Sunningdale near their home, for pocket-money. That often meant playing truant but proved lucrative for Gary, who caddied for the legendary Michael 'Queenie' King in many money games. Gary's involvement with Barry Lane came when he bumped into the Berkshire professional while they were both doing their Christmas shopping in 1989. 'Barry asked me if I could work for him the next year but I rather think he thought he was talking to my brother Guy, who had been on his bag before,' says Gary.

STAN MERCER (PETER BAKER 1993)

Liverpudlian Stan Mercer is another caddie who matriculated from the professional golfing ranks. Mercer harboured hopes of Cup glory himself when serving as an assistant professional at Bootle from 1979 to 1983. He switched to caddying in 1986, having written a letter to touring pro Robert Lee, who arranged for Mercer to caddie for the American Rick Hartmann. Mercer then worked with Irishman Paul McGinley, but in 1992 switched to Baker's bag. The young West Midlander had begun his career spectacularly but gone into a decline until teaming up with Mercer. A runaway 1993 Dunhill Masters success was augmented by victory in the Scandinavian Masters and runner-up in the German Open, which clinched the pair's Ryder Cup debut.

MICK DORAN (COSTANTINO ROCCA 1993,1995; LEE WESTWOOD 1997, 1999; DAVID HOWELL 2004, 2006)

Englishman Mick Doran hardly spoke a word of Italian but his world revolved around Italian golfers for much of the early part of his caddying career. After going on tour straight from school in 1987, Doran teamed up with Alberto Binaghi. Then in 1989 he moved to Costantino Rocca. The pair had to suffer the desperation of the 17th green at The Belfry for two years and then deservedly savoured the triumph of Oak Hill in 1995. After parting company with Rocca in 1997, Doran took over brilliant young Englishman Lee Westwood's bag less than three months before the 1997 showdown in Valderrama. He was also by

Westwood's side at Brookline in 1999 before the pair parted company. He joined David Howell for the 2004 encounter.

THE ACTION

'The tension around the green was unbearable. He gave it a solid rap. In a split-second I thought he'd done it, closed it down. "Good old Costa!" As soon as it got near the hole, though, it gathered speed and took off.'

It was a Ryder Cup littered with stories of injuries and mishaps, which in some cases happened well before the match. Sam Torrance injured himself the month before in a bizarre accident walking in his sleep. Bernhard Langer was never fully fit, suffering an injured neck, and nearly did not play. Captain Bernhard Gallacher had to put Ronan Rafferty on standby.

There was a report that Ballesteros's bad back may not last four pairs matches and a single. Then Torrance, having fought to get fit from his original injury, fell foul of an infected ingrowing toenail. For a second Ryder Cup in succession the 'envelope' had to be used.

Rookies in the European team acquitted themselves well, but an inconsistent game-plan took its toll in the end after Europe had put their noses in front by the Saturday afternoon. With Langer and Ballesteros asking to be left out, the latter causing the break-up of his influential partnership with José Maria Olazábal and a dagger to the heart of the home team's morale, the huge Belfry crowd witnessed an American fightback.

The US team had been briefed by their president: 'Bring back the Ryder Cup', although the staunch Republican side had been loath to meet Democrat Bill Clinton before flying out to defend. They obeyed the president's command, however, albeit helped this time by significant failings by the Europeans rather than by the sort of frenetic determination shown at Kiawah Island in the previous campaign.

Straight away the 1993 encounter was thrown into controversy. US captain Tom Watson, a player used to success in Britain after five Open Championship victories, declared that he would not worry about crowds being over-partisan – the clapping of opposition missed putts had always rankled with the Americans at The Belfry – and urged his team not to worry either. The highly respected captain, revered by many British golf fans, was anxious to build bridges again after the often unseemly débâcle of 1991.

Watson got off to a bad start. He decided he did not want his players bothered by the usual autograph-signing stints during the gala dinner, telling would-be signature-seekers that menus could be signed later, not at the function. Torrance asked Watson for his autograph – and was politely refused.

Watson told Torrance that if he did it for him, then the team would be flooded with requests from the gala dinner guests. Torrance stalked off, accusing Watson of snubbing him – and the press got to hear about it. The next day the episode had blown up into a diplomatic storm. However, Gallacher defused the situation admirably, saying, 'If that's going to be the only major incident of the week, that'll be fine.'

The bruised pride of Torrance was healed, just as an unusual injury had in the weeks leading up to the Cup meeting. Accident-prone Sam had crashed into a huge flowerpot, apparently while walking in his sleep when staying, ironically, at The Belfry during the English Open, and had badly bruised his sternum. Doubts over his fitness eased and the Scot arrived at the place of his earlier misfortune clear of any bruising – but suffering from a painful ingrowing toenail.

When Torrance and his caddie Malcolm Mason waited over two hours for fog to clear on the opening day before they could begin their foursomes with Mark James against Lanny Wadkins and Corey Pavin, the Lancastrian bagman was far more worried about the toe than any bruised chest or pride:

'Sam was well over the chest injury because he took a couple of weeks off from golf altogether, and his little kerfuffle with Tom Watson got blown out of all proportion by the tabloids. He did have a problem, though; a septic toenail. He'd thought he'd be able to play because it didn't affect his swing and he was walking reasonably OK. We went to the range every day and he was striking the ball nicely.

'Bernard Gallacher was very good at asking caddies for advice. He always wanted to get the full input from the whole team, which included the caddies' input as well as that of the players. He was always coming round asking what we thought. Sam and Bernard are very good friends and perhaps that didn't always work when they discussed situations, and so I came into the picture. I told Bernard that Sam was fit to play but I did mention that he's not a very good foursomes player; he's a much better fourballs player. Bernard thought about it, I guess, but decided to put Sam in straight away in foursomes with Mark James. Sam was fine swinging the club and making any kind of shot but he was definitely struggling when he walked. Any distance and he was in pain. It definitely played on his mind and we lost the match.'

Two overwhelming victories by Europe brightened up the grey morning for the home supporters, however. Ian Woosnam was to tot up four points out of four in the foursomes and fourballs, doing so with two partners, Langer and Peter Baker.

On Woosnam's bag again was Phil 'Wobbly' Morbey, who witnessed first hand the opening morning pulverising of Paul Azinger and Payne Stewart:

'Obviously Bernard wasn't going to put Woosie and Faldo together because they hadn't gelled at all well at Kiawah Island. I said to Woosie, "I hope we're paired with Bernhard because if we happen to miss a green, he's going to chip it stiff. It'll be a great pairing." Gallacher must have felt the same because that was how we started.

'We absolutely hammered Azinger and Stewart 7 and 5. Woosie didn't hit the ball that well but Langer's short-game was brilliant. We knew Langer had got neck problems but he didn't show it much and he didn't put a foot wrong. Whenever we missed a green, you could be sure it was Bernhard chipping it close.'

Faldo and Montgomerie were also in commanding form, brushing aside Faldo's old adversary Ray Floyd and Fred Couples 4 and 3.

Chosen to partner Faldo, whom he had quoted as his role model, Montgomerie fully justified Gallacher's decision to pair Europe's most successful Ryder Cup player with the man who would be European No. 1 at the end of the season.

The partnership came as no surprise to Montgomerie's caddie Alastair McLean:

'Faldo's his own man and I don't know whether he really respects any other golfer, but for some reason he did have a certain amount of respect for Monty, even though he did things his own way. I don't know why he cottoned on to Monty. Faldo was a fitness freak and, at the time, Monty was a food freak. Their aims were the same but they seemed to be opposites.

'They practised together and I think Gallacher had made up his mind that they'd play together. On the very first day's practice they did 27 holes and I don't think any other combination did that. They played 18 and then nine holes of foursomes in the afternoon, perhaps enabling Gallacher to confirm the pairing in his own mind. There had been a clash of No. 1s between Faldo and Woosnam and it was obvious they wouldn't play together, and the decision by Bernard was proved right because Faldo and Monty got off to a great start by beating Couples and Floyd.

'I know there was a lot of rivalry between Faldo and Floyd. Nick was very fired up to beat them and although Monty wasn't a bit-player by any means, Nick was extremely fired up about beating the Americans, trying so hard on every shot, anxious to get Monty going and continually geeing him up. All week it was like that. Monty played well in foursomes but in the fourballs, although he made his share of birdies and solid pars, Nick was the dominant partner. While Monty might be three- or four-under, Nick might be six- or seven-under.'

A huge blot on the morning's proceedings for Europe came when Ballesteros and Olazábal suffered only their second defeat since starting a brilliant partnership in 1987, their first loss in foursomes, as they went down to Tom Kite – a satisfying win over his old foe – and Cup first-timer Davis Love III. It left the match all-square after the morning session.

In the afternoon, two of Europe's first-time Cup men were given their chances. Peter Baker joined up with great friend Woosnam for victory over two more rookies, Jim Gallagher Junior and US Open champion Lee Janzen.

For Baker, 1993 represented his comeback year. The cheerful, talented, young West Midlander had promised much when beating Faldo in a 1988 playoff at just 21 but then laid low for five years. Victories in the 1993 British Masters and Scandinavian Masters, though, had set up his Ryder Cup chance.

The final hours before his debut were harrowing for Baker, as his caddie Stan Mercer reports:

'Peter's daughter Georgina had been ill at the start of the week with flu and an ear infection, but he was right on the doorstep and kept constantly in touch. Then on the Thursday night she was taken into hospital because they thought it might be something more serious. Somebody said to me in the caddie hotel, "Peter Baker might not be playing now because his daughter's been taken to hospital." He'd gone from the players' hotel to the hospital to check how his daughter was, and when he was satisfied that she wasn't in danger and she had gone to sleep, he left her with his wife Helen by her bedside.

'It was a worry to Peter the next morning in case she had meningitis, but he got some promising reports from the hospital and, if anything, I think it cheered him up and he played even better in his first match with Woosie. Helen came out to the course and gave Peter the thumbs-up about Georgina – and he relaxed and played even better then. By the weekend, his daughter was out of danger. Helen had insisted he went out there and played, and he responded.

'Peter really had his eye on the greens and read them perfectly whenever he played with Woosie. Woosie admitted that Peter was carrying him. When he's got his eye in like that, he doesn't need any help from me in lining it up. It's only when he's not sure that he asks for a second opinion. He didn't need one for most of the week, though, and I was able to just leave him alone. He is a very good reader of greens.

'He thoroughly enjoyed playing with Woosie because he was on top of his game and playing with a great friend. With Woosie not being on top of his game, it spurred Peter on to better things. I remember Woosie saying, "Keep it going, Pete. You don't need me." Bakes holed some big putts in the one-hole win over Gallagher and Janzen. It was a tightish match and although Peter played really well to make five or six birdies, it was his putting which edged it for us.'

Barry Lane had won the European Masters title in Switzerland three weeks before the Ryder Cup, to show he was on song, after virtually assuring himself of his place before 1993 even started. Lane's caddie Gary Tilston, identical twin brother of Guy, who helped Eamonn Darcy to Ryder Cup success in 1987, was delighted to be paired with Langer on the first day as they took on Lanny Wadkins and Corey Pavin:

'Langer's my favourite player in the world. He's the ultimate professional and the easiest of guys to get on with. It was just about the easiest baptism Barry and I could have had. I think every Ryder Cup captain tends to put the rookies in with players who have experience, and Bernhard has the ultimate in experience.

'I felt sick going to the first tee. When they announced "Barry Lane, Europe" it brought a lump to my throat. I couldn't swallow – and neither could Barry. But he nailed a great shot and then hit in to only six feet, so I felt great that we actually got the clubs right. He didn't quite make the putt, but it was a good start. I normally help line up the putts when Barry's not sure but he and Bernhard did it together for their match. I don't exactly agree with that, because as a pair you have got to the Ryder Cup without anybody else being involved. And I think it should stay that way. Only the player and the caddie know the pace the player's likely to hit the putt.

'In the end I had to ask Pete [Coleman, Langer's caddie] if he could have a word with Bernhard because he was coming over every few minutes to talk to Barry and give advice and I knew it was only likely to make Barry a little bit more edgy. For instance, on the second Bernhard didn't hit very close and Barry hit inside Wadkins to about six feet again. Pavin was in to four feet. It was Langer's turn but he asked Barry, "Would you like to go first?" He did, even though I knew he didn't really want to. He missed it and we ended up losing the hole. It was a bit of a battle after that, although Barry played exceptionally well. He was four-under with his own ball when we lost on the 16th.'

Europe's top partnership soon took care of that setback. Ballesteros and Olazábal were not the force of previous Ryder Cups but they still managed to turn the tables on Kite and Love in the afternoon.

The day was elongated due to the morning fog. That left Faldo and Montgomerie's match against Azinger and Couples unfinished when finely poised, Azinger having missed a putt in the darkness on the 17th which would have put the Americans one-up. On the Saturday morning, Faldo holed a brave ten-footer on the last to halve the match and ensure Europe kept a one-point lead.

Faldo and Montgomerie quickly breakfasted en route to the first tee, and then went straight out and won one of the three foursomes matches which put Europe in the ascendancy by early Saturday afternoon, Wadkins and Pavin this time the defeated Americans. Montgomerie's caddie McLean gives the main details:

'The Friday-afternoon fourballs was a great match against Azinger and Couples. It was really dark by the time we got to the 17th and we couldn't believe we'd gone as far ahead as 17. Even on the green it was very hard to see. Azinger had a pretty straightforward putt of about 12 feet or so. He putted but couldn't even see the line of it. And he missed. They had that one to go one-up with one to play.

'If they'd left it until the morning they could have seen the line properly. I was very surprised the Americans opted to carry on. We'd made our par and they had the putt for a birdie to go one-up and they knew they couldn't go any further because it was far too dark to play 18. That was crucial to the match. If that putt had gone in it would have been a huge blow. Monty and Nick would have gone to bed a bit down and then got up knowing they'd got a fight on their hands to avoid losing – on the toughest hole on the course.

'In the morning, Monty was a bit cold and hit his drive into the water and that left Nick against the two of them. He did fantastically well to hole from about 12 feet after hitting his second shot long. Getting the half gave them a very good feeling. They then just had time for a bacon sandwich and a few putts before heading for the first tee again. We had a tough match against Pavin and Wadkins. Pavin was very competitive that week and Wadkins is a bit like Floyd: he gets under people's skins and can wind them up. It was another pair they badly wanted to beat.

'Monty and Nick were buzzing for the foursomes. If Nick's putt had missed earlier on it would have been a different story; it would have put a whole new complexion on things and I don't know what would have happened. They'd had a win first time together the previous morning and then had got a really good half in a tough, tough match. Then they were straight off again, full of confidence.

'They were chatting to each other and in great spirits. It all came down to a brilliant putt by Monty on 16 to finish them off. We were up in the top-right part of the green with the pin bottom-left and Monty ran this huge putt right through the ridge with about 20 feet of break, down to about a couple of feet and it was all over.'

On an encouraging morning, Langer and Woosnam took out Couples and Azinger and Ballesteros and Olazábal continued their winning ways with victory over Kite and Love again. Only Baker and Lane had to accept defeat for the home team, slipping to Floyd and Stewart. But Europe had a three-point cushion.

Then came the two withdrawals that many pundits reckoned had a great bearing on where the Ryder Cup would head the next day. Ballesteros and Langer, two of Gallacher's icons, pulled out of the afternoon fourballs.

Ballesteros's withdrawal was no surprise to caddie Foster:

'In total contrast to 1991, Seve couldn't hit a cow's arse with a banjo. He'd gone. His confidence was low . . . too many swing thoughts . . . Only Seve's magnificent putting and José's sheer determination to get something out of their matches kept their heads above water and kept them winning. They played Davis Love and Tom Kite three matches in a row. Kite and Love still had to play great to win the first time and then Seve absolutely putted the lights out in the afternoon. It must have been devastating for the Americans.

'On Saturday morning Seve was all over the place. Whenever he teed off he just put it so far in trouble it became exciting for the crowd – in the tented village, down banks, in bushes. José kept chopping out, Seve sank the putt. They just hung on by sheer guts. Seve just binned the world. They won two and one and it must have been so disheartening for the guys playing them. But it was only papering over the cracks for Seve. After 12 holes on Saturday he was hitting it so badly. His back had seized up and he just could not hit the ball. How they won was a mystery. I'm not a great golfer, but I fancied beating him myself – until we got to the green.

'It was no surprise when he was pulled in the afternoon. It was his decision and Bernard Gallacher did the right thing to agree to withdraw him. Bernard got a lot of stick in the press for allowing Seve and Langer to pull out, but in the case of Seve he had no other choice. Seve's back was that bad he couldn't swing, and he had no confidence. He went straight to Bernard and told him, "Look, my swing's terrible and I just can't hit the ball. You've got to leave me out." You can't point the finger at Bernard because José and Joakim Haeggman didn't work out. Joakim had to have a game before the singles and Seve just wasn't fit.

'He had lessons off two or three people that week, just searching, really, for a swing. But he didn't have a clue, to be honest. I could see it, standing alongside him. They all tried, coaches, players . . . advice was raining in.'

Langer also asked to be rested for Saturday afternoon. Gallacher's compliance with the requests caused great criticism from the pundits. However, Langer's caddie Coleman believes the captain had no other option:

'Bernhard had been in doubt through injury for a month before the match and there was a lot of worry that he wouldn't play. He had a neck injury which had been going on for a long time and which had got worse and worse during the German Open a few weeks beforehand. I had to keep in touch while he rested the injury and then he had some light practice a week or so before The Belfry. He decided he was fit enough to play and I had no doubts he was. Anyway, Bernhard can be an even more dangerous opponent when he's not totally fit. He's definitely one about whom you could say, "Beware the injured golfer!"

'The foursomes matches with Woosie worked out well and his short-game was terrific, but all along he didn't feel as though he was hitting the ball long enough. I suppose it was to do with the neck. He didn't talk too much about the injury but it was obviously something that must have contributed to his being shorter off the tee.

'That was the case in the fourballs and he told Bernard Gallacher he wouldn't be any use to him on the Saturday afternoon because he wasn't hitting it long enough. And Bernard had to find a game for Rocca and Haeggman. Seve was hitting it all over the place, so I think it had to be done, leaving out Bernhard and Seve. It was logical.'

Some hasty rejigging of the pairings clearly affected the Europeans. Faldo and Montgomerie went down to John Cook, from whom Faldo had stolen the 1992 Open Championship, making his debut, and Chip Beck, also playing his first match of the week. James and debutant Rocca lost heavily to Pavin and Gallagher. Olazábal and his new partner Joakim Haeggman, the first Swede to play in a Ryder Cup, also conceded to Floyd and Stewart. However, Gallacher had carried out his promise that everyone would get a match before the singles.

The one European win came from Woosnam and Baker. After hearing his daughter was out of danger, Baker went to work on The Belfry greens with gusto, as caddie Mercer witnessed:

'Peter was really on fire. I can remember going down the fairway and overhearing Couples saying to Azinger, "I'm so embarrassed!" That's because Peter was completely destroying them. He holed a 40-footer on the fifth, might even have been 50 feet because it was in before anyone had time to measure or to think about it. Then a 25-footer went in on the next and he followed up with two 12–15-footers on the eighth and ninth.

'By the time we went through the turn it was virtually over. You could see Couples in particular was getting niggled. They couldn't do anything about it, though. Pete was banging them in from all over the place – eight birdies in thirteen holes – and they slaughtered Couples and Azinger, who were just about America's toughest pairing, six and five.'

As well as Ballesteros and Langer, there was further worry for Europe on Saturday night before the singles draw, despite knowing they would take a one-point lead into the finale.

Optimism for the stricken Torrance – who had been typically nicknamed 'Pus in Boots' by his close friend Feherty – proved not enough. Reports saying he would appear the next day, which caught a few early Sunday newspaper editions, proved to be wrong.

Late on the Saturday night, Gallacher had to inform his opposite number Watson that there were serious doubts over Torrance playing. An American might need to be withdrawn. That would mean half a point each. Wadkins persuaded Watson he should be the man to stand down, having come into the Cup as one of the American wild-cards. The veteran Cup-campaigner knew he was taking a chance on not getting a singles match, aware that Torrance might be a doubtful starter, but put his own esteem to one side.

Thus, Watson placed Wadkins's name into the envelope, the system which was devised to prevent last-minute changes by the captains when the draw was finalised. In this case, though, the draw had already been made and Wadkins was down to meet Ballesteros. The meeting between the veterans of numerous hard-fought matches would never take place.

Torrance's caddie Mason was not immediately aware of the Saturday-night drama concerning his player. However, he was to discover to his dismay the next morning, he would not be in action:

'During the course of Friday, Sam had the toenail removed – a very painful operation, and I know he thought that was going to be the end of his problems. The trouble was, though, that the dressing around the toe made it almost impossible to get a golf shoe on, so I wasn't surprised when we couldn't play on

Saturday. We practised but you could see Sam was struggling a bit. He was very optimistic he'd be OK for Sunday, though.

'I travelled back to the caddies' hotel on Saturday night with Lanny Wadkins's caddie Bruce Edwards, a good friend of mine over the years, and he asked me if Sam would play, obviously knowing that Lanny had volunteered to be put in the envelope. I told him that Sam was playing as far as I knew, and that he was going to dose himself up with painkillers and hope the toe had eased. Lanny knew Sam well enough to know that if Sam could play, he would. I was sure Sam would be there.

'It was only when I got to the course the next morning that I heard Sam was out. As I walked up to the practice putting green, Lawrence Levy, one of the photographers, said to me, "Unlucky, Malc." I said, "What do you mean?" He said, "Sam can't play." Lawrence, God bless him because he died a couple of years later, was a terrible wind-up merchant and I didn't really believe him. I went up to the players' room and Sam said, "I'm sorry, but I can't play." I was devastated.

'He'd been over to the range that morning, needing a buggy to get over there. He'd hit balls for half an hour and that was fine. But when he tried to walk back, he knew he was done for. It was only 200 yards maximum but when he hobbled back he was in agony, his foot was throbbing so much. Bernard, being the professional he is, told Sam, "I don't want you playing if you're not fully fit. I'd rather get half a point than lose a full one with a half-fit player."

'I heard some of the Americans say that Sam should get a buggy to play, but I knew Bernard wouldn't go along with that because it wasn't professional. Sam wouldn't have wanted to go down as the first professional to play a Ryder Cup match in a buggy either, but it wasn't even put to him. Bernard made the decision. Sam was heartbroken. He'd worked so hard to get into the team. He's never been picked – he's qualified for all his Ryder Cups. And here he was, just a half-point to show for all his hard work.'

An evening of conjecture about Torrance's fitness could not have helped the European cause as players deliberated over the draw. It thrust Woosnam and Couples together in the first encounter.

Woosnam came desperately close to bagging all five points. He was two-up with six to play at a time when Europe looked well in command, up in all the first five matches.

As Couples fought back, so America got on top. Woosnam had to pull out all the stops to at least save a half, not much consolation for caddie Morbey:

'It was a match I never thought Woosie could lose, even when Freddie fought back coming in to be all-square playing the last. And it all came down to the 18th. Fred got up to the green, I knew, with a nine-iron, glad to make it after what happened in 1989 at The Belfry. But the wind was changing all the time and we must have been there for a long while choosing our club to hit in with. Wedge-nine, wedge-nine, it seemed like an eternity. In the end I said, "You'll have to hit nine or you might not get over the last tier." It was a lot of pressure, knowing we could get it wrong right at the death and lose a match we'd always been favourite to win.

'Woosie hit just inside Fred, a great shot. Fred missed his putt, got a tap-in. We had a putt of about 25 feet to win and get that first point – one that Ian well deserved. When he hit it three and a half feet past, though, I just cringed.

'Freddie came over to me, put his arm round me and said, "You know I'd love to give Woosie this putt and just walk off with a half, but I can't. It's the Ryder Cup." He's such a great bloke, Freddie, and I knew that's what he wanted to say to Woosie really. But he'd never have been forgiven if it had cost his team the Cup. Fred's such a gent, though. There's no venom like some of the others. We have a good fight but there's no hostility. I said, "I know, Fred; I understand." Woosie holed the putt and I went off the green in tears. I knew Woosie had the chance to win his first point but to knock it that far past . . . It must have seemed like a ten-footer to him, and I knew he was so nervous. It took real guts to hole that putt.

'It was so disappointing for Woosie not to make his first singles point. Not many people have won all five points in a Ryder Cup.'

After not getting a match on Saturday afternoon, Lane was determined he would break his duck in the singles. When the draw came out he found himself second match away against Beck, who had, with Cook, toppled the powerful partnership of Faldo and Montgomerie. Caddie Tilston expected a tough encounter in the quest for that elusive first point:

'It was no surprise when we didn't get a match in the final fourballs. What was surprising, perhaps, was that Ballesteros and Langer didn't come out. We'd understood they would be playing. The withdrawals left Bernard with a lot fewer options than some people realise. He didn't have many rabbits left in the hat by Saturday afternoon.

'By now both Barry and myself were relishing the atmosphere and really looking forward to the match. Barry will be gutted if he never plays the Ryder Cup again. He wants another chance to get the right result next time, because you couldn't fault the way he played.

'Barry was something like four-under-par for the first nine. He's three-up and hits a great seven-iron on to the apron of the 14th green. When he's under the cosh he likes to hit it harder, not wanting to hit soft shots, so it was a good club. He decides to putt but three-putts. That was a real blow, going back to two again. It was with his little putter, which he'd had for five years. It's a tiny little thing with a ladies' head on it. Nothing unusual. He hits a ladies' driver as well. But his 31-inch putter didn't work too well on the 14th. He left himself too much to do with his first putt, about four feet. Beck hit a wonderful putt from the back of the green.

'At the par-five 15th Barry hit a good drive but just leaked his second shot into the bunker. Beck hit two career shots to about 40 feet. Barry stiffed his bunker shot for a certain birdie and had a quiet grin. But then Beck holed his huge putt for an eagle. The grin went a bit. That was a really heavy body-blow this time. How quickly a lead can go. All he did was three-putt a hole. Then he'd even birdied the next. Barry hadn't done that much wrong. From what we said to each other I know Barry realised he wasn't cruising but after he got three-up he was talking about not doing anything silly, just closing his man out. Now here he was, only one-up just two holes later. The tide had turned suddenly and here we were under the cosh.

'Now the 16th is a hole we've always had trouble with. It's a two-tier green left and right, lower tier on the left, higher tier on the right, instead of front and back. And we always seem to hit it on the wrong tier. So he was determined to get it on the correct tier, which was the top right. He overcut his second shot, it caught the tree and his ball came down just in the front fringe. Beck wasn't particularly close, but Barry hit a weak chip and then Beck holed a four- or five-footer to get back to all-square. Game on. Barry said to me, "I cannot believe it. I'm playing the golf of my life and I haven't really missed a shot, yet I'm only level with him."

'On 17 Barry hit a bad drive and then hacked it out just short of the cross ditch which was about 175 yards short of the green. Beck hit a lovely lay-up, leaving himself about 100 yards. We're going in with five-iron third shot, so we're up against it. Barry hit a very good approach, probably 20 feet pin-high-left. Beck spun back to the front-edge. To my great relief they halve. As we walk to the last tee, Barry comes out with his favourite matchplay expression in this kind of situation: "That was all a bit of a waste of time. We might just as well have come out and played only the 18th!"

'The 18th's one of the world's best matchplay holes. Beck hits a good drive in the circumstances. Barry bails out a bit and goes in the bunker right of the fairway. We didn't have much choice other than to go for it. Although the flag was 35 yards on, the actual carry wasn't that much. And the shot was on. It was 160 yards carry and we hit four-iron. Anything other than going for the green would have given him the edge. As Barry tends to do sometimes, he hit it fat. His ball pitched on the bank – and fell back into the water.

'It was just about the most demoralising thing that could happen to a player and his caddie. Give Beck his due, he missed the green just off right, but chipped and putted for victory. He was the perfect gentleman in winning. Barry was inconsolable, though. He had to get away. And I had to get away. I must admit to a few tears.

'If you lose one-down coming from behind you can bear it, but when it's in your grasp and it's taken away, then it's very hard. Barry took it hard, and felt he'd let the team down. I took it hard because we were very experienced. Maybe not in Ryder Cup, but very experienced at matchplay. It's never over until it's over, whether it's Ryder Cup or Sunningdale Foursomes. We knew that. Again Barry said to me, almost choking, as we went off the 18th, "I can't believe it's happened. I haven't won a point and I've played some of the best golf of my life."'

Directly behind Lane came Montgomerie, battling hard to get the better of the reigning US Open champion Lee Janzen and put Europe back in front. Confidence oozed from the by now well-blooded Montgomerie early on and nervous apprehension from the relatively fresh Janzen told immediately. Early blows to Janzen were to have an effect on the outcome of their singles match, but so, too, was Montgomerie's knack of holing from huge distances, as his caddie McLean witnessed:

'Monty came to the first tee on Sunday knowing he'd already had a good Ryder Cup. He had played four matches and won two and a great half. His nervousness could be channelled in the right direction. Janzen had played one match and got beaten. Although he was US Open champion, when he stood on that first tee he couldn't channel his nervousness in a positive way. He bogeyed the first two holes. Monty made solid pars. They aren't the hardest holes in the world, by any means. Monty's nervousness wore off and he was confident; Janzen's nervousness wore off – but he was now two-down.

'Giving Monty two holes' start is a lot to make up and it took a long time for Janzen to get one of them back. In fact it was very close from the second onwards and Janzen got it back to all-square on 14. But it all swung Monty's way on 15. Janzen easily outdrove Monty, by at least 25 yards, and could reach the green comfortably with a long-iron. Monty was in between a three-wood and a two-iron because of his drive. A two-iron would put him on the absolute limit. Monty hit this fantastic shot from where he was. It snook through all the bunkers and reached the green. He was about 45 feet away. Janzen wasn't put off in any way, though, and he hit a comfortable iron to about 20 feet.

'We were definitely in three-putt territory, but Monty took a big breath and hit the line absolutely perfectly. It rattled in for an eagle. Janzen missed his 20-footer.

'Janzen had always been favourite to win the hole, and here we were one-up again. And at 17, Monty had the chance to close it all down. Lee was chopping about on the right and struggled to make par. Monty hit a great sand-iron from 90 yards to leave himself a four-footer for a birdie, but missed it.

'He told me he could have done without going to 18. It's a great hole for this kind of situation. Monty hit three-wood off the tee and had 190 again, and wanted to hit five-iron. I told him it was six because he'd already air-mailed his six-iron 190 yards at the 14th and he'd hit a six the previous hole the same distance. The water at the closing hole tends to elongate the carry, though. He'd carried it the previous hole the same distance and the holes all go in a similar direction, so I wasn't worried about the carry. His six-iron was perfect for distance, pin-high but just about a foot off the green on the right. Janzen hit a pretty good shot on but with a tier to negotiate for his birdie and we saw it as a good two-putt rather than one.

'Monty putted from off the green to about two feet. He was just about to mark the ball when Janzen gave him it. He couldn't believe it and said to me,

"There's no way I would have given anybody that putt, not in this situation." A huge relief came over Monty. Then Janzen missed his putt. I couldn't believe it either. Two feet in the Ryder Cup? And it had a little break in it. It was very sporting of Janzen. I'm sure Monty would have made it but, Christ, it saved a few grey hairs!'

When Baker received the all-clear on his sick daughter on Sunday morning, it took away all doubts as to whether he might have to pull out of the last day. The other American wild-card, Floyd, had persuaded Watson that, like Wadkins, he should stand down should Baker be unable to play.

Lifted both by relief that his daughter was recovering and by his performance the afternoon before, Baker then had to address his next problem. He had drawn America's most feared and determined competitor that week, Pavin.

Pavin hit the headlines Sunday morning after his exploits the day before, 'slam-dunking' a nine-iron straight into the cup without a bounce on the fifth for an eagle-two, the shot of the week. He earned labels like 'vindictive' and 'the assassin' from journalists who remembered Pavin's 'Desert Storm' antics from two years before, and the general view was that whoever found himself matched against the never-say-die Pavin would be against a formidable foe, as caddie Mercer appreciated:

'We couldn't have had it tougher. I winced when I saw we'd got Pavin, but Peter was in defiant mood when we met up on Sunday morning. "He's only human and he can be beaten just like anybody on the day" was his way of looking at it. But it was the first time that week that I got the vibes that he was slightly nervous. It didn't help, I suppose, on the first tee when Lanny Wadkins came up, started massaging Pavin's shoulders, and said, loudly enough for Bakes and me to hear, "This is just going to be a walk in the park."

'Perhaps he was doing it to relax Pavin, or perhaps it was done to try to demoralise Peter. I don't know. It certainly didn't prove to be a walk in the park, that's for sure.

'It was a great match and it was a fast match, too – tee, fairway, green and then they'd both be about 10 or 12 feet. Pavin would miss and Bakes would go in, Bakes would miss and Pavin would get his. It was a really great advert for Ryder Cup golf, up and down all the way. And Pavin proved a really nice bloke, unlike my idea of how he'd be. The Americans had heard about Peter's daughter and sent a note round hoping she was getting better, and the first thing Corey asked was how she was. He chatted a lot, too, to Bakes and me, and Peter found him a great guy. They've been firm friends ever since.

'We knew it was going to be down to the closing holes and Peter showed a lot of character to come through. He was one-up at 17 and playing really solidly, but I knew the hole would be a key one because it had to be played as the par-five it was. Peter wasn't going to be able to reach it in two. We played a wedge just off the green to about ten feet, though, and I thought we'd got it there and then. How the putt stayed out I'll never know, but we had to take half there.

'So, going down the last we were just in the semi on the right and Pavin was down the middle. Bakes wanted to hit a six-iron in to a flag that was on the middle ledge. But he was so pumped up, I didn't want him on the top ledge, so I told him to take seven-iron. We had 180 yards but we're in the semi-rough, so the ball's going to get a lot of forward spin, and he was so pumped with adrenalin and the huge crowd around us was adding to that. The way he'd been striking the ball, so sweet out of the middle of the club, no way could it be six.

'Thankfully he took my advice and took a seven. He hit it just past the flag but in a good spot 15 feet away. Pavin came up way short and putted up to about four feet. Then Bakes hit another great putt, great pace, great line. It was slightly left to right but it went in – bang. Goodnight, God bless!

'I looked up at the scoreboard. Barry was up, Rocky was up. Haeggman was just behind us and he'd just won. I thought, "We're going to win this." I felt great for Peter. He'd done himself proud on his debut, giving 110 per cent. He'd beaten the toughest of opponents and played as if he'd been in six Ryder Cups.'

Haeggman's victory was the third in succession for Europe. It came after he had just missed the water on the 18th with his drive and his opponent Cook had gone in it with his approach, after they had been all-square coming to the last.

It was, though, the last win of the day for the home team. From being three points up, Europe suffered five successive defeats to lose their way.

One of them was really hard to take for The Belfry gallery. Ballesteros, a shadow of his 1991 self, lost on the 16th to America's virtual unknown Jim Gallagher Junior, no surprise to the Spaniard's caddie:

'His game was as low as it could go and he went out in the singles on a hiding to nothing. He could have been playing Lanny Wadkins but we got Gallagher after the envelope. It could have been anybody, to be honest. In fact Seve did well to hold on until the 16th. He hit 2 greens in the first 12 holes, bogeyed the first four and went out six-over. Horrendous. Nobody expected Seve to lose to somebody like Gallagher – except me. And deep down, Seve probably did as well. His game was that bad. He just couldn't compete.

'It was a terrible time to be caddying for Seve. Not that he was ever on my back for his problems at that time. He knew how badly he was playing. He was a different man from the one who had made four and a half-points at Kiawah Island. For me, I'd rather have been with Seve when he got no points out of the week but Europe won. I was devastated.'

The outcome was in doubt until Rocca's match was over. It was to prove a miserable time for the gentle man from near Verona.

He had drawn Davis Love III. The American had had his share of problems off the course. His seven-months-pregnant wife Robin, accompanying him to The Belfry, had over-tired herself out course-walking, and, on the Friday, doctors thought she may have brought on a premature birth. When his wife's condition stabilised, however, Love was in a good frame of mind for his match.

Rocca and caddie Mick Doran were ready for their appointment with fate too, even though both knew that they had been thrown in at a crucial part of the draw, a position that puzzled Doran, as did a later procrastination by the European captain:

'I don't know what the thinking was behind putting Costantino in the lower half of the draw when he'd only had one match, and a defeat at that. But he would have played anywhere, he was so keen to get a Ryder Cup point. And he played really well. That surprised a few people. There was never more than a hole in it either way. On the back-nine he holed a couple of brave putts and a really long one from off the green on 14 to get in front. He kept one-up to the 17th and he thought he was going to do it, he was playing so well. He seemed to be driven along by the crowd, who were giving it the old "Rockee, Rockee, come on, Rockee" by the time we got on to the tee.

'It was quite windy and Love had the advantage with his draw. Costantino hit his drive right, a bit blocky really, and had to lay up short of the water with a six-iron. He then hit a three-iron in to the green to about 15 feet. That was the one that could have won us the Ryder Cup. I knew from the people there that we had this one to win the match. Faldo looked as though he was going to win and Ollie was down, so that meant we were tied at that point. Costantino's result was the big one. I don't know whether Costantino realised. He didn't say anything about it, asking only if it was fast or slow, and so on.

'Bernard Gallacher was there and I expected him to say something to Costantino, like the putt was fast, or whatever. He didn't offer anything. Haeggman had had a putt from there earlier and Woosnam as well. They'd put it straight past. You'd have thought the captain might come up and say, "Woosie and Joakim had this putt and it's a fast one." It's not as if Costantino wouldn't have understood, even though his English wasn't fantastic in 1993. He would have understood the meaning of, "This is going to be a fast putt!" Not a word, though.

'We lined it up together, as we nearly always do, and Costantino hit it, not expecting it to speed up the way it did. The tension around the green was pretty unbearable. He gave it a solid rap. It looked really good at first and I thought it was going to go in. In a split-second I thought he'd done it, closed it down. "Good old Costa!" As soon as it got near to the hole, though, it gathered speed and its pace took it away from the cup. Then it just took off and went nearly five feet past.

'He knew this one was fast. He's not too strong under pressure and just got over it, and there it was from nowhere, the hole gone. It could have been game, set and match, even if he'd two-putted out. Now we were all-square going down the last. Costantino was very upset because he'd played the hole really well until the putting. You're certainly not choking, as some people said, when you hit a brilliant three-iron like he did to 15 feet against a strong breeze.

'When we got to the 18th tee Gallacher came up and did say something this time. He told us it was straight downwind. We already knew that. I wanted him to hit a three-wood. He didn't want to hit three-wood, saying it was driver. But I made him. He blocks it a bit right, turns round and says, "It was the wrong club. I told you it was a driver." But it wasn't the club. Haeggman hit the driver in front of us and he'd been lucky not to go into the water.

'It was only a three-wood flick, but he didn't like it. We get up there and Love is down the centre of the fairway with just a nine-iron or wedge or something like that. We're sat by the bunker, not lying great, got a two-iron to it. We just carry the water and then pitch-and-run with a seven-iron. It looks good but just misses the flag and runs past about 15 feet again, maybe just a bit longer.

'Davis comes up way short, about seven feet or so, and that leaves Costantino under the cosh again. If he can get his for par, then Love's will be a real pressure putt. But he just misses it, and it goes 15 inches past. Love thinks about it a second but then gives it. Nobody can bear to watch, really, but you just know Love's going to sink it. He does and it's all over. Love doesn't even have a chance to shake hands after just standing there with his arms in the air. Wadkins is shouting something and the American team go mad. Costantino knew it was all on him and he looked away, then trudged off, already close to tears. When the putt went in I could see him shaking with emotion.

'Love did manage to catch up with Costantino and put his arm on his shoulder, but what can you say? Seve came over and tried to console him. He put his arm round Costantino and tried to tell him it was a team game and he hadn't lost it. But Seve was in tears as well, so it was a pretty emotional finish, with the crowd almost quiet.

'It was cruel to blame him. The press gave him so much stick the next day. So much pressure. It can make or break a bloke's career. He did come back from it, but it could have finished somebody else for good. There's so much pressure on players' shoulders, it's unbelievable. Quite a few players don't want to play in it because of that. I think everyone takes it a bit too seriously. It's only a game!'

The win that was to clinch America's success fell to Floyd against Olazábal, whose caddie Renwick was dismayed at his man's defeat, one he had not expected:

'I'd fully expected them to be shaking hands well before coming down the stretch. We'd played against Floyd the previous day and he'd hit it all over the place. But José didn't play that well and Raymond played exceptionally well, shooting the lowest round of the day.

'We still had a chance at the end when José chipped in to keep the match alive and I thought when he birdied 17 there was still a chance, as we were now only one-down and we'd been three-down with four to play. The half was going to be no good, so he went for it, turned the club over just a fraction and pulled it into the water. That gave Raymond the glory of winning the last and the Cup, and he deserved it.'

Floyd's success did indeed ensure the victory, because the ailing Langer had already succumbed to Tom Kite out in the country.

When the draw had put together Faldo and Azinger, The Belfry gallery awaited in great anticipation the meeting of old protagonists. Azinger had partially redeemed his collapse at Muirfield in 1987 to help Faldo to the Open Championship, by keeping out the Englishman to win the US PGA Championship title weeks before this Ryder Cup.

For much of the time over their last five holes, the outcome of their singles threatened to decide the destiny of the 1993 Ryder Cup. When Faldo holed in one at the 14th, only the second in Ryder Cup history, the ace helped keep Europe's heart beating and caddie Sunesson living in hope:

'It was a tough match against Azinger. He can be an awesome competitor in Ryder Cup matches. Nick had been the backbone of the side and the match lived up to expectations. There was nothing in it all the way to the 14th and we were all-square. We saw Ray Floyd up ahead nearly hole his shot and that got quite a reception from the huge crowd around the green. Nothing like what was to come for Nick, though.

'We decided on a six-iron. It was 196 yards, and it looked good from the second Nick hit it, straight down the line. I even shouted "Go in," something I never normally do. And it did go in. The noise from around the green was deafening, and I just hoped that the team realised it was Nick's hole in one, and that it would keep the spirits going.

'It put us one-up and it wasn't all over. Pretty soon, though, it was. We could see the Americans all running about on the 18th celebrating, and we got the word it was over. It was pretty much an anti-climax really. Then when Azinger birdied the last to get the half, it made it a very sad end.'

HOW WE WON THE RYDER CUP
BACK AGAIN

1995: UNSUNG EUROPE TURN THE TABLES

OAK HILL, ROCHESTER, NEW YORK, 22–24 SEPTEMBER
USA 13½ EUROPE 14½

CAPTAINS: Lanny Wadkins (USA)
           Bernard Gallacher (Europe)

(European names first)

Foursomes (morning):
N. Faldo and C. Montgomerie 0, C. Pavin and T. Lehman (1 hole) 1
S. Torrance and C. Rocca (3 and 2) 1, J. Haas and F. Couples 0
H. Clark and M. James 0, D. Love III and J. Maggert (4 and 3) 1
B. Langer and P-U. Johansson (1 hole) 1, B. Crenshaw and C. Strange 0

Fourballs (afternoon):
D. Gilford and S. Ballesteros (4 and 3) 1, B. Faxon and R. Jacobsen 0
S. Torrance and C. Rocca 0, J. Maggert and L. Roberts (6 and 5) 1
N. Faldo and C. Montgomerie 0, F. Couples and D. Love III (3 and 2) 1
B. Langer and P-U. Johannson 0, C. Pavin and P. Mickelson (6 and 4) 1

Foursomes (morning):
N. Faldo and C. Montgomerie (4 and 2) 1, C. Strange and J. Haas 0
S. Torrance and C. Rocca (6 and 5) 1, D. Love III and J. Maggert 0
I. Woosnam and P. Walton 0, L. Roberts and R. Jacobsen (1 hole) 1
B. Langer and D. Gilford (4 and 3) 1, C. Pavin and T. Lehman 0

Fourballs (afternoon):
S. Torrance and C. Montgomerie 0, B. Faxon and F. Couples (4 and 2) 1
I. Woosnam and C. Rocca (3 and 2) 1, D. Love III and B. Crenshaw 0
S. Ballesteros and D. Gilford 0, J. Haas and P. Mickelson (3 and 2) 1
N. Faldo and B. Langer 0, C. Pavin and L. Roberts (1 hole) 1

Singles:
S. Ballesteros 0, T. Lehman (4 and 3) 1
H. Clark (1 hole) 1, R. Jacobsen 0
M. James (4 and 3) 1, J. Maggert 0
I. Woosnam (half) ½, F. Couples (half) ½
C. Rocca 0, D. Love III (3 and 2) 1
D. Gilford (1 hole) 1, B. Faxon 0
C. Montgomerie (3 and 1) 1, B. Crenshaw 0
N. Faldo (1 hole) 1, C. Strange 0
S. Torrance (2 and 1) 1, L. Roberts 0
B. Langer 0, C. Pavin (3 and 2) 1
P. Walton (1 hole) 1, J. Haas 0
P-U. Johansson 0, P. Mickelson (2 and 1) 1

THE CADDIES

TIM LEES (DAVID GILFORD 1995)

Six-handicapper Tim Lees from Sandbatch was inspired to try his hand briefly at caddying after watching Severiano Ballesteros win the Open Championship at Royal Lytham and St Anne's in 1988. The Rolls-Royce engineer caddied in his spare time but in 1990, while caddying part-time for Andrew Murray, Lees met up with David Gilford during practice rounds. When Murray became Gilford's manager, Lees teamed up with the softly spoken Crewe pro, temporarily at first, but then became a full-time caddie as he gave up his job. In 1993 the pair had ten top-ten finishes and two wins in the first ten events of the year, but Gilford did not quite make his Cup place. Two years later the Cheshiremen were in. A European Open victory in 1994 set Gilford on the road to Oak Hill. At the end of 1995 Lees decided to return to Rolls-Royce.

Former Bootle taxi-driver Bryan McLauchlan came into European Tour caddying late in life, not taking up Philip Walton's bag until the year before the Irishman's brilliant 1995 season. The pair were an instant hit together and before long the studious Liverpudlian and the dedicated Dubliner were in the winner's enclosure.

McLauchlan's first task in Girona was just to keep his feet as his man won the Catalonia Open in gale-force winds. It put the pair on the road to Oak Hill and when Walton overcame the formidable Colin Montgomerie in a playoff for the English Open title, the new player–caddie partnership was already eyeing a 1995 Cup place in America.

THE ACTION

'Philip only had to get his close. I whispered to him that the putt was going to come off the left. He took a deep breath and told me, "Bryan, I've got two putts for it. I think I'll take them."'

To Irishman Philip Walton went the honour of performing the final act which brought the Ryder Cup back to Europe. The visitors to Oak Hill, Rochester, NY won with a display of remarkable cool and resilience in a department in which they had often been found wanting – the singles.

It was a victory that, arguably, should not have been. America were at home on a course which could be said to have been purpose-built for the home team's ambitions. Oak Hill was a traditional US Open venue, with dense rough, tight fairways and the usual lightning-slick greens.

The Americans had at the helm one of the most experienced and doughtiest Cup campaigners of them all, the fiercely competitive Lanny Wadkins. European captain Bernard Gallacher, though, had the experience of two narrow defeats to call on, having been persuaded to take up the cudgels again after initially retiring from duty following his terms of 1991 and '93.

Despite fielding five rookies, the US side had strength at the top, with US Masters champion Ben Crenshaw and US Open winner Corey Pavin. And Curtis Strange had won the last time the US Open was played at Oak Hill. Gallacher had only two first-time players, not exactly neophytes. Philip Walton had savoured past triumphs against similar opposition in the Walker Cup. Per-Ulrik Johansson was from the Swedish school of excellence that had put team golf high on its priority list.

The Europeans were unsettled by events leading up to, and following, selection.

The decision to switch to only two wild-cards, like the US team, proved controversial, and left Gallacher in an invidious position. Nick Faldo, Ian Woosnam and the troubled José Maria Olazábal were all needed as 'picks', and the in-form Swede Jesper Parnevik, acquitting himself well on the American tour, was also in the reckoning, four men for two picks. Gallacher had already said that Faldo was going to play. Three men, one pick. Parnevik was going to prove a luxury Gallacher could not afford. Two men, one pick. Olazábal, a fortnight before the Ryder Cup, was a man who could walk only 12–13 holes before hobbling in agony with foot problems, at the time diagnosed as rheumatoid arthritis. By the Monday morning of 11 September, just a week before the team was due to fly out, Olazábal admitted he was not fit enough to play. One man, one pick.

However, after all that, Woosnam was then dismayed to find himself not quite at the top of his game when he arrived at Oak Hill – and decided he might be better left out of foursomes.

Gallacher had more worries. His top twosome was Faldo and Montgomerie. Faldo had shrugged off reports in British newspapers that he had split with his wife Gill – who none the less accompanied the rest of the team's wives on Concorde – and that a divorce was pending. Gallacher hoped it would not affect his prize possession's game.

It proved an unconvincing start by the two European stars, who did well in the end to fight back against Corey Pavin and Tom Lehman and keep their defeat to only one hole.

Montgomerie felt the layout would favour him. But as he set the tournament in motion it did not mean the reigning European No. 1 was without nerves. As caddie Alastair McLean reveals, there was no question of who chose the club to start off the 1995 Ryder Cup:

'Having experienced 1993 at The Belfry, I knew there was a great deal of pressure on everybody, not just Monty and the guys hitting the clubs. And that definitely included us caddies. You make one mistake and it could cost the team the whole shooting match. So it was a trifle nerve-wracking on the first tee at Oak Hill and I was half thinking that I'd sooner it had been Nick having the first drive. They'd laid out the course American Open-style, and I knew a few of the European guys hadn't any experience of that kind of layout. Monty had enough and he always said if he were going to win a major it would be a US Open because of his accuracy. With Monty being one of the straightest hitters in the business, he got the dubious honour of hitting the first tee-shot.

'Monty and Nick weren't scared of anybody in the American team. You could see Monty was tense, though. It was more through excitement than real fright, but as the seconds drew closer to hitting off he got more and more nervous. With the huge crowds, the occasion. I can tell you, my hands were shaking, too. And I could feel the hair on the back of my neck bristling, standing up inside my baseball cap.

'By now, though, we'd been involved in playoffs in majors and plenty of nailbiting moments in Europe, so I expected him to settle down pretty quickly. However, he was still really nervous as the big moment came and he wanted to hit a driver. Monty said to me, "I want to hit the driver because it's the biggest club in the bag and I've got less chance of missing the ball altogether with it!"

'It may well have been a driver for some, but a good, strong three-wood was, I felt, the ideal shot. This would save us getting into any trouble at the end of the ball's run, and save Nick being in trouble. Monty was so keyed up, though, and he was insisting on the driver until I had a few more quiet words. Then he agreed and took the three-wood – straight down the middle and in an ideal position. The terrifying moment was over for both of us. The only trouble was that Lehman took a driver and killed it. He was right down the middle as well, only much further up. I didn't know what to think then.

'When we got down there it hardly mattered that Lehman had got the extra distance because we'd put Nick in a pretty good position. It wasn't a great iron in by Nick, though, and they got much closer, about ten feet, and Lehman holed for a birdie. Nick made more mistakes and Monty was carrying him for a good while, unlike 1993 at The Belfry when it was the other way round.

'We got to four-down but I kept thinking all along that things were going to swing our way. You get so used to the two guys playing so well, that it was hard to swallow the fact that they were getting beaten easily. You could see that Nick was getting niggled by the way he was playing and you can't let your guard drop against Pavin at all, he's such a competitor.

'It started raining heavily and made us feel pretty miserable. Nick and Monty started to claw it back, though. A big putt by Monty on the sixth got us going and the opposition played the seventh and eighth badly, so we were back to only one-down coming to the turn. Then Nick holed a long one on the 13th and we were all-square.

'I thought we might have it then. It was really chucking it down but they were both concentrating well. Then Nick hit a really poor drive down the last. Monty got it back on line but then Nick played a poor chip and the hole was gone. So was the match.'

To win the match, Lehman had to wait for a few minutes while the 18th green was 'squeegeed', following the incessant rain which dogged the first day's play. It has been said that true Scots golfers can only play well when it's lashing down with rain and blowing a gale. That meant the downpour of Friday should suit Sam Torrance. But would it suit his partner Costantino Rocca? And would the Italian, who was accused of fragile nerves at The Belfry two years previously, blend with the easy-going Scot?

Rocca's caddie Mick Doran sensed there was empathy between the two as soon as the practice sessions began:

'There had been talk of Seve Ballesteros playing with Costantino to help with

127

the language difficulties but it would have been daft to partner them just because of that. And there would have been less chance of Costantino getting a match straight away. In the last practice game Bernard Gallacher put Costantino out with Sam and they just clicked; their games seemed to suit each other perfectly. Bernard asked the caddies their opinions a lot during the week, and when I talked to him I said it would be great if they went out in foursomes for the first morning, because they'd hit it off so well.

'The next day they went out against Haas and Couples and did the business. It wasn't a surprise to me. They are a perfect match. They both like a smoke, so they could offer each other a fag on the way round, kept the talk going and made it a real team effort. They're both down-to-earth blokes. Sam likes a bet and Costa has a similar personality. He's not a great betting man, but he did put a few bob on himself to win the PGA Championship at Wentworth, and won the money.

'They didn't play spectacular stuff but they were really steady and got well ahead with some solid pars from about the middle of the front nine. It was great for Costantino to get his first point. He'd suffered badly after 1993, carrying the burden of it all on his shoulders. And he'd lost an Open in between in a playoff with John Daly. He was determined to get back into the Ryder Cup, though, and show people he was good enough. I was very pleased for him.'

While it was a relief for Rocca to seal his first point and prove he could play under the pressure of the Ryder Cup, it was also a delighted Torrance who picked up his first point of the last two encounters. Torrance was in the throes of his best year on the European Tour, constantly swapping places on top of the Order of Merit with Montgomerie and making the team in a canter. A victory the week before Oak Hill in the British Masters underlined the brilliant form the veteran Scot was in.

Caddie Malcolm Mason studied the form with his regular betting partner – and the runners and riders that Gallacher might team up – before they enjoyed success in the opening clash:

'Sam was playing the best golf of his career and was full of himself by the time we flew out to Oak Hill. We practised with so many different partners – James, Monty – I think Bernard had pre-set ideas of his teams but he was trying out everything. Ballesteros and Rocca always seemed a likely two-ball. David Gilford looked as though he was going to be just making up the numbers, but then he and Seve were put together in practice and they gelled. Seve just takes over and he's not only a good player but probably the best caddie in the world as well. He caddies for people he plays with. He's such a magician with shots, he expects others to play them as well, and invariably he gets the shot out of them – when they didn't know they had it in them in the first place. He gets them to play the shots they didn't even believe they could play.

'After all the mix-and-match in practice, Sam said, "I think I'll be all right playing with Rocca in fourballs, but I don't know about foursomes." This is because Costantino's another one who manipulates shots. You might be thinking seven-iron and he's thinking of just cutting a five-iron with a shot that just can't be done. Occasionally he comes up with some mysteries, but he normally knows his limitations and knows which shots will work. That worked very well, but it was curious that we won both our foursomes, which we thought might be difficult for our pairing, and lost the fourballs we thought we'd walk.'

The pairing by Gallacher which was the worst-kept secret next to Montgomerie and Faldo was that of the long-time friends Howard Clark and Mark James. Clark returned to Ryder Cup action with his third successive different caddie. On the bag this time was Ronan Rafferty's caddie from 1989, Stuart Dryden, finally coming to terms with his task after a worrying period:

'We had 1989 US Open yardage books which showed the sprinkler positions, trees right and left of the fairways, all the usual markings. But all our boys went straight out on to the golf course when they arrived, wheeling and measuring, putting in numbers and positions we noticed weren't in the books we were given. We had to have it absolutely right and the way yardages are done in the US is definitely different from the way we do it in Europe. The caddies did it pretty well to a man. Shows how thorough and professional they are.

'For instance, at the first there was a stream maybe 40 yards short of the green and they didn't have that number in the books. If we drove into the rough and got a fairly decent lie, we'd want to know how far it is to carry that stream. Sure enough, it happened exactly like that during the week. Howard drove in the rough, got a semi-decent lie and wanted to know exactly how far the carry was. With a player like Howard, you wouldn't dare take a chance on not having that kind of fact at your fingertips.

'Two weeks before at the Lancôme Trophy in Paris the tension was really building up and I felt it with Howard. I did a useless job because I just didn't come to terms with the tension he was expressing and I really got caught up in all the pressure. I was hopeless on the golf course, and felt intimidated all the time. Howard was struggling with his game and that was the last thing he wanted at that stage. He didn't want to be looking for a swing two weeks before going into a Ryder Cup match. I felt I daren't say anything. He wasn't asking me too much on club selection, and when he did I didn't have all that much confidence I could get it right. My mind was not attuned to doing the job. He missed the cut and I admitted to him I was completely hopeless. He wasn't impressed, obviously.

'I went home for a week instead of doing the British Masters and just hoped I'd get it right when the chips were down. Even going over, I was apprehensive. The Ryder Cup's become such a big animal since 1985. Even the luxury of Concorde, a once-in-a-lifetime treat, didn't allay all my fears and I spent most of the trip working out how I could get it right and do the job to the best of my ability.

'Howard had no intention of playing any holes on the Monday, although Woosie and Sam played a few. It was down to business on the Tuesday – and the tension was there again. I really struggled to sleep a lot that week. Howard was really wound up, even in the practice rounds.

'Despite his demeanour he was keen to play and he and Mark had had a good record in the past. But they struggled against Maggert and Love. Howard's game was so-so, but he was definitely struggling with nerves. On the sixth, par-three, Howard hit a really poor shot. He felt he was a little bit between clubs and he was a bit indecisive and hit a hook shot into the stream which should never really have been in play. From that moment on, they were gone. Mark couldn't really say much about it. Then he stood on the next tee and hit a stone-cold top himself. If you see your opponents do that, it's got to give you a lot of confidence and it was all over by the 15th. Howard was boiling. He had wanted so much to play well but his game wasn't really there. We finished up playing a lot of practice from then on – a lot of the time with Mark.'

With the eclipse of one of Europe's most experienced pairings, it was left to Langer and Johansson to cancel out the morning's deficit with a filibuster success in lashing rain against Ben Crenshaw and Curtis Strange.

Gallacher took his decision to give the German and the Swede another match in the afternoon fourballs before the heavier rain set in and the match was elongated. With his men three-up and six to play, it seemed a wise move – until they had to fight for their success in the strength-sapping deluge. For Johansson and Langer there was huge relief at a last-hole triumph, but then Langer's caddie Pete Coleman realised there would be no respite before they had to lift themselves to higher plains of endeavour:

'We knew we had to go out again because the teams for the afternoon fourballs had to be in by midday and we were still well out on the course at that time. Because we were three-up I suppose Bernard thought it was going to be all over fairly quickly, so we wouldn't have any trouble turning around. But we ran into trouble after the 12th. It was all a bit of a mess, the back-nine, and we had lost all three holes by the time we came to the 18th. But Bernhard made sure we got the point with a 20-footer on the last. It was a great putt because the green was so unpredictable after having all the water on it.

'Everything was soaking and Bernhard and Per were very tired – in fact, Per looked absolutely whacked. But there we were, expected to go straight out and play the fourballs. They took all our wet gear, and we were absolutely soaked to the skin, gave us some dry stuff and something to eat on the run, and we were out there again after only half an hour's break. It was hardly surprising they couldn't get it going again.'

Langer and Johansson's morning success had brought the teams level, highlighting the importance of that final putt by the German, but then they capitulated 6 and 4 to Corey Pavin and Phil Mickelson. Theirs was one of three defeats for the Europeans in the afternoon, which left the visitors 5–3 down.

Shining through the gloom, though, was a spectacular success for just about the most unlikely combination, on paper, ever seen in a Ryder Cup. Unlikely, that is, unless you think like Bernard Gallacher.

Ballesteros's game was in erratic shape but he could always rely on his conjuring tricks. It would need the steadiest of men alongside him. There was nobody in the team steadier than part-time cattle-breeder Gilford. To complement his own enigmatic genius against Peter Jacobsen and Brad Faxon, Gilford's caddie Tim Lees witnessed Ballesteros milk his man's talent for all it was worth:

'We played with Seve in a practice round and he was great to David, encouraging even then. He told me how much he liked the way David played and I knew how much Seve respected his game. We just wanted to get out there and prove it. David had been very hurt by the way things had gone in 1991 at Kiawah Island and he was dying to put the record straight. He doesn't like to talk too much about it, but he told me that. He'd got a point to prove, so he wanted to get out there and prove it as early as he could.

'His chance came in the afternoon on the first day. Seve was over straight away when the pairing was finalised, chatting and encouraging before we even went out. He knew he was hitting it all over the shop, left and right, didn't really know where the ball was going. He knew it was David who was going to be doing the hard work. On the first tee Seve put his arm round him and said, "Come on, David. You're the best player in the world. As long as you believe it, you're the best." Right away you could see David respond.

'David is very quiet and lets his clubs do the talking and that was one thing I'd been slightly wary of. He might enjoy the banter coming from Seve, but would it change his game? Because he's not used to a lot of chat on the golf course, would it tend to unnerve him or spoil his concentration? He wasn't carried away, though. David's very level-headed and he knew how he planned his game. He said to me as we were walking down one of the early fairways, "It's great to have Seve so enthusiastic, but I've got to play my own game as well." I think Seve respected that, although I doubt David would have said it to him. It was just understood. Seve seemed to back off when it was needed and he didn't interfere much in club selection; he let me get on with it with David. It worked the other way with Seve, though, and geed him up like I'd never seen him before.

'We got in front when David birdied the sixth and then Peter Jacobsen made a big mistake on the seventh. He either forgot or didn't realise Faxon had gone in the water and picked up his marker, thinking we'd halved and his putt wasn't needed. In fact he'd got a four-footer uphill, just the sort the pros love, for the win. He knocked our ball away to concede, so they finished up with nothing.

'Seve and David were a bit shocked at first. They didn't even realise what was going on until we heard Brad sort of gasp, "What are you doing, Pete?" Then the referee, who'd obviously been counting, called the hole to us. They walked off counting their luck and the opponents' heads went down a bit then, I think. It put us in the driving seat and that hole was the key to our winning.

'The 13th just about did it for us. Seve had gone out of the hole again and David was in the right fringe just off the green with about 18 feet to the hole. I knew he wouldn't want to chip it or pitch it, because that's not his strong point. And it must have had at least ten feet of break on it, right to left. Seve had been reading the putts with him all the way round and they took a long time discussing this one. I hadn't got involved with lining up at all. Who needs to when Seve's around?

'David looked really cool and got a lovely stroke on it. It took what seemed an age to bend towards the hole and then dropped. As soon as it went in, the two of them hugged each other. In fact, Seve was so chuffed that he squeezed David so tight he knocked his hat off. I'll never forget the looks on their faces. When we came in with the win there was so much pride on both their faces. I guess Seve was proud of what he'd been able to achieve with helping David and David was proud of his point. I guess you could say he'd proved his point!'

Plenty more team members had points to prove. Torrance and Rocca had gleaned a point from their opening match, but then became one of the three pairs to concede defeat on the opening afternoon. Worryingly for Gallacher, his top pairing of Faldo and Montgomerie also went down again.

Each year since the 1985 revival, though, there had been a golden spell on the Saturday when Europe came good. Again it was to be the second-day foursomes where the Europeans excelled, enabling Europe to climb back level with their hosts.

To Gallacher's relief, Faldo and Montgomerie at last gelled well enough to dispose of Strange and Jay Haas but the revelation came from Torrance and Rocca as they overwhelmed Davis Love III and Jeff Maggert. It was a rather poignant success for Rocca and his caddie Mick Doran as they celebrated a hole in one:

'Costantino had been desperate to come good after what had happened in 1993. He told me that before we got to Oak Hill. Now we're matched against the player who beat him at The Belfry two years before, Davis Love. Did he want to win!

'It was strange because Costa normally gets very nervous before a match, yet he wasn't nervous at all for this one. I knew what it meant to him, with it being Love, but he seemed right on top of things. He and Sam worked out where they were going to hit their tee-shots. I don't know whether they'd planned it all that hard but it worked out that Costantino had the tee at the short sixth.

'We were already three-up so they're feeling confident. Costantino pulls out a five-iron. It's only 167 yards but I know how he likes to play cut down shots a bit differently from how you would imagine, so that wasn't a surprise. We discussed it and thought five would be a bit too much, though, especially as there was trouble behind the flag. We decided instead it was a little six.

'So he has a couple of waggles with his six-iron, nods OK and hits it lovely. It pitched on the front, big right to left, and in it went. There was no holding him. He was hugging Sam, really excited. I knew we couldn't get beaten from there. It was pretty special and he deserved it. To have it happen against Love as well . . . You just sort of felt that it was fate or something.'

If Rocca had hit into the cup with joy in the morning, it was positively running over in the afternoon when he and Woosnam fashioned a point in the fourballs – with Love again in the opposing duo. Before that, Gilford's fortunes, too, went back on the upward curve as he continued to enjoy his Ryder Cup week.

Whereas Ballesteros had been the mentor to Gilford on the first day, this time it was Langer with the helping hand. The Cheshireman's caddie, Lees, however, was not a bad judge of reading between the lines himself.

'It didn't work so well the second time he played with Seve because the pair of them got more and more anxious as they saw the Saturday fourballs slip away. Seve started asking me about my yardages more and got involved in David's club selection, but it all got away from them in the end. Everything they tried worked against them, and that time Seve's enthusiasm was probably counterproductive. Instead of letting David get into his own private bubble and do his thing with me, Seve tried to get him to do it the way he thought, and it didn't work out.

'With Bernhard, though, it did work for the Saturday-morning foursomes against Pavin and Lehman. Bernhard's a bit like Seve, very inspirational and very Ryder Cup orientated, wanting to beat the Americans. The difference was that they were carrying each other because Bernhard played well, chipped in on the 12th and did his bit, half and half.

'It was good for David in another way, playing with Seve and Bernhard. Because they are two of the world's top players, we had enormous crowds following us every day. Having such a big gallery around him all the time stood David in good stead when it came to the singles.

'As well as being straight, David's other strength is mental. He plays a bad shot and forgets about it. He is one of only a few players that can do that. He'll tell you himself he's not the most talented, especially around the greens, and it was tough round the greens that week. When he played with Bernhard he showed his mental strength most of all, and that helped them earn their point. It was a bit of a dodgy start, but David just put it out of his mind and on the second he hit an eight-iron to about 18 inches. We had a three-iron in to not much more on the next and you just knew it was going to be all right from then on. He played some great irons and so did Bernhard. They were a great team.'

Woosnam and debutant Philip Walton, having their first outings of the week, were Europe's only losers in the morning. It put a dampener on the first Ryder Cup encounter for Walton and bagman Bryan McLauchlan:

'It was a long wait before getting the nod from Bernard. The uncertainty of it really gnawed at my stomach and I know it was hard for Philip. Bernard did ask Philip which he'd prefer playing – foursomes or fourballs. Philip told him fourballs but that didn't make a lot of difference because we ended up playing foursomes. Neither Philip nor Ian played at their very best and they didn't seem to gel, although they got a lot out of their match and encouraged each other. Peter Jacobsen, who's one of the nicest guys I've ever met, and Loren Roberts did gel well. We could still have easily got a half out of it, but we didn't. Perhaps if we had, things might have turned out completely differently. It was all fate that week.'

Whereas Walton did not get another chance, Woosnam made up for their defeat in the afternoon by accompanying Rocca to that second heady success over Love, who had Ben Crenshaw in tandem for the Saturday fourballs. Theirs was the only victory, however, as the balance of power swung America's way.

The first Europeans to fall were Torrance and Montgomerie. This new partnership, splitting Montgomerie and Faldo, was a result of Scottish scheming, felt Montgomerie's caddie McLean, another man from north of the border:

'Faldo and Monty hadn't had a great deal of success in the fourballs for some strange reason. In fact, the best they'd done was a half, so the move to team up Sam and Monty was on. Monty favoured it but the pushing to match them up actually came more from Sam.

'He and Costa had got hammered in fourballs as well and Sam had more to do with the change than Monty or Nick. I think all the Scots got together – Sam, Monty and Bernard, a sort of gathering of the clans – and decided on the change. Sam's like Braveheart with golf clubs and he gets everybody fired up, so the thinking was that maybe he could get Monty fired up to win a fourballs for a change. They were Nos 1 and 2 in Europe, so it was quite some pairing.

'As it turned out, the opponents, Brad Faxon and Fred Couples, did some of the most incredible dovetailing you'll ever see in a Ryder Cup. It was unbelievable. Monty and Sam would have beaten anybody on earth that day, otherwise. When Freddie was chopping about in the trees, Faxon would make a birdie and when Fax had his ball in his pocket, Freddie made the birdie. The Americans call it "ham and eggs" when it happens like that, and Monty and Sam certainly had too much on their plate. They made a lot of birdies, too – but they seemed to do it on the same hole all the while. It was just incredible the way it worked out, and very frustrating for us. The other guy could be completely out of the hole and his partner would rake in a huge putt across the green to win.

'Fred and Fax really went to town after the turn, birdieing the 10th, 11th, 12th and 13th by dovetailing. We got worn down in the end and it was virtually all over from the long 13th, which summed up the way the round went. Sam had hit a super shot in to a few inches, almost holing out, and had a certain birdie. Fax is out the hole and Freddie has a 30-foot chip across the green from inside quite heavy fringe, with about eight or nine feet of break on it. He binned it for the half.

'It caused the loudest cheer you've ever heard in your life from what seemed like all of the 30,000 crowd at our hole. Freddie was running around the green "high-fiving" it with Fax. It was bedlam. But it was a wee bit depressing for us because that was about it.'

If it unsettled the European camp to lose the first match out, especially one which featured the top men off their order of merit, then it was little compared to the events at the end of a day of frustration for the visiting team. Europe's most experienced pairing of Faldo and Langer looked as though they could edge a stirring point. But then, as Faldo's caddie Fanny Sunesson remembers, one of those cruel twists of fate worked against Europe, bringing the highly charged home crowd to a crescendo:

'The crowd was huge anyway, but the gallery just got bigger and bigger around us and we knew how important our result was going to be. A point and we'd be into the singles level, but if we lost then Europe would be two-down going into the final day.

'Nick just couldn't get the putts to drop again. He'd had the same problem when playing with Colin in the fourballs. The ball just wouldn't go in the hole. Then on the 13th a putt finally went in, although he was in reasonably close anyway, about seven or eight feet. A birdie brought us back level because Pavin had birdied the 12th.

'Pavin played awesomely all week and he was carrying his partner. We couldn't shake them off and it stayed level coming to the last. Nick was on in two and looking pretty good, has about an 18-footer for a birdie. Pavin's in the hollows in some pretty long rough. But he hits a really great shot just on the fringe, leaving himself a tough little pitch shot because the hole's running away from him slightly. Roberts is on, but a long, long way away. We had a great chance of winning the hole if Nick could find another good putt.

'Even when Roberts ran his up close enough for the four, I still thought we could make the birdie we needed, and even if we didn't, the half was surely safe. Then Pavin chipped in, just pitched low and ran hard. It tried to get out of the hole and spun round, but it dropped. You have to feel gutted. We lined up Nick's putt and he didn't hold back. It ran past the cup and we'd lost the hole from nowhere. The noise was like nothing you've ever heard on a golf course.'

Pavin's lucky break left Europe with their backs to the wall at the start of singles day at two points adrift. Pavin's heart-sinking chip-in deflated the 3,000 European supporters in a capacity 25,000 gallery. It was the first time since 1981 that the USA had led going into the last day. With their traditional penchant for singles, America looked as though they were going to inflict the first decisive defeat since 1981 at Walton Heath.

Gallacher mused long and hard upon how his opposite number would put out his men, rethinking, guessing and double-guessing. He would have the erratic and self-destructive Ballesteros out first 'because you can't lose us the Ryder Cup from that position, Seve', and his two rookies out last. Some thought it too much of a gamble. A highly likely Ballesteros defeat would mean Europe going three-down straight away. This could very well leave the onus on the lower half of the draw, including the two rookies, to seal the victory.

It was a gamble by Gallacher, who hoped it would not come down to Walton and Johansson. He loaded his strength in the middle and when Wadkins' team was matched with Gallacher's, it was felt the European captain had pulled off a significant coup.

When Ballesteros duly lost his match to Lehman, savaging the Oak Hill rough, ironically it was to act as a spur, because the Europeans knew they now had to fight from three points down. It was something of a morale-booster that Ballesteros had not been crushed something like 8 and 7, which is what he would have been but for his remarkable ironplay. And it was also because Ballesteros almost immediately went back out on to the course to launch a one-man crusade to urge his team on.

The inspirational Spaniard spent the rest of the afternoon frenziedly charging about from one match to another, throwing in advice – wanted or not – to Gallacher, egging his team-mates on from the wings and cajoling and pleading with the golfing gods to take Europe's side.

Superstitious Ballesteros had had his own strategy for victory – to persuade Gallacher to let the team go out on the last day in blue, his lucky Open-winning colour, instead of the green outfits that had been planned. It would be hard to persuade Ballesteros afterwards that his colour switch wasn't a contributory factor to America being blue by the end of the day.

While Ballesteros was still out there steadily defoliating the rough, though, Clark was on his way to Europe's opening success, the first of the magnificent seven victories registered in the afternoon as Gallacher's game-plan succeeded in just the way he had prayed it might.

Clark's caddie Dryden was looking for a change in fortune after taking part in nothing but practice since the first morning. Oak Hill's 11th hole provided the lucky break:

'Come Saturday he was hitting balls on the range with no idea whether he was going to play that day or not. Bernard probably had an idea which players he was going to play. But he hadn't relayed it to Howard, who was particularly jumpy, not knowing whether or not he would be playing. I'm running about asking what the team is and Bernard's sending messages back to keep ourselves prepared. Howard's like a cat on a hot tin roof!

'I had a pretty terrible night, tossing and turning, worrying about how things were going to go. I'd gone back to my hotel thinking if Howard really decides to have a go at me out there, then there was really no way we could win. I'd struggle to add and subtract on the yardages, never mind work out which clubs we should be playing.

'I was churning up and glad that we'd at least got an early start. I'd woken up at 4 a.m. and couldn't get back to sleep again, so I just got up and got myself prepared. The bag was checked – enough balls, and so on – and we went to the range. Howard was hitting the ball reasonably well and, after all, we were playing with Peter Jacobsen. He wasn't going to be aggressive. It would be a tough match, but there are no undertones of gamesmanship or too much patriotism with Peter. That helped.

'We were ready for the off, so I said to Howard, "Take a couple of deep breaths. Let's go and do the best we can." He hit a great drive down the first, got on the green a bit short and I had to tend the flag. Ridiculous thoughts went through my head: "What happens if I can't get the flag out of the cup when the ball comes at it?" I pictured in my mind the horror of the ball striking the flagstick and getting a penalty. But Howard rolled up a good putt and we made a half.

'Then on the second he hit into the left rough. He asked me where the flag was and I said it was short right, but he then hit a bad shot with a one-iron because of thinking about the pin position instead of just trying to make the left of the fairway. That left him with a difficult third and he still didn't make the green. Peter was on in two. Then Howard chipped in from quite heavy fringe for a four – and another half. That lifted him. If he hadn't done that, I really don't know what might have happened because it would have been a bad way to lose it. His chipping was good because he nearly chipped in at the third as well.

'We were all-square coming to the sixth, a hole I was not all that keen on. We'd had a bit of a trying time during the practice rounds at this hole. Once, Howard hit into the water on the sixth with an eight-iron. I rested the club on the side of the bag while he asked for another ball, not thinking he'd want the same club because he'd come up short. But instead of going for a seven-iron he took the eight. Then he had a go at me for not cleaning his eight-iron! Well, we got the shot away OK this time, but Peter won the hole with a birdie.

'Howard's short-game was razor sharp to stay with Jacobsen. By the 11th we're one-down, having lost the tenth, and so it's Peter's honour. He hits into the left-hand bunker. We've got a "standup" six-iron shot, no great debate necessary. We don't have to worry whether it's five-iron or six-iron. I hand him the six-iron. It's covering the flag all the way. He turns away and picks up his tee-shot. The television cameras pan in on his face. He looks disgusted!

'Now, as the cameras get to him he looks totally distraught, and that made a lot of people confused. It was only him expressing how he felt. My impression was that he'd made a beautiful swing and had hit a pure golf shot. He just said to me,

"What more can I do? I made a great swing on that." He knew he'd hit it pure and that from there he was in the lap of the gods. Just goes to show the camera can lie! I just thought to myself, "That's all I can do as well," and the ball went in the hole.

'Then Howard went AWOL. The euphoria of the hole in one got to him mentally and he was out of there. I had to say to him on the 12th tee, "I think we should get tuned back in a little bit now. It was nice what happened but we only won one hole out of it." Sure enough, he'd gone in the rough. Pete was on in two and eventually Howard had an eight-footer for a half, a really slippery putt, but he made it. He hadn't missed a putt he'd needed to hole all day. Peter thought he was going to get the hole straight back, but they halved.

'At 13 we hit three-iron off the tee and a three-iron second shot which leaks into the heavy rough. He nine-irons it up short, leaving 70 yards. The green slopes really heavily from back to front, so you don't really want to get it behind the hole. It was a little bit down-breeze and I thought he may think this is a full sand-iron. He did and hit it nicely, and thought it was a really good shot. It finished up about six yards behind the flag. I didn't realise at the time, but he was pacing his yardages. And he turned round and said, "That was the wrong yardage." I said, "Howard, I know for a fact that I've measured from that sprinkler," pointing to the sprinkler spot. "I have no reason to think you've had a wrong number." He then said, "Well, why am I behind the flag? It was a good shot." I suggested it was because it was a little down-breeze. He accepted that and hit a wonderful putt which didn't quite go in, so we went one behind.

'On 14 he gets his tee-shot away and then comes at me again. "That had to be a wrong yardage." I said, "Look, Howard. That was the 13th. We're now on the 14th. We've still got a job to do. How about we just get on with it?" He said, "Yes, I guess you're right." He won the hole to a Jacobsen three-putt. So we got on 15 all-square. He took quite a while before deciding it was a six-iron. To me it was a six-iron all day, never anything else. By now I was thinking quite clearly even though the tension was building. We'd had a little incident on 13 that he'd tried to carry on at 14 but I felt in control. I was churning up but trying to show a calm front, as if it was just another round of golf!

'They both par 15 and on 16 Howard hits a lovely drive and Pete's in the right trees. Now we're one-up. At 17 they both hit good drives. Peter goes first and hits the green. We are debating whether it's a six- or a seven-iron. I said to Howard, "Where do you think all the trouble is?" Howard said, "Short." So I said, "Well, there's your answer." He hits a six-iron just off the left fringe, putts it down close and has it conceded. Peter putts up. Half. So now the big one.

'We're just in the right rough, and Peter is in the fairway after a really good drive. Once again, is it four or five? I thought all the trouble was past the flag and said I liked the five-iron. He said, "Right. I'll have to go with that." He hits the green and, importantly, is underneath the hole. He rolls up his putt to about three feet. Peter thought he'd holed his putt for the halved match. I thought he had. The crowd thought he had. It brushed the lip but somehow failed to drop. Now we've got a three-footer coming downhill, left to right. It's for a pretty crucial point. The first point for Europe.

'Afterwards he told me he could hardly feel his hands they were so numb but he hit a pretty good putt and in it went. I was in shock. I went on my haunches, a little bit overcome. And I shed a couple of tears, even though we weren't even close to winning yet. We'd drawn the first blood. Howard said to me later, "You did a good job. The one thing you did best was to look so calm. I knew you were nervous but outwardly you were really calm."'

Clark's great friend James followed up with a decisive victory over Maggert to bring the week round for the pair, who had been cooling their heels since defeat on the opening day. James pitched in from a bunker's edge on the fourth just as Concorde flew over on its way to collect the European team.

While James set up his victory with the super sand-shot, Woosnam was trying to win his first Ryder Cup point in the singles. Woosnam's game had definitely perked up by the Saturday session, caddie Morbey felt, after an anxious time on the practice range. That was much to do with his run out with Walton:

'Woosie and Philip played quite well in the foursomes and were unlucky to lose by one hole, but the match did them both a lot of good. Ian gave Philip a lot of encouragement and helped him on one or two things and he also found his own game again.

'When I saw the draw I thought, "We're going to win this. On paper, we've got a great chance. The draw has come out just perfect for us." It was a real result having Seve with Tom Lehman. Lehman was in great form, very confident, and I felt he could beat at least half the players in our team. Seve would have lost to anybody, the way he was carving it into the undergrowth, so we were taking out one of their best men.

'I couldn't believe we'd got Fred again. When I met up with Woosie all he could talk about was getting it right this time. Woosie was always up on Freddie and I really thought we were going to do it this time. But Fred just scrambled like you've never seen at the end.

'On the 15th Fred misses the green way left and it looked as though there would be no way he could stop a ball with the pin being on the back right. But Freddie just launches a sand-iron into orbit and gets the ball to stop at about six feet, a wonderful shot. He's so good at them. Woosie's up on the top and rolls down to three feet – and Fred holes out. What an up-and-down. Fred looks as though he's going to go two-down with three to play. Then on 16 Fred's in the trees, but hits an unbelievable shot out of them to save par and save himself going two-down again.

'The 17th was the hole that did Woosie for his point, though. It's a huge par-four and you just don't expect anybody to make a birdie on it. Fred hit a huge drive, though, of about 300 yards. Woosie went through the green – just. Fred hits an eight-iron to about fifteen feet. When Woosie chips down to four feet I'm thinking half; I'm thinking one-up playing the last and here we go for our point at last. Freddie then holes his 15-footer and it's all-square. Even then, when Fred snap-hooks way left and we're just short of the bunker, I think we might have it because we get on to 18 foot and Fred's in the bunker. He hits out to six feet past and so Woosie can do it.

'The putt looked great all the way. How it missed just defies belief – defied gravity. We were in the air ready to celebrate when the ball just whiskered past. Ian couldn't believe it and held his head in his hands, on his knees. We'd still got it, though, if Fred missed his. He said afterwards that if it had been uphill he might have just tweaked it left. He'd been struggling with his putting all week. This one he just had to set rolling. It went in. We were gutted.'

While Rocca was this time having to accept defeat against Love, having had the better of the American all week, Gilford was grinding out a lead on Faxon. It had been a satisfying week for Gilford, who was able to banish the misery of Kiawah Island from his memory with two points in the bag before he carved out his and Europe's destiny in the singles.

The unassuming Cheshireman assumed a position of strength in Gallacher's line-up to play out a thriller of a match, undecided until the last telling putt. Gilford's role in the European hierarchy came as no surprise to his caddie Lees:

'We were halfway down the field and it was no surprise to us. Bernard made it quite clear on Saturday night, before the draw, how he was going to play it. He regarded David as one of the stronger players and he wanted his strong men in the middle of the field.

'We'd already played against Faxon, knew his capabilities, knew he was a very strong player, and had a lot of respect for him. The first nine was very nip-and-tuck and then halfway round the back-nine David moved a couple ahead, giving us a bit of a cushion. I was wary about the crowd, thinking back to Kiawah Island and all the hullabaloo at the last few holes. I didn't want us to be going down the stretch level because I thought he might struggle against the home crowd. The gallery were very close to you, especially around the tees where it was quite claustrophobic, and it definitely affected concentration. They were extremely partisan. Not rude, but extremely intimidating, with lots of banter and shouting out. Not very nice at all and it would be easy to be unnerved by them.

'So I was very pleased when David got himself two ahead by the 12th, a good springboard. We were still one-up by the really long par-four 17th and here we had a chance to close it down, but he missed a longish, tricky downhiller with a right-to-left swing. I say "he" because I've only ever read one putt with David. That was at the US Masters on the last green on the last day – and we missed! I never know how hard he's going to hit it or how true the greens are; it's down to his feel. He's a pretty good putter above six foot anyway. He needed a solid one from about that length to save on 17 in the finish.

'Having halved the 17th, he hit an accurate drive at 18 right in the middle of the fairway. He had 204 yards to the flag, the ball a bit above us. Before he asked for the club I knew what he was going to do. We didn't have a two-iron in the bag and he'd have to absolutely flush a three-iron to make the green. He didn't have a lot of options. He's got quite a lofted four-wood and his idea was to take a bit off it and fade it in. He flushed it and it pulled. I think that was because of adrenalin more than not hitting the shape he'd wanted. It looked miles big but wasn't really. If it had pitched on the green on the correct line it would have been in the fringe, 30-foot long at the most.

'He asked me where it had gone and I had to tell him just by the back of the stand and bounced back. Now he's faced with the sort of shot we'd been dreading at the end, from the bad stuff at the back of the green. We breathed a bit of a sigh of relief when Faxon's went in the left bunker. He's faced with a tough, tough shot bearing in mind the green's eight feet above where his feet are. We walk up the green not too disheartened.

'When we get to the ball, though, nightmare of nightmares it's on tight-packed mud – mostly caused by players jumping up and down watching their team-mates play out the last – and there isn't much of a shot. A yard in front and he goes into very thick rough, five yards, straight down the hill, it's into the semi. Then the green runs very fast away from him. David didn't really have a choice on how he played it. He got a wedge out and tried it behind the ball but there was no way he could play an orthodox chip. Even Seve could have had 50 goes at it and not got it right. In fact, I could see him dancing around, chasing after Bernard. I knew he was dying to tell David how to play it. Fortunately, David wasn't aware of him, being too engrossed in the shot. I think Seve was urging Bernard to go and tell David how to play the shot – his way. We'd had plenty of that in our matches together!

'It was close to being pretty good, the way David decided to play. He took a six-iron and tried to bump-and-run it low and bounce it once in the long stuff, hoping for it to release down. He just quit on it a bit. If it had got into the first cut of the semi it would have been quite close. He stubbed it a bit and it danced into the thick rough. It left him a better shot actually because now it was sat up quite nicely. There's a lot going through my head, though, because Faxon's played a pretty good bunker shot, got close to nipping it in, but he'd left himself a treacherous six-footer across the break. He's got to sink the putt to win the hole for the half, though. I tried to tell myself that we were still in the driving-seat, even though I could see some of the European contingent not daring to look.

'David makes a nice chip but the ball's gathered speed near the hole and

141

gone about nine feet past. He had a look at the putt from both sides and at this stage I went walkabout. I wandered around doing anything, looking at the scoreboard, anything. I didn't really want to get involved in case he asked me what I thought the line was. I didn't want the responsibility so I looked the other way.

'I then forced myself to watch the shot. He stood over the ball and halfway to the hole it was in. The line, I could see now, was two balls on the outside edge and it was never going anywhere else. His only problem would have been not hitting it hard enough up the hill. It slid in. It absolutely destroyed Brad Faxon. His face dropped. He had a really tricky putt, one that he would only have got maybe four times out of ten. This wasn't going to be one of the four.

'When it missed I thought, "Take that, you American sods." Not because of what happened at Oak Hill, but because David had finally laid the ghost of '91. That was it for me. I went off to pack the bag and let David bask in his glory, although, as usual, he wasn't saying much.'

The victory lifted Europe's spirit again as the scoreboard showed the visitors in a strong position now that Gilford had ensured the point and refused to settle for the half. Montgomerie was on the point of sealing victory against Crenshaw while Gilford and the Europeans went through three or four different moods up ahead on the last green. Montgomerie's caddie McLean, like many, had been delighted when he saw the draw the evening before:

'We all thought Gallacher had done a great job. He'd done the complete opposite to what everyone had been thinking. He had loaded the middle-order, and put Seve out first just to get him out of the way, but after that it was a masterpiece of thinking. Hats off to Gallacher.

'We were against the US Masters champion, playing on US Open-type greens, so we had to be wary of his putting capabilities. But at the same time Crenshaw hadn't had much of a year since winning at Augusta and everyone expected Monty to win. So there's a lot more pressure on him. If Seve, Jesse or Howard got beaten then it was different because they'd not been playing that well. If Monty got beaten it would be bad news. The whole basis of Bernard's draw was that the middle-order guys should win. Actually, Crenshaw didn't putt at all well for someone with his reputation. He played well but didn't hole anything.

'It was a bit nerve-tingling; by the time we played the 14th it was still anybody's match. Monty pushed his tee-shot into the right rough but just managed to creep his approach shot on to the green, front left, 60 or 70 feet away, with about eight or nine feet of break on the line. Crenshaw had hit the fairway and then the green to only 12 feet. I'm absolutely certain Crenshaw thought he was going to go one-up but Monty got this fantastic fluke.

'There was no way I could help him with the line, because it was so far away anything could happen on the way to the hole. On fast greens like they were,

Monty likes to do the lining up on his own. That was OK by me. Caddies often end up having to read the most difficult putts so they are nearly always bound to get them wrong. Some really awkward ones, he will ask me to look at. This one he didn't.

'He bent his putt down, just trying desperately to make sure it was only a two-putt from that distance, make sure Crenshaw had to putt. It bent right into the hole. Perhaps I shouldn't call it a fluke, but it was the sort of putt you could only dream about under those conditions. Monty had done exactly the same thing to Lee Janzen in the singles two years before at The Belfry, and it had a similar result.

'You have to think of the psychology of it all, as far as Crenshaw is concerned. Here he is, even with all his experience, now faced with a putt for a half – when he must in his mind have already been counting himself one-up. He missed his putt. The old killer-instinct then came out in Monty. A great five-iron at the short 15th ensured he made par and it was followed by a 3 on 16 with a shot in to four feet to go two-up.

'The icing on the cake was still to come. It came on 17. Monty hit a superb drive on the toughest hole on the course. He debated for a good while whether he should play safe and take the three-wood or even the two-iron. But we agreed on the driver. I know he was thinking that he was one of the straightest hitters in golf and why should he worry. He said, "Oh, what the hell; let's go for it." He absolutely killed it straight down the middle. It must have been one of the longest drives there all week. It only left him an eight- or nine-iron in and it's over 450 yards. He hit it in to about six feet for a three and it was all over. Three-three-three finish. Not bad under pressure.

'But it was the 14th that did it. He did it all on his own. If I'd got involved with the putt it might not have gone in. I could have seen a yard of break, he seven or eight feet. Then he would have been in two minds. He just guessed – and what a guess.'

Directly behind Montgomerie was his former pairs partner Faldo. Faldo and Strange were re-enacting their 1988 US Open playoff. Again Strange looked to have the upper hand but by the time Montgomerie sealed victory, Faldo was producing the grandstand finish which saw him beat his arch-rival, getting in front for the first time on the last green.

Strange had found a glimmer of vintage form and threatened to make his first point of the week, needing only to hold his head after leading Faldo one-up with three to go.

With Philip Walton in the ascendancy behind, Faldo knew he had to somehow beat Strange. His caddie Sunesson remembers his final approach, which became 'Shot of the Year' in Europe:

'Curtis had a good run, chipping in at the sixth, and got back ahead at the 11th with another birdie-two after Nick pulled it back. It stayed that way with just the last three holes to go. We could tell from the scoreboard how crucial our match was going to be. Sam was nearly there and Philip was two-up.

'At the 16th Nick nearly holed a 20-footer for par, but the putt just stayed out to keep us one-down. On the 17th Nick hit the fairway but with a horrid stance, a downhill lie, and he went into the sand. Curtis couldn't make the green and both of them had eight-footers or so, Curtis just outside Nick. Curtis missed his and Nick holed a good putt. All-square.

'So it was all down to the last hole. You could feel the whole of the course seething with tension. The spectators looked frantic but you have to keep your mind on the job. Nick just turned it left, not so good, and Curtis was down the middle. We were in the rough by only 12 feet or so, but the ball was down and Nick could only play short. His ball just came off the fairway into the short semi. Curtis then came up way short and put his ball into the bank in front of the green. We then had 93 yards to go, the distance was that precise. I have it as a permanent record in my yardage book, Nick's great shot into the last. It was the middle-wedge, and he just got the most perfect stroke on it, pitched nicely and ran to about four foot just left of the hole with an uphill putt. Curtis went a foot past us with his chip.

'He went first [with Faldo's eyes jammed tightly closed] – and missed. Our putt was left to right, horrible, not the sort of putt you want at that stage in any tournament, but this was the Ryder Cup and this one had to go in. We read the line together and I lined him up on the putt from behind as I'd done a lot that week.

'Nick had shown fantastic nerve at the end and he rolled it in. The scenes were unbelievable. Seve's holding him and crying like a baby, Nick is too, and so's Bernard – we're all very emotional. It only needs Philip to finish it off.'

Before Walton's memorable finish Torrance cruised in, rarely looking troubled against Roberts, closing down the match. That was pleasing for Torrance's caddie Mason:

'Thankfully we never had to go down 18 all week. We'd finished all our matches before it. I think it's as tough a finish as The Belfry, without water. Sam was always in a comfort-zone and he shut out Loren with a great approach shot to birdie 16, needing a putt of less than three feet. We halved 17 for the point and by then we were more interested in what was going on ahead with Faldo's match. Faldo's a giant. We watched the shot and putt on 18. His win was a killer-blow for the Americans.'

Langer had reached the point of no return with Pavin and Johansson could still halve with Mickelson. None of this mattered, however, if Walton kept his nerve. The Irishman, one of the three European 'broomhandle' putter-users, along with Torrance and James, looked to have swept Europe to the very brink of victory.

Then the luck of the Irish seemed to desert Walton. Even his rock-steady caddie Bryan McLauchlan began to wobble when he looked up at the scoreboard and realised it all depended on their match:

'Philip was very determined he was going to get something out of his Ryder Cup and was very dedicated with his practice, trying out a few things he needed to work on. One of those things was the way to pitch and chip out of the rough at Oak Hill, which was a real killer. Woosie had given him a tip and he worked on it.

'To play well on the last day was a dream not only for him but for me as well, and when we got to two-up on Jay Haas I was almost floating along. We were holding it and things were looking good. A few glances up at the scoreboard, though, set the nerves jangling, knowing just how crucial our match had become. It was nerve-wracking then, dry-mouthed, hands shaking, head spinning – and that was just me. Philip seemed as cool as a cucumber. I was going through cigarette after cigarette. It's hard for anyone to understand what a player goes through in these kinds of situations. Perhaps the caddie understands better than most. I knew Philip must be heaving inside but trying not to show it.

'We get to the 15th, 186 yards to the pin. Philip says, "What do you think?" It was a tough shot. We decided on a solid six-iron. Not many people would expect to be playing a six-iron over 186 yards but I knew he was so pumped up. He stiffed it six feet just left of the flag. It was a downhill putt. He rolled it in. Lovely.

'At that stage, three-up with three to play, as a caddie you feel as though you've done your job. The whole reason for being there doing such a job is to see your man win. You have to be dedicated, not sidetracked by anything. Only see one thing – your man winning. So we're dormie-three. I can't explain how that felt at that stage. We can't lose. Whether you're wanting to or not, you mentally drop your guard.

'Philip played 16 beautifully. Down the left-hand side, plonks it in the middle of the green. Lovely. Jay misses the green right and goes in the trap. Surely it's all over now? And the way things were, we had a shrewd idea what that might mean: the Ryder Cup. Haas splashes out – and into the hole! Well, there's nothing we can do about that. Okay. No big problem. We're still two-up with two to play. No problem.

'Neither of them hit good tee-shots on 17, both going into trees on the right. Philip asked me what I thought, was it a four-iron or a five-wood? I said the way we were lying it would be better to hit the iron. He did but came up a little bit short. Then he made a lovely chip-and-run to about eight feet. Now we really know this is for the Ryder Cup. It was a left-lip putt but Philip just pulled it slightly, and it brushed the lip but didn't drop. He missed his par. Jay was on in two and got his.

'So now we're only one-up with one to play. The agony of it all isn't lost on me, I can tell you. Philip must have been churning inside. It's Jay's honour, of course, and he hits into the trees on the left at 18. We go right. We get down there and we're short of the trap, in highish rough but it's in a clump of grass trodden down by the spectators. It's well down but not so bad that we can't risk the wood in.

'Over on the other side, Jay seems to be taking forever to make up his mind. Hanging around waiting for him made Philip a bit edgy. So I handed him the five-wood and suggested he practise his swing to take his mind off the job in hand for the moment, while the opposition gets sorted out. Finally, Jay punches out of the trees, hooks out, and can only lay up. Philip hits and it looks as though he's gone on to the bank in front of the green, but we're not certain. The crowd's making a hell of a noise but I can't tell whether it's for us or whether it's a sort of relief because we might be in trouble.

'Haas hits his third up on the green – and his ball disappears! Surely he couldn't have pitched in again? Philip was thinking the same thing. There wasn't a rule saying it couldn't happen again. Why not? This is golf, after all. It's amazing the things that go through your head. I was wondering if the papers the next day would be screaming how luck stole the Ryder Cup from under Philip's nose and from out of Europe's hands at the death. My face must have looked a picture of misery. I wondered if Per-Ulrik could do his bit now.

'Suddenly the ball reappears. Philip and I look at each other. Total relief. I couldn't stop shaking, though. We knew, because it had come back into view, that he'd screwed back off the green. When we get up to the hole I can see that our five-wood, which I'd thought would get us up all the way, had caught the front and dropped back into the grassy bank. The ball's nestled down and we have an uphill shot. When I say nestled down, that is an understatement. It was buried so deep, we nearly stood on our ball looking for it.

'Philip had had a tip from Ian Woosnam, though, on how to play out of rough like this, especially the rough near the green. Woosie had finished second here in the US Open and had plenty of experience of that kind of rough, whereas Philip hadn't. In fact, the tip had paid off all day. The worse the rough, the better Philip started playing the little pitch-and-chip shots. This was the big one, though. It had to be perfect. Short and he's still in; long and he's got a frightening putt down.

'He just nicked it out perfectly. It looked almost as though it would stop, and then ran up to about 12 feet. Jay played his fourth, and went a good five feet past. Philip only had to get his close. I whispered to him that the putt was going to come off the left. He took a deep breath and told me, "Brian, I've got two putts for it. I think I'll take them." That's what he did. Afterwards he told me his legs were shaking so much he didn't know whether they were his or John Travolta's. But he rolled up to about four inches. Jay came over and shook his hand.

'Now it really was all over. I was just overwhelmed. All I could think of was that I'd better get the flag back in. Philip was stunned. Then turmoil. Slaps on the back, Bernard lifting Philip up. I was in a trance, dazed. I didn't know quite what to do, so I just walked off the green up the path to the locker-room. People were reaching out for me, screeching in excitement, I was slapped on the back as I went through them – it was like collecting the FA Cup!

'After a struggle, I finally made it to the locker-room and put the bag down. Then it hit me. I filled up and had a little weep. "Christ!" I thought. "What have we done? We've made history. They can never take that away from us now. We won the Ryder Cup!"'

HOW WE WON 'EL' RYDER CUP

1997: THE FASTEST BUGGY IN THE WEST

VALDERRAMA, SOTOGRANDE, 26–28 SEPTEMBER
EUROPE 14 ½ USA 13½

CAPTAINS: Severiano Ballesteros (Europe)
Tom Kite (USA)

(European names first)

Fourballs (morning):
J.M. Olazábal and C. Rocca (1 hole) 1, D. Love III and P. Mickelson 0
N. Faldo and L. Westwood 0, F. Couples and B. Faxon (1 hole) 1
J. Parnevik and P-U. Johansson (1 hole) 1, T. Lehman and J. Furyk 0
B. Langer and C. Montgomerie 0, T. Woods and M. O'Meara (3 and 2) 1

Foursomes (afternoon):
J.M. Olazábal and C. Rocca 0, S. Hoch and L. Janzen (1 hole) 1
B. Langer and C. Montgomerie (5 and 3) 1, T. Woods and M. O'Meara 0
N. Faldo and L. Westwood (3 and 2) 1, J. Leonard and J. Maggert 0
I. Garrido and J. Parnevik (half) ½, P. Mickelson and T. Lehman (half) ½

Fourballs (morning):
C. Montgomerie and D. Clarke (1 hole) 1, F. Couples and D. Love III 0
I. Woosnam and T. Bjørn (2 and 1) 1, J. Leonard and B. Faxon 0
N. Faldo and L. Westwood (2 and 1) 1, T. Woods and M. O'Meara 0
J.M. Olazábal and I. Garrido (half) ½, P. Mickelson and T. Lehman (half) ½

Foursomes (afternoon):
C. Montgomerie and B. Langer (1 hole) 1, L. Janzen and J. Furyk 0
N. Faldo and L. Westwood 0, S. Hoch and J. Maggert (2 and 1) 1
J. Parnevik and I. Garrido (half) ½, T. Woods and J. Leonard (half) ½
J.M. Olazábal and C. Rocca (5 and 4) 1, F. Couples and D. Love III 0

Singles:
I. Woosnam 0, F. Couples (8 and 7) 1
P-U. Johansson (3 and 2) 1, D. Love III 0
C. Rocca (4 and 2) 1, T. Woods 0
T. Bjørn (half) ½, J. Leonard (half) ½
D. Clarke 0, P. Mickelson (2 and 1) 1
J. Parnevik 0, M. O'Meara (5 and 4) 1
J.M. Olazábal 0, L. Janzen (1 hole) 1
B. Langer (2 and 1) 1, B. Faxon 0
L. Westwood 0, J. Maggert (3 and 2) 1
C. Montgomerie (half) ½, S. Hoch (half) ½
N. Faldo 0, J. Furyk (3 and 2) 1
I. Garrido 0, T. Lehman (7 and 6) 1

THE CADDIES

JOHN MULROONEY (JOSÉ MARIA OLAZÁBAL 1997)

Bray butcher's assistant John Mulrooney decided to carve out a career in caddying and in 1993, four years into his career, he did a temporary stint on José Maria Olazábal's bag. When, 18 months later, Dave Renwick and the Spaniard went their separate ways, 'Johnny Muller' was hired on the recommendation of the respected Billy Foster. In the second week of a trial, Olazábal won the Volvo PGA Championship and the job was Mulrooney's. Olazábal also won the World Series, but then he gradually succumbed to foot problems. To Mulrooney's crushing disappointent, Olazábal had to withdraw from the '95 Ryder Cup. But when Olazábal made his glorious comeback in February 1996, it was with Mulrooney by his side, as he was when the golfing story of the year ended with an emotional finale at Valderrama.

TIM 'TOFFY' KING (PER-ULRIK JOHANSSON 1995, 1997)

'Toffy Tim' King tired of working in fund management in the City after graduating in chemistry from Oxford University, and he took up caddying. After six months as a club caddie at Wentworth, he met some of the regular tour caddies who persuaded him to tour too, christening him with his nickname after hearing his accent. In 1989 he worked for Colin Montgomerie but gave himself only a year before he knew he would have to go back to the City. By the time he took up his place alongside Per-Ulrik Johansson at Valderrama for his second Ryder Cup, Toffy was in his ninth year of caddying, having teamed up with the Swede at the start of 1994.

KEVIN WOODWARD (IGNACIO GARRIDO 1997)

Zimbabwean Kevin Woodward was 47 when he featured in his maiden Ryder Cup, but he first got the call of the rake just over 20 years before. A visit to Turnberry in 1977 for the Open Championship left the banker with a British grandfather hankering for an open-air life. He teamed up with compatriot Nick Price for a second place in the 1982 Open and the pair went off to America. He later also carried for another fellow-countryman, Mark McNulty. After retiring for 11 years, in early 1996 he stepped in for the final round in Dubai when Ignacio Garrido's caddie was unavailable. The following week he took up his position full-time. Woodward planned to retire again from the bags that year, but, spotting the young Spaniard's potential, stayed on.

ALEJANDRO MOLINA (COSTANTINO ROCCA 1997)

Argentine Alej Molina from Cordoba took over Costantino Rocca's bag the week before the 1997 Open Championship. He got the job on the recommendation of Eduardo Romero, himself a former caddie from Cordoba. Alej had no trouble reading either Rocca's game or his lines because he still harbours hopes of playing professionally himself as a low-handicap golfer. He is the nephew of Florentino Molina, who played on the European Tour in the '50s and '60s. There was no problem with language either. Rocca understood Molina's Spanish when they paired up for Valderrama and Molina could converse in Italian.

THE ACTION

'Costantino somehow knew he was going to draw Tiger Woods for the singles. It was all he could talk about the week before the match. When their names came out together, he was up for it.'

For Severiano Ballesteros, the triumphant lifting of the Ryder Cup on home soil was achieved after a memorable fightback by the US team who had looked dead and buried after the weather-affected fourballs and foursomes. The Americans showed true grit and quality when it came to one-on-one, just like Europe had done two years previously. But, whereas Europe had turned the tables, this time America had just too much to do.

As you would expect of golf's most charismatic figure, victory for Ballesteros was not achieved unremarkably. Not only was it won in breathtaking style but it was won in breathless fashion as well. The 1997 Ryder Cup will be forever remembered as the one where Ballesteros commanded the European forces from several holes at one time. It was a victory overseen from the fastest buggy in the west. Seve somehow managed to be in three places at once.

But Seve's driving force was not just his buggy. It was his desire to play every shot. At times he had to be told to back off. His enthusiasm and will to win, however, rubbed off. His attention to every detail imaginable paid off.

Perhaps most of all, though, it was a Valderrama hole which was part-brainchild of Ballesteros that was to enable him to celebrate an emotional success 18 years after he and Europe made their Ryder Cup debuts. Ballesteros himself revamped the original 17th hole. It was to prove the 1997 catalyst to winning in much the same way as the final hole always seems to at The Belfry.

Europe blooded five rookies, America four. Lee Westwood, Thomas Bjørn, Ignacio Garrido, Darren Clarke and wild-card selection Jesper Parnevik all became vital cogs for Europe. America started favourites, but were they not two years before at Oak Hill? This time, though, they held three aces in the shape of a trio of 1997 major winners. They had the most talked-about player in golf, US Masters destroyer Tiger Woods. They had Justin Leonard, the Open Champion who had come through at Royal Troon to pip Clarke and Parnevik. They had Davis Love III, who took the US PGA title a few weeks before Valderrama. However, Europe had a trump card they could perhaps use against all 12 of the American hand: Valderrama itself. Having played the par-71, 6,819-yard, Andalusian course remodelled by Robert Trent-Jones for the last nine years when Valderrama hosted the prestigious end-of-term Volvo Masters, all the European players knew its dangers and, mostly, how to counteract them.

They knew about the intimidating and inhibiting par-5 17th, about its hidden humps and necklace of rough added by Ballesteros in 1995, ready to catch the 300-yard drives of such as Tiger Woods. They knew of its awkwardly slanted island green, which tips down into a protecting lake. Of its out-of-bounds which snakes into play on the right. Of its back bunkers that leave no shot. They knew of its potential to turn a Ryder Cup.

American skipper Tom Kite, Ballesteros's old foe, realised what a great advantage course knowledge would be and urged his men to visit the southern Spanish layout while they were in Europe in July. Only half of his team took his advice.

On paper the USA had the best line-up since the awesome 12 of 1981. And when linchpin team member Mark O'Meara took the Lancôme Trophy a fortnight before the Ryder Cup, it appeared to underline America's supremacy – and to make Ballesteros even more determined to win.

There was another reason for the smart money to go on the US team. In the month leading up to Valderrama, Europe were in turmoil. The row centred around the diminutive Spaniard Miguel Martin, who had suffered an injured wrist as far back as the week before the Open Championship. Even though he did not strike a ball in anger after that, he stayed in the automatic top-ten places after qualifying was complete. Jesper Parnevik and Nick Faldo got the wild-cards a week late after Martin had been given a deadline to prove he was fit to play. Martin was ousted and he was replaced by the 11th qualifier in the points table, José Maria Olazábal. Martin refused to accept the decision, despite an unfavourable prognosis on his wrist, and threatened litigation. Subsequently there was a compromise when he was still unfit to play. He had all his full Ryder Cup member rights bestowed on him. However, he did not appear on the official team photograph taken on the week of the match. One was taken with him and the team and another, the official one, without him. Soon after, he left for home.

By the time the players were well into practice, however, the Martin affair was pushed under the carpet. Ballesteros reckoned his was a better team than the one that had won on American soil for the first time, the stalwarts of 1987. Come what may, he would be doing everything in his considerable power to prove himself right.

Ballesteros took gambles. Some came off. One ploy which did seem to work was encouraging his trial pairings to play against each other for £100 stakes. That got the European team into competitive matchplay right away!

Again the Europeans were one big team, with few expenses spared on the caddies, as Colin Montgomerie's caddie Alastair McLean points out:

'It was just like Oak Hill. The PGA made us all feel part of the big team again. They put us all up at the same hotel, we all flew out to Valderrama in "Club" seats on the same aeroplane. So straight away you're all in it together. The Americans didn't invite their caddies along on Concorde and they were all arriving in dribs and drabs. Our camaraderie was much, much better, and started us off on the right foot.

153

'Tom Lehman's caddie Andy Martinez had asked Tom Kite if the American caddies could travel on Concorde because the Europeans had the last time. He was told if he wanted to get a ride on Concorde he should go and caddie for someone in the European team!'

When the first day came around, it looked a safe bet there would be little action. Hours of torrential rain waterlogged the course and play looked out of the question until at least mid-afternoon. However, a miraculous mop-up operation and the remarkable drainage system at Valderrama meant that less than two hours were lost. Then the first four protagonists strode to the first tee in front of a huge, jostling, fairly evenly-partisan gallery still dodging occasional rain droplets falling from the cork trees which envelope the course, sometimes to claustrophobic proportions.

In an emotional start, Olazábal, who two years before had wondered if he would ever play again, and Costantino Rocca took on Davis Love and the left-hander with the exquisite putting touch, Phil Mickelson. The opening format was fourballs, the change brought about by Ballesteros to try to give Europe an immediate advantage.

Love set the 1997 encounter in motion, straight down the middle. First man to play for Europe was the gentle giant from Bergamo, Rocca. He had admitted the day before that he was probably more nervous this time than during either of his two previous appearances. Not as nervous as his 26-year-old caddie Alejandro Molina, however:

'With being Argentinian it was going to be very strange playing in a match which Americans and Europeans were desperate to win. Costantino took me to one side and told me he wanted me to be very concentrated for the week – extra, extra concentrated. It's hard to believe, but he had this feeling he was going to play Tiger in the singles matches and he was already working himself up for that. I don't know how he knew, but he did. All the time, he was saying that he wanted to beat him, wanted to play his best.

'Costantino was very focused. Nothing was going to break his concentration for this match. It was as if he was blinkered, like a horse. We talked over every situation that he could think of happening out on the course, sometimes in Spanish, sometimes with a mixture of Italian and Spanish.

'We practised with Olazábal and Thomas Bjørn, and Costantino made some money because the players had been asked to bet on their games by Seve so that they would be keener to win!

'When it came to the first match I just knew we were going to be out first because I knew Costantino had asked for that, if he was going to be picked to play. I was very, very nervous, but only for the first hole. Costantino could feel I was nervous and told me "Tranquillo; don't look at the spectators. Just concentrate on the game."

'Davis Love holed a long putt on the first but that was no problem because at the third Costantino hit a six-iron to less than a metre to get us back to all-square. It was very even until suddenly we were fighting to stay in the match after they went two-up and Costantino was out of it on 12. His ironplay is so good, though, and we got it back to only one down when he hit a great seven-iron to the 13th, about three metres. Nobody else made the green.

'I could sense we were going to win when José Maria pitched in for a two at the next to get us back all-square. Costantino was really buzzing then. He played a great bunker shot at the 15th to keep us level and, at 16, a wonderful 9-iron to about a metre. We were in front for the first time. It was real pressure then but on the 17th José Maria hit a great iron into the green and kept us one-up.

'We looked as though we were still going to have to take a half, though. On the last Costantino missed from quite a long way and even though Olazábal made a fantastic tap-in four from the bunker, Mickelson was in very close. I hardly dared look, knowing what a good putter he is, but he missed and we had our point. Costantino was so excited.'

In the intervening period since appearing in his last Ryder Cup, before foot problems cheated him of 18 months of his career, Olazábal had taken on a new caddie. He was an Irishman, John Mulrooney. Mulrooney had lost his chance of appearing with Olazábal at the previous Ryder Cup because of the Spaniard's crippling foot injuries, so this one meant a great deal to him:

'It was fantastic when Ollie came back. He won in his third event back after starting in Dubai at the end of February and always looked as though he was going to, hitting the ball great for someone who'd been out of competitive golf for so long.

'He always looked as though he was going to make the Ryder Cup team but it didn't quite happen. That was, I feel, because he practised so hard with his driving that he rather neglected his putting.

'It paid off in the end with his driving, but I think he just missed his qualifying place because he struggled with his putting, normally the better part of his game. He left a lot of putts short, and went through a really poor spell between the Masters and the US Open. That's where he lost out. And at the BMW, he played really great but putted absolutely terribly. Two putts going in and he would have made his place automatically.

'But he was putting all right by the time Valderrama came round and his feet were never a problem by then, not 100 per cent but never affecting his concentration or his game. I'd never been in any doubt we were going to be there. If he didn't make it, I knew Seve would pick him.

'It was marvellous when we all met up at the airport hotel and flew over together. There was a great team feeling. Practice was pretty special, too. They were playing for 100 quid – and taking it quite seriously because of that. We played with Rocca against Woosnam, Parnevik . . . we swapped around a lot, but from what I remember Ollie was nearly always in the money!

'It was a big moment for me when we went first group out. But I only had two really nervous moments – when they called out Ollie's name on the tee and at the 18th on the last day.

'I soon got over my nerves. There was no problem working with Alex, Costantino's caddie, because most caddies work off each other in tournaments all right whether they can speak each other's language or not.

'Our match against Mickelson and Love was always pretty close and you always felt it would need something really special to turn things one way or another. That came at the 14th. It's a blind shot up because you can't see the bottom of the flag. Ollie hit this beautiful wedge second shot in from 133 yards and we saw the crowd go mad. He'd holed it for an eagle-two. That got us back level and I felt we were going to win then.

'You need a bit of luck as well as being accurate with a shot like that, but when he made the 17th for an eagle chance, I knew Ollie was well and truly back. It meant a pretty certain half and he followed it up with a fantastic pitch out of the bunker on the last to 18 inches. I'm sure that put too much pressure on the Americans in the end.'

Ballesteros had indicated he would split up the long-term Faldo–Montgomerie partnership and he paired autumn with spring, putting Faldo with 24-year-old Westwood. It signified Faldo's 11th Ryder Cup appearance, breaking Christy O'Connor's record, and the new mix looked to have paid off until the Englishmen were eventually pipped by an unexpected twosome. Everyone expected Fred Couples would team up with his regular World Cup-winning partner Love, but he won instead with Brad Faxon.

Westwood had a reliable man on the bag to help for his debut, the highly experienced Mick Doran, Rocca's former caddie. The pair had a hilarious start to the match:

'Most of us had been round Valderrama so many times, we knew it like the backs of our hands. That was a big point in our favour, because the American caddies made mistakes just like their players during the week.

'Lee was obviously chuffed he was going to get straight out in the opening fourball, but I could hardly believe what Seve did with him on the range before going out with Faldo. He came up to Lee and said "Put this in your ear." Seve handed him some cotton wool. I guess he didn't want Lee to be worried about all the noise at the first before the match.

'Well, we fell about. We couldn't believe he could be serious. So we went up to the practice green with these lumps of cotton wool dangling out of our ears, saying to the others, "What do you think of this, then?" Apart from it being a shame to miss some of the buzz from the atmosphere at the first, Lee's not the sort of player who'd be overcome by it anyway. So the cotton wool went in the dustbin!

'But I was very surprised that Seve put us in with Faldo. We hadn't played a couple of rounds together to let them get to know each other, only eight holes. There didn't seem to be a lot of chemistry between them, so I wondered what was going to happen. It obviously worked out in the end but I didn't think it was going to be a good partnership at first. We got in front through Lee birdieing the second and third and it stayed that way until the eighth.

'Faldo did talk a lot and came up with plenty of advice, as he would because he's been out a few years. He tried to tell Lee what to do on a few holes, which was expected of him. On number eight, though, he told Lee to hit a three-wood off the tee when he'd been hitting two-iron every day in practice. He took Faldo's advice and blocked himself out. We lost the hole.

'I said afterwards, "Just play your own game." They seemed to get on really well together but sometimes Nick's advice wasn't the best. And they struggled together on the greens in the first round, misreading them. They definitely didn't gel there and that cost us in the end. Faldo got us back with a 20-footer on the ninth but between them they missed short ones on the tenth that would have put them two-up and makeable ones on the 11th that could have closed down the match.

'Couples and Faxon took advantage and got in front at the 15th when Nick three-putted, and stayed there. So I thought the Faldo partnership was due for the chop.'

Parnevik and Johansson were put together for the first morning. Johansson's caddie was again 'Toffy Tim' King, his bagman at the 1995 Ryder Cup. When King got to the 16th his fingers were tightly crossed:

'I'd learned a lot from Oak Hill, like keeping energy levels up because the matches can be a grinding-out process. You have to keep fit mentally as well as physically because after practice players and caddies can feel drained. For instance, two years ago we played in heavy rain on the first day and just keeping everything dry was a grind.

'Practice had been interesting. Seve was always around, lurking. I remember playing the 16th on the first day of practice. The hole doglegs right and the fairway cambers from right to left, always a very tricky drive. Per's never really liked the tee-shot there and often hits it right, maybe in the trees right, and there's no shot from there.

'Seve was in his buggy, watching things. Per hit it in the trees and Seve came up to him and said, "Per, I know you know this, but I have to tell you, there is no shot from the right-hand side; the left-hand side maybe you can hit the green." Per said "Yes, I know that, Seve. I have played here before, but thank you very much anyway." Seve said, "Okay; I just want to remind you of this."

'Anyway, the next day of practice, we get to the 16th. Seve's not around, or so it seems. Per tees up . . . hits it into the trees right. We get to the ball, and suddenly this buggy screeches to a halt . . . Seve, as if by magic.

'He says, "Per. I tell you yesterday. You don't remember about these trees?

There is no shot from here." Per says, "Okay, Seve!" Well, it didn't put Seve off picking Per to play with Jesper for the first fourball. It was widely tipped the Swedes would pair up.

'For this opening match, Per played some very good approach shots indeed, matched any kind of shots the Americans could come up with, and his two birdies on the eighth and ninth got us in front after we'd been behind all the way from the first.

'Maybe Per wasn't quite on his game off the tee, though, and he'd missed a few drives. On the 11th he hooked his drive and the hole was left to Jesper to make the half that kept us in front. I was standing by the side of the green because we were pretty well out of it, when I heard this "pssst, pssst, pssst!" I looked round and it was Seve beckoning me over.

'He said, "Come here, sit down, sit down. I don't think Per's playing so well today." I said, "Well, he's made some great approach shots but maybe his game's not quite so good off the tee as Jesper. Jesper's playing better."

'Seve then said, "Yes. This afternoon in the foursomes, I don't think I'm going to play Per. But don't tell him anything or he will get disappointed." I said, "Okay, that's fine." To my astonishment, Seve carried on, "But I need someone else to play with Jesper. Who do you think – Garrido or Woosnam?"

'I stood there flabbergasted, couldn't believe he'd asked me this question. I said, "Garrido, probably. I don't know." He thought for a minute and said, "Don't forget; don't tell Per anything. He must still focus and concentrate." Then he was zooming off after saying, "Good luck. You are going to win this match."

'Seve was fantastic with his encouragement to everybody all week. I did wonder if he'd be right after the 15th, though. We'd gone two-up when Per hit a great nine-iron in to about three feet on the 14th, another one of his great approaches. But then Lehman pitched in on 15 to bring it back to one.

'Then when we got to 16 – Per hit in the trees right again. I think that pretty well made Seve's mind up on the foursome pairings!'

King and Johansson could rest easy in the afternoon. Despite inevitably losing the 16th, Parnevik's raking winners on the last two holes ensured Europe would at least share the morning honours.

There had been home disappointments, like Colin Montgomerie and Bernhard Langer succumbing to Tiger Woods and Mark O'Meara. The European defeat surprised Montgomerie's caddie Alastair McLean, who had been optimistic of a bright start. He and Montgomerie had been raring to go after finding practice tedious:

'Monty wasn't keen on too much practice. He got bored with it. It was important to go with the team, he felt. But because the Europeans played the course every year, they knew the course inside-out and all this extra practice wasn't necessary. His practice at a tournament, for instance, is nine holes on a

Tuesday and the pro-am, so this constant extra practice left him bored with it all. I was bored. I knew where I was going; he knew where he was going.

'We practised mostly with Langer because I think we all realised he was going to be playing with him. One day it was suggested we pair up with Garrido, but Monty's attitude was, "Hell, if I'm not going to be playing with him, why practise with him?" We played against players whom he might be paired with, like Darren Clarke, just in case Seve wanted to switch at half-time. There was obviously a chance we would be playing with Darren.

'It was Langer in the draw, though. Monty wasn't worried about him being slower on the course. He felt it might encourage him to think things out longer. But I thought we'd never get started. The rain was unbelievable on the first day. The course didn't look as though it could be played that day at all. The job the greens staff did was incredible. I said to Monty at the seventh that it looked as though it had never rained and yet it was torrential all night and all morning.

'Langer and Monty just didn't play that well in the first match but O'Meara played fantastic golf. He was the man who did the damage. Woods probably played as badly as Monty and Langer.

'Seve, though, came up as early as the 11th and asked Monty and Bernhard if they wanted to play together in the foursomes and they both immediately said yes. They were three-down at that stage, too, both struggling with their games, but very anxious to put it right in the afternoon, keen to play again.'

Keeping faith with Montgomerie and Langer and Faldo and Westwood paid off handsomely as the foursomes, which ran into the next day, ended with Europe just in front.

A last-hole birdie by wild-card Janzen earned him and debutant Scott Hoch a one-hole victory over Olazábal and Rocca. With the opening foursomes incomplete because of darkness, honours were even. Rocca and Olazábal's narrow defeat was offset by Montgomerie and Langer crushing Woods and O'Meara. Woods was anything but a tiger, often fazed by the tightness of Valderrama, even though he was one of those who had made the July trip to familiarise.

Knowing his man's resolute mood – Montgomerie marched straight from the 16th to the practice range and had his lunch brought out to him by his wife – and the real strength of the experienced Scots/German partnership, again made Montgomerie's caddie McLean optimistic on Friday afternoon, especially as he felt that Woods might be the weak link:

'Whether it was fate or Seve guessing well, as it turned out we were again drawn with Woods and O'Meara. This time Woods is hitting half the shots, so it doesn't matter how well O'Meara's playing. If Woods is hitting half of them and not hitting them awfully well, you feel you've got a much better chance this time.

'There wasn't any real key point to our win. Monty and Bernhard just played solid, solid golf. Couple of good pars, then a birdie, couple of pars, birdie – and par can win holes at Valderrama. They were never going to get beaten.

'O'Meara did play well again but Tiger was often in the rough and he wasn't really a happy soldier. You felt he was trying too hard, being the boy wonder.

'Another reason for Bernhard and Monty combining so well – and Langer was hitting every second shot, so that made him twice as quick – was because they both really helped each other out all the way round.

'In fact I didn't get involved much. It's difficult to when you've got Coleman with you. He always says his piece, and Langer's so precise and methodical he does everything for everybody anyway. And with Monty knowing what he's doing, you've already got three guys running the show. It was hardly worth putting my tuppence in! Langer must be the best partner in the world to have in foursomes, working out the putts, what type of shot to hit. He's tireless.'

Although the match stood at 3–3 overnight, Europe had their tails well and truly up because Faldo and Westwood, fighting back from being one-down after six, stood at two-up with three to play against debutant Justin Leonard and Jeff Maggert, both playing their opening games.

After another mop-up on Saturday because of further rain, Westwood returned to the course following another near two-hour delay with one object in mind – to hole the nine-foot birdie putt his partner had set up on 16 before the premature halt to play. The putt went in for Westwood and Faldo, the six-times major-winner now breaking Billy Casper's all-time Ryder Cup points record by earning his 24th Cup point, to mop up their match.

That nine-footer had not proved so easy in the long wait before Westwood went out to wrap up the match, though, as caddie Doran remembered:

'There was a bit of an argument about what point we should come in off the course on Friday evening. At the 16th, Faldo asked Maggert and Leonard if we were going to finish off the hole and they said yes. So Faldo hit a great second shot into the green to about nine or ten feet.

'Then Tom Kite came over and said the Americans weren't going to finish the hole. Faldo and Lee certainly weren't happy about that. Obviously they had a great chance of finishing the match there and then. They were hot. They'd played great after the seventh, where they saved par from a bunker to get back all-square.

'So they had to go back the next morning. We had more bad weather so we couldn't start again. Lee knew what he had to do, though, and so he practised the putt over and over again. Believe it or not, it hardly went in more than a handful of times from a load of attempts. But he went out on to the course and sank it just like that. It was a break of four inches from left to right, and it went in as sweet as a nut.

'We'd had a long time to think about the line but the last time we'd seen it out on the course it was nearly dark. So it was a great putt of Lee's, and it really

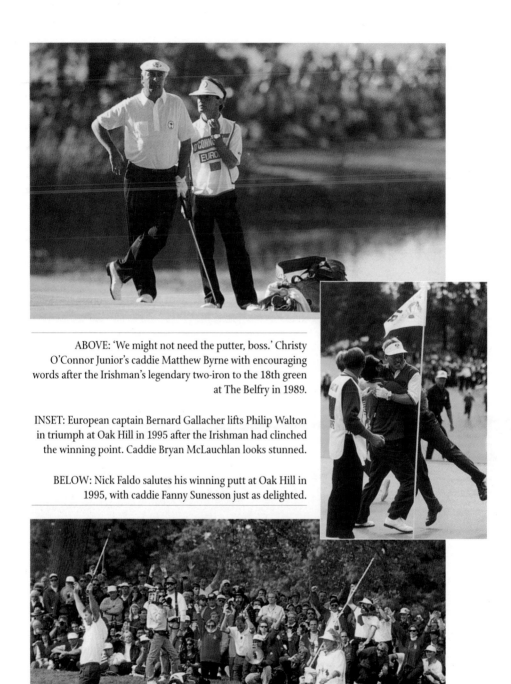

ABOVE: 'We might not need the putter, boss.' Christy O'Connor Junior's caddie Matthew Byrne with encouraging words after the Irishman's legendary two-iron to the 18th green at The Belfry in 1989.

INSET: European captain Bernard Gallacher lifts Philip Walton in triumph at Oak Hill in 1995 after the Irishman had clinched the winning point. Caddie Bryan McLauchlan looks stunned.

BELOW: Nick Faldo salutes his winning putt at Oak Hill in 1995, with caddie Fanny Sunesson just as delighted.

ABOVE: Europe's successful 1995 caddies, with Fanny Sunesson holding the Ryder Cup.

MIDDLE: The 1993 Belfry line-up.

BELOW: The 1985 Belfry 'team' (© Phil Sheldon).

ABOVE: The 1987 caddie line-up before Andy Prodger (centre, back row)
got himself locked up (picture courtesy of Dave Musgrove).

BELOW: Seve Ballesteros, to be captain in 1997, holds Tony Jacklin's arm aloft at Muirfield
Village ten years earlier. Sam Torrance, winning captain in 2002,
is just behind Jacklin.

ABOVE: The infamous invasion of the 17th green at Brookline in 1999.

INSET: Niclas Fasth gets the line from caddie David 'Magic' Johnstone, before being denied glory by Paul Azinger's bunker shot on 18 at The Belfry in 2002.

BELOW: Padraig Harrington acknowledges The Belfry gallery in 2002, with veteran Dave McNeilly by his side.

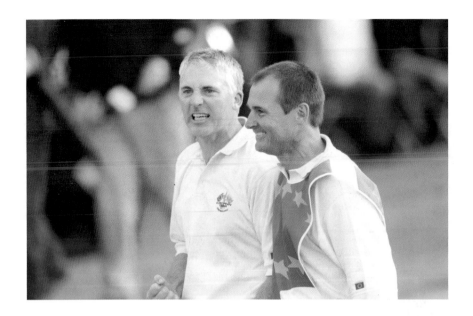

ABOVE: 'Yessss! Tell them who I beat.' A grimace from Phillip Price and a grin from his caddie Cliff Picking, both of delight, after the Welshman had overcome Phil Mickelson – a defining moment in 2002.

BELOW: Sergio García is all fired up in 2002, flanked by caddie Edoardo Gardino, wearing his bandanna made from Europe's flag, and Lee Westwood's bagman Dave Renwick.

ABOVE: Victorious 2004 captain Bernhard Langer celebrates
with the triumphant Oakland Hills caddies. Back row, l to r: Craig Connelly (Paul Casey),
Langer, Russ Holden (Langer's caddie); Middle l to r: Darren Reynolds (Paul McGinley), Owen
Craig (Thomas Levet), Ronan Flood (Padraig Harrington); Bottom l to r: Mike Kerr (Miguel
Angel Jiménez), Christian Donald (Luke Donald), Mick Doran (David Howell), John Graham
(Lee Westwood), Alastair McLean (Colin Montgomerie), Billy Foster (Darren Clarke), Glen
Murray (Sergio García), Mick Donaghy (Ian Poulter).

BELOW: Europe's victorious 2006 team. Each player's caddie is below him. Debut pair Robert
Karlsson and Gareth Lord are on the extreme left; Henrik Stenson and Grant Berry are on the
extreme right. Phil 'Wobbly' Morbey, returning to the Ryder Cup fold, is fourth from right.
Centre: Captain Ian Woosnam with his bagman Martin Rowley.

took the wind out of the Americans, who were hoping to go on. I'd helped with the lines on the greens in the foursomes. Fanny said to Faldo, "Get Mick working on the greens," because I can read greens. And Faldo did ask me a couple of times to read the line.'

After Ballesteros had dropped Johansson it had been time for Ignacio Garrido to take the Ryder Cup stage, a historic moment in itself. The Madrid youngster was following in the footsteps of his father Antonio, who by a twist of fate had partnered Ballesteros in Seve's Ryder Cup debut 18 years previously. Garrido joined up with Parnevik to take on the formidable Lehman and Mickelson, and their foursome ended in darkness, too, all-square at the 12th.

Zimbabwean caddie Kevin Woodward had no doubt Garrido would measure up in his first Ryder Cup to ensure Europe stayed in the ascendency:

'I'd seen the huge potential in Ignacio and decided to postpone my retirement from caddying at the end of '96, and it was fantastic to be seeing him rise to the occasion at Valderrama.

'But it's funny because at Wentworth during PGA week in May, they told a number of us to get measured up for Ryder Cup outfits. At the time he was lying 30th in the points table with only just over three months to go. So I didn't bother going to be measured because I really didn't think he had a chance.

'After his great run from late June, though, I had to rethink and it was a little worrying for me, at any rate. It's now a team I've got to think about. If you make a mistake it's not just for your player – it could influence the whole team.

'As a Zimbabwean I obviously had very little experience of the Ryder Cup so I went and spoke to a couple of Spaniards who had a lot, José Rivero and Manuel Pinero, and they gave me some good advice. Also, I sounded out some of the top caddies like Pete Coleman for the odd little bit of information. I was going in with a new boy and I was completely new.

'Ignacio wasn't overawed when we got to Valderrama and stayed levelheaded, which seems to be his way. I wanted to be part of the team so I decided to do my bit by trying to get the guys together, when we were travelling, going out to eat, doing things together as a group. We had 12 individuals. I wanted to keep us all together for team spirit.

'Practice was enjoyable. We had to play for money. We played with Faldo, Darren Clarke and Woosie. Interestingly, Garrido never once lost his money. They either won or halved, so he didn't have to dip into his pocket, which made him happy because the bets were £100.

'It proved he was in good form, so I was a little surprised he didn't get in for the first fourballs. But I was even more surprised Seve blooded one of his new youngsters in foursomes. It showed how good he thought Ignacio was playing, though. Playing with Jesper was an even bigger surprise, because they didn't really know each other. Jesper had been playing in America so they were virtual strangers. But it worked out well. For a start, Parnevik didn't resent losing his Swedish partner.

'Ignacio had played against Mickelson in the Dunhill Cup and Lehman was easy-going, so it was a nice experience. But we took a little time to settle down and we were behind by the fifth and two-down after seven. We got it back at the eighth, though, and it was all-square after 12 with the light gone when we came in. Mickelson wanted to go on but Lehman wasn't bothered either way. I think Jesper was very keen to stop because he wears contact lenses and the 13th is down in the trees, so the light would have been very poor.

'When we went back in the morning Lehman hit a marvellous shot out of those trees on 13 to 4 feet and the Americans went ahead, but that didn't last for long. Jesper hit a cracking shot to less than three feet on the next.

'There were chances for both sides then. Seve was darting about all over the place and he was very animated with Ignacio in Spanish. I'm not sure what went on. I don't know what Seve thought when Jesper gave Mickelson a putt of over two feet on the 17th for the half!

'It all ended on a really nice note because both sides gave each other two-footers on the last and I guess the half was the fair result.'

That half, taking the match to 4½–3½ in Europe's favour, was a prelude to America's worst Saturday in the history of the Ryder Cup.

It didn't look that way by early afternoon, when America led in three fourballs and were all-square in another. But the Americans were to feel the full force of three players in particular who had a point to prove after waiting in the wings: Ian Woosnam, Thomas Bjørn and Darren Clarke. Three remarkable fightbacks by Europe left America without a win all day. And it was to leave Kite's men just too much to do in the end.

For the second round of fourballs Ballesteros threw in Clarke for his debut alongside Montgomerie. They hung on tenaciously to beat Couples and Love right at the death. The Europeans never got in front until the infamous 17th. That was enough for them to take the point. But it wasn't plain sailing when Cap'n Seve came along, as Montgomerie's caddie McLean points out:

'We'd got back into it after the Americans had gone two-up after the turn, including a pitch-in by Fred. We got it back to level through Darren hitting this wonderful shot in to the 14th to about a foot.

'Monty had mothered Darren along. Darren had missed a three-footer on first, so Monty lined up most of Darren's putts for him. It was the Langer influence brushing off on Monty from the previous matches. Now it had moved on to Monty and Darren. Who knows, somewhere down the road Darren might do it for someone else. Monty enjoyed being mother and it also helped settle him down, kept him quite relaxed.

'Monty and Couples both holed great putts on 16 to keep us still all-square by the 17th, but then we were in the left and right rough. Seve came spurting out and there was a lot of conversation, which ended with Darren having a pop at the green. It was never going to get on. It was a silly decision. Neither of them could reach the green. They both should have laid up, so we had two birdie attempts instead of one. I'm sure they all agreed on it, but I think Seve again thought he was playing the shot himself, instead of a lesser mortal.

'Darren went in the water. That now left Monty on his own against the two Americans, Love on the fairway and Couples in the rough. Fred lays up and Davis goes for it. Davis goes right at the back of the green.

'Monty's laid up but then there's more talk with Seve and Darren drops his ball by the side of Monty's lay-up. He was allowed to do that because he can go back as far as he likes. He goes first to give Monty an idea of how the ball's going to spin on the green, and hits it to about 12 feet. Freddie asks him to mark it but everybody thinks he can't do that because he's 80 yards away in the rough.

'Rather than get into an argument with the opposition, they call in the two captains. Kite says the ball's got to be marked if it's requested. Seve says, "No, no, no; you cannot ask for the ball to be marked." They end up calling John Paramor [European Tour referee] and Darren has to mark his ball.

'Seve's not happy, I'm sure, because he must have felt a bit humbled. And you think perhaps the Americans are trying it on a little bit, trying to upset the flow. Monty pitches in to eight feet. Freddie doesn't get anywhere near the flag and neither of the Americans could make birdie after two chips, so it's left to Monty to hole his to put us one-up.

'His putt was above the pin, which was on the front of the green, right, with a vicious borrow. It seemed about four feet. It was one of those putts where we've always agreed if the greens are that fast, like Augusta, US Open, he's on his own. It's completely feel. He's the one who's got his hands on the putter. I can give him an idea but at that speed it's so much feel. How can I tell a man to putt four feet wide on a putt eight feet long?

'He holed it, and it was a huge, huge putt. It took the pressure off and halving 18 was no problem. I walked straight from the 18th to play in the foursomes. We had ten minutes for a chicken sandwich and a can of Coke and then we were off again.'

As Montgomerie and Clarke were clinching the first Saturday fourball, another rookie/veteran partnership was sealing victory just behind them. Woosnam, stung at having to wait until the third round of matches before he could swing into action, teamed up with Denmark's first Ryder Cup player, Thomas Bjørn, to outdo Leonard and Faxon.

Ballesteros realised that Woosnam was not fully in synch with his driver and knew the risks of pitting the sometimes-headstrong Bjørn alongside him. But it all worked well in the end, as Bjørn's caddie Martin Gray divulges:

'We were getting a bit of a pasting on the greens early on. Leonard and Faxon have got to be two of the best putters in the world. Everything they looked at seemed to go in. Then Leonard holed a wedge-shot at the fourth. But we were hanging in even though Woosie was struggling with his driving. He had been all week. He was fairly subdued for him, not bubbling like normal. He'd been pretty pissed off at being left out until that time. He wasn't brilliant in practice but as an experienced bloke you'd have thought he'd have got a start before this. But Seve knew best. And I don't think he did too bad a job in his selections; everything knitted in. Thomas birdied the eighth, though, with a great tricky downhill ten-footer, and that seemed to fire them up. With it being his first match, Thomas got a lot of confidence from that.

'It was see-saw right up to the 15th, then Woosie drained a real long downhiller for a two and that really set him off then. He was high-fiving with Thomas – the best he could, little Woosie – and they'd got a real good spirit going.

'At 17 Thomas hit a pretty good drive: Woosie had laid up so it was down to us. I'd given him his yardage but Wobbly came running up shouting I'd given him it from the wrong sprinkler. Thomas is stood over his ball by now, hitting a three-iron off a down slope, most important shot of his life, and Wobbly's jumping up and down saying it's the wrong sprinkler, wrong yardage! So Thomas steps back and looks at me. I just say, "No, it's the right yardage," and then Woosie steps in and says, "Martin, just have a re-check." I say it's right and so Woosie turns round to Wobbly as if to say, "Piss off out the way, Wobbly."

'Thomas hits a really solid three-iron to the middle of the green – two-putts it for four. End of match.'

Kite had decided to go in with his big guns on Saturday morning for what he rightly felt could be the session that decided the outcome of the 1997 Ryder Cup. Faldo and Westwood also added insult to injury to Woods and O'Meara, just like Montgomerie and Clarke and Woosnam and Bjørn, never leading until the end.

Westwood's four-birdie run from the ninth and a vital birdie by Faldo on 16 brought Europe to two-up playing the seething 17th, when they had been two-down after eight. When Westwood crashed his second shot on to the island green just eight feet from the flag, it was a killer blow because Faldo had made the green too. In trying vainly to hole the eagle putt to claw back, the Tiger watched in horror as his ball rolled up and over and then off the sloping green into the water, drowning any chance of even a half for him and O'Meara. Faldo was able to celebrate another record after chalking up his 23rd win, one better than Arnold Palmer.

In contrast to Faldo and Westwood's fightback, Olazábal and Garrido held the upper hand over the opening nine holes against Mickelson and Lehman and reached the turn one-up. Then, though, the Americans came fighting back and stood one-up with the crunch holes to come, the tricky downhill and doglegged 16th and the hole where dreams flickered and rekindled all week, the capricious 17th.

Olazábal, playing some of his best golf since coming back from injury, birdied the 16th to bring it back all-square. Then came some of the most extraordinary twists and turns of the whole Ryder Cup, as the Europeans held on for the half, richly deserved, if only for one outstanding flash of brilliance from his man Garrido at the 17th, felt bagman Woodward:

'Ollie's ball had trickled into the water, so Garrido went with a three-wood to make sure he hit the green. But it was always too much club and it went into the back bunker. The green sloped down from it after a longish patch of woolly stuff. Short and he has just as difficult a job still to come; long and he's in the water. No shot, we all thought.

'Lehman had finished up below the green a long way away, but Mickelson had hit this wonderful two-iron out of the rough to about seven or eight feet and I'm sure, walking up to his ball, even the pro's pro that he is, he was thinking, "Okay, we're one-up going to the last."

'That was reckoning without Garrido's determination. I didn't get the chance to say anything to him, not that I could anyway. He obviously had it in his mind what he needed to do. He looked so confident, didn't look as though he was worried about the shot.

'I think the fact that it was such a difficult shot took a bit of the pressure off. His ball was sitting well, hadn't rolled back into its own indentation, but it was on a steep downhill lie. He splashed it out on top of the plateau, it checked and then started going right because he'd hit it with quite a bit of slice. It checked in just the right spot, only released on the down slope, and rolled about ten feet past. The crowd went mad. But not as mad as when he finished off the job and holed it!

'That then left Mickelson in the chair. He'd got a tricky, downhill, slippery putt for the eagle and he knew now he was going to have to hole it to go to the 18th one-up. And with Lehman three-putting from down off the green, he knew he couldn't afford to roll it past any length in case he three-putted as well and they went to the 18th one-down.

'Suddenly, from looking as though there was no way America could fail to win the hole, he must be thinking he mustn't make a nonsense of this. He did slip it past and he must have been relieved to get the one back. But it was a huge psychological blow for Ollie and Ignacio.

'At the 18th three of them were bunkered and Lehman was a long way from the flag on the green, so it needed something special again from the sand. Garrido did it again, although it was Ollie who made the par that won the half. Ignacio played a wonderfully cool pitch out eight feet and Ollie hit to 15 feet. After Lehman needed two putts and Mickelson missed from 20 feet, Ollie drained his, knowing they had another chance.

'Garrido's performance at the end was fantastic for such a young player making his debut. I'd thought somewhere along the line he might show a little bit of nerve – not fully commit himself or not show complete confidence in his own ability – but nowhere did he. I was very proud of him.'

The men Kite had labelled his 'A' team reeled to a 3½–½ setback in the fourballs from which they were never to recover. They now trailed by 4 points at 8–4. And worse was to come.

Because of the morning delay, only one of the afternoon foursomes matches finished, but that extended Europe's lead to five points. Reunited, Montgomerie, who had turned straight round after his fourball, and a fresh Langer, were only ever behind at the first hole against Janzen and Furyk. But it came down to the wire to ensure that point, even though it only needed a bogey to do it after the Europeans went to the last having been pegged back to one-up on the 17th.

There was a little conflict of ideas with the captain, according to Montgomerie's caddie McLean, before, at 8.25 p.m., darkness cloaked Valderrama and gloom descended on the American camp:

'We'd just lost the 17th and Monty and Langer were stuck in the rough behind trees on the 18th. The Americans were on the fairway in pretty good shape. It's very dark. Seve comes rushing over in his buggy and tells Monty and Bernhard how to play the shot. He suggests a little shot through the trees, a two-iron, I think he wanted them to hit.

'It was at that point where they said, "Seve, get in your buggy and bugger off!" The pair of them decided that the only way they could do it was Langer chipping out to leave Monty the 100–105-yard shot in. From that distance he's pretty good, and that gave them a chance to make four still.

'Langer chipped out, left Monty 102 yards. Monty hit his wedge up to five feet. Brilliant. They had a great chance now for par. The Americans were a good 50 feet away after playing in, and Janzen whacked it past 15 feet and Furyk missed the putt. So they conceded without Bernhard having to putt.

'I'm sure, though, that Monty and Bernhard deciding they would do it the methodical way and not Seve's cavalier way would have salvaged them par. And it won them the match. If they'd listened to Seve they could have been pinging around in the cork trees all night!'

When that match ended the three others had to give best for the light out on the course, evenly poised. Faldo and Westwood, pairing up for the fourth time, were a hole down to Hoch and Maggert. Parnevik and Garrido, back together, were all-square with Leonard and Woods. Olazábal and Rocca were one-up on Couples and Love.

In the last match, Rocca hit the Americans with a huge psychological body blow just before play ended when he pitched in from beside the bunker on the long par-four seventh. Soon after that birdie, which hauled Europe in front, the hooter went to bring in the combatants. By then, Faldo and Westwood had surrendered a three-up advantage but Parnevik, also with a little chip-in on seven, and Garrido were hanging in to keep Europe still five points to the better by nightfall.

As he mused on his singles pairings on at last awakening to clear blue skies, Kite acknowledged on Sunday morning it was 'backs against the wall'. His hope was that his side could reduce the 9–4, 5-point deficit in the three matches still to finish.

When Rocca and Olazábal came back to hammer Couples and Love out of sight, though, hope did not spring eternal, although at least he took some solace from Hoch and Maggert edging out Faldo and Westwood at the 17th. Would he at least have to only worry about being four points behind if his main man Woods and Leonard could steal it from Parnevik and Garrido? Not if Garrido, his bagman Woodward, and the penultimate hole, had anything to do with it:

'It was the 17th again which proved the key hole. Leonard hit on to the plateau on top of the green, with the pin down in the middle, bottom-left. Garrido put Parnevik within wedge distance but Parnevik had to be careful not to screw it back too far, so he hit with a little bit of draw with his sand-iron. He gave it just a bit too much, though, and it trickled over the back of the green.

'So we're over the back in three and they are on in two. Once again the advantage was with the Americans, as it had been the last time Ignacio played the hole. But lucky for us, we'd had a similar shot to play the year before in the Volvo Masters at Valderrama to a similar pin and chipped it into the water. And in the practice round we'd actually gone to the 17th and practised that shot to get the pace right so we didn't put it in the water again.

'We were about two feet off the back of the green. Nacho said, "We'll have to do something special here." I said, "No, nothing special; you've just got to chip it close." I think I might have already pictured in his mind, Tiger making at least a four.

'It was a pretty good chip again, only about four feet past. Tiger hit his putt about 20 feet past, down the plateau, down the slope. A bit more pace and his ball would have gone in the water again. Now they are 20 feet past and we're almost a given four feet. Leonard missed; Jesper holed. Again the 17th proved crucial – and crucial for us. The Europeans were on the point of losing the hole and got the half.

'At the 18th Nacho drove into the left rough, a little bit unfortunate because it trickled in close to a tree. When it was on its way, though, the Americans were asking each other where it was. I didn't want to admit it was in the rough so I said in a loud voice to Garrido that it was on the fairway. I don't know whether it swayed the guys – they're so experienced – but I did try!

'When we got down to the ball Seve joined in the discussion on how Parnevik should play the shot, but Jesper had it all under control and said, "Don't worry, Seve. I know what to do." Between him and his caddie, they'd been in that position many times before. They were confident of hitting the green and the Americans looked in real trouble in the trees.

'We could smell victory. But then suddenly the boot's on the other foot to the 17th. They hit a wonderful shot on and now the pressure's on us to save the match. Parnevik kept his cool superbly, though, hit on from 138 yards and made the green. We both two-putted. A very hard-earned half.'

Half a loaf to Tom Kite, though, was little better than no bread at all. Whereas he had crumbs of comfort from Hoch and Maggert in early-morning, he now had to swallow the fact that Europe were five points ahead at 10½–5½. They only needed three and a half-points from the ensuing singles to keep Sam Ryder's trophy, and four points to win.

But he had to tell himself – quite rightly as it dramatically turned out – that it was not all over. He planned an immediate recovery operation and placed his heavy mob at the top of the draw.

Ballesteros must have felt he only had to put the icing on the cake. But, not wanting to write a recipe for disaster, he decided on a mixture of experience early on and at the end of his list. The menu could hardly have been more mouth-watering.

First pair out were Woosnam and Couples, remarkably playing their third match against each other in successive Ryder Cup singles. Honours were even over 1993 and '95, when both matches were halved. Woosnam had never won a Ryder Cup singles.

He was not about to break his duck. Instead Couples broke his heart. Woosnam, after bogeying the first, hardly played badly. Couples played supremely well, lying seven under par when matters came to an end after only 11 holes. Couples' 8 and 7 victory equalled the record in the Ryder Cup, set eight years previously by his current captain Kite.

As Couples and Woosnam returned to the clubhouse, the scoreboard showed the US ahead in nearly every match. Could the outcome really be in doubt? Rocca and Johansson had to stem the red tide.

Johansson's caddie King wondered if their match would get to the 16th:

'We'd both been surprised that Per wasn't picked for the fourballs on the Saturday because we felt he wouldn't be picked for the foursomes anyway. So he practised hard on the Saturday because he wasn't sure what was happening. He said, "Seve hasn't told me anything." He was feeling a little bit distraught, a bit upset. My advice was to just sit tight and not worry. I told him I thought Seve was going to keep his cards close to his chest, anyway.

'With all the delays it had been difficult to know what to do but my advice to Per was to get ready as if he was going to be picked for the afternoon. "Get 100 per cent tuned up. If you're not picked, don't worry." All those stories about Per and Seve being at loggerheads because of him not getting another pairs match, though, were all nonsense.

'He was really pumped up for his singles. Per was happy to be off second and against such a good opponent, and a really nice bloke, as Davis. Being last off at Oak Hill was quite a nerve-wracking affair in his first Ryder Cup. And he wanted to get out early, especially after all the waiting around of Saturday.

'There was a nice touch from Seve in the morning. He produced a little sheet, which his caddie Julian Phillips gave out to all the caddies, which he wanted us to give to our players and read ourselves. It was eight to ten reminders – just "focus, concentrate", obvious things, but I thought it was great because it did make you concentrate your mind on the job ahead. And it made you think at least the captain was thinking about you. Per had a look at it on the practice green just before we went out and I think it did register in his mind, things like "Don't get too excited; don't look at the scoreboards; just play your own game."

'At the first Per was on to about 30 feet and one of the things you don't do at the first is go through the green, but Love did. And, as happens in matchplay, he went and chipped it in. You must always expect the opposition to do the most amazing things like that in matchplay.

'Seve's advice not to get excited came back to me and Per didn't get excited. He just came straight back at Davis with a cracking shot in on the next and repeated the feat at the fifth to go one-up.

'It stayed pretty tight after Per lost the tenth to a big putt from Love. The 13th's a tight tee-shot. You can't hit too far or you can be blocked out by the trees. For us it's a three-wood, eight-iron, but I couldn't believe it when Love, who had the honour, pulled out a driver. He pulled it long left and caught a massive flyer over the green and had to take a penalty. Per stiffed it on 14 and Love missed the 15th green to make it three-up.

'When we walked from the green, Per said, "You know what I'm going to say now, don't you?" I said, "I know exactly what you're going to say. We've got to think we've got to win the next three holes!"

'"Exactly right. Even though we're three-up, we've got to imagine we've got to win the next three holes," he said.

'You can guess what happened at 16. His tee-shot hit the trees on the right! And who should be there when we got to the ball? None other than Seve! He put his arms out wide and looked at me askance as if to say, "What is he doing there?" Per caught sight of him out of the corner of his eye, so Seve said "Per, what is happening? I tell you all week . . ." Per said, "Well, I'm a little bit closer to the fairway this time, even if I am in the trees."

'Per made a great four because he hit an eight-iron forward, chipped on and sank a 15-foot putt and Davis missed his birdie from 10 feet. So I guess Seve was pretty satisfied after all.

'What made the day was that we could then go out and watch other matches, which we hadn't been able to do at Oak Hill.'

Psychologically, a defeat of Woods in the third match could prove priceless.

Rocca was ready to cage his Tiger. Hadn't he already decided he would be the one who would stalk him, days before the dramatic finale? Caddie Molina found his man's premonition had come true:

'Costantino somehow knew he was going to draw Tiger Woods for the singles. It was all he could talk about the week before the match. When their names came out together, he was up for it.

'Seve just came over and said, "Costantino, you will have to play Tiger." I think Rocca, even though he had felt it would be him, was at first nervous. So was I when I knew. But he soon settled and when we went to the practice green he was already thinking ahead.

'He says to me, "Okay, this is a big day. We're going to beat this guy and we must be into it straight away. There can't be any letting him get away to a good start or it's going to be difficult, because he will always be a danger at the par-fives."

'When we get to the tee, I think he wanted me to show Woods and his caddie and the gallery that we were not afraid of Tiger's reputation. He was as good as his word because he went one-up straight away with a great shot in to about one and a half metres. It was a big moment for me because Costantino wanted to go in with a hard wedge but I said, "No, it's better with a nice easy nine-iron." He listened to me. I felt good. And it really relaxed him, then, although it didn't spoil his concentration. It was important for both our nerves!

'At the par-three, the third, we both agreed it was a six-iron and we got on nicely with that. Tiger looked as though he was only one club less and it was too much because he smashed his tee-shot right over the back, even over the gallery. So that was another hole up and us both feeling even more comfortable.

'Tiger didn't birdie the first par-five at the fourth and Costantino made solid par, so that was a bonus, especially for me. I'd told him to go for the green with his second shot and he said "Are you crazy? If I miss on the right I go into the water and he's got the hole." He laid up and he was right. Woods missed the green when he tried to get on. He then hit in a beautiful shot to less than a metre for birdie. A great let-off for me.

'The real bonus came at the short sixth, though, and for me again. I made a mistake because Constantino wanted to go with a seven and I told him eight. He came up short and plugged badly in soft ground. But he got relief and chipped and putted to save par while Tiger missed his birdie putt. Another let-off for me.

'Then the ninth hole was very important. They both hit three-woods but Tiger was yards and yards past us with a simple shot in. We missed the green with a three-iron, but Tiger also missed. Costantino, though, then sank a big putt, about three metres, to save his par and Woods missed his from well under half that. It was a big hole and it really fired up Costantino. It did me as well, because I helped with the putt. He asked me what I thought and I said, "One and a half balls to the right." He agreed and took that line.

'That took us four-up and when we missed a birdie chance on 11, and Woods made his to take it back to three-up, I thought about Costantino's words over the par-5s. It was important to hang on because the 17th might be very important, but Costantino was definitely playing the best golf. Woods had to save at the 14th and 15th, so we stood three-up with three to play.

'Knowing how the scoreboard was, though, it had to be the full point because we could be in trouble otherwise. It was raining hard and Costantino missed the drive on 16 on the right in the trees. Seve came out and told him to lay up but I told him that was not good, we should go for the green because there were people behind who could stop the ball or we could go into the bunker. There's more chance to make par from there than laying up well short.

'Rocca agreed, so he took a one-iron and hit from beside a tree, finished at the back of the green. Woods missed the green as well and also his putt from a couple of metres. Costantino chipped to a metre and made it. Fantastic. It's all over. We hadn't wanted to go to 17 with Tiger.'

Every half-point looked as though it were going to prove vital. But when Leonard came out of the blocks against Bjørn, there looked little chance of Europe getting anything out of this match.

Seve was on tenterhooks, advising, cajoling, nursemaiding. It was too much for Bjørn. His captain would only unnerve him if he carried on that way. Something had to be said, remembers caddie Gray:

'We were both fairly happy we'd been drawn against Justin. He's the Open Champion but there's nothing intimidating about him. He just knocks it down the middle, knocks it on the green – and knocks it in. There's something sneaky about that! But we'd beaten him in the pairs, there was no mystique about him and Thomas knew he could beat him.

'I think Thomas was fairly nervous setting off on his own and right in the thick of it, then Leonard went and drained about a 25-footer on the first. I thought, "Here we go. I've seen this before: watching Leonard's arse up in the air all day, picking the ball out of the hole."

'Anyway, Thomas hits a really good tee-shot at the second, then, with the breeze hurting, came off a nine-iron and came up short. He turned round and snapped my head off. I couldn't understand it. But I realised he was under the cosh a bit . . . first Ryder Cup singles . . . he might just be a bit excited . . . just get on with it, Martin.

'He knocks it six feet past and misses it. We were just walking off the green when Seve rushes up and he just about dived on him going into the tunnel to the third. Seve says, "Thomas, Thomas, I thought we'd agreed in the team meeting, play the man, not the medal. Play the man, play the man, do not play the course, Thomas."

'Thomas looks across and nonchalantly waves his hand at Seve and says,

"Seve, I'm all right. Leave me alone." Seve's just about to say something else and Thomas stops him, saying, "Seve, I'm all right. Just leave me alone."

'Well, Seve took the hint. That was just about the last we saw of him until the 16th. I don't know what Seve thought Thomas was trying to do at the second – trying to hole his chip or what, I don't know.

'Well, it just went on. Leonard canned a big one on the third and then he nearly repeated his previous day's feat on the fourth. Suddenly we're four-down. I think we were both in shock. The Americans in the crowd, and there seemed to be a lot of Leonard fans, were going mental. But I knew Thomas would come back. It was a case of getting him to believe it. He went so quiet and introverted. I felt it was the wrong way to go about it. I wanted him to get fired up.

'He hit a pretty manky tee-shot on the next, to the right. He started jumping up and down and raving. I thought, "This is more like Thomas. At least he's showing a bit of emotion." Then he hit a beautiful six-iron, just came down the ridge nicely to about four feet. Leonard was in the trap. Thomas banged his putt in. It took a lap of honour before it settled in the cup but I thought, "That's it; we're off and running now."

'At the eighth they were both stymied by an overhanging tree branch. Thomas nicked one over, Justin tried the same but plugged in the trap. Then on the ninth we hit a four-iron to 15 feet and rammed it in really positively. A great birdie and we were only one-down.

'As I was putting the flag in I looked back and there were Darren and Billy both waving their arms because they'd seen Thomas get the birdie. So I waved the flag to them. It was nice to see them cheering us on. On the tenth, though, we made a bit of a balls of it. Then he plays the 11th better. Then at the 12th it was Leonard's turn to make a balls of it and that was very encouraging.

'The 16th was a big hole. They both hit into the trees right. Thomas chips out sideways but then hits a great eight-iron to about four to win the hole, a great shot under pressure. All-square. That was the first time we'd seen Seve again. He was going ballistic on his buggy. We knew then it was going to be an important time if Seve was giving us airtime! Just looking at the boards, it looked pretty tight, and it suddenly dawned on us that if Thomas could win it could just kick us over the line.

'Thomas hits a good drive at 17 and as we walk up the fairway my legs are like jelly. I thought, "This is all I need." We're the first match to go down 17 and it was like a football crowd around the lake. It wasn't enjoyable at all.

'A good three-wood would have probably seen him just over the water but it didn't come into the equation. He asked me how far we'd got to the water. I look at the yardage book. It's just a blur because my hand's shaking like a leaf. He says, "Martin, Martin, how far have I got to the water?"

'I tell him it's 160 metres and he says, "What am I going to hit?" Just anything came from my lips. I said, "Eight-iron?" I knew that wouldn't reach and he could hit it as far left as he liked, he wouldn't go in the water. And he did pull it. But it was absolutely perfect for the next shot in. Leonard laid up past us. It was starting to rain, pretty murky. The crowd was going mad.

'We'd done a lot of work beforehand at that hole, the caddies had. Checked a lot of sprinkler yardages and stuff like that. So the yardage book showed hundreds of numbers around the area we were at. I wished I'd got a neater yardage book. I checked it twice and then went back to Thomas. He said, "Are you sure?" I went back and checked for a third time.

'He'd got 87 metres to the pin with just a little bit of breeze against. Well, he hits his sand-iron about 90 metres, so if he absolutely flushed it he'd come up short and then spin all the way back into the water, so it'd got to be a really, really soft wedge. He hit his wedge 110 metres, so he had to take a hell of a lot off it.

'So he pulls the wedge and I'm thinking he's got six past the pin but if he goes through, no way can he get up and down. I just couldn't believe he could hit a wedge so soft under the pressure he was under. The adrenalin must have been absolutely pumping through him like crazy. But he hits the shot and as soon as it pitches the crowd go absolutely mental. We're both in shock that he's hit such a good shot, frozen. We managed to squeeze a little grin out, just a little one. He's hit in to about six or seven feet, and Leonard's followed him on to about ten feet. Walking round the lake I looked across at the crowd . . . I had prickles up my neck, I was floating. It felt as though my hair was floating a foot above my cap. A weird, weird experience.

'We got on to the green. I cleaned his ball. I felt Thomas was nervy. Leonard just looked ice-cool. No way was he going to miss his putt. But he did. Then it came home. We've got a chance to win this. Everything went absolutely quiet. All you could hear was the pump, pumping water back into the lake.

'Thomas holes the putt. The place erupts. Seve's jumping up and down, nearly dropping his walkie-talkie. Everybody's off. I'm still stood on the green. I had to jog myself. The crowd was pouring across. I hastily jammed the flag back in, but it was a struggle to get up to the tee with the bag.

'It was bedlam but I managed to squeeze through. It was probably an iron or a three-wood off the tee at 18, but Thomas had been hitting his driver well all day, so he said, "Do you think driver's all right?"

'His aim was to hit over the trees and cut it but he hit it absolutely straight, absolutely killed it, hit a tree. When we get to the ball it's not a brilliant lie but we think wedge to hit over the tree, try and get a bit of a flyer to the front edge of the green, or the bank, short.

'Leonard's already hit into the trap and I've gone back into the crowd to watch him over. Seve grabs me. "Martin, what is he doing?" I tell him he's going over the trees. "Is he crazy? He could take five, six, seven, eight," says Seve.

'He drags me from near the crowd and we go to Thomas and Seve says, "Thomas, I think you should spend a little time thinking about this. It is a very difficult shot. A five could win the match." Thomas still thought he could chip over the trees but Seve persuaded him to chip out sideways. That wasn't easy either because he had to chip out of fairly thick rough, under a branch through more thick rough, but then stop it running into trouble on the other side.

'He turns it over into the rough. That leaves him a chip and run with a six-iron and he's short. He nearly holes it but leaves it to about five feet. Leonard's made a mess of his bunker shot, left himself eight or nine feet still. If he missed it, then it would be very interesting if Thomas has a five-footer to win the match. But it wasn't to be. Leonard holes his. It was so disappointing.'

Who, then, would be able to seal it for Europe? Clarke never really looked like outdoing Mickelson, and despite a brave battle back, the Ulsterman lost his match and with it his chance of winning a Ferrari. The sportscar-mad Irishman had been promised a Ferrari by his club manufacturers if he won at least two full points.

Parnevik was never in it against a Mark O'Meara continuing his blazing form, but Olazábal stood on the brink of glory behind, poised for a victory that would provide his happy ending.

Olazábal, just over six months after returning to the game and making light of his once career-threatening injury, was playing his fifth match out of five. Coming to the last few holes, he held the upper hand against Janzen. The once-stricken Spaniard looked as though he was going to cap a wonderful comeback to the top echelon of golf by winning the match that would ensure Europe kept its hands on the Ryder Cup.

With three holes to go, Olazábal was two-up. But then his compelling story of courage against all odds had to wait a while before it could be written, as his caddie John Mulrooney found out:

'Ollie had a marvellous week and a great singles. He impressed me so much. For the first time I started thinking he was really back, back, that is, in good enough shape to win majors. He played some of the best shots, gutsiest shots, I've ever seen him play. He relished the Ryder Cup and looked a different person, taking on shots he wouldn't normally do and totally unworried about either his old foot problems or his golf. A lot of the time I felt like a spectator.

'The Americans always looked uneasy, struggling with the pressure, but on the last day it all seemed to change. I could see it changing and thought our match might be very important. Neither of them was bothered or intimidated by anything, though, and the match was pretty even until José Maria took over after the turn and he was looking pretty good with three holes to go.

'At 16 he always tries to cut a driver up the left side because if you miss it right you're blocked out by trees. If you miss the fairway left you still always have a shot to the green. He hit it up the left, but the fairway slopes right to left and his ball pitched on it but just trickled into the rough because he didn't cut it quite enough. It rolled in by just an inch, the worst place to go because it's always lush there. He had a bad lie, sat down, and it didn't look good at all.

'Janzen missed right and didn't look as though he had a shot to the pin, but he blasted at the stand on the left side of the green. I think he was trying to hit the stand to get a drop. He found the bunker and the bunkers are actually better than the rough around that green.

'We knew we had to get it close because Janzen had made some great up-and-downs out of bunkers all day. We tried to figure whether we could get the ball close enough to the green to make it worthwhile us going for it. It was always going to come out heavy. The fairway was 25 yards short of the green and then there was more very lush, heavy rough, so if he had a chip he wanted to be as near to the green as possible so it would be easier to judge. So we discussed leaving him short off the fairway instead by laying up to get up-and-down from there. We were always struggling with this lie.

'He decided it would be worthwhile having a go. It came out terrible, just scuttled along the fairway downhill and went into the rough by two feet. It was starting to look as though this wasn't to be our hole. Janzen made a great bunker shot, stiff again. We came out heavy as expected, got on to 20 feet and needed two putts to his one. But it wasn't any big deal because we were one-up going to the 17th.

'Neither of them could get on for two and both had putts of about 20 feet. Janzen left his on the high side of the hole because he'd laid up in the rough. His was a difficult one, downhill and a left-to-right putt. He was just inside Ollie and we went first and missed.

'Then José Maria came over and said in English over and over again, "Please don't hole the putt, please don't hole the putt." Janzen holed it. The ball was going like a rocket. It was a do-or-die situation. He knew it.

'There was a huge cheer went up on 17. There always seemed just as many American spectators as Europeans all week. It put a tremendous amount of pressure on us now going to 18. I for one was looking at the scoreboard and I knew we needed only one more point. It was likely it was going to be his putt which won the Cup, and it would have been a great way to finish off coming back to golf. He probably wanted that more than anything in his life.

'He'd been struggling with his three-wood for months. He changed halfway through the year but it was still poor, had been all week, all day. We needed it on the last.

'Janzen missed his, caught it out of the top of the club, and skied his three-wood a bit but straight down the middle, and he said, "That'll do me." I knew José didn't want to hit his three-wood and if he'd asked me I'd have told him "one-iron". That's what he took.

'He had to get it up high, but the shot he was hitting was a low pull-hook and all I could see was it going into trees, leaving him no chance of making the green. Sure enough he pulled it into the rough, and got a bad lie again. The flag was only on eight yards, so even if he did make the green it was probably going to run right through to the back. He hit a seven-iron second and pulled it pin-high. Janzen, though, killed it off, hit in to only about three feet.

'José did his best and produced a great chip to try to put the pressure on, but he must have known in his heart of hearts that Janzen wasn't going to miss the putt. So did I. He was the one guy I'd have preferred not to have got in the draw. He's such a cool customer and never misses the pressure putts. He didn't.

'It was such a shame for Ollie. Maybe it would have been better if they'd been all-square with three to play. Janzen had nothing to lose. That putt on the 17th was the killer.'

Help for Europe, though, was close at hand. Langer had left Kiawah Island in misery after that agonising miss against Hale Irwin which denied Europe its fourth successive tenure of the Cup. Just like 1991, as caddie Coleman surmised, a five- or six-footer was going to decide on which side of the Atlantic the Ryder Cup would reside:

'I looked up at the leaderboard and we were down in a lot of matches. Bernhard knew full well our match was going to be vital yet again. But he carried on hitting a lot of good shots, playing consistently, regardless.

'Number seven had proved a very vital hole. We went two-up there with two very good shots and we thought it would take a top-class effort from Brad Faxon to get back from that position. When he made a mess of the eighth we were cruising, didn't have to do anything spectacular. But in matchplay you can't rule anything out and by the 13th he'd clawed it back, hitting a great shot into the 12th for a birdie when we got into trouble there.

'He wasn't really playing that well and by the 14th, the crucial hole in the end, we'd got it back to two-up. Faxon messed up again and needed four to get on to the green, while we were on for two and took two safe putts to get down. Bernhard wasn't going for anything at that stage, just grinding out a result.

'Once we were up all we had to do was make sure we didn't three-putt and stay two-up, which we were at the 17th. It maybe sounds a bit dull, but that's all we were concentrating on there as well.

'Both of them laid up because Faxon couldn't have got on, you wouldn't have thought, in two, and it was that which finished him off. Bernhard hit a lovely little wedge above the hole and Faxon needed two putts. We knew the putt down from about six feet was a slippery one. Take no chances. He ran it down to a few inches. That was it. Now we couldn't lose.

'All hell broke loose. There were caddies in the lake, people crying . . . unbelievable. Bernhard took it in his stride but I knew what he was feeling inside. Inside he's a very emotional person. Outside he's as cool as a cucumber. I'd say he was pretty pleased with the irony of it all, but quietly so, even if everybody else was going crazy. Six years previously it had been Bernhard or nothing. We still had players out on the course, even though it was looking good. You like to think that Bernhard's win provided the fillip for Monty.'

But the win still had to be achieved. Seve's thirst for victory had to be slaked. Westwood had lost his chance to Maggert's superior putting skills. That was typified when Westwood hit the flagstick on two occasions to leave his ball only inches from the hole, but then saw Maggert ram in big putts to sink his hopes. The American went three-up by the turn and it was all over by the 16th.

As the pair shook hands the course was still shaking to rapturous applause signalling a Montgomerie success at the 14th. The European No. 1 had finally caught Hoch, at 41 the oldest US Cup player that week but, none the less, a Ryder rookie. It was a crucial act. Behind, Garrido, playing last, had succumbed to a Lehman barrage of six birdies in ten holes from the second, beaten in much the same way as Woosnam had been earlier. Faldo was two-down, still not putting at his best, with opponent Furyk chipping and pitching at his very best.

As Montgomerie presses home his advantage at 16, Faldo hits to inches on the 14th. It looks as though it is one back, but Furyk pitches in to dash that hope. At the short 15th a magnificent four-iron by Faldo leaves him a mere three feet, with Furyk bunkered. Furyk chips in. Almost as if resigned to defeat through lady luck as well as at the hands of his opponent, their match comes to an untidy and frustrating finale when Faldo three-putts from only five feet on the 16th.

Up ahead, though, it is fever pitch. The rain returns to Valderrama and Seve's industrious, trusty caddie Julian Phillips distributes the brollies, but Montgomerie, as his caddie McLean observes, is ready to put a dampener on American hopes:

'Monty did well to be only one-down at the turn when he could easily have been three-down. He made a really good up-and-down from the flower-bed on the fourth, nearly in the houses, for instance, for a half, and he was just scrambling well.

'It was still the same after the turn but now the pressure's on because we've been looking at the scoreboards dotted around the course and all you can see is these bloody red numbers up there, not much blue. As we play 14 the scoreboards are just red. We have to do a count. We need to know how important this is becoming. Ollie had somehow lost. We knew we just had to win this match. By that time, for instance, Bernhard hadn't won his match. We could lose this and that would be a disaster.

'He was still pretty calm and I felt like he moved up another gear then, decided he had to do something when he saw we were in trouble. Hoch hit a bad shot on 14 and never looked like making the four, but Monty hit the green for a solid par. So Monty had been struggling up to this point, could have been dead and buried, but he'd hung in there and won this hole. That gave him a big fillip. He holed another good putt on the next when they both missed the green. Then we got in front. At the 16th Hoch made a complete mess of it but he still made Monty take a putt of only 12 inches, if that. Things like that only make Monty more determined.

'It could all have gone wrong then, though. At the 17th we're laying up with a three-iron to leave us 80 yards to the pin after Hoch's lain up in the right rough, where anything could happen. You assume the guy's going to dob it in the water or airmail the green. But Monty pulls his three-iron and he felt it was going in the stream but it didn't, even though the body language from the crowd nearly frightened me to death. It did leave him a funny distance, though, not a favourite distance, 61 yards. What made it worse was Hoch hit this unbelievable shot in, really, really close.

'So Monty's got a pressure shot. He knows he can get a good swing on his L-wedge 80 yards and it'll stop dead. This one has to be cut up so he can stop it quickly. It hit the ridge and backed off to 20 feet. He hit a great putt but the ball only shaved the rim and the hole's gone because when we'd got up there Hoch's only four inches from the flag. We all know he can miss short ones but Monty's had to give him this one.

'All-square and now we're the only match on the course. Everybody's cheering because we've retained the Cup. I don't know why people get excited at retaining – it's still only a half, you've not won. Monty thinks like that too. He wants to win. The pressure is just unbelievable now. Hoch hits what he thinks is a good shot, a nice high draw on what looks like a good line.

'We've hit a three-wood every day but Monty's pumped up. It's lashing with rain now. We're both soaked to the skin. Monty absolutely creases this three-wood. The swing was just perfect. He said he didn't feel a thing. When they say that, you know they've absolutely nailed it. His ball was right in the middle of the fairway.

'Well, Hoch must have caught a tree and he's not as good as any of us think. But we saw his ball as we walked by, just in the semi, and we felt he was still going to make the green. Monty's absolutely killed this three-wood, though. We're way down, where most people would be with a driver. Hoch mishits his shot. I don't know whether the pressure got to him, but he's pulled it into the trees this time. There are so many people gathering I can't even see where he is for his third shot.

'It's an absolute perfect distance for Monty, 142 yards to the pin, nine-iron. If he duffs it, he'll still get on. If he hits a good shot, he could hole it. If he nails it, he can't go off because there's still plenty of green behind the flag. It took a lot of weight off his mind that he didn't have to manufacture any kind of shot, and it made my job a lot easier, too. When I say there's only one club to hit, he goes ahead and hits it. He could stand there all year and hit a nine-iron. It was absolutely an unbelievably perfect distance. He pulled it a wee bit, maybe to 20 feet, pin-high-left.

'Then all the crowd moved in. It was pandemonium. I had to fight my way through them. I just couldn't get through. I grabbed this American cameraman and ripped his wire from his sound recordist and told him where he could go! I know he's just doing his job but I'm supposed to be on the green with Monty.

'Hoch pitches up but it's awful, only just makes the green. It's Monty's putt just. I knew all he had on his mind was "Two putts, nothing else, just two putts." Because that wins the lot. We line it up, left-to-right with about a foot of break. I close my eyes as usual, thinking two putts and it's a big celebration. He putted it to a few inches.

'Just as he was going down to mark it, Seve asked him to concede Hoch's putt. Monty was a bit dazed, not even sure whether he'd been given his putt. He was so absolutely wrapped up in his match, absolutely focused.

'Whether Seve said it and it had just gone right past him, or whether he couldn't believe what he was hearing because he was wanting to win his match, I don't know. But he came wandering back towards me. At that point Tom Kite came over and said, "Yes, just concede this putt." So Monty, who'd by then marked his ball, said, "Right, OK, Scott," and Scott said, "Yes, OK, pick your marker up." It was a halved match.

'I think maybe the next day he was disappointed. But on that green he was just relieved that Europe had won the Ryder Cup.'

HOW WE LOST THE RYDER CUP AGAIN

1999: NO TEA PARTY FOR EUROPE

BROOKLINE, MASSACHUSETTS, 24–26 SEPTEMBER
USA 14½ EUROPE 13½

CAPTAINS: Ben Crenshaw (USA)
             Mark James (Europe)

(European names first)

Foursomes (morning):
C. Montgomerie and P. Lawrie (3 and 2) 1, D. Duval and P. Mickelson 0
J. Parnevik and S. García (2 and 1) 1, T. Lehman and T. Woods 0
M.A. Jiménez and P. Harrington (half) ½, D. Love III and P. Stewart (half) ½
D. Clarke and L. Westwood 0, H. Sutton and J. Maggert (3 and 2) 1

Fourballs (afternoon):
C. Montgomerie and P. Lawrie (half) ½, D. Love III and J. Leonard (half) ½
J. Parnevik and S. García (1 hole) 1, P. Mickelson and J. Furyk 0
M.A. Jiménez and J.M. Olazábal (2 and 1) 1, H. Sutton and J. Maggert 0
D. Clarke and L. Westwood (1 hole) 1, D. Duval and T. Woods 0

Foursomes (morning):
C. Montgomerie and P. Lawrie 0, H. Sutton and J. Maggert (1 hole) 1
D. Clarke and L. Westwood (3 and 2) 1, J. Furyk and M. O'Meara 0
M.A. Jiménez and P. Harrington 0, S. Pate and T. Woods (1 hole) 1
J. Parnevik and S. García (3 and 2) 1, P. Stewart and J. Leonard 0

Fourballs (afternoon):

D. Clarke and L. Westwood 0, P. Mickelson and T. Lehman (2 and 1) 1
J. Parnevik and S. García (half) ½, D. Love III and D. Duval (half) ½
M.A. Jiménez and J.M. Olazábal (half) ½, J. Leonard and H. Sutton (half) ½
C. Montgomerie and P. Lawrie (2 and 1) 1, S. Pate and T. Woods 0

Singles:

L. Westwood 0, T. Lehman (3 and 2) 1
D. Clarke 0, H. Sutton (4 and 2) 1
J. Sandelin 0, P. Mickelson (4 and 3) 1
J. Van de Velde 0, D. Love III (6 and 5) 1
A. Coltart 0, T. Woods (3 and 2) 1
J. Parnevik 0, D. Duval (5 and 4) 1
P. Harrington (1 hole) 1, M. O'Meara 0
M.A. Jiménez 0, S. Pate (2 and 1) 1
J.M. Olazábal (half) ½, J. Leonard (half) ½
C. Montgomerie (1 hole) 1, P. Stewart 0
S. García 0, J. Furyk (4 and 3) 1
P. Lawrie (4 and 3) 1, J. Maggert 0

THE CADDIES

DAVE McNEILLY (PADRAIG HARRINGTON 1999, 2002)

Northern Irishman Dave McNeilly was in a rut working in an office, so in 1981, aged 30, he set out for America with the intention of buying club parts and reassembling them back home for sale. That wasn't successful, so, after meeting up with doyens Dave Musgrove and Pete Coleman in Florida, he switched to caddying. During a four-year stint with Nick Faldo, Faldo became European No. 1 and at that time the legendary anecdote was spawned, about Faldo pulling out a wad of notes when he saw Dave's shoes were falling apart – then handing him the rubber band holding the cash. McNeilly insists the yarn was 'totally fabricated'. They split in 1985 and McNeilly then worked with Nick Price for six years. Marriage encouraged McNeilly to forsake the fairways for seven years until fellow Ulsterman Darren Clarke arranged the partnership that was to take McNeilly and Padraig Harrington to the Ryder Cup.

Chicago-born Ten Broeck put aside allegiance to America to carry out his professional duties by the side of Jesper Parnevik as he and Jerry Higginbotham (Sergio García's caddie at Brookline) followed in the footsteps of Nick De Paul in 1987 as Americans to shoulder European Ryder Cup bags. Ten Broeck, the youngest of eight golfing brothers and sisters, gained a scholarship to the University of Texas, where he had a highly successful collegiate golfing career. After turning professional in 1977, he was a US Tour pro for 12 years, his highest US order of merit ranking of 96th coming in 1989. In 1999, five years after losing his card, Ten Broeck picked up the bag of Parnevik, a close neighbour in Jupiter, Florida. In a meteoric start they won first time out and by the time they played their second Ryder Cup, Parnevik had clinched four US Tour titles.

EDOARDO GARDINO (MIGUEL ANGEL JIMÉNEZ 1999; SERGIO GARCÍA 2002)

Gardino, though born in Argentina, is of Italian and British stock and was intensely proud to represent Europe when he made his Ryder Cup caddying debut in 1999 alongside Spaniard Miguel Angel Jiménez. His perfect English was first taught by his maternal grandmother, who was born in Liverpool, and honed at English school in Buenos Aires. Pro-golfer Gardino's first taste of the European Tour came when he caddied for his friend Angel Cabrera in 1996. Gardino, fluent in French and Italian as well, made an unsuccessful foray on the Canadian Tour in 1997 and returned to caddie for another fellow Argentine, José Coceres, moving on a year later to Jiménez. Gardino was playing on the Alps Tour when he got an emergency call from Sergio García to caddie in the 2002 match.

RICCI ROBERTS (ANDREW COLTART 1999)

Yorkshire-born Roberts emigrated to South Africa with his parents in the late 1960s, where his family helped in the development of the Sun City complex. Sport-mad Roberts was first attracted to the cricket scene and has many an absorbing and hilarious tale to tell of his time in 1981 as a locker-room attendant during the famous Ashes tour of that year. On taking up caddying, Roberts had spells with Nick Price, Mark McNulty, Jeff Hawkes and Derrick Cooper, then teamed up with Ernie Els in 1992 to form one of the most successful player–caddie partnerships in golf. Two years later Els won the first of his US Open titles with Roberts by his side and then they did it again in 1997. Their greatest day so far, though, came with a memorable and dramatic success in the 2002 Open Championship. The pair took a break from 1998 to 2001 and in 1999, Roberts teamed up with Andrew Coltart.

JERRY HIGGINBOTHAM (SERGIO GARCÍA 1999)

Veteran Higginbotham actually caddied for the 1999 American Ryder Cup captain Ben Crenshaw in the 1970s. However, he is most remembered as the man who possibly preserved Mark O'Meara's 1998 Open Championship victory. Higginbotham refused to give up the search for O'Meara's apparently lost ball at Royal Birkdale and it was discovered with only seconds remaining. Earlier that year, Higginbotham was by O'Meara's side when he won the Masters. After the pair parted company in 1999, Higginbotham's experience earned him the bag of Sergio García. In their first event together, the Byron Nelson Classic, García finished third, and soon after won the Irish Open. When the 19-year-old Spaniard was only just edged out of the US PGA Championship by Tiger Woods, García's place in Mark James's team was assured. Higginbotham did not think twice about being an American caddie on the European team.

THE ACTION

'The emotion I can understand, but I still had a putt to try to make and that display should not have happened. No matter how much emotion is going on you have to keep your feet on the ground.'

With few lessons learned from the 'War on the Shore' in 1991, the 1999 Ryder Cup developed into a 'Battle of Brookline' in which the massed American ranks of supporters spat venom at those they considered not rivals, but enemies. In the end, it was a pyrrhic victory. The loser was not only Europe, but golf.

On the final, ignominious day, when the 17th green was invaded by over-zealous American players and their caddies and wives, fêted by wild-eyed supporters driven to extremes by those who should have known better, for a second time in eight years Samuel Ryder must have turned in his grave. America won the 1999 Ryder Cup with a courageous fight back when they looked down and out, but on the 17th, dignity took a back seat. Not since the Boston Tea Party had Massachusetts witnessed such xenophobia.

There was no doubt that the US side had been stung at losing to Seve

Ballesteros's team in 1997. The US wanted the Cup badly and the American media clamoured for success this time. US golf fans demanded success too. And that was the root of the sorry scenes at Brookline, when the leafy glades of the Country Club turned into gladiatorial arenas, with the crowd baying for blood.

Mark James's Europeans knew it would be difficult to retain the Cup against a team of superstars led by Ben Crenshaw, with Tiger Woods, the world No. 1, as their talisman. Europe's task, too, was not helped by controversy leading up to the match.

The Ryder Cup's most successful performer of all time and the man with most appearances, Nick Faldo, had a much-publicised falling out with captain James, over whether he deserved a wild-card or not. Then James rather dropped a bombshell over one of his wild-cards. US Tour-based Jesper Parnevik was a natural choice for a pick, but there was surprise over his second pick, Scot Andrew Coltart. Coltart had finished in 12th place in the Ryder Cup table to Robert Karlsson's 11th, and the highly-experienced Bernhard Langer was many pundits' preference.

James was to be vilified for picking Coltart and then not giving the Scot a game. Coltart's first experience of the cauldron of Brookline was when he had to take on Woods, a highly charged and partisan gallery, and either short-sighted, or devious, officials.

Whatever the wrangles and arguments over the European side were, by the time the match began they were as one. That counted for the caddies, including two more 'Yanks in the Camp'. After Nick de Paul in 1987 at Muirfield Village, this time Jerry Higginbotham and Lance Ten Broeck put aside their feelings for their country and the Americans swore allegiance to the USA's opponents Sergio García and Jesper Parnevik. Ironically, these two Europeans never lost a match in the pairs and proved to be the visitors' most successful partnership. However, in another inglorious episode in the infamous 1999 Ryder Cup, Higginbotham was to eventually pay for his part as a European caddie – in blood.

With seven rookies in the side – Coltart, García, Jarmo Sandelin, Paul Lawrie, Jean Van de Velde, Miguel Angel Jiménez and Padraig Harrington – the Europeans were up against it. That was despite Lawrie being the reigning Open Champion after winning the major title dramatically at Carnoustie in July, and García already established as the most exciting young player in the world after finishing runner-up to Tiger Woods not long before the Ryder Cup, in the US PGA Championship. America had only one man making his debut and he was David Duval. Duval was hardly likely to be cannon fodder. Earlier on in the year he was briefly world No. 1 before giving way to Woods.

Europe arrived at Massachusetts determined to prove doubters both sides of the Atlantic wrong, captained by a droll, ironic man with a stubborn streak. And if Colin Montgomerie could provide the inspiration, Europe would have a chance to beat the odds. However, the player who was on the brink of chalking up his seventh successive European order of merit success had one major foe – the American gallery. Montgomerie, often derided in the US media, was the American crowd's favourite British bear to be baited.

His long-serving caddie, Alastair McLean, knew his man would be in for a torrid time. But not even the astute McLean was prepared for the torrent of vitriol that poured out on his player, right from their opening foursomes with Paul Lawrie:

'We had a bunch of new guys and you obviously don't know how they are going to fare, but Europe's was a pretty experienced team. As usual, the Americans were unbelievably strong but, also as always, the Europeans' great strength was playing together as a team. The Americans tend to play as individuals. We may have looked weaker on paper but as a team, I knew, we were stronger.

'You had the feeling, even before we went to America, that Monty would play with Paul. Here we have one player who has borne the brunt of course leadership in a Ryder Cup for a long time and a player who's come out on top in a major. And they are both Scots. Experience and confidence. What a combination that was.

'Jesse [Mark James] just let them get on with it and I wasn't surprised that they were the top match. But that really is a hairy, nerve-wracking experience. Monty by no means shirked his responsibilities by letting Paul hit the first shot, but he was rather happy to do so. That's when Paul found out it was a completely different experience to winning the Open – opening bat for the Ryder Cup side.

'Paul's first drive was, understandably, kind of a nervy drive, a sort of "cutty" thing off to the right into the rough, but you have to have a strong will to take on that shot. Monty had been the first to drive off at Oak Hill in 1995 and that's when I felt the hairs rise up on the back of my neck. For such a scary moment, though, Paul did really well.

'It was four of us against the Americans, then. Paul's caddie Paddy [Byrne] and I, and the two players. Most of the time, though, it seemed like us four against the world. But we had a great time, just laughed at the American gallery all the way round, the way they were behaving, what we were hearing . . . "Go home, Europeans," was one of the mildest shouts. Wouldn't have been much of a match without us! We just thought, "What a bunch of ignoramuses."

'When Monty was playing with Paul, it was no problem. The two players, and Paddy and I, could just let it bounce off us. It was funny. We could make fun of them, because they thought they were getting to us and they were not. Plus, Paul and Monty played wonderful golf. That was the way to beat the crowd, and on the way try to beat Duval and Mickelson, but it was hard to do that. The better Paul and Monty played, the worse the crowd seemed to get.

'What really settled the game down for us, though, was Monty's calmness on the greens at the start. After that, understandably, nervous drive of Paul's, Monty hit a six-iron out of the rough and couldn't quite get to the green. Chippy [Lawrie's nickname] knocked it up to about ten feet and Monty holed it, for the half I think. The Americans had gone long and chipped back and Duval holed a good putt as well. Our opponents were nervous, too, remember.

'On the first three greens, Monty holed putts of around ten feet each time. We could have lost holes but didn't. And seeing Monty putting well, Paul felt he could relax and play his own game. They felt confident knowing that, even if they mishit shots, they could still get halves against Duval and Mickelson. And when they played good shots they could beat anybody.

'Duval and Mickelson were probably the strongest pairing in the US team but Monty and Paul never let them get on top.'

Europe were off to a flyer, a 3 and 2 success for Montgomerie and Lawrie did, in the end, quieten the crowd. Before the second match got underway, there were plenty of questions floating around the Country Club. How would the crowd handle having two American caddies on the bags of Parnevik and García? Former US Tour pro Lance Ten Broeck was with the Swede and veteran Jerry Higginbotham by the young Spaniard's side in Europe's second match away against Tiger Woods and Tom Lehman.

As Higginbotham maintains, García, at 19 the youngest player to appear in a Ryder Cup, openly showed no fear of Woods, whom he had run so close at Medinah in that year's US PGA Championship:

'I just knew what a great talent I was with when the kid played his first tournament with me on the bag, the Byron Nelson Classic. Tiger Woods had shot a 61 in the first round and Sergio said, "I'm going to come after him." Sergio then shot 62 in his first competitive round with me! He finished third and Tiger was seventh.

'Then we went over to Europe. He had a great win in the Irish Open. Even though the kid was a rookie, that kind of got a monkey off his back, made a statement. It also boosted his Ryder Cup points. At the US PGA Championship he played great the whole week and the kid really had it together. I thought he should have won and he only lost by one to Tiger. He had no fear of Woods.

'That clinched up the Ryder Cup and Sergio was made. All he wanted to do was play in the Ryder Cup. Every day it was: "I gotta make the points, I gotta make the points." I think he probably would have been picked but he made it on his own, which was pretty cool. He'd played a few practice rounds with Jesper so it wasn't a surprise that Mark James picked them to play together. They meshed together really good. Jesper took him under his wing.

'I don't think Mark James was real happy about me being in the side as an American caddie, neither me nor Lance Ten Broeck, but I didn't really care what he thought, or what anybody else thought. Sergio was my boss. And it's just a golf match. I'm going around the world with the guy, so why not the Ryder Cup? I was part of his success and I might as well reap the benefits. I got a lot of needling by the other players and caddies on the US team. They were calling me "Benedict Arnold".

'Well, it couldn't have been better for the start of the Ryder Cup, as far as I was concerned, and as far as Sergio was concerned. We were playing Tiger Woods, just what he would have wanted. As far as Sergio went, he wasn't afraid of anybody. It was "bring 'em on". He'd love to play Tiger head-to-head every day.

'But Parnevik and García were such a good mix. Sergio's short-game is so good and whenever Parnevik would get into trouble, Sergio would be there. His imagination is so good.'

Unlike Higginbotham, Ten Broeck had thought long and hard before deciding not to sit out the Ryder Cup and let someone else take over Parnevik's bag:

'I wasn't sure how I would feel, as an American in the European camp. I wasn't sure if I should be doing the job, to be honest. I approached some of the American players on the team. I distinctly remember asking Hal Sutton what he thought about me carrying Jesper's bag in the Ryder Cup. Hal and I were of the same age group and had played a lot together. He said, "Why shouldn't you? You're his caddie, you might as well be working for him."

'When you looked at the big picture, I didn't think it was that big a deal. Some people, over-patriotic people, were handing out flak to me and other caddies gave me some grief, but I really didn't care about those people's opinions. I didn't feel I was doing anything wrong. It was just a golf match, not a war.

'Anyway, there was no real trouble out there. You could understand some of the crowd being upset by an American caddying on a European side, but I just got on with the job and switched off from anything the gallery might have been shouting.

'I thought the partnership between Parnevik and García was a great team. The way they were both playing, the way they matched up and fed off each other's games, it turned out to be a great pairing. At that time, I don't think many of the Americans wanted to play them. I guess we drew two who were equipped to give them a game and it was a great opening match, the foursomes. Both pairs played well but Parnevik and García played just a little bit better.

'Woods and Lehman went one-up immediately when Lehman chipped in at the first, and they were two-up after the fifth, but, you know, I didn't feel they were really worth the two-hole lead. The putts wouldn't drop for either side early on and there was nothing in it for shot-making.

'Sure enough, we got it back and then the key hole was the 12th. That's where it all turned. Sergio hit a fantastic chip to about four feet. Tiger sensed he'd need his birdie putt to win the hole and ran it about nine feet by with a rush of blood. Lehman missed the putt and Jesper made the four-footer. We were up.

'I remember Parnevik then made about a 12–15-foot putt on 16 to keep us one ahead and then Sergio hit a wonderful approach shot on the 17th, about eight or nine feet, and Jesper holed the birdie putt to close them out. It could have gone either way without a couple of good shots and putts, great golf and really exciting.'

Parnevik and García's 2 and 1 success got Europe off to the best of starts and while the top two were battling to victory, a complete rookie partnership, Padraig Harrington and Miguel Angel Jiménez, were holding their own against yet another formidable partnership, Davis Love III and Payne Stewart.

Harrington had claimed his place with a courageous second place in the last event to count for points, but despite his obvious resolute qualities, was not expected to be immediately on duty, as caddie Dave McNeilly observes:

'José Maria Olazábal was, we all thought, going to be the one to play with Jiménez, but the more the practice days went on it became apparent that Padraig was a strong player and he should be playing foursomes. Because Olazábal wasn't playing that well, he was held back for the fourballs, where any mistakes would not be highlighted so much. Jiménez was happy enough with that, when Jesse broke the news that Padraig would be his foursomes partner and not Ollie.

'They had a real ding-dong with Davis and Payne but we could have won it. Padraig had a six-foot putt on the last for the point but he missed it, so it was a half. Padraig was disappointed with himself but he'd played well. It's a team game and he was soon on the up. Outwardly he was fine anyway. We had plenty to cheer us up for the afternoon's fourballs. As soon as I knew we wouldn't be out, I guessed that we would be mixing in practice with supporting the team, though!'

Jiménez had secured his place long before that, and that was good news for his caddie Edoardo Gardino.

Gardino was born and bred in Argentina, but his family roots were pure European and he was proud to be part of Mark James's bid to retain the Cup. The young caddie, just 24 and a professional himself now, had spent weeks rehearsing how he should tackle his Ryder Cup debut:

'Jiménez was already sure of his place by the time we went to the US PGA Championship and his tenth at Medinah made doubly sure. He was really looking forward to playing in the Ryder Cup. He told me how he just missed a place in 1995 by only a few thousand points. He had a lot of passion and a lot of heart going into the Ryder Cup.

'I was very excited by going to Boston. It surpassed anything I'd expected, better than the Masters, the Open, any of the majors. The ambience was fantastic and I knew it was going to be very competitive. There was sportsmanship between the teams, but a feeling like it was a little war. I felt European. My father was born in Italy and came to Argentina when he was four and my mother's mother was born in Liverpool. I was living in Switzerland and I was feeling like a European guy!

'There was plenty of drama right away. Harrington wasn't going to play and Olazábal had the choice of being Jiménez's partner. But Mark James came to Olazábal and said: "Are you going to play with Jiménez? Do you feel like playing in the foursomes?" Olazábal said: "I am not hitting the ball well enough to play in the foursomes. I will play in the fourballs."

'So we practised foursomes with Harrington. I had a laugh at Miguel Angel during the practice with Padraig. It's no secret that Jiménez is a very, very tight person. When we practised for foursomes, Harrington was using the Maxfly ball and Jiménez the Titleist. So in the practice we switched balls halfway round, so that the two could decide which ball they were going to use in the foursomes [alternate shots]. We were playing with Clarke and Westwood and when we arrived at the 18th they started throwing head covers, balls, towels, all kinds of mementoes to the kids in the crowd. Jiménez approached me and said: "Throw all his [Harrington's] balls," the Maxflys. He didn't even want to give up a ball!

'They played together well in the foursomes. We should have won but they didn't play the 17th very well. Jiménez blocked Harrington out with one of his only poor drives and Harrington could only chip out on to the fairway. The pin was seven yards on, a little bit uphill into the wind, a very easy shot from about 35–40 yards. But he wasn't sure what to do, whether to use a three-quarter lob and make it pitch by the hole and stop . . . he was very unclear what to do. In the end he chipped with a seven-iron, a terrible shot 15 feet from the pin. Harrington misses and we lose the hole. That meant all-square going to the last. Then Harrington missed from about six feet, so it was really a combination of a couple of bad shots and an unlucky putt or they would have got the point they deserved instead of just the half. They complemented each other very well.'

The final foursome of the morning saw two great friends and management stablemates paired together for Europe. Lee Westwood and Darren Clarke were two of Europe's brightest young stars and the teaming up of the two burly youngsters was a natural one for captain James.

They had two pretty determined, and highly experienced, caddies on their bags. Westwood was with fellow Englishman Mick Doran, on his bag at Valderrama in 1997, and Costantino Rocca's carrier for 1993 and 1995. On Clarke's bag was the Englishman who had helped take on the Americans as far back as 1987 and, despite his youth, was serving in his sixth Ryder Cup, the unflappable Billy Foster:

'Darren couldn't wait to get out and play. He'd been playing well and he was,

I think, excited about playing with Lee. They'd been at it hammer and tongs through the year and, with being so close, stablemates and such, were a good "tag team".

'I could see us needing a bit of support, though, because the atmosphere from the American gallery was incredible. They seemed really up for it. It was good to see a lot of European support therefore. We were going to need it.

'Darren and Lee were in good spirits and we got off to a good start – we were two holes up after four. But then they got on top and I don't think we won another hole after that. Sutton and Maggert played really well to win by the 16th.'

Defeat did not sit well with Doran, who had had to face defeat against the US in his first Ryder Cup in 1993, but who had taken great delight in helping to win on American soil, in 1995 particularly. Doran had a little grudge to settle with a certain cadre of security guards at the Country Club.

'You just want to get over the Atlantic and beat them on their own ground. We'd done that at Oak Hill and we dearly wanted to do it again. It had felt good enough winning with Lee at Valderrama in '97, but winning in America would be something special.

'It wasn't a very pleasant experience, though, much of the time. We caddies were parked a long way from the clubhouse when we got into work. There's a hole running right across from where we parked, and, with early starts, we needed to walk across it to get to the clubhouse in the morning to get there as quickly as possible. All the caddies turned up around the same time and walked across the grass, otherwise it's over 200 yards' walk up on the right. Even first thing in the morning there were security guards screaming, "Keep off the grass." I thought, "Get me out of here."

'I just knew Lee would be playing in all five matches and we knew right from the start that Lee and Darren would be the partnership. Sure enough, they were teamed up against Hal Sutton and Jeff Maggert. Sutton, in particular, looked really fired up, fists pumping when they won a hole. You have to expect that, but as the matches wore on it started to turn ugly. Players were definitely inciting the crowd.'

It was a promising start for Europe and Montgomerie and Lawrie were soon back on duty after a quick lunch. They looked to have the better of Love and Justin Leonard, but a last-ditch birdie by the Americans forced the half.

Following on from Montgomerie and Lawrie were Parnevik and García. Parnevik's caddie Ten Broeck only had eyes for his player's stunning performance in a one-hole win against Jim Furyk and an ultimately miserable Phil Mickelson:

'Jesper just played unbelievable golf over the front nine in the afternoon. Mickelson and Furyk played great, but Parnevik shot 29 on the front nine. That's better-ball, but it was a great performance. Jesper had five birdies and an eagle on the front nine. I remember him holing out with a nine-iron on the eighth hole for an eagle. It still needed a little help from our opponents, though. Mickelson missed a couple of short putts, one on the 16th and another on the last. That was the difference between them.'

As their countrymen were put on the back foot, there was little chance for mixed feelings for either Ten Broeck or García's caddie, Higginbotham, who witnessed one fellow American's tears:

'Sergio was so fired up. He lived and breathed the Ryder Cup and trying to win. When Parnevik pitched in, he ran across and picked him up bodily. He was so excited. You know it was such a good mix, the two of them. They really ham-and-egged it throughout the week.

'Mickelson was really down at missing that putt on the last, about five feet it was, from memory. You could see the tears streaking his face. He wasn't very happy with himself. Phil misses a lot of putts. It's always said that the guy's such a great putter, but he does miss them now and then.'

Following Parnevik and García were Jiménez and Olazábal. While Jiménez had already had a taste of action, Olazábal, again uncomfortable on the tee, made his first appearance. The reigning Masters champion had been the one to rule himself out of the foursomes.

Jiménez's caddie Gardino was delighted with the way his man handled the tough match, but shocked in one instance at the antics of one American 'fan' during their 2 and 1 success over Maggert and Sutton:

'On the 17th, Olazábal was in the rough on the right, virtually out of the hole but still making the chip because you never know what might happen. He could still chip in for par. This American guy comes right up to him and yells, "Pick up the ball and put it in your pocket." We were all shocked. José Maria just took it in his stride. In fact, he laughed. I guess then we all thought it was quite funny.'

The way the draw worked out, arguably the day's most thrilling encounter was in prospect for the fourth and final match of the afternoon – Clarke and Westwood versus Woods and Duval, Europe's young contenders for places in the world's top bracket against two men who were regarded as the current best in the world.

While relations between the crowd and the European team, and often between the players, were not at their best, Clarke's caddie Foster was delighted when the afternoon's 'big match' turned out to be a very pleasant encounter indeed:

'Out of all the Ryder Cups I have been at I would say Kiawah Island and Brookline were the most "tetchy" between the teams. There was quite a bit of heat through the week. I wouldn't say the players were having a go at each other, but there were a couple of unsavoury moments. There was a slight atmosphere amongst the players and a hell of a lot of atmosphere with the crowd. The

European team were pissing into a 50mph wind if they wanted good reactions from the crowd!

'The match against Duval and Woods was against the norm of the week. There was a very good atmosphere between the players, a lot of respect. They all got on really well and we all had a right good laugh; well, as much of a laugh as you can have. They had a real friendly game, there was some good golf played and it was nip-and-tuck all the way.

'I remember them going one-up when Tiger holed one off the green straight after the turn but Clarkey got it straight back at the 11th and it stayed even right to the last two holes. Clarkey then birdied the 17th to put us one-up. He holed about a seven-footer, not bad because it was getting very dark. Then Duval slashed it way right off the tee on the last, Clarkey missed it right, Lee missed the fairway. Tiger was the only one on the fairway, but he hit his second long left in the back bunker and par was good enough in the end for us to take the point. It was a great morale-boosting victory for the team.'

In the fourballs, only Montgomerie and Lawrie did not pick up a full point for Europe, who took the afternoon matches 3½–½, taking the aggregate score to 6–2 to the visitors. James and his men had grabbed the match by the scruff of its neck. Europe had matched their feat of 1987 at Muirfield Village, where they had gone on to secure their first win on American soil.

The US team awoke to stinging rebukes in the papers, having received a pep-talk from Crenshaw the night before. They came out fighting – and ready to whip up strong support from their home gallery.

Montgomerie and Lawrie were first ones out again, this time playing against Sutton and Maggert. As Montgomerie's caddie McLean remembers, Sutton, in particular, soon charged up the partisan gallery:

'Sutton was punching the air and whooping up the crowd. That wasn't called for. It happened. His kind of behaviour was not the way I was brought up to play golf. It was almost like a complete lack of etiquette. He didn't really need to do any stirring. He was playing ever so well. Maybe the crowd had started to get to Monty and Paul as well.

'Sutton was almost unbeatable around that time. In foursomes you have to rely on your partner, but before and after the Ryder Cup, Sutton played awesome golf. He had to be America's top man in the 1999 match.

'On the second day, the European crowd could see the American gallery was having an effect, so they tried to be a little more vociferous, but they were getting drowned out. Every time there was support, a shout from Europeans in the crowd, Sutton would wave his arms to gee up the American crowd. And at this stage they didn't need much geeing up. That caused a lot of screaming and shouting. Hal Sutton caused a lot of that. Monty and Chippy did their best but they were undone in the end by a better pair – and the crowd, I guess.'

To offset Montgomerie and Lawrie's narrow one-hole defeat, Clarke and

Westwood won out in the country as they disposed of Furyk and Mark O'Meara, the latter playing for the first time in the week, 3 and 2.

That heavy defeat in the second match dampened the home gallery's enthusiasm for a little while, but a superb display of power and accuracy by America's and the world's top man, Woods, soon had them hollering in the ranks.

Woods was in supreme form as he and Steve Pate, also playing for the first time in the week, ended the hopes of Jiménez and Harrington of pulling off their first point. If Woods had played with a stronger partner than Pate, the man who missed the 1991 singles and had to be 'enveloped' at Kiawah Island, the margin of victory might have been greater, argues Jiménez's caddie Gardino:

'I saw Tiger as a god. He never missed a shot. If he had been playing with somebody like Mickelson, we would have been walking back by about the 12th or 13th hole. For instance, at the par-five up the hill, the 14th, I think, he left Pate a four or a five-iron. Jiménez chose a three-wood to get there and wasn't going to make it.

'Every time he needed to, Tiger left the ball in the middle of the fairway absolutely perfectly and every time he needed to hole a ten-foot putt to tie the hole and avoid losing it, he made it. He never failed under pressure. Jiménez and Harrington played well enough, but Tiger ran the show and, even though it was foursomes, he made such a difference to the outcome of the match.'

McNeilly, on Harrington's bag, thought the very presence of Woods was worth several shots and when the world No. 1 strode to the 18th tee, he seemed determined to capture the point for America by hook or by crook:

'It was a gargantuan battle against Woods and Pate, which we only lost at the last hole. There was a tremendous atmosphere and I, particularly, was very excited to be playing against Woods.

'Woods just kept doing the right things all the time and got his partner out of trouble while keeping up the pressure on us. He kept his side in it all the way to the 14th and then, with his length off the tee and Pate hitting the green, they made eagle to go one ahead. Padraig and Miguel tried their best, but it was Tiger's great drive at the last that finally won it for him and Pate. On the 18th Woods hit a cracker straight over the left trap, very long. It left Pate only a wedge. He knocked it in to about eight or ten feet, and you just knew Tiger would make the putt.'

Europe just would not relent, however, and retained their four-point advantage well before Woods' virtuoso display added the home point. That was because Parnevik and García had overwhelmed Stewart and Leonard 3 and 2 to add some vocals from the visiting gallery. Thus the European tails were still up going into the afternoon fourballs. By the end of the day, the status quo was maintained, but not before a few unsavoury incidents which came in the opening fourball, won by Mickelson and Lehman, by a hole, over Westwood and Clarke. The initial problems came when Clarke and Westwood seemed to be paying too much attention to detail while playing their match, according to Westwood's caddie, Doran:

'It was a real grudge match in the end, not a very pleasant experience at times. Mickelson and Lehman started getting annoyed because Lee and Darren were practising afterwards on the green. You could see niggle creeping in and so could the crowd. Lehman holed a massive putt and went absolutely mad, completely over the top. He's punching his fist. It was definitely OTT.

'Clarkey and Westwood didn't let that put them off. They again played a couple of practice putts. When we got to the next tee, Mickelson had already teed off before we got there!

'Lehman definitely incited the crowd, without a doubt. He was running up to the hole and fist-pumping, not quietening the crowd down when Clarkey's got a putt, or when Lee was putting. That was totally out of order.'

Clarke's caddie Billy Foster gives his version of the distasteful scenes in the match:

'There was a lot of "bad blood", let's say. On the ninth green, Darren had about a three-footer up the hill for a birdie and looked like winning the hole. They were a couple up at the time and Darren was thinking he was probably going to win the hole. Then Lehman holed a 20-foot putt down the green and let's just say he was a bit over the top. He ran down the green, jumping up and down about two foot from the hole, punching the air like a demented thing. It was uncalled for and his celebration was way over the top for a mature, experienced golfer. Clarkey holed his putt, though, and gave him the "Ulster Dead-eye".

'The next hole was the real unsavoury moment for me, though. They'd won the tenth to go three-up and Clarkey and Westwood held back and had a couple of practice putts. When they got to the 11th tee, Mickelson had already teed off, without them being on the tee. It was ungentlemanly, to say the least.

'For me, who's done seven Ryder Cups now, it left a bad taste in the mouth. The Ryder Cup's supposed to be a gentleman's match. Brookline was very disappointing in that aspect.'

As in the morning, America fashioned a good start as Mickelson and Lehman overcame Westwood and Clarke by the 17th, chalking up a 2 and 1 success. In the following match it was tight, too, and there were the occasional outbreaks of catcalling from the American gallery as Parnevik and García failed to win for the first time, having to settle for a half with Love and Duval.

Parnevik's bagman Ten Broeck couldn't help noticing the barracking aimed at García, who was in the early throes of a habit that eventually turned into an obsession:

'You could feel the atmosphere was uncomfortable but we were heavily involved in trying to win, so I didn't take much notice of any crowd trouble. That was until we got to the 14th. Here somebody in the crowd really took exception to Sergio's habit, where he kept regripping, shouting out: "Hit the ball, Spick," before he could take his shot. Sergio backed off and he sat down on the ground for two or three minutes. Whoever the impatient guy was, he had to wait even longer then!

'It was a shame, really. Sergio wasn't using gamesmanship. We had a great match otherwise and they were very evenly matched. A half was definitely the right result and, really, apart from the one incident, there wasn't so much trouble.'

García's caddie, Higginbotham, remembers the uncomfortable saga thus:

'It wasn't only his regripping habit. At that particular hole I was trying to size up the yardage and Lance had a different yardage. It was a matter of four or five yards difference, as I recall.

'So we're all trying to get sorted out, looking at sprinkler-heads for definition and all, and then the crowd started to get a mite restless. When Sergio was under a little pressure, too, he would give the shaft about ten regrips. The regripping wasn't that big a deal at the time. That came later. Anyway, look at the shots he could hit after all that regripping. I just don't know how he could bring himself back into focus!

'The crowd was noisy and we started taking tally of the shouts that were likely to disturb the players. Us caddies didn't get too much heat. There were a few times, though, when we did get a bit of unpleasantness. We would be walking through the crowd, going to the driving-range for instance, with our European outfits on, and we'd take some flak. There were a lot of fans who knew me because of my success with Mark O'Meara, and I heard a few comments like "Higgy, what you doing on the other side?" I'd just laugh and say: "May the best man win." I heard "Benedict Arnold" a few more times but I just laughed it off.'

Regrettably, Higginbotham could not always laugh it off, though. After the Ryder Cup had finished he was in a bar enjoying a couple of beers when he got recognised again. When he was challenged to explain why he'd chosen to caddie for Europe against America, this time Higginbotham lost patience, especially as his adopted team had lost. He gave his inquisitors short shrift. What happened next, though, showed just how far certain 'fans' were prepared to go in their xenophobia over the match. Higginbotham finished up with two black eyes, a swollen jaw and six stitches in a head wound. He ended up in hospital on the Sunday night and spent six hours there before setting off with García for Europe and a playoff victory in the German Masters.

'It was at my hotel when it happened, a couple of hours after we finished at Brookline. There were plenty of people in the bar and I got recognised. The guys didn't like the fact that, as an American, I'd caddied for a European.

'They were all pretty drunk and this one guy must have had a bad day because he carried it on and said a couple of things to me I didn't like. I defended myself and said a couple of things back. Then suddenly, "boom-boom". He got on the blind side of me. I fell over and hit my head on the way down.

'But it takes two to tango. I guess I should have walked away.'

While Higginbotham and Ten Broeck were helping Parnevik and García to a half with Love and Duval, another tense battle had developed behind as Olazábal and Jiménez teamed up again. It was tense for Europe because Olazábal still could not find his game, as Jiménez's caddie Gardino recalls.

'Olazábal played very badly in the afternoon and Jiménez was often on his own against Leonard and Sutton. We did well to get a half. Jiménez kept us going and we were one-up going into the 14th, the par-five. Then Olazábal snap-hooked a terrible drive and had no chance of getting to the green, not even in three. Jiménez had to lay up with his second shot, about 85 yards out, and Olazábal was still 50 yards short with his third shot.

'Leonard hit his third shot to about ten feet, a very, very fast putt. Jiménez hits in a poorish shot, pitches about four or five yards short of the pin and rolls all the way back about 25 or 30 yards short.

'When Miguel Angel's ball spins back off the green, there is a huge cheer from the gallery. Is it bad sportsmanship? I don't know. It happens in a football match. The fans cheer and jeer. And that's how this Ryder Cup was a little bit, like a football match. It's not always that they are clapping because you've hit a bad shot or missed a putt, but that your team is winning a point. It's absolutely understandable.

'Anyway, from there Miguel Angel makes a very good chip to about eight feet past the hole, also very, very fast and on the same line as Leonard's ball. So Leonard has a fast ten-footer for birdie and Jiménez a fast eight-footer for par in front of him.

'Leonard misses and Jiménez holes his, downhill and at enormous speed, to keep us one-up going to 15. We tie again, Jiménez just missing a putt of 20 feet for birdie to win the hole.

'Then Sutton nearly holes in one at 16. I remember there was a huge grandstand on the left at the 16th, nearly the length of the hole, 150 yards long. It really impressed me. It wasn't golf, more like a football match! It was something awesome. Jiménez and Olazábal both had chances to hole birdie putts but they were under so much pressure. The noise from the fans in the stand when Sutton tapped in his putt to win the hole was absolutely unbelievable.

'So we go to 17 all-square. The gallery is going mad. But we manage to tie the 17th, so it's all to play for on 18. Jiménez hit a very, very good shot into the 18th, a five-iron from the right edge of the fairway in to about 10 or 12 feet. Sutton and Leonard both missed the green but Sutton then chips so close from the bunker it is given for the four.

'Jiménez then has a putt to win the match. He hits a beautiful, beautiful putt, but it somehow stays on the edge. It was one of those putts that should have had just a fraction of break but it didn't move. I was so disappointed for him and for me. I always helped him read the putts.

'It was just one of those moments in the match. But for a centimetre we would have kept the Ryder Cup, might have gone and won it. You can say that about a lot of key points. Anyway, we were very disappointed to get just a half. Jiménez had played his heart out.'

By now the European members of the gallery were making themselves heard occasionally because the Americans' great figurehead Woods was under the cosh. Europe's all-Scot partnership of Montgomerie and Lawrie was to provide the final telling blow of the afternoon and send the away supporters home to their hotels euphoric.

Montgomerie's bagman McLean was not only happy with the 2 and 1 outcome to Europe, but also with the behaviour of their American opponents Woods and Pate. During the whole week vitriol was spat at Montgomerie's wife Eimear, and his father James, recovering from heart surgery, was eventually forced to walk off the course in the singles because he could not take the undeserving taunts thrown at his son. Woods and Pate were blameless, however, maintains McLean:

'Pate was ever such a nice lad, behaved ever so well. Tiger did as well. On the course Tiger just wants to play golf, beat whoever he's playing. He doesn't get involved in the hoo-ha. Pate was the same, ever so laid-back.

'The noise and the antics from the crowd were terrible, though. There was hardly a hole went by where Paul or Monty didn't have to back off a shot. It seemed to happen all the time. But it wasn't Steve Pate or Tiger's fault that the crowd were behaving badly. It could have been because Hal Sutton was egging them on that they became a bit noisier, but Pate and Woods were excellent.

'We heard things from the crowd but, because we were inside the ropes, we couldn't see things. I know there were bad scenes. I heard from my friends that there was fighting; they were having to be pulled off people. Fans were right in each other's faces and tempers were getting badly frayed at that point. It was toe-to-toe.

'That's not a golf match. It's complete lack of respect for the players. It was ignorance of golf and complete lack of etiquette. I don't know whether the crowds over in America know anything about golf but they certainly didn't show they did. It was like one of these ice-hockey matches where they are screaming and shouting and baying for blood almost. All they're doing is hitting a little white ball around a field. It's not a blood sport.

'Amidst all the furore, Monty and Paul are trying to win a match and their opponents are trying to do the same – respectfully. It was tight all the way. Then at the par-5 14th we made a vital half to keep us one-up.

'Tiger knocked it on in two, of course, bombed it on with probably just a five-iron. Paul and Monty couldn't even reach but they both chipped up well to give themselves birdie chances. Tiger then missed the eagle putt from only about 12 feet and then Monty holed from six feet for the half and to keep their noses in front.

'One-up with four to go and you knew that Woods' length for the remaining holes didn't give them any great advantage.'

Europe finished the day with their 4-point advantage intact, with the matches 10–6 in their favour. That meant only 4½ points were needed from the 12 singles matches for them to win and retain the Cup, 4 points to draw and still hold on to it, as they had in 1989.

Many in the European camp dared to hope that the visitors' lead was unassailable. For Andrew Coltart and his caddie Ricci Roberts, it at least alleviated some of the crushing disappointment at not getting a game in the foursomes or fourballs:

'If you ask me was I surprised that Coltart was a pick, I'd say, "Yes and no." Jesse asked me a couple of times how Andrew was playing and I told him he was playing good and trying hard. But the closer it got to selection, I think the pressure was telling on him a little bit. He had a chance at the final tournament to count for an automatic place, the BMW International, to really get in there but let it slip on the Saturday. He still had a chance to play his way in on the Sunday but it just didn't happen, even though he shot a 66. I thought when Robert Karlsson got himself into 11th place, and Andrew was in 12th spot, Jesse was going to go for Karlsson.

'So I was a little surprised – but over the moon, actually. I was so happy for him because I knew how badly he wanted it. I was happy because it was something I'd never done before. I've been fortunate in the years I've worked with Ernie [Els] that I've been able to do most things, and I thought the Ryder Cup might be something I wouldn't be able to achieve.

'The way practice went it looked as though the opening foursomes and fourballs were pretty well set and I didn't expect we'd play the first day. I thought he would have got a game the second day. But then on Saturday morning, when Europe still had a good lead, Jesse obviously told him the news and then came to me and said: "I'm sorry, but he's going to sit out this afternoon as well." He explained, something along the lines of: "I've got to try and amass as many points as I can."

'I tried to console Andrew. He was extremely disappointed that he wasn't going to play at all until the singles. I tried to justify it by gently explaining that it was a team game and that whatever it takes to win, you've got to do. If it so happens that he sticks with the same guys and amasses a big lead, then that's the way it's got to be. The object is to win.

'It's easy to criticise in hindsight. If Jesse had done things differently and we'd lost, then people would have said: "Why didn't he just stick with what he had?" It was a Catch 22 situation.

'The one thing that surprised me, though, was, if he's used him as a captain's selection, then why not play him? Why didn't he go for Langer if he was going to do something like that? Andrew was obviously picked on the thinking he would play with Monty or Lawrie. It could be that Monty and Lawrie turned out so good, and so did other pairings, that Jesse felt he couldn't change those pairings. I don't think it was in his thinking initially that he wouldn't play the three guys. It turned into a roller-coaster effect. A couple of the guys were obviously getting tired but I guess he wanted them to carry on.'

James had gambled over the fitness of six men: Montgomerie, Lawrie, Westwood, Clarke, Parnevik and García, whom he played in all four pairs matches so he did not have to change a winning team. So three debutants would get their first taste of battle only in the singles – Jarmo Sandelin, third man out and pitted against the world's best lefthander Phil Mickelson, Jean Van de Velde, out fourth, and matched against the highly experienced Love III, and Coltart, with the seemingly impossible task of trying to get something out of a tie with the world's best golfer.

Many in the European camp thought it was all over. They began to sing 'Before the Fat Lady', much to the disapproval of Lehman's veteran caddie, Andrew Martinez. As he tried to get off to sleep, he wondered if the Saturday-night revellers might live to regret their pre-singles party:

'We were all staying at the same hotel and on the Saturday night I was kept awake by people upstairs stomping around, making an awful din on my ceiling. There were caddies above us but I don't know whether it was them making the noise. They seemed to be on the roof. I felt they might be celebrating prematurely. It was quite a ruckus and I felt like going up there and cracking a few skulls.

'Yes, we were getting a trouncing and that doesn't feel good, but I thought: "Get real; it's just a golf tournament." I knew we had to make up a huge deficit but traditionally we play well in the singles and I didn't think it was beyond us when I saw the pairings. The draw was all important.

'We were first out against Lee Westwood and Hal Sutton was to play Darren Clarke. Personally, I thought Clarke and Westwood had looked dead on their feet when they finished on Saturday.

'Then Europe's next three guys hadn't hit a shot in the match, and they were expected to play against three of our top guns – Mickelson, Love and Woods. I could easily see us coming out of the blocks and getting points on the board. I felt the guys making all the noise upstairs might get their comeuppance, as you do when you celebrate prematurely. You don't count your chickens . . .'

If some in Europe's ranks counted chickens, in direct contrast to their captain, who refused to gloat at a four-point lead, America's method of sabre-rattling was a little crass, too. Crenshaw, insisting on Saturday night that he still had a 'good feeling' about the outcome, recruited president-to-be George 'Dubya' Bush to talk to his players. The governor of Texas read them the 'Alamo Address'. This inspired Sutton to jump up and launch into his own frenzied battle cry. It was hardly surprising that America's players went to bed that night more ready for a backs-to-the-wall fight with Santa Anna and his Mexican army than a golf match. The rather vulgar aspect of Crenshaw's patriotism was shown, too, when America sported their final-day shirts – plastered with gaudy montages of photographs of winning US Ryder Cup teams of the past.

It was true, though, that the American backs were to the wall. They had to rewrite the record books if they were to overcome a four-point deficit. However, wily old campaigner Martinez had summed up the final-day scenario perfectly. Right from the start it went horribly wrong for Europe, as Westwood fell behind to Lehman. The noise from the home gallery was deafening at times, recalls Westwood's caddie Doran, almost unnerving:

'All you could hear, all around the course, was "USA, USA, USA." You think to yourself, "Change the song, for God's sake!" The chanting was incredible, more like a football match than a golf match. I think it definitely affected our players, to tell the truth. Without a doubt it played on your nerves, as well as your ears. I went to sleep that night humming it!

'Lee didn't play all that well and that was a pity as we were first out, looking to get something on the board. Lehman played all right; Lee just couldn't get into it. He didn't tell me he was tired but I did wonder. You just never know how you are affected mentally. I think he was capable of playing all five matches. But with "USA, USA, USA" dinning into you all the while . . . As far as I remember, though, Lehman had stopped his antics while we were playing the singles. Fair do, he got America off to a good start.

'It was an important result. As we finished at the 16th, it looked very bleak on the scoreboard. I went off to the clubhouse to watch the finish on the television. It soon became obvious we were going to struggle to get the points we needed, even for a tie.'

Obvious it became as Westwood's 3 and 2 defeat virtually coincided with Darren Clarke's end as he lost out to Sutton 4 and 2. Sutton remained on fire for the whole week, one of the sparks that lit the gallery's inferno.

Clarke's caddie Foster could hardly believe how Europe were wilting, although he acknowledged his own man was nearly spent by the time he teed up for the singles:

'It seemed to be a case of "Stand up and be counted and fall over the line," but it was crucial we got a result out of those first two games, with three rookies going out 3, 4 and 5. But it was just a sea of red and confidence just built and built for the Americans. Fair play to them, they outplayed the European team on the Sunday.

'Darren was shattered. He'd be the first to admit it. He played quite poorly, really. He won the first hole, chipped in, and was psyched up for it – but whatever he tried, he couldn't pull anything off. Sutton played steadily and beat him.

'You can't look at things in hindsight, though, and criticise Jesse. Nobody was complaining on Saturday night.'

As Clarke was losing out 4 and 2, there was little to cheer behind. The normally extrovert Sandelin could not use his typical bravado and flamboyancy to any effect. The man who favours huge winged collars, garish colours and Italian belts buckled even earlier, going down 4 and 3 to the staid Mickelson. Van de Velde, the man who had held a world audience spellbound as he faltered and threw away his major title chance at Carnoustie that previous July, had no answer to Love and succumbed even further out in the country, sliding to a 6 and 5 demise.

It would need a monumental effort from Coltart, 66th in the world, to claim one of the four points needed for at least the tie. Initially it went well for him but then, as caddie Ricci Roberts reports, a cruel hammer-blow took the wind out of the Scot's sails, before an incident at the ninth hole that further tainted the 1999 Ryder Cup:

'At the end of the second day, the feeling was that we just needed a couple of our big guns to go out and win and it was game over. We only needed 4½ points. With 12 players, you had to be thinking we were going to get those points.

'When we saw the draw, I thought it was quite ironic that Mark hadn't picked Andrew, and then he gets thrown into the lion's – or the tiger's – den! I thought, "This could be a total massacre." But as far as Andrew was concerned, I had the feeling he was elated when he'd taken it all in. I guess he was thinking, "Well, I have nothing to lose now." He was determined to give it his best shot. And there's no doubt, we've seen it time and time again, the best player in the world can be beaten by somebody right down in the rankings when it comes to matchplay. In Andrew's defence, he played really, really well. I felt sorry for him, because he could have taken Tiger all the way to the 18th.

'He had a lot of pressure, because it wasn't just Tiger he was playing, but the gallery. In all the tournaments I've been at in my life, it was the worst I've ever seen. Supporters are expected to get behind the team, and they are expected to be biased, that's fine, but when you resort to heckling players and trying to put them off, that's over-stepping the mark. It came as a shock to me because over the first couple of days I thought the crowd had been fine. In fact some of them had remarked on how our guys were much more polite than the Americans and how obliging they were, signing autographs, for instance. The American players just wouldn't sign autographs. Then the American players got into the spectators and the crowd turned on us. It wasn't everybody. You get bad apples in every bunch. Some of them were totally out of control. We had two of them slung off the course during Andrew's match.

'Once he'd got over the initial stage of nerves, Andrew began to play really well. Woods won a hole around the middle of the front nine, fourth or fifth, but Andrew was hanging on more than gamely. Tiger just seems to be able to produce little acts of magic, though, as if he's waving a wand at his opponent.

'At the eighth, Andrew hit into about 12 feet and Tiger missed the green, right. We were really up for it then. Wouldn't you just know it, though? Tiger chips in from about 45 feet. It had looked for all the world that Andrew was going to win the hole one minute, and then the next he's fighting to save the hole.

'Well, he missed the putt when he had been looking like squaring the match. All of a sudden he's two-down. It was very deflating. Then came the real body blow. On the ninth, Andrew pulled the ball left off the tee. Now that week there had been some rain and on the left side of the hole it was very wet. Fifteen yards left of the fairway there's a big rock outcrop. Tiger's bombed it over this sort of false canyon. We go down there, to where we think the ball is, and this marshal says: "No, it's further up there, in the bushes, up in those rocks." I looked at my yardage book. It has to be 265–270 yards to carry it to where he was indicating.

'Now Andrew does not carry the ball 265–270 yards. It's not possible. There were no spectators on the left-hand side; we're looking and looking. I kept saying: "There's no way the ball can be here. It's not possible for it to be here."

'Eventually the officials said "Sorry, your time's up." Sam [Torrance, James's joint vice-captain with Ken Brown] was there and he took Andrew back on the golf cart.

'Andrew hits his next one down the fairway. I was standing about five yards off the fairway. This marshal says, "There's a ball here, a 'Titleist Three' with a blue stripe on it." You could see the ball was plugged. But if it's plugging from 240–50 yards, it goes in at an angle. This ball was plugged straight down. The ball had been stood on purposely. There was no question about that. You could see somebody had stood on it. And the ball was at least 12 yards from the rocks – where they were telling us to look.

'Well, it took us three-down. It was an uphill battle all the way from there. When we came in and looked at the scoreboard, I thought, "Where are these 4½ points going to come from now?" We needed a miracle.'

That miracle certainly wasn't going to come from Europe's sixth man, Parnevik. The Swede never even got as far as Coltart, who lost 3 and 2 to Woods, and was crushed 5 and 4 by Duval. Parnevik's caddie, Ten Broeck, felt exhaustion played a major part:

'Oh, yes, he was tired all right. I didn't think he was physically tired; mentally he was done. He had the energy physically, but mentally he just wasn't there. I don't know as it was a mistake to keep playing Jesper and Sergio because they got 3½ points. The only second-guessing I could possibly have about the tactics was his [Mark James's] line-up for the last day. Jesper and I were talking on the range on Sunday and looking at the board. We wondered where the heck Europe was going to come up with four points out of the twelve matches. It was just the way they were lined up. It didn't look good for Europe.

'By the time we were on the third or fourth hole, the scoreboard was all red, for the home team. From what I've learned about Ryder Cups, momentum is a huge thing. Whoever starts winning the early matches then it feeds over to the rest of the team.

'In our match we were lucky to halve the first hole. Jesper had to hole a 20-foot putt for par to do that. Then he lost six of the next seven holes. It was over early and over quickly. I looked in his eyes. He was empty. He was done. He was fried. He didn't have to say anything to me.'

Opponent Duval's relief at holing the ten-foot birdie putt that closed out Parnevik on the 14th was starkly visible. Duval had been heartily criticised for calling the Ryder Cup match purely 'exhibition' not long before the encounter and he had been slated in the press for his apparent lack of will for a fight. His response was to thump the air with his fists and run the length of the gallery, slapping palms and cocking a hand around his ear, exhorting the crowd to cheer to near-hysterical proportions. If it had been a cauldron before for Europe, it was now a bubbling cooking-pot – and they were the missionaries!

With a wipe-out in the first six matches, Europe's flagging chances now rested with the bottom half of the draw. Hope still sprang eternal, especially with all but one of the last six matches looking close.

Harrington was taking on the double-major champion O'Meara and trying to beat one of the world's greatest short-iron exponents at his own game. Harrington's caddie McNeilly had a little secret about his man's improved chances:

'We went to the BC Open the week before Brookline, had a reasonable tournament, but it was mainly to get acclimatised. Padraig also had a very important wedge session at a really nice course called The Links. This session was instrumental in wholly improving his short game. Mark O'Meara is probably regarded as the best wedge player in the world and Padraig definitely outplayed him in that department.

'We were at what we thought would be a crucial stage in the match. It was bound to whip up quite a frenzy in the crowd. Padraig had got off lightly at first, probably because of being in Boston and him being Irish. He got a little bit of flak, but not to the same extent as Monty. In fact Padraig was quite well received. It was more of an enjoyable experience for us than some, but even he had to put up with the shouting and screaming in the end.

'It was the most excitement I've ever experienced in golf. The foursomes match the day before had been exciting enough and a fantastic atmosphere, but the singles was something else. You could tell how much the whole affair had swept into a fervour because all the American players were coming to our match to shout on O'Meara. It looked as though everything might hinge on our match. This was the one for the money, or so it seemed.

'We'd been in reasonably high spirits on the Saturday night because we were favourites to win now, but I think in the back of our minds we realised the fatigue factor might come into play. When you think of Jiménez, for instance. With us, he had gone through sheer hell on the Saturday morning. He then had to go back out again. We were exhausted and Jiménez had to go out and play with Olazábal, and play brilliantly to get a half. So, OK, we had a substantial lead points-wise, but the team had nothing left in the tank.

'Padraig was pretty fresh. Mentally, too, he seemed a lot more into his game. He had started working with Jos Vanstiphout, his sports psychologist, at the BMW International and once again Jos's midas touch was in evidence, as in his very first week, Padraig finishes second and secures his Ryder Cup spot.

'On Sunday before the match with O'Meara, Padraig reminded himself of what Jos was telling him to do, the usual stuff, focusing and the like. You couldn't say Padraig was playing golf thinking about swing thoughts, he was thinking more about how to stay relaxed and focused and keep his concentration levels high.

'He played brilliantly. It stayed really tight the whole way through. O'Meara's short-game certainly kept him in it, but Padraig bettered him. At the sixth, they both had wedge shots from exactly the same place from the middle of the fairway and Padraig came out better and went one-up. To have upstaged the wedge-master must have been rather a gratifying feeling for Padraig.

'The greens had turned really hard and fast. I think that was instrumental, too, in the Americans dominating the last day. It was noticeable that when the greens had been slower over the first two days, the Europeans had prevailed.

'O'Meara got it back to all-square. We came to the par-5 14th and both of them had laid up with a shot of about 95 yards. O'Meara was first in, hit what looked to be a really nice shot, but all of a sudden there was a loud gasp from the crowd. It was obvious he had gone long. The green was so hard his ball had skipped into the back trap. It was impossible to play a good shot from there. He would be absolutely dead.

'Padraig went up and examined the green. Of course he got flak from the crowd, shouting about slow-play and all. But gee whiz, he was in one hell of a position. Olazábal was four-up in his match and looked to be coasting against Leonard. Ours looked the critical match. The crowd were unbelievable. Every single time we finished a hole and walked to the next tee, it was like going back into the ring in a boxing match, with the crowd screaming and shouting at us. It really was nerve-tingling stuff.

'After walking back, Padraig decides to play 20 or 30 feet short. O'Meara comes out of the bunker, impossible shot, hits it long. Padraig has this four-footer to win the hole. He asked me, "What do you think this is?" and I said

"Gee, you more or less just have to get it started, it will depend on gravity after that!" It's maybe left half. He sets the ball off and there's a scream from the back of the green: "He's missed it." Everyone goes crazy. He's hit it six feet past. Now we're in a completely different situation. This is for the half now and to stay all-square. My brain is saying "shut down". I don't know how Padraig could stand it – the notion of trying to collect yourself to hole this return putt. If he misses this, his whole world could crash around him – a four-putt in the Ryder Cup? Somehow he holed it. He showed tremendous nerve. That was the only way to quieten the crowd. They still weren't quiet, though.

'We're still all-square going to the 16th, the par-three. Mark James came over and said everybody had been hitting seven-irons. But we know, with the wind blowing from left to right at the 15th, here we must be hitting into the wind, so it's got to be a six. O'Meara still had the honour. He took out a six-iron. Padraig's longer than O'Meara. O'Meara's ball looked right down the throat. Padraig and I looked at each other, thinking he was going to birdie. It was short and in the bunker. Padraig hits a really good shot to about 15 feet. O'Meara makes a wonderful up-and-down from the bunker to keep it all-square.'

'At the 17th Padraig hit a good second shot and had a long putt. O'Meara then hit a marvellous chip to about eight feet. Padraig rolled up to about three feet. O'Meara's fast downhiller went in. The crowd went crazy. Because of all the commotion, O'Meara gave Padraig his putt. With everybody running around and screaming the odds, it was not only a decent thing to do, but a brave thing.

'On the 18th, Padraig hit one of the best shots of his career. It's such a tough driving hole, but he hit such a long, straight, tee-shot and left himself only a wedge in. O'Meara pulled his tee-shot and then couldn't carry the trap. He pitches on but makes bogey. Padraig has hit to about 10–15 feet. He wins the hole. That was it, all over.'

It was, though, getting close to being all over for Europe. Crucially it was certainly all over for García, not because of tiredness, according to caddie Higginbotham, but through a deadly opponent:

'We ran into a buzz-saw called Jim Furyk. All of a sudden we were four or five down. We couldn't get on track. I don't think Sergio was played out. It's hard to be tired when you're 19. He might have been a bit worn down mentally, but I don't think so. He was playing golf every week at the top notch. Anyway, it's the Ryder Cup and I don't care how tired you are mentally or physically, everyone rises to the occasion.

'In my opinion, we just ran into a Jim Furyk on his "A" game and there was nothing he could do about it. He never made any mistakes. Sergio tried to make a comeback later in the round but it didn't happen.

'Apart from a couple of instances I've talked about, the crowd treated us pretty good, but Sergio got quite a bit of ribbing on Sunday. The crowd were shouting: "Where's Jesper? You need your partner. You're going to lose. You need your buddy to help you win." It got to him a couple of times. He tried to wave to them, tried to stay positive, but there was a lot of heckling.

'Sergio and I and some of his friends and family walked down the 18th and cut over to the 17th fairway on the dogleg, when Olazábal and Leonard were hitting their second shots. We saw Leonard make that putt and all hell broke loose. There was not much said between our group. Sergio was pretty much bombed out. President Bush [senior] was standing there with Tim Finchem [US PGA Tour Commissioner]. I had my European Tour gear on, but I said "Mr Bush, Sergio would love to meet you."

'He said he would love to meet Sergio, who was standing 20 feet away. So I took President Bush over and introduced him to Sergio. Maybe it was not the greatest moment to do it, but it was kind of cool Sergio meeting one of the presidents of the United States.

'There were a lot of tears, though. The locker-room was not a real fun place to be afterwards.'

Jiménez soon lost out to Pate, the second of Crenshaw's wild-cards, 2 and 1, to deepen Europe's gloom. Caddie Gardino witnessed an emotional finale:

'Jiménez played badly. He really felt the pressure. Pate didn't play that well, either. It could have gone either way. When I looked at the scoreboard on the 10th we were already 12–10 down.

'Pate holed a putt of 25 feet for par on the 13th and Jiménez missed from three and a half feet for par, so we are one-down. Then at the long hole, the 14th, Jiménez misses a birdie putt of six feet, so we are still one-down. Jiménez then misses another birdie chance on 15 and the crowd is in a fever because the board is showing just how close it is.

'We know how important it is for Jiménez to win his match now. He is trying but cannot get the putt to get level. Then on the par-three, the 16th, Pate birdies. We are now two-down. Jiménez can only par the 17th. We've lost. I worked out things frantically. Now we can only tie. I wanted to stay there to see if Olazábal could square the match.

'Olazábal was not in the fairway. The pin was up on the slope and he could not pitch it all the way up. He hit a good shot but it did not release enough and stayed short. Leonard hit a better shot but his ball spun back a lot. He had to go first from about 50 feet. This was our last chance to halve the whole match.

'When Leonard hit the putt, I watched it roll on and on. It was like being stabbed when it went in. I felt like crying. You get very emotional. You really want so much to win that everything hurts. But Olazábal still had a putt to halve the hole. I couldn't believe it when the American players ran out on to the green. That was unforgivable. All the cheering for bad shots, that's the game. There's a lot of competition. It's understandable. But when the thing is not over yet . . . that is unforgivable.'

Olazábal could be forgiven for being in a state of shock as he watched the extraordinary scenes on the 17th green. It was bad enough losing what had seemed an unassailable lead. He had been four holes ahead of Leonard with seven holes to go. And an off-colour Leonard did not look like a man who might turn things around. Then Olazábal lost two holes to par and subsided to Leonard's subsequent two birdies, the second with a putt of 40 feet. Suddenly their match was all-square.

At the 17th, as Gardino rightly observed, Leonard's ball spun back much further away than Olazábal's and he was left with a putt of around 45–50 feet. If he holed it, then America were on the brink of claiming the half-point that would enable them to claim back the Ryder Cup. Only on the brink, mind you. He holed it.

All the pent-up anxiety of the home side was released. Hysteria took over. The green was invaded by players, caddies, wives, hangers-on. Some people were on the pitch. They thought it was all over. It wasn't.

Olazábal waited, dismayed by the antics, knowing he could still be Europe's hero if he could only gather his wits after the invasion, part of which took place over his very line in to the hole. After what must have seemed like a cacophanous eternity, the Spaniard missed his 20-footer. That should have been the time for celebrations and not before. American exuberance would then have been expected, even though Olazábal and Leonard still had a hole to go in their match.

It is to Olazábal's great credit that he at least won the 18th to earn a consolation half.

His caddie at Brookline declined to contribute to this book, but Olazábal's reaction at the time says it all:

'It was very sad to see, an ugly picture. The emotion I can understand, but I still had a putt to try to make and that display should not have happened. No matter how much emotion is going on you have to keep your feet on the ground. You should show respect to your opponents.'

Despite Lawrie racking up a 4 and 3 success over Maggert, by the time America started celebrating, the result of Montgomerie's match against Payne Stewart was academic. Montgomerie's caddie McLean knew pride was at stake, a chance to show the American gallery they had not beaten Montgomerie.

McLean very nearly didn't even make it to the course, though:

'It all nearly went very wrong for me on the Sunday. The day started by almost getting arrested by the Massachusetts police!

'We were getting a wee bit late and I went speeding up the wrong way, coming to the course. There was me, Paddy [Byrne, Lawrie's caddie], Adam [Hunter, Lawrie's coach] and my fiancée as she was then, Ilona, in the car. There was quite a lot of traffic building up outside the club. We'd driven the same road every morning and I knew there were two lanes going up to this intersection. I knew one was the right lane and one the wrong lane. The right lane was full of traffic and the wrong lane was empty. I went for it, steamed up the wrong side and cut somebody up at the end to get in. Trouble was, in the queue was a police car!

'I'd seen the policeman face to face because when I pulled up in the wrong lane I pulled up right next to him, thinking, "God, I'm doing the wrong thing here." But then I decided, "Bugger it, I'm going for it anyway." He pulls out, comes up behind me, lights all flashing. He pulls me over, jumps out of his car. He says: "What makes you think you can drive like that in the State of Massachusetts? Produce your licence. Get out of the car."

'I told him I didn't have my driving licence and the car was by courtesy of the tournament. He was by then starting to get really awkward. He was upset that we'd looked over at him and still made a break for it. I explained how we were running a bit late, but he wasn't interested. He didn't care who we were. I knew what I'd done wasn't right but we were almost at the gate of the club. I think he was ready to take us down to the police station, but he eventually relented, much to the relief of Paddy and I.

'If that was a bit of a laugh, when we got over to the driving range, it was anything but funny. The big screen wasn't good reading. Monty said: "Goodness. Look what's happening out there." You could see some of the guys pulling a hole back but they'd still be two- or three-down. It was looking very bleak. It's difficult enough to have to go out and play, but knowing you've got to win at all costs is a different pressure again.

'It was situation normal when we began the singles against Payne. Monty must have backed off four shots in the first four holes because of bad behaviour from the crowd. He was fired up but, to be honest, I saw a different side to him – the way he controlled himself under a huge amount of baiting and just rudeness. He handled himself admirably, pulled back from shots, regrouped, and went ahead and hit good shots.

'He went up early in the match, after about seven holes, and that helped him. He really wanted to win this match. In his fifth tough, tough, game, though, the crowd were getting to him a bit. On the ninth he had to pull away from a shot because somebody in the crowd shouted out very loudly, "Why don't you f*** off, you c***?"

'Payne Stewart had already said something to the crowd before this but at that point Payne was dismayed with the crowd's behaviour. He was embarrassed. He tried to find out who the culprit was, they found him and he was hoofed out.

'Monty lost that hole, I'm sure because of that. His concentration had been affected, I'm sure, and he lost the next one as well. He was beginning to lose it now. It really was disgraceful. But he gathered himself and fought back, got it back to one-up. Then we lost the 15th and even Payne was punching the air at that point. As much as he had tried to help Monty with the crowd, he got carried away as well. It's the moment. It's the way the tournament is nowadays.

'The whole outcome was now really, really close. The matches Europe were up in, they really had to hang on to. So I guess Payne was thinking he'd done his bit. He'd now clawed back into the game. That kind of euphoria by a player is understandable, that's fine. He has his punches in the air and that's it done and dusted. On we go to the 16th tee. It's still a golf game to the two of them. It's not war, like some of the crowd seemed to think, not a punch-up.

'Then Monty went one-up by the 17th. We were standing on the 17th fairway behind Ollie's match with Justin Leonard, and watched what went on in front of us. We couldn't believe it. It was just too much for words. We were dumbstruck. When everybody cleared the green, José missed the putt. We knew that was it all over. You do feel flatter now.

'Monty was still determined to win his match – to make a point. And it wasn't just to give a reply to the crowd. He'd already been robbed of a win at Valderrama and he had the feeling, "They're not going to rob me again. I'm one-up. I'm going to beat this guy."

'Bearing in mind the conditions he had had to play under and the duress he had been under, there was no way Monty was going to say: "Okay, we'll make it a half. You've been great supporters, great golf fans . . ." He was determined to make a point by beating Payne Stewart and getting his own back.

'Monty showed real steel and determination to do exactly that. I was very impressed that he could go on and win and make his point. He comes under a lot of fire from the press, public, whatever, that he doesn't handle himself well, but nobody in the world could have handled himself better than he did that week, especially that last day. It was unbelievable what he went through, how he survived it. He came out of it bigger than any of the idiots outside the ropes who were shouting and screaming.'

HOW WE REGAINED THE RYDER CUP

2002: THE POSTPONED MATCH

THE BELFRY, ENGLAND, 27–29 SEPTEMBER
EUROPE 15½ USA 12½

CAPTAINS: Sam Torrance (Europe)
              Curtis Strange (USA)

(European names first)

Fourballs (morning):
D. Clarke and T. Bjørn (1 hole) 1, T. Woods and P. Azinger 0
S. García and L. Westwood (4 and 3) 1, D. Duval and D. Love III 0
C. Montgomerie and B. Langer (4 and 3) 1, S. Hoch and J. Furyk 0
P. Harrington and N. Fasth 0, P. Mickelson and D. Toms (1 hole) 1

Foursomes (afternoon):
D. Clarke and T. Bjørn 0, H. Sutton and S. Verplank (2 and 1) 1
S. García and L. Westwood (2 and 1) 1, T. Woods and M. Calcavecchia 0
C. Montgomerie and B. Langer (half) ½, P. Mickelson and D. Toms (half) ½
P. Harrington and P. McGinley 0, S. Cink and J. Furyk (3 and 2) 1

Foursomes (morning):
P. Fulke and P. Price 0, P. Mickelson and D. Toms (2 and 1) 1
L. Westwood and S. García (2 and 1) 1, S. Cink and J. Furyk 0
C. Montgomerie and B. Langer (1 hole) 1, S. Verplank and S. Hoch 0
D. Clarke and T. Bjørn 0, T. Woods and D. Love III (4 and 3) 1

Fourballs (afternoon):
N. Fasth and J. Parnevik 0, M. Calcavecchia and D. Duval (1 hole) 1
C. Montgomerie and P. Harrington (2 and 1) 1, P. Mickelson and D. Toms 0
S. García and L. Westwood 0, T. Woods and D. Love III (1 hole) 1
D. Clarke and P. McGinley (half) ½, S. Hoch and J. Furyk (half) ½

Singles:
C. Montgomerie (5 and 4) 1, S. Hoch 0
S. García 0, D. Toms (1 hole) 1
D. Clarke (half) ½, D. Duval (half) ½
B. Langer (4 and 3) 1, H. Sutton 0
P. Harrington (5 and 4) 1, M. Calcavecchia 0
T. Bjørn (2 and 1) 1, S. Cink 0
L. Westwood 0, S. Verplank (2 and 1) 1
N. Fasth (half) ½, P. Azinger (half) ½
P. McGinley (half) ½, J. Furyk (half) ½
P. Fulke (half) ½, D. Love III (half) ½
P. Price (3 and 2) 1, P. Mickelson 0
J. Parnevik (half) ½, T. Woods (half) ½

THE CADDIES

DAVID 'MAGIC' JOHNSTONE (NICLAS FASTH 2002)

The caddie with the magic touch to his name began caddying at the tender age of ten at Turnberry, during his summer holidays and at weekends, to earn some extra pocket money. Electrician Johnstone served five years in the Royal Air Force and then, while rewiring the home of 'Turnberry George' Sprunt, Paul Broadhurst's 1991 Ryder Cup bagman, he was urged to try the European Tour. He began his caddying career in 1993, significantly serving Russell Claydon and Michael Jonzon before joining Fasth and helping the young Swede to the second place in the 2001 Open that took them to the Ryder Cup. His nickname is that of the superstar basketball player but was also approved by his mother. 'She said I could make my wages disappear in three days!'

Englishman Picking celebrated ten years in the caddie ranks when he appeared in his first Ryder Cup, alongside Welshman Phillip Price. Picking had worked in the motor industry, but jumped at the chance of caddying for former European TPC Champion Ross McFarlane, a member of his club, as a holiday job. Picking, a four-handicapper, soon decided on a full-time caddying career with McFarlane. Picking then joined up with David Carter and the highlights of this stint came when Carter beat reigning European No. 1 Colin Montgomerie in a playoff for the 1998 Irish Open title and then teamed up with Nick Faldo to win the World Cup for England. After the pair parted company in 1999, Picking again became a free agent. Then, in 2002, after the much-publicised head-hunting of Price's caddie Andy Prodger by Montgomerie, Picking took over the Welshman's bag.

J.P. FITZGERALD (PAUL McGINLEY 2002)

Fitzgerald, who prefers to use his initials instead of his name, John Paul, and his fellow Irishman McGinley teamed up full-time five years before the 2002 match, one of several touring partnerships formed between good friends. While he is now a professional caddie – he took over Darren Clarke's bag at the start of the 2003 season – Fitzgerald gave up his job working for a Dublin computer company after being persuaded to go on tour with McGinley. Playing off a handicap of two shows Fitzgerald is a useful man to have on the bag. He proved that in 2001 by helping McGinley become the eighth-best player in Europe while sealing his Ryder Cup debut. McGinley's memory of a certain vital putt that he had holed before on The Belfry's 18th green was jogged by his trusty caddie – and the rest is now history.

THE ACTION

'We read the putt. I said to him: "We had this putt two years ago at the Benson and Hedges International." I reminded him it didn't break as much as we thought.'

There was much to do, bridges to build and wounds still to heal, if the Ryder Cup were to reinstate the sportsmanship and accord that its inceptor had intended. The breathtaking encounter at The Belfry, scene of Europe's mould-breaking victory over the USA in 1985, meant Sam Ryder's soul could rejoice this time.

After the horrific events of 11 September 2001 in America, it was fitting that the postponed match will be remembered for its vibrant and thrilling golf. And that was a great relief to many pundits, who feared a decline in future enthusiasm for a match that was prevented from being played through terrorist acts in New York and Washington the previous year. There were more important issues in the world to digest than arguing golfers and unruly crowds.

In the opposing captains, the affable but avid Sam Torrance and the dignified but determined Curtis Strange, the Ryder Cup had two adversaries who would make sure the event was no life-or-death encounter. They were also two men who would ensure that it would be no anodyne go-through-the-motions exhibition either. With their preparation and communication before the match and their leadership during it, the 2002 Ryder Cup developed into one of the most pulsating affairs in the history of the competition, rightly called 'The Friendly Ryder Cup'. In the opening ceremony – marked by silent respect for the victims of the 11 September atrocities – Torrance pledged that the tradition of the Ryder Cup, and the game of golf itself, would be preserved. Strange pleaded for the spirit of the match to return. Their wishes were to be respected by the players and the gallery.

When the previous year's tragedy left America's team stunned and unwilling to fly across the Atlantic, the match was rearranged, with the same 24 players keeping their places. America had a slightly more experienced team, with three rookies, Scott Verplank, none the less one of Strange's two wild-card choices, Stewart Cink, and 2001 US PGA Champion David Toms. Europe's team contained four first-timers, two Swedes, Pierre Fulke and Niclas Fasth, Irishman Paul McGinley and Welshman Phillip Price. The home side, though, was a much more unsung outfit compared to America's stars.

Progress in 2002, after the postponement, did not change that scenario. It was true that some of the US team were off-colour leading up to the match, but a greater part of the European side were struggling badly in the months building up to The Belfry clash.

Colin Montgomerie, frequently struck down by troublesome back spasms, was not even certain of playing – just a week or so before the match. Montgomerie was not the only one struggling with injury. Bernhard Langer, making his tenth Ryder Cup appearance after a wonderful campaign to regain the place he lost in 1999, had had back and neck problems for many years. The German, too, kept the physiotherapists busy.

Another European with injury woes was Padraig Harrington. His most serious problem was a bad neck strain, incurred around US PGA Championship time, just a month or so before the match, that had caused him to drastically change his practice schedule. In the end, though, the super-fit Irishman won his fitness race, although his injuries and niggles in the weeks leading up to the Ryder Cup were still to inhibit him during the week.

Torrance's job was to knit his nationalities together and coax, cajole and convince his players they were good enough to beat anybody. Once again, by the time the match got underway, his side were no longer a mix of English, Scottish, Welsh, Irish, Swedish, Spanish, German or Danish, but European, not a side of 12 individuals playing in a team, as the visitors seemed to be. For instance, Tiger Woods wanted to practice early in the morning ahead of his team-mates. That could not have helped US team-bonding.

Woods needed plenty of practice to work out a strategy for the hosting course. Torrance, as is the home captain's prerogative, had ordered the rough on the Brabazon layout to be grown into the fairways around about the length the world No. 1 could be expected to drive. All the fairways were narrowed to try to neutralise the bigger-hitting Americans. The greens were not cut too short and the 311-yard par-four tenth hole tee was pushed back to discourage the visitors from going for the island green and racking up not only a glut of birdies but setting up eagle chances as well. Every fair and legal advantage Torrance could gain, he took.

Europe's captain was determined to finish where he had left off in 1985, when he holed the winning putt at The Belfry that finally ended America's domination of the Ryder Cup. Torrance had already changed the opening day pairs format, reverting back to a fourballs Friday morning favoured by Seve Ballesteros in 1997 at Valderrama. Ben Crenshaw had opted for a foursomes opener in 1999. The Europeans felt they could get off to a better start by opening up with fourballs instead of foursomes. It was to be a wise switch.

First up for Europe were Darren Clarke and Thomas Bjørn, playing Tiger Woods and Paul Azinger. Clarke had beaten the world No. 1 at matchplay in the Accenture World Golf Championship Matchplay in 2000 and in 2001 Bjørn had mastered Woods to win the Dubai Desert Classic. The crowd were in for a treat.

Azinger might have seen it all before but nerves showed for the player who just loves beating Europeans at the Ryder Cup, as he launched the 2002 match with a slice over the gallery's heads into long rough. Woods's two-iron took him into the right fairway bunker. Bjørn then settled his nerves with a composed three-wood to the left-hand side of the fairway. Clarke, though, then sent his opening drive with a three-wood into the same bunker as Woods. So the 34th Ryder Cup began.

There had been a small earthquake not long before the match in the West Midlands, prompting the staging staff to double-check on all the foundations and fittings of the numerous stands and equipment set up around The Belfry in the time leading up to the start of the match.

When Clarke's caddie Billy Foster arrived on the first tee he could feel the earth shaking again. He was soon trembling with anticipation after a wonderful shot from his man:

'I'd been telling Ken [Ken Comboy, Bjørn's bagman, who was making his caddying debut] just what to expect from a Ryder Cup, that it makes the British Open and Masters feel like caddying in a pro-am! But even I wasn't expecting the atmosphere when we walked to the first tee. It was sensational, unbelievable. Walking down the steps of the first tee, I've got to admit it got to me. My eyes had filled up with tears by the time we got to the tee. It was scary, but enjoyably scary.

'I don't how the players were feeling, especially the opposition. The gallery was boisterous all right, but this time in the right way. Their support was just fantastic, but it was a fantastic sporting atmosphere. It was the best Ryder Cup of all time for that.

'Ours was a dream draw . . . first game of the Ryder Cup and playing Tiger Woods. It could hardly have been better. Both our players were really up for it – and so were both their caddies, I can tell you.

'We had just over 150 yards from the bunker. It was a reasonable lie but Darren hit a magnificent eight-iron, came out perfectly with just enough club behind the ball to sand. It landed on the edge of the green and rolled on about seven or eight feet, pin-high. In the circumstances, it was a fantastic shot.

'Azinger had somehow found the green and I know we still had Thomas to come, but it was a wonderful blow from Darren with everything going on around us. The atmosphere was just electric, everyone willing Europe on. And it was still early morning, not long after eight o'clock!

'It was a great feeling to start like that but no sense in getting carried away. We've got a lot of work to do and Woods, you certainly know, isn't going to take that lying down. So it proved. He hit his approach shot very nearly stiff at the next.

'Darren kept his cool, though, and he holed his birdie putt to keep us one-up. Then he rolled in another on the third, three in succession.

'Clarkey and Thomas were really psyched up for it and they holed a lot of good putts on the way round on the first morning. I wouldn't say they dominated the match but they were certainly very confident. They kept their noses in front and then Thomas hit a great shot in to two or three feet and they were two up with two to play. You sort of fancied your chances then.

'Thomas really had his putting boots on. He'd holed one from about 40 feet earlier on and I thought he'd won us the match on the 17th. His putt from about 20–25 feet to wrap it up somehow seemed to go right over the hole, though, and didn't drop. Of course, as you'd expect, Woods then canned his from about 12 feet to take us to the 18th.

'Then Azinger stiffed his at the last but then good old Thomas did the trick for us, rolling in a 25-footer. It was a great win and a great boost for Europe. No disrespect for Tiger, but if the lads beat him in his first match it's a real feather in the team's cap. It's a great confidence-booster because of Tiger being far and away the best player in the world.'

Bjørn's awkward 25-footer did indeed do the trick. His birdie putt on the last, for a one-hole win, put Europe 3–0 up. Westwood and García and Montgomerie and Langer had already completed 4 and 3 successes.

Westwood's partnership with García proved another master-stroke by Torrance. The European captain had been warned by Jesper Parnevik that the Swede was going through agonies with his game and would be a high risk. But who then to pair with García?

The slump that Westwood was in, as his decline from European No. 1 to also-ran continued, gave no cause for optimism and it was assumed that he would play alongside Darren Clarke, his stablemate and partner of 1999, possibly just for fourballs. Instead of relying on Clarke to fire Westwood into a potent force, though, Torrance plumped for the volatile and ebullient García. Torrance's hunch that the young Spaniard would galvanise Westwood worked admirably.

As far as García was concerned, all he wanted to do was to win points whoever he was with. However, there was one small problem for García. His regular caddie was dogged by illness and was unfit to appear. Cue a call on the services of Edoardo Gardino, the Argentine golf professional who had caddied for Miguel Angel Jiménez at Brookline. The diminutive Argentine showed his pride in a novel way, wearing a flamboyant bandanna made out of the European flag:

'After 1999 I finished with Jiménez because he was very tight with the money, and I went back to caddie for José Coceres. I needed to play, though, so I decided to join the Alps Tour in Switzerland in 2002 and I was also giving some lessons at Crans sur Sierre, where I live, when Sergio called me. He told me his caddie Glen was ill and asked me if I could do some weeks on the bag with him. I was then able to enjoy my second Ryder Cup, caddying for Sergio. It was like a present from God.

'The aura at The Belfry was out of this world. It was a very emotional atmosphere. Now that I've played one Ryder Cup in America and one in Europe, I realise what a big advantage it is to be at home.

'I was so proud to be there and I had a great idea. I saw this very good-looking girl wearing a bandanna. I told her how attractive it looked and asked her where she got it. She told me she had made it, so I said to her, "If you make me one I'll wear it for the matches." The day after she comes and finds me on the range and gives me the bandanna. For protocol, I went to Sergio and asked him what he thought and did he mind if I wore it? He said, "No, no." He liked it. I was in the locker-room putting it on in the morning to go out in the first match, when Willie Aitchison [Europe's veteran caddie-master] spotted me. He said: "Oh, no. You cannot wear that. We are not Americans. You'll have to take it off." Then David Garland [Director of European Tour Operations and one of the top Ryder Cup officials] came up and said: "No, no, don't take it off.

He can wear that. It's absolutely lovely." So I wore it and it brought us good luck.

'Parnevik didn't want to play, so before the matches they were trying to get Sergio to play with Langer because they were not really sure about Westwood, who was also playing quite badly. The thinking was that Sergio would respect Langer. He might get annoyed and lose his calm with someone else, but not Bernhard.

'They practised together on the first day, but then on the second day's practice they put Sergio with Lee and they did very well and had fun playing together. Sam noticed that. Then we went up to the driving-range and Lee, who was there working with his dad and Pete Cowen [Westwood's coach], was struggling with his swing a little. Sergio told him to try to come more from the inside . . . this and that. He was trying to help Lee play to his best. So after that Sam decided to pair them together. It was a brilliant move. Lee and Sergio and Langer and Montgomerie were the strongest pairs.

'Against Duval and Love, Lee and Sergio did so well because they did everything together, worked things out so well together. The team talking for Europe was so much stronger. Sergio and Lee were like one player. When one is to play, the other is there, saying this and that and helping. The other two played much more on their own. In the 15 holes we played, Duval and Love maybe only discussed things one or two times, whereas Lee and Sergio were doing it all the time. Their partnership was much stronger. They were never really under pressure. Sergio, as he did all week, took on the tenth and went in the water but we still made a half, and it was virtually all over when Lee birdied the 12th to take us two-up.'

Montgomerie's caddie Andy Prodger was delighted at such an overwhelming opening success against Jim Furyk and Scott Hoch, as he registered his first Ryder Cup point with a player after an absence of 13 years.

The pair had come together in the May after Montgomerie and his long-serving bagman Alastair McLean parted company and Prodger left Welshman Phillip Price's bag. The move had not been with Price's approval and much diplomacy had to be observed around the Benson and Hedges International – ironically at the Belfry venue – to avoid a fall-out between two of Europe's Ryder Cup players.

Playing with Langer and his old friend Pete Coleman was a bonus. As Prodger reveals, Montgomerie's ploy of letting Langer take charge worked ideally. However, practice did not all go according to plan, although a relaxed Montgomerie handled one potentially embarrassing moment with aplomb. This Ryder Cup was not going to be any confrontation with the gallery:

'Our relationship didn't get off to a bad start in the May, finishing second to Tiger Woods, especially with Colin's bad back, but the season leading up to the Ryder Cup was a real mixture – course records and disasters. The majors were very disappointing.

'The back was always a problem. He tried different ways to get round the problem on the course. All he could do was to exercise and rest in equal measures. For someone like Colin, though, the word "rest" isn't in his vocabulary. He was always going to play the Ryder Cup unless the guy who looks after his back said he couldn't. His specialist was actually at the Ryder Cup all week, making sure he could play. Just a few days before the match there was still doubt. If his back had seized up at any time, he would have had to pull out. Colin and Sam spoke before the Ryder Cup and Sam told Colin he wanted him to play all five matches if it was at all possible. Sam said, before and after, that Colin was his "rock" for the tournament.

'We had a bit of a laugh in practice. Colin missed the green at the par-three 12th hole and before he could chip to the green, this guy in the crowd said, "I think I can chip this on, no problem." Monty overheard him and said: "Well, come on then, show us what you can do." The guy chips it a foot! Now Montgomerie's got to play his chip. He couldn't get anywhere near as close. Colin took it all in good part. He was very relaxed and had such a good rapport with the crowd, and it was a good way to loosen up.

'There were times of worry, though. On the Thursday morning, when we'd played just nine holes, his back was not very good. As soon as we came in at the ninth hole, he went straight off for treatment because his man had arrived from Fulham. His back was manipulated and it was fingers crossed then.

'We practised with Lee [Westwood] on the first day and then with Bernhard [Langer] for the rest of the time. Sam told him he was thinking about Westwood and Langer for partners, but Westwood got a good relationship going with García.

'Langer was always only playing four matches, though, so I wondered who we were going to get for the spare one, assuming that Colin would be on duty all the way through.

'Colin and Bernhard are such a competitive pair, you knew they were going to blend well. When one was out of it, the other one was in, but one point was crucial to the partnership. We let Langer be the captain! What he said went. He ran the show. Colin's got a lot of respect for him, so he had no qualms about that.

'Bernhard's a real stickler to detail, as everyone knows. Montgomerie doesn't mark his ball at all, but Langer always puts one dot beside the number. So Peter had to mark up all the balls, ours as well, to make Bernhard happy!

'For the fourballs, it's crucial that one of you is in the hole all the time, both of you if possible, and it worked out that's exactly what happened on the opening morning. And you have to hole putts at crucial times, and they did that, too.

'They needed to be at their best to beat Furyk and Hoch. The Americans were very determined. I remember Furyk taking off his shoes and rolling up his trousers to play one shot in the hazard.

'Monty putted well all week and he put them three-up, then Bernhard made a two with a great putt, about 25 feet, at the 14th, the par-three, and it was virtually all over.'

Six weeks before the match, Langer's caddie Coleman was *hors de combat*, nursing a broken right shoulder. Although he doggedly went against medical advice and resumed duties a fortnight before the Ryder Cup, Coleman still had to be rested for some of the practice rounds, and Torrance's former caddie, and Belfry assistant, Malcolm Mason, stood in. Coleman explains how he nearly missed the 2002 triumph:

'It was one of those very unfortunate things. I was in my garden picking some blackberries. The family had picked all the reachable ones but there were a few juicy ones left at the top, so I put up a ladder. It tumbled over and I fell on my right shoulder and broke it. When I went to the hospital, they said it could be eight to twelve weeks before I could work again. Luckily I got back within five or six weeks. I was in pain but I was bored with being at home!

'I had to let Malcolm do some of the practice sessions, though. It's probably the hardest week of the year. I was there Monday and you practice Tuesday, Wednesday, Thursday, probably with extra clubs in the bag. I did Tuesday and I was aching a lot. If it was going to pan out that we played 36 holes on the Friday, I wouldn't be in a fit state to go the full week. I had a nerve pulling on the side of my shoulder, which was causing a problem, and the physio people told me it was best to rest it, so Malcolm took over. I did nine holes on Thursday.

'It was a much more comfortable Ryder Cup for the caddies this time. The Ryder Cup's been up and down for me. I've been doing it since 1977 and some of the treatment we've had along the way has not been the best and other times it's been great. When they put us on Concorde we felt part of the team and the result proved it worked. But previous years when we were at The Belfry we were at a hotel down in Walsall somewhere, which meant an hour's drive in the morning and an hour and a half to get back at night. You're getting back at 8.30–9 p.m. and then having to get a meal, then getting up again at 5 a.m. – to me that wasn't fair treatment. You have to remember that, regardless of all the people involved around the team, the team is 24 people. We are the other 12. So you shouldn't have 12 people at The Belfry and 12 people staying over 30 miles away. So I for one was very happy we were billeted in The Belfry. If they hadn't done that, I wouldn't have caddied.'

'It was strange. Three years before Bernhard had been left out of the team and this year everybody wanted to play with him. We thought we were going to have a pairing of García and Langer at one stage, but I think Monty's strong personality won the day and he got what he wanted.'

As it was, Coleman very nearly missed out on Friday's start with Langer anyway. The night before, the German contacted Torrance as late as 10 p.m. to warn him that he had a neck strain and only had 85 per cent movement when moving his body left. He was not able to turn properly. Torrance had already gone to bed. He had to jump up and try to get hold of physiotherapist Dale Richardson. After a long search, Richardson was contacted, collected by car and brought to The Belfry. Just after midnight he managed to free Langer's neck spasms. He then had to stay the night at The Belfry so he could treat Langer in the morning. The draw had already been made. Torrance had everything crossed that his most senior player would be fit. He was.

Coleman went to bed on Thursday night blissfully unaware of his player's problem and only found out when he met up with him on Friday morning:

'Bernhard told me about his neck problem on Friday morning. It had apparently happened when he was trying to sleep. He'd lain awkwardly and it had progressively got worse. He told me they'd done some good work on it and he was going to give it a try. You could see he was still anxious on Friday morning. All you can do, though, is practice and see how it goes. He got through all right on the range, so he was ready to go.

'When we did get going, Monty and Bernhard were never really behind. In fact I don't think they were all week. They never had to press the panic button. That helped their thinking, enabled them to be a bit more positive. When Bernhard plays a normal golf tournament he's one for missing the green on the safe side and playing the safe shots, but when he's playing fourball and you're both playing well, he really goes for flags.

'Furyk and Hoch played well but Bernhard and Monty were just a class above them. Monty putted great. I think Monty felt more secure with Bernhard giving him lines and reading the greens with him. We were both helping Monty. And when Monty gets in a good vein of form he's pretty unbeatable. If ever there was something to do, Bernhard would push Monty forward to try to do it first, before him, then if it didn't work out, he would be the one with any pressure. But Monty just never played any bad shots to worry about.

'We got such fantastic support from the gallery, as well. The European crowds are just fantastic. American crowds, sad to say, give too many verbal insults to the players sometimes. You could always tell when a European player had played a good shot or holed a putt because the cheers were long and loud, but they cheered good shots from the Americans as well. The home crowd certainly gave us a boost. We had a good loud crowd. Having someone cheering for Monty, instead of slinging abuse at him, was a great fillip for him.'

So Europe were three points to the good. Could they make it a clean sweep? As the final match progressed, Harrington and Fasth gave Europe every chance. Harrington's caddie McNeilly knew his man had prepared himself to be a major cog in Europe's battle machine this time:

'He felt as though he was going to make a big contribution to the team and his experience at Brookline gave him positive feelings about this match. He felt he was an important part of Sam's strategy, advising, playing a major part in the team. Padraig had suggested that the greens should be kept slow, for instance, because the Americans would be better on faster greens. At Brookline he had taken a back seat and let it all just happen.

'Padraig has a lot of respect for Niclas. He'd played with him a few times and admired what a cool customer he was. He certainly wouldn't be scared, making his debut. When our match got underway, Niclas was to the fore as well. He holed some very important 15-footers, keeping things tight, while Padraig helped keep them in it towards the end of the round after they had gone 3-down after 11.

'I thought he'd done it on the last and we were going to halve the match, but Padraig's putt did a complete horseshoe around the hole and somehow stayed above ground. He was bitterly disappointed – we were both lost for words and shattered at that bit of bad luck.'

Fasth's caddie David 'Magic' Johnstone was, like the Swede, making his Ryder Cup debut. The Scottish bagman's young charge had sealed his place with a surprise second place in the 2001 Open Championship at Royal Lytham and St Anne's. If no one had heard of Fasth up until then, Johnstone was willing to bet he would become a household name at The Belfry:

'Finishing runner-up at the 2001 Open got Niclas into the Ryder Cup team and changed his life. It got him into the world's top 50 and the Ryder Cup in one hit. He went from nowhere to somewhere in the space of four days.

'Pete Cowen had told me the week before the Ryder Cup at Mount Juliet that Padraig had asked to play with Niclas in the fourballs and we practised with Padraig on the first day, so I was pretty sure that we would be playing on the Friday morning.

'On the practice putting green on Friday morning, he said to me: "Look, I know you're going to be nervous, I'm going to be nervous. Let's just double-check everything, get it right." I said: "Here, I've nothing to be nervous about. Just you worry about yourself. I'm fine." Off we went. It was a bit nerve-racking walking on to the first tee, but once Niclas had got the first tee-shot away, we were fine. I was pretty calm. At the end of the day, he's got to hit the shots.

'He played very well. The Americans got off to a great start, though, birdieing the first two holes. Toms holed a ten-footer on the first, after Niclas played a good shot out of the rough to 15 feet but missed the putt. Toms then birdied the second as well, so we were two-down early-doors.

'We then birdied the third to win the hole but Padraig was a bit out of sorts, really, and we were always chasing the match. Padraig didn't make his first birdie until the 14th. He was absolutely robbed on the last hole. He hit a fantastic putt and it was in all the way until the last foot when it broke a bit to his left. It caught the edge of the hole and did a 360-degree turn. You could see him welling up. He knew how much it meant. Three and a half to a half sounded much better than 3–1.

'That was pretty much the first day over for me . . . afternoon off, a few beers, cheer the boys on. We were all together. It was very sociable and friendly. There was a great camaraderie between both teams, caddies and players.

'At the end of the day it was back to the caddie room: "Well done, well done, commiserations," whatever the case may be. We had a few more beers. I'd say the European caddies were the dominant force in the drinking department over the Americans. If it was down to the caddie drinking stakes, we wouldn't have had to play the singles!'

Torrance was satisfied with 3–1 to take into the afternoon foursomes. Clarke and Bjørn had a quick turn round because they were also first out together in the afternoon foursomes. This time they went down, to Hal Sutton and Scott Verplank, 2 and 1. Soon after that setback, Europe regained their three-point advantage as García and Westwood again proved an irresistible combination, winning by the same margin against Woods and Calcavecchia, another telling blow against the world No. 1.

The afternoon honours swung back to the visitors, though, when Harrington and his new partner Paul McGinley lost out against Stewart Cink and Jim Furyk. McGinley was making his Ryder Cup debut, but he had tasted success with Harrington in 1997 at the World Cup, which they won for Ireland at Kiawah Island. Theirs was a natural partnership for Torrance, who quietly encouraged McGinley to put aside swing worries. While he had been in brilliant form in 2001, when the Cup should have taken place, he was at a fairly low ebb coming into the 2002 match, as his caddie J.P. Fitzgerald knew:

'Paul lost his way technically. I'm sure it was definitely not the thought of playing in the Ryder Cup that made him play poorly, more that he had lost the path of his swing. But the week of the Ryder Cup Paul seemed to forget about his swing problems. That was down to Sam, I think. Sam certainly lifted Paul to a level of performance he hadn't found in the previous couple of months. Sam did that, I feel, to all the players.

'Paul's form in practice was OK – not sensational, not bad. We practised with Padraig, Parnevik and Langer. We knew the night before the match started that we would be going out in the afternoon foursomes, so that was something to really look forward to.

'We both soaked in the atmosphere on the Friday morning and when it came to Paul's time on the tee it was a great moment. To me the highlight of the day was Paul hitting his first shot. I was hoping he would hit it 240 yards with a 5-wood – and he hit 260. Obviously that was pure adrenalin, but he hit a great shot up the fairway. That was a very special moment, with so many Irish tricolours, and so many Irish people standing around the first tee.

'Paul carried on hitting the ball really long, especially when it came to his tee-shots, but gradually the Americans started to get on top. I remember Cink producing a fantastic chip to a few inches on the ninth to put them one-up at the turn and after that we struggled. Padraig and Paul made a couple of mistakes and it was all over by the 16th.'

McGinley was disappointed, but Harrington's feelings went further than that, as caddie McNeilly remembers, resulting in Harrington missing the next round of foursomes:

'You could see that Padraig's form was really getting to him. He was getting disappointed in his game, frustrated with his form. He certainly wasn't hitting the ball as he would have liked. Things weren't really happening for him and it was starting to affect him. As a result of that, he decided he would not play the following morning. He told Sam he needed rest.'

While it was all up for Harrington and McGinley, Montgomerie and Langer still harboured hopes of bringing in a point for Europe against David Toms and Phil Mickelson. As the two caddies, Prodger and Coleman, remember, it was quite a match, much to do with a change in tactics, according to Coleman:

'Because of my shoulder pain I was off on the Wednesday, but when we practised on the Thursday, it caused quite a lot of hard thinking. In the end, when we played the foursomes on Friday afternoon, they actually reversed what they had been practising earlier.

'Bernhard is a great wedge player, so you've got to play to his strength there, and Monty's a good long-iron hitter, for instance, so they were working on that on the Thursday. That brought the playing of the tenth into question. If you're not going for it, you need a good wedge player to be playing the second shot. For the 12th, which is a long short hole, you need a good long-iron player on the tee. By the time they planned for Friday, they decided that Monty would play the even holes. It was the reverse of those tactics the day before. When they played the nine holes on Thursday, they realised they had to change round.'

Tiredness probably played its part in the senior European pair getting caught, feels Prodger:

'We came right out of the boxes really well and we were three-up, but as the match went on, you could tell the pair of them, Monty and Bernhard, were getting a bit tired.

'Around about the 15th hole the opposition suddenly went up a gear as well and there was a big turn-round. It was Bernhard's drive and he sliced it just short of the bunker on the right-hand side. They could reach the green in two and we couldn't, so we lost that hole to a birdie. Mickelson chipped in at 16 for another birdie and then the Americans birdied the 17th and all of a sudden we're all-square.

'Montgomerie hit a great drive at 18 and we got the advantage back because Mickelson took a driver on the last, and we thought that was too much club for him. Sure enough, he went through the fairway and in the rough. Toms, though, managed to get it on the front of the green. The pin was right at the very back. Langer's hitting a five-iron. Peter said: "You just need to draw it a bit." It looked like he was aiming a bit too much to the right to me, but he hit it straight and it went to the right of the green, rolled down the bank a bit. It was not a tough chip shot for Colin but, under those circumstances, they are all tough.

'Mickelson then caused a lot of gasps in the crowd and we all looked at each other a bit wide-eyed, because he opted to chip up from down the front of the green. He was easily 100 feet away, so I guess he felt he was going to get closer by chipping, even if it did raise a lot of eyebrows. I'm sure I remember Curtis actually hiding his eyes when he realised what Mickelson was going to do!

'He chipped well past, about 12 or 15 feet. Colin then played a rather average pitch to 15 feet by. They both then missed the putts and it was a bit of an anticlimax having to settle for a half. It was kind of a deflating ending to the round, but a half is a half and we're still undefeated. As Monty said, at least we didn't lose. The way Mickelson and Toms were going in the finish, we had to be happy with the half in the end.

'That was the feeling when we had a chance to relax later. We were a point ahead and on schedule. We caddies were well treated during the week. We had an open bar to eight o'clock, so we could chat away and discuss how tactics went and the like. It all helps. I felt that the European caddies were more of a team than the Americans, just like our players were.'

The half in the end, saved by Montgomerie and Langer in the face of the American fight-back, ensured Europe led 4½–3½. When Saturday dawned, a new European partnership was born for the opening foursomes of the day. Phillip Price, who had hung on like grim death to his place in 2001, was paired with Pierre Fulke, also making his debut. Swede Fulke had been one of the earliest qualifiers for his Ryder Cup spot, by virtue of a magnificent few months at the end of the 2000 season and the start of 2001. A total rookie pairing was a big gamble by Torrance, who stuck to his promise of giving everyone a game before the singles.

On Price's bag was the Englishman who took over following the very public head-hunt of the Welshman's previous caddie Prodger, four-handicapper Cliff Picking. Picking knew just how anxious Price was to prove he was worth his place, as one of the more unsung members of Europe's Ryder Cup 12:

'Phil's mood leading up to the Ryder Cup was one of nervous expectation. He was so keen to perform well. He'd earned his place by right and he wanted to prove himself, not just get carried on by the rest of the team, so he was delighted when Sam gave him his chance.

'He was struggling a little with his form all year, really, so that was a big concern, but he had worked so hard with his coach, Denis Sheehy, and his sports psychologist, Alan Fine. It was tough enough justifying his place, but being out of form as well placed a huge demand on him. Phil tried so hard in the weeks leading up to the Ryder Cup to get it right. What happened to him was more deserved than a lot of people will ever know.

'It was a real baptism of fire for me, too, but it was great to have such experienced caddies around me . . . Billy Foster, seven Ryder Cups, Andy Prodger . . . we all had plenty of really good chats that week. They all knew what it felt like to be doing your first Ryder Cup. The job was made easier by the advice I got and the way all the boys pitched in together. Staying on site was such an advantage. We were one big family.

'We practised all week with Pierre, so it was pretty obvious who we would be playing with. Phil seemed to take on a new air as soon as he arrived at The Belfry. He was far more confident, and the practice went really well. Whether it was the crowd, the event, whatever, I knew he would play well that week. We practised both formats, fourballs as well as foursomes. While theirs were two contrasting styles of play, they blended really well.

'On the first day, when we didn't play, Sam said it would be a good idea if we walked around with the matches and soaked up the atmosphere. It was a good idea. We got a real feeling of how everything works. For Phil, and me for that matter, it was a vital thing to do because no matter how much you imagine what it's like standing on the first tee and having your name called, you have no idea of the enormity of it all. It's like standing in the middle of Wembley and having your name called out by the crowd. We had passes, so I did a bit of both – walked around with the gallery and also ducked inside the ropes, to soak it all up.

'When we knew the draw, I sat down with Pierre's caddie John Hort and we swapped ideas on how we should play it. John might have been a Ryder Cup novice but he's been around a long time and has a lot of experience. Sam told Phil he would play before Sunday and that put Phil at ease. He didn't want to go to the Ryder Cup just to play on Sunday.

'It helped that the team had got off to a good start on the Friday. Phil was keen to get stuck in and make his contribution. So was I. We'd drawn Toms and Mickelson. Little did I know what a huge part Mickelson was going to play in Phil's week. Phil and Pierre had discussed who was going to take odds and who would take evens, on the tee, and Phil was quite relieved Pierre decided to hit off on the first. We joked about that. Pierre was fantastic, though. He showed very little nerves at all. I think Phil fed off that.

'We lost the first hole to a birdie, then got it back with our own on the third. There was nothing in it. By seven, eight and nine, we felt we were gaining the advantage. We went one-ahead with a birdie at ten. Phil had the honour of doing that. It was a seven-iron off the tee for him and then Pierre hit a wedge to about 10 or 12 feet. Phil being the putter he is, he rolled it in and that was a huge boost. That week Phil didn't need any help from me on the greens. Some weeks he does, but if he's happy with the lines and the speed he just goes ahead by himself. He knows The Belfry well enough. In it went. You could see the Americans were a bit rattled by not being in front.

'We had a very good chance to go two-up on the 11th, but Pierre missed from 6 feet unfortunately. Then on 12, Pierre missed from 10 feet. If we'd made those two putts we would have been going down 13 three-up.

'The turning-point came at 13, 14 and 15, where we had a little wobble. The Americans played the stretch well. We bogeyed 13 and 14 and they were one-up. Then on 15 we knew we were at a disadvantage. The Americans could get on in two and we couldn't. Pierre hit a great drive, but Phil felt he was really pushing himself trying to match the Americans and hit a poor shot. Mickelson stiffed a three-wood to a couple of feet.

'Two-down, but we still stood on the 16th tee thinking we could turn the match around. Although Phil missed the fairway and the Americans were in the middle of it, Pierre hit a fantastic recovery shot to the front of the green. David Toms then misjudged his approach shot and left his ball stuck right under the lip of the bunker, practically an impossible shot. When I walked past it I couldn't resist a little chuckle to myself. I thought there was no way they could get the ball out, even Mickelson. We're going to win this hole and go to 17 just one-down. But Mickelson, being the player he is, somehow manufactured a brilliant shot to within three feet. After the match, Mickelson's caddie admitted even he was amazed how Mickelson got the ball out of the bunker. In all the years he'd been working for him, he was still impressed with the recovery shots he can make.

'That was a huge disappointment. You don't count your chickens, but we thought we'd won the 16th once we saw the position of their ball. Two-down with two to play. Unfortunately, Phil then had to go for a hit-or-bust five-wood out of the bunker. It didn't come off, and we ended up losing the match on the 17th.

'But they had acquitted themselves well. Phil told me he felt he could compete in the big arena. He felt part of the team now. To Phil that was very, very important. Starting from cold on Sunday would not have been the same thing.'

Disappointment for Price and Fulke with a 2 and 1 defeat was quickly followed by an overwhelming victory for America. Woods, playing with his eighth different partner in Ryder Cups, and Love III won 4 and 3 over the strong Clarke and Bjørn partnership. Woods had drawn his first blood of the week. That put the Americans in front for the first and, subsequently, only time, taking the score to 5½–4½ in their favour. There was soon delight for Europe, however, as they hit back through García and Westwood, who overcame Cink and Furyk by 2 and 1.

The overall match was becoming tighter and tighter, with neither side, by now, giving an inch. García and Westwood were punching the air with delight one moment, but Cink and Furyk refused to bow.

Europe went one-up by the turn but it took two significant acts by the revitalised Lee Westwood, marked in the memory of playing-partner García's caddie, Gardino, to decide the issue:

'The key to winning in the end was the par-five 15th. Sergio hit a good drive and Lee hit a superb three-wood to the green. We two-putted from there, and we needed to. Furyk holed from 20 feet or more to tie the hole.

'Lee's contribution was very necessary because that meant we were still one-up, and then he holed a great putt on 16. That took us two-up because Furyk missed their putt. Two-up and that was pretty well that.'

It needed a win by Montgomerie and Langer if Europe were to regain their advantage. Hoch and Verplank were the opponents for the Europeans. It was another meeting between Hoch and Montgomerie. The home crowd was bound to be noisy, but, as Montgomerie's caddie Prodger points out, the gallery proved to be an extra weapon:

'We were still stinging a bit at being caught the day before, and I'm sure they were going to make sure it didn't happen again. But it nearly did! Just like the day before, we were out of the boxes, one-up after four and two-up after ten. Then Hoch and Verplank hit back. They won the 11th and the 15th and I wondered if we were going to miss out this time.

'It came down to a magnificent shot by Bernhard on the 17th. He hit a seven-iron to five or six feet and the roar was the loudest I've ever heard on a golf course – and I've heard a few. I didn't have to wait long to hear an even louder roar. It came when Monty holed the putt to put us back one-up playing the last. It was a noise I will remember for the rest of my life.

'This time we made sure of par on the last and that was good enough. That's as good as our opponents could do. There were the roars yet again. It was great for Monty particularly. The crowd was loud but fair, even the Americans said that. The noise of the crowd definitely helped. As Curtis Strange said, the crowd was our 13th man.'

Langer's caddie Coleman was, by now, in considerable pain with his shoulder injury, but he knew he would be off duty in the afternoon:

'Bernhard told Sam he could not play 36, 36 and then 18 holes, so it was agreed he wouldn't play in the fourballs. Bernhard put a lot into the morning match. It was a very high-class match. Monty putted very well to keep us in it and then Bernhard hit a great shot on the 17th to virtually win the match. I think we were six-under-par and that, for foursomes, is very good quality golf.

'Bernhard lifted himself to a higher plain that week. It was the best I'd seen him play all year. It shows what the Ryder Cup means, even to someone like Bernhard, who's seen it all before.'

Langer and Montgomerie's fortitude meant that Europe ended the morning with their noses still in front, leading by 6½–5½. Sticking to his intention of trying to give everyone a match before the singles, Torrance called up Jesper

Parnevik to play with Fasth in the fourballs against Calcavecchia and Duval. It was a different Parnevik to the high-flyer who had blended so perfectly with García in the previous Ryder Cup. Parnevik's form had drained away and so had his confidence in the summer and autumn of 2002. As Parnevik's caddie Lance Ten Broeck divulges, his man doubted he should be going to The Belfry, although the American maintains that stories circulated in the media about Parnevik asking to be replaced were exaggerated:

'Jesper mentioned to me a couple of times that he should call Sam up and tell him he was not really playing well enough to play. Mind you, whenever he said it, we were on the golf course, during a tournament, where he had maybe hit a few bad shots and was having a bad time of it. People say things like that on the golf course when things aren't going well. They don't really mean it. It's a bit like having a fight with your spouse. You say things you don't really mean! Somebody might have overheard him and I think that's how the stories got about.

'Anyway, we talked about it and decided it was not really in the spirit of the game to pull out like that, just because you're not playing as well as you'd like. My opinion was that the team was picked, the match was postponed because of dreadful circumstances, but if you're on the team, you're on the team. I don't care if you're shooting 90s, you're still on the team and you go ahead and play. I don't agree with players who are playing badly dropping off and making way for someone who's playing well.

'Jesper was still ready to go and he was a little disappointed, in fact, that he didn't play until Saturday afternoon. But Sam watched the practice rounds with the other co-captains and I think they just considered him too much of a liability to play in alternate shots especially. He was driving the ball wildly. He got his chance with Fasth, though. I'm sure Sam was determined to give everyone a game, so it was a relief that we were going out.

'Fasth played tremendous golf and Jesper played so-so, but they outplayed Calcavecchia and Duval over the front nine and their defeat was a tough loss. Even though he wasn't at his best, Jesper made three or four birdies. That kind of golf course, you should make a lot of birdies. It wasn't that difficult a course.

'The ninth hole caused the swing against us. We could have gone back to three-up there, but Calcavecchia holed a great putt to hold it at only two. Calcavecchia then played really well on the back nine, carried on holing a lot of putts, and gradually that wore us down.'

Fasth's caddie Johnstone feels that the Swedes should have racked up a point in the match, never mind suffering defeat, cursing, particularly the tenth hole:

'We came out like a train and we were three-up after seven. It could have been five- or six-up. On the fourth hole Calcavecchia holed about a 25-footer for a half and on six the Americans holed about a 25–30-footer for another half.

Then Jesper holed about a 25-footer on seven to put us three-up; we certainly could have been five-up standing on the eighth tee. The Americans won the eighth and then Jesper missed a real good chance on the ninth that would have taken us three-up at the turn.

'On ten, though, Duval opted to go for the green – and he greened it, 15–20 feet away. Niclas thought we should go in with seven- or eight-irons off the tee. He said to Jesper, "I don't mind going in with a wedge. I'm wedging it quite well." I couldn't understand that. I thought, "One of you has got to go for this."

'We went first, hit a seven-iron. I said to Lance, Jesper and Niclas: "Jesper's got to go for this. He's got to take it on." We were in the middle of the fairway, presumably wedging it on and having a putt for a three, but you couldn't leave the opposition with that kind of advantage. They had a certain two putts for a three and a good chance of a two.

'Jesper took it on, hit a good shot. He was really unlucky. It pitched on the green but didn't have enough cut-spin on it and finished up going into the water just where the green comes in a bit further. It was desperately unlucky. If his ball had stayed on the green, I'm sure we would have won the match. We would certainly have stayed two-up and maybe even gone three-up.

'Such is golf and such is life. Niclas hit a bad wedge-shot, hit the trees and also went into the water, leaving Jesper to try to pitch in from the other side. Even then it might not have been enough, and we had no chance. That proved a very important win in the end. The Americans won the 12th and played fantastically altogether on the back-nine. They birdied something like seven holes and that was hard to live with. They went from playing rubbish to playing fantastic and turned it round.'

That defeat squared up the match, but help was soon on hand for Europe in the shape of Montgomerie and his new partner Harrington, gaining revenge on Mickelson and Toms, a relief to Montgomerie's caddie, Prodger:

'We'd made up our minds we wanted to beat these two this time. They'd snook a point off us the previous day. We were fully aware of how the overall match was looking and Colin, I can tell you, was very much up for beating them.

'In the fourball you've got to have someone in on every hole, if not both of you. Harrington and Montgomerie played their parts perfectly. Montgomerie putted well all week, so he was going to make lots of birdies, we hoped, and Harrington had been making lots of birdies, so if it all went to plan, they shouldn't get beaten. It was a well-thought-out partnership and Monty had actually asked for Harrington.

'As with all Monty's matches, we got in front early on and then it was up to the opposition to try to catch us. Colin birdied the second and then we had to hold them back as they came back at us.

'Colin holed a long putt for birdie on the 14th. I was involved. I do get involved in putts, but it's more agreeing with what he sees. It's the same with club selection; I don't say a lot until asked. But I had made up my mind for this week, if it was wrong, then I'd say so. It's very important that if you've made up your mind on something, you go with it. You have to choose your moments. It's a bit hard for a 5 ft 5 in. person to start making out to a 6 ft 3 in. person that he's better than him!'

Harrington had been so dismayed with his form that he was happy to sit out the morning foursomes, having practised the night before until darkness descended on The Belfry. Practice had by no means made Harrington perfect but his determination to back Montgomerie to the hilt was undiminished, as his caddie McNeilly points out:

'Monty only had about a 20-minute turnaround after another gargantuan battle, barely enough time for any lunch, whereas Padraig had had all morning to prepare. He knew it was going to be crucial for him to be on the ball early on while Monty recovered.

'Padraig did that job well. He began very strongly, birdied two of the first five holes. Then Monty's game kicked in. He started taking over then. Padraig became a little bit of a back-seat passenger but he had contributed a very important part of the match. He allowed Monty to recover and get himself back into the right frame of mind because he must have been shattered after his morning match.'

Torrance felt he had just the pair to set Woods back on his heels again, the deadly duo of García and Westwood, with three wins out of three to their names. Another defeat for Woods, to take Europe two points ahead, would be a wonderful morale-booster.

As García's caddie Gardino recalls, all went according to plan for a long while. Then came two devastating moments late on, when the rivalry between García and Woods was plain for the enraptured onlookers to see:

'This was a great, great, great match. It was a wonderful exhibition of golf. They all played marvellously. The golf was very aggressive. On the tenth, Sergio was always going to go for the green. He had decided he would do that every time in the fourballs and in the singles, not in the foursomes. He hit on to the green first and then Lee said he would go for it, too, and also landed it on the green. They were both on, about 30–40 feet from the pin. Tiger then had to get on from the tee as well.

'It was still very close but we were just ahead. Then on the 15th, the long hole, Lee is on the green in two and Tiger is also on in two. We are one-up. Tiger putts up from a long distance and leaves it "given", no more than a foot or so. Is it given, not given? When Tiger looks to Sergio to see if he should pick up his ball or not, Sergio does a bit of an arrogant thing and turns himself around and starts walking, without looking at Tiger. So Tiger goes towards the ball to mark it. Sergio picks his ball up and throws it to him, quite hard. Tiger catches it, turns his head and looks at Sergio with the eyes of a killer. Tiger didn't like it at all. It was disrespect from Sergio to the best player who's ever played this game.

'Well, the 15th was halved in birdies and then on 16 Tiger hit a superb shot to six feet, but Lee holed from 15 feet for a birdie three. So Tiger's putt is to save going two-down with two to play. He holes it to stay only one-down. It was all so dramatic.

'On the 17th Tiger misses his drive and hits into the rough, but hits a superb approach and is only three feet from the pin in three. Sergio is on the green in two. Tiger wasn't going to miss his putt, but then Love chips in for the birdie four. It's up to Sergio now to try to win the match, but he three-putts. We are devastated. From being favourites in the hole, we've lost it. It had looked sure that the worst we could do was a half on 17. Now we've lost it and the match is all-square.

'On 18, Tiger gets away a big drive to take the pressure of his second shot, which covers the flag all the way. Sergio finds the back of the green with his second. He's a little too aggressive with his putt because he wanted to hole it and win. He gave it a little bit more than he meant to and it went 12 feet past. Lee also hit a very, very aggressive first putt and his went four feet past. Sergio misses his and then Lee misses his, too. Tiger two-putts. We lose the 18th to a par. It is heartbreaking. It was our match all the time.'

Having succumbed to a seven-birdie Woods, it was now vital that Europe should get something out of the last match, McGinley and Clarke versus Hoch and Furyk.

The match was back to all-square, so Europe now had a fight on their hands to avoid being down before the singles, traditionally America's trump card at Ryder Cup. Originally the final European pairing was expected to be Clarke and Bjørn again, but there was a surprise in store for McGinley and his caddie Fitzgerald:

'On Friday night, Paul just said he'd see me next morning. We'd been told we wouldn't be playing at all the next day. He was really disappointed. I was disappointed too, but I didn't show my feelings to him. I felt he'd acquitted himself quite well, but I realised it was a team game and we were all playing for each other. You had to stand by the decision.

'I said to him: "Well, look, just on the off-chance, let's go and practice." He had it in his mind to, anyway. I was watching the screen and could see Thomas Bjørn was struggling, playing with Darren. I said to Paul, "I have a feeling Thomas is struggling with his game." He'd said so the night before. "You've got a good chance of partnering Darren, so let's get ready just on the off-chance that happens.

'Apart from winning the Ryder Cup, that was my highest moment – when Derrick Cooper [one of Torrance's assistants] came over to us on the green on the Saturday morning and said, "You're out last, playing with Darren." The thought of playing with Darren made me really excited, and I'd have been equally happy playing with Padraig. They'd been successful enough in the

World Cup, but I'd known that option was out because I understood Monty had wanted to play with Padraig. So to get another chance, and this time with Darren, was fantastic.

'I've never seen Darren so fired up. Early on there were birdies flying everywhere. There was a big disappointment at the eighth, when Paul and Darren were both on the fairway and they had one ball in the rough and one in the water – but won with a birdie.'

(It was hardly surprising the European pair lost the eighth. Torrance revealed later that McGinley had come to him on that hole and reported anxiously that he was using a driver that was banned on the American tour. The Irishman was concerned his driver was illegal, bearing in mind the match was against the US. It also put the wind up Torrance for a time, before he confirmed what he'd 'confidently' told McGinley, that the driver was legal because the match was being played under European Tour rules.)

'We were still two-down with five to play. I think Scott Hoch is the best competitor I've ever seen. The scoring was phenomenal. Both sides, I think, were round in 62 better-ball, but Hoch was brilliant. Darren chipped in on 14 when he'd lipped out a short putt at the previous hole for birdie. That was crucial. We might have had too much to do if it had gone three-down with four to play. They had the better chance to birdie. Furyk had hit to about eight feet and we had both missed the green, but Darren chipped in and it was so important to win that hole.

'Paul birdied 15, another critical point. He hit a lovely eight-iron third shot to about 10 or 12 feet to make sure we got the half. Then on 16 he hit a seven-iron second shot to about two or three feet for another birdie. Fantastic. We were now all-square, but we were in for disappointment at the 17th. Hoch holed a 20-footer and won the hole. Darren was in a better position. He had an eight-footer for birdie but, unfortunately, missed it.'

With darkness fast closing in, a tactical ploy that was crucial in keeping the match at 8–8 by the end of the day came at the 18th fairway. As Fitzgerald reveals, it was not conceived by McGinley, nor Clarke, and even if the advice came directly from Torrance, not even by the European captain:

'So we're one-down again. The last was playing very tough, into the wind off the left. The tee-shots were OK, but it was Darren to play in first because Paul had the longer drive. The Americans still hadn't played. Bernhard Langer was out on the course watching, and he said to Sam that it would be good for Paul to play first and try to put pressure on the other boys. It was good advice. As it was the European team's go first, Paul was quite within his rights to do so, and he did. He hit a tremendous four-iron, 200 yards, pin-high about 20 feet away. It certainly did put the opposition under pressure and, thankfully, they both took five while Paul got down in two putts for the halved match.

'The European team were on a high and the 18th green was quite a sight, with everybody congratulating each other. We were all very excited. All the caddies went back to begin forecasting who was going to be playing who in the singles.'

The match was tied. Pundits, knowing America's strength in the singles, went in for some forecasting too. It was going to be a victory for the visitors, was the general consensus. That was without reckoning on crystal-ball-like foresight and Wellington-like strategy from Sam Torrance, who loaded his top guns in the first half of the draw. Torrance wanted a fast start. Playing in previous Ryder Cups, and being vice-captain in 1999, told the wily Torrance there was only one way to win the singles – ram home an early advantage and hope that the later players, arguably not quite as experienced or fancied, could pick off one or two points, too.

Torrance's strategy worked to perfection. The first name he put in the draw was Monty's, the Rock. Next he went for his young matador, García, whose youthful vigour and appetite for beating Americans would surely not be diminished by an unexpected and disappointing late setback the previous day. In third berth he wrote in the name of Clarke, his strongman, a player who had already proved himself the best in the world when it came to matchplay. All his first three men had played in all four pairs matches, so there was a risk that tiredness could play its part. But this was on home soil. The trio would be lifted in body and spirit by the crowd, Torrance knew. A rested Langer came next. Langer's record of ten Ryder Cup appearances spoke for itself. Torrance had gambled with his most reliable and proven players for his opening quartet.

Following on, he gambled further. In the middle of his draw he placed three men who could beat anyone in the world on their day, Harrington at number five, Bjørn in sixth spot, and Westwood playing seventh. Westwood seemed to have mastered his wayward ways, visibly lifted by the occasion. Doubts about erratic play were only in the minds of Harrington and Bjørn, both of whom had stepped down at one time during the pairs matches. Torrance had the utmost confidence in them. They were his back-up trio.

In 8th, 9th, 10th and 11th spots in the draw came the rookies, Fasth, McGinley, Fulke, and Price. Torrance's theory was that his first-timers could get a huge boost if they saw plenty of favourable blue figures on the board early on. Tail-end Charlie was the out-of-sorts Parnevik. If Parnevik could get anything out of his match, it would be a bonus. Surely it would not come down to the last match? If it did, Torrance was sure Parnevik would not let him down.

When the American names were matched, there was a huge gasp. Tiger Woods had been backed in last, to face Parnevik. Did Curtis Strange think it would come down to the last match? European followers were sure it would be all over by then. Woods seemed to be in a wasted slot.

As fate, and the pen of Strange decreed, Montgomerie was up against Hoch. The two had already met twice during the week but, more significantly, the last time Hoch had played Ryder Cup singles had been against Montgomerie.

Montgomerie's telling three-wood shot from the 18th tee at Valderrama had decided the destiny of the 1999 Ryder Cup. The three-wood was also in favour this time – several times over – as caddie Prodger divulges:

'When Colin saw the draw, he was looking for his name in position seven. He looked down there first, but he couldn't find his name at all! That was because it had been put in as just "Monty". When he did twig it, he was shocked that he was first off.

'On Sunday when he got down on to the range, not surprisingly he was first one there. The stand behind the range was full, and, apparently, it held 7,000 people. He hits one shot and there is enormous applause. Well, he thought he couldn't keep doing that, every shot getting clapped like that, so he pulled somebody out the crowd to hit a few balls. That went down well with all those watching from the players' room and the caddies' room. It loosened everybody up straight away, calmed a few nerves, I guess.

'We got on to the first tee and the roar from the crowd was amazing. We decided we would hit three-wood. That's his favourite club. It was probably too much club, but at least him and his club would be as one, as it were. He was confident with it and he ripped it 305 yards, left only a sand-iron to the green.

'He actually didn't hit a very good sand-iron, only half hit it. First of all, he'd had a wedge in his hand and I said, "No, a sand-iron's more than enough." Then he only half hit it, to about 30 feet, but he holed the putt and that got him off to the start he and everybody on Europe's side wanted. There was another almighty roar as the first blue figure went up on the board.

'They both had birdie chances on the second but both missed, then on the par-five Hoch hit a very good third shot and won the hole to make it all-square. They halved the fourth. Hoch was fighting a hook every time we played him, though, and on the fifth he blocked his tee-shot and had to come up short of the green on the right-hand side, because the rough was quite thick. He made a good chip. Colin said to me: "This guy's a gritty player, isn't he?" I said: "Yes, but if he's got one flaw it's his putting." He missed a four- or five-footer and that took us back to one-up.

'We were three-up by the 12th. I said to Colin on 13, "Your three-wood will leave you a perfect lob-wedge." So we took three-wood and did finish in perfect position for a lob-wedge, which he then nearly holed. Hoch was in the right rough and then went a bit long with his approach, so we went four-up. That just about did it. Monty closed it down with a four-iron to about 15 feet on the 14th.

'I looked at the scoreboard and saw that we were up in all the first six matches. Colin looked over at me and said: "At this time in Brookline, we were down in the first six matches. Perhaps it's going to be our turn this time."

'We had a bit of a rest and then I went to the 18th around about the time Fasth and Azinger and McGinley and Furyk were coming up. I was down at the front of the green with Sam, hopefully ready to congratulate him.'

By the time Prodger took his place, the roars of the crowd might have left those not in the know thinking that Birmingham was experiencing its second earthquake in a month. Twelve good men and true, led to the water, were drinking copiously. Torrance, by then, was probably already rehearsing his eloquent accolade to his team, which would take its place in golfing history.

Montgomerie's heady opening 5 and 4 success was timed at just before 2 p.m. – 1.56 p.m. to be precise. It was a whirlwind victory for the European talisman. Forty-five minutes later, give or take a couple of minutes, Harrington was claiming a similar 5 and 4 success over Calcavecchia. Such an overwhelming victory by Harrington was a remarkable turnaround in form by the Irishman whose swing and form had been seriously affected by injuries leading up to the Ryder Cup, problems which at one time put his appearance in as much jeopardy as Montgomerie's. Harrington's caddie McNeilly was, unusually, apprehensive about how his man would perform when they took to the first tee:

'Padraig still wasn't 100 per cent happy about how he was playing. Once again we'd gone through another gruelling session on the range on Saturday, right to 7.30 p.m. – in fact, until we couldn't see the ball. It was too dark. He felt his ball-striking was very poor. Normally he's a great driver but his driving was poor. He really was struggling. I think it was one of the few occasions I was actually nervous for Padraig.

'Going into the singles I actually felt worried because I knew, with the way he'd finished off on Saturday night, that he was just so disenchanted with how he was playing. He didn't really have a clue how to get things working satisfactorily at that point, no key. That was no way to be going into an important singles match. But it was unbelievable how Padraig managed to focus on trying to hit some sort of golf shot. He ended up deciding to hit everything with a cut. He'd lost his alignment. Looking back, it all went back to the US PGA Championship when he injured his neck. His whole system had got screwed up. It took a long time for him to recover from it and he was by no means recovered at this stage. I mean, there had even been serious doubts whether he would even be able to play. This was all related to that injury.

'Somehow, though, he got something working. He hit a great drive down the first. Then he hit a wonderful nine-iron in to about five feet. I'd been rolling balls all over these greens to check out the breaks and subtleties and he said to me, "What are you thinking with this one?" I said, "It's a double-breaker. This is going to be left-half." Padraig shook his head and said, "Oh my goodness, really? I see this as a right-to-left putt." I said, "Well, you can go straight if you want, but don't go down that right side." So he hits down the left side, hits a good putt. Of course, it breaks right-to-left. When I saw the replays of that hole, everybody's putts were from the right-hand side. Well done, David. "How 'we' won the Ryder Cup?" That was my contribution!

'At the second he hits a wedge into four feet. He has it to win the hole. I said, "Right, OK." I'm giving it the full run down, looking all over this putt. It's a pretty straight putt, no problem. But there has been way too much analysis going on. This is not the way we normally work. He misses the putt. It is not a good way to be starting out, missing chances like this.

'On the third hole, he's got a putt from about 20 feet. I say to him, "Look, I tell you what, let's just let you go about your own thing here because it really looks as though this isn't working out. It's way over the top and I think you should just carry on and do your own thing." He said, "I think that's a good idea." I thought ,"Fair enough." As it happened, Calcavecchia made a pretty ugly bogey and Padraig two-putted from 20 feet for his par, so we were one-up.

'He'd played great approach shots at the first two holes and missed the chance to win them both, and he didn't have to do too much to win the third. He then played really well. He hit a great seven-iron into about ten on the fifth, but Calcavecchia made a mess of that as well, so it didn't make any difference.

'At the seventh Padraig holed about a 20-foot putt from the back of the green for birdie, but probably the key hole was the eighth. We were off to a very good start but Padraig hit a bad drive, pulled it left, into the water. Calcavecchia took a three-wood off the tee. It was into the wind, short because of taking the three-wood, and he missed the fairway. Bogey was always on the cards for Calcavecchia then.

'As he left the tee, Padraig said, "You know something, if I can make bogey here, and he makes bogey, this is going to be such a big moment in this match." Padraig really ground it out, took a drop, took his time getting the drop he wanted. He had to come in with a five-wood on a hole that would normally have been drive and six-iron or seven-iron. He hit a good five-wood from the left rough, underneath the trees, into the left trap, not a bad result from what was a very difficult shot. Meantime, Calcavecchia had narrowly put his approach shot into the burn at the front of the green. I think his ball actually struck the wooden parapet and he'd missed the green by about 30 yards.

'Calcavecchia then hit a fantastic chip on to about 12 feet. Padraig hit a great bunker shot. Calcavecchia missed his putt. Padraig's got a very difficult five-foot putt but he holes it. There's the half that he wanted.

'That just gave him such a lift and on number nine he took charge completely with a birdie. His putt there was going like a train, though. It really rattled the hole and would have gone at least nine feet past if it hadn't dropped. That's four-up. He was never really in any danger after that.

'Number eight won it for him. Even though it was a bogey, because he came out of the hole with something, it kept his momentum going. He cruised from there. At 14 he finished it off in style. He hit a brilliant shot in to about seven, eight feet, holed the putt and that was it.'

Just ten minutes after Harrington's closure of his match at the 14th, Langer sealed his 4 and 3 victory over Sutton. As Langer's caddie Coleman observed at the time, the German's afternoon off the day before had done both of them the world of good. Apart from his own man's exhilarating display, Coleman reckons there was an attitude problem in the American camp that did not help team harmony:

'Bernhard looked completely fresh and ready for action and, I must admit, I was grateful for a break on Saturday afternoon. My shoulder had been throbbing like mad. There's only one way to describe Bernhard's performance: phenomenal. He hit the flag out on every shot and won his match in some style.

'The night before we were all over the moon with the draw. Having Monty, García, Clarke and Langer at the top put us all in a great frame of mind. They were the players who had been out there and done it. If we were going to have a chance to get some blue up on the board, that was it. It worked out exactly as Sam wanted. Once you get those blue figures up there and the crowd sense we're getting on top, it's such a great spur for the guys who've never been in a Ryder Cup before. I thought it was top-class planning by Sam. Curtis was out-thought.

'I know it's easy to say in hindsight, but I'd have wanted Tiger Woods out first, to try to get you off to a good start and then get him out there to urge on your team. Then again, you had to wonder whether that would have worked. I didn't like the attitude of Tiger – going out playing a practice round on his own and dressing differently from the rest of his team. His caddie didn't have the official bib on. The Europeans dressed properly, as befits a team competition. I don't think the Americans were a unit like us.

'When our singles started we were disappointed at first. At the second hole we hit it 18 inches–2 feet and missed the putt. I thought, "Oh no, not one of those days." Then at the next we hit it to two feet again but holed it. He kept the birdies coming, four in six holes and Sutton was done. He'd been well beaten the first time we played him in the 1985 singles and he was again. Bernhard was hitting it that close all day. I don't think there was anybody out there, including anybody in his own side, who would have beaten him.

'After we finished, I drove home. I needed to get back as soon as I could because my wife wasn't very well and my shoulder wasn't too good. I listened to the finish on the radio and celebrated in spirit, in the car.'

Within minutes of Langer finishing, García allowed a strong position to evaporate against Toms. García's caddie Gardino takes us through the enthralling encounter that saw the American team build up their hopes. Again, it was the tenth hole that provided the watershed:

'Sergio had played well all week. He had been very disappointed at losing on the last hole, especially as it was Woods, the afternoon before, but by the evening I think he was over it and couldn't wait to play the next day. We got off to a great start and he was two-up after the first nine. David Toms is a superb player and very, very good under pressure, so we were not taking anything for granted.

'On number ten, Sergio likes to hit the driver. That was the shot he really felt like playing there all week. Not many people wanted to take it on because of the tee being back, but Sergio was comfortable going for the green. He hit a good drive and his ball catches the right edge of the bunker, pin-high. It finishes up just one yard from the bunker. If it had gone in the bunker, he would have made a three, no doubt about that. But he was on a downhill slope a yard past the bunker and with all the grass across the ball, so it was difficult to control that shot. It was fast. He hit a little bit in front of where he wanted to land the ball and left it 15 feet short. He missed the putt. Toms had laid up and got close with his wedge. He made birdie. That was a blow. We went to the 11th only one-up.

'At the 11th, Toms hit a wonderful second shot, nearly made a two. His putt was given. Sergio then missed from eight feet for the half and suddenly he is now all-square. They are playing wonderful golf, but Toms has the edge and by 17 Sergio is still one-down and he just misses on the left. He was long and his ball just ran out. He has a difficult lie and hits a six-iron, just catches part of the bunker and the ball finishes up in the sand. It was a real shame because it was going to have a lot of roll. If it had carried another yard instead of just catching the bunker, his ball would have rolled right up to the pin. He has a 25–30-yard bunker shot and plays it really well. His ball finishes up within four or five feet, pin-high, but he misses the putt.

'That means we go to the last still one-down. Sergio desperately wants to get something out of the match and puts everything into his drive. It hooks, though, into the water. That's it all over. He catches the next one heavy; Toms only needs to make the green. He does. Sergio concedes the hole from the middle of the fairway. It was a great match, though. Sergio was five-under up to the 18th tee and Toms was six-under.'

That took Europe back to only two points ahead and within the next 15 minutes that situation did not alter, as Clarke and Duval finished off an epic struggle, sharing a point. Clarke's caddie Foster had a good feeling about the way things were going to go when he glanced up at the scoreboard:

'We got great vibes straight away when we saw the draw. It was almost the reverse of Brookline. You looked at the draw and felt there was every chance of making at least five points out of the first six matches if we had a good day. And if there are four or five blues on the board, it's going to give the rest of the team a whole load of confidence. It could be a snowball effect.

'In fact, it was a bit disappointing for Darren because he should have made more than half a point from his singles. He just missed everything. He'd be the first to tell you that he should have won the match fairly comfortably, 3 and 2 maybe, something like that. He kept setting up the chances and then missing them by missing the putts. Then Duval came back at him and it almost looked like we could lose the match in the end. On 17, Darren holed a 20-footer to stop going one-down. They both made good up-and-downs to halve the last and halve the match.

'It was paramount not to lose that match, though. It was a big half-point because there might have been a bad effect on morale in the end if we'd lost two points out of the first three matches, even with all the favourable scoring at that stage. The momentum may have been lost with the loss of a whole point in our match.'

Within 20 minutes of Clarke stepping off the 18th, his earlier partner Bjørn was taking Europe three points ahead again. A great show by the Dane saw him two-up by the turn against Stewart Cink. Then the American fought back to cut the deficit to only a hole by the 15th. Bjørn refused to be rattled, however, and, showing no signs of the fallibility that had seen him replaced by McGinley in the previous day's fourballs, he closed the match down with a wonderful shot to five feet on the long 17th. A 2 and 1 success for Bjørn took the match to 12½–9½ in Europe's favour. Just over half an hour later, the lead was only two points again, as Westwood lost his match by the 17th to Verplank, fully justifying Strange's faith in picking him as a wild-card.

On the course, though, a pivotal match of the bottom half of the draw was nearing its close. Price and the then world No. 2, Mickelson, were around the 15th hole and Price, confounding all predictions and odds, was in the driving-seat against the deadly left-hander. Price's caddie, Picking, knew his man would have to be in the perfect frame of mind to win and that's where a little sports psychology helped:

'I thought "fantastic" when I heard the draw, first because we were playing Mickelson, No. 2 in the world, second because I felt it could either come down to us, or the match in front, or the match behind.

'Phil did say to me he didn't want to be lost in the middle of the field. He wanted to count. He phoned me very excited, very keen to get out there. All the European caddies got a huge boost from the draw. We thought Sam had got it right and Curtis had got it wrong.

'On Saturday night I was very nervous and didn't sleep. I didn't really sleep well all week, not because of being nervous on my first Ryder Cup but because the adrenalin was flowing so much that I didn't want to sleep. Darren Clarke had said to Phil that there was no feeling like the Ryder Cup. Phil agreed, and I said it went for the caddies as well.

'We caddies were sharing among ourselves the checking of pin positions and bits and pieces on the course. By the time we were ready to go out, I had all the information I needed – pin placements, spaces behind the pin and to the sides, and carries. But before that, I went to the gym, just to get away from the razmatazz. It was important for me to have a few quiet moments on my own, thinking out how I wanted the day to go.

'I met up with Phil on the range. Phil's not a great practiser before he plays. He only needs about 40 minutes to warm up. A good thing with him during the week was that he didn't really change his routine. Alan Fine, his psychological coach, was around all week and he was a big influence in keeping Phil mentally in place. He was there for Phil on Sunday. I had a little chat to Alan, too. We worked on how to keep Phil motivated and focused on what he had to do, and not let him get distracted. We have a few keys we use, just a few positives, to keep Phil focused and his mind on the job. Alan reminded me I had to come out with the right phrase at the right time to encourage Phil, take his mind off any negative thoughts he might have. It worked fantastically all week. So rather than hit thousands of balls and wear himself out, Phil readied himself that way.

'When we stood on the first tee, I thought, "How on earth can Phil take the club back?" There must have been so much adrenalin coursing through his body. He managed to make contact, not the greatest strike in the world, and got down the first to halve with a par. Mickelson missed a good birdie chance.

'The fourth was a bit of turning point mentally. Phil hit a poor drive into the bunker and Mickelson was on the fairway. Knowing Mickelson was going to make at least par, we tried to take on a shot we probably wouldn't have chanced in a tournament. It hit the lip of the bunker and found the rough. Mickelson was in the middle of the green. Then Phil hit one of his best shots of the day, a five-iron. It was only about 150 yards to the flag, but Phil's great at manufacturing shots and he hit out of a very poor lie to about 12 feet. I thought it was a wonderful shot, although the gallery probably didn't appreciate how good it was. He then sank the putt and they did appreciate it then because Mickelson missed his birdie chance.

'That was a very, very good four for Phil. Visibly, it shook Mickelson. I could see that clearly. He didn't expect Phil to par that hole and thought he would win it. I think it was at that point that Phil Mickelson realised he had a game on his hands. It wasn't going to be a walk in the park.

'On the fifth, Mickelson hit a poor drive and was never really in the hole. First blood to us. Then, if the fourth was a key hole, the sixth was even more so. Mickelson was in the middle of the fairway; Phil's ball was on the edge of the hazard. He was actually standing in the hazard and couldn't ground the club. Mickelson hit to what looked about three left of the flag. We had been talking about how Phil could play his safely to the middle of the green. After Mickelson had hit, Phil said to me, "How close has he hit that?" I said, "It's very close." He said, "Perhaps we've got to reassess this shot." I agreed we should try to match Mickelson's shot or perhaps at least try and get it a bit closer than we had intended. Phil sucked in his breath and hit a fantastic shot, an eight-iron, just outside Mickelson's, about four feet right of the flag. The ball had been above his feet, he couldn't ground the club and he'd hit a once-in-a-lifetime shot. I told him: "You've just hit a career golf shot."

241

'We walked up to the green. Mickelson was very close. I was surprised Phil didn't give him the putt, he was that close. Phil went ahead and rolled his in for the three. He didn't say anything to me, he was so focused, but I was saying to him, "Make him play, make him play," words like that. He didn't need to answer me. I could see he was taking it in and he'd already made up his mind anyway. He asked Mickelson to putt. Surprisingly, he missed it. That was huge for us. I said to Phil afterwards, "Why did you make him putt?" He said: "Well, anybody can miss a three-foot putt, even Phil Mickelson." It wasn't three feet, actually. It was probably shorter than that.

'They looked like halving the seventh. But I said to Phil, walking down to the green, "You've got him rattled, making that birdie, keep the pressure on. Make him play, make him putt out." Mickelson was shaking. Uncharacteristically, he hit his first putt about 15 feet past the hole. It's a difficult green but it was a very poor putt. We won it with a par. From looking like being all-square for three holes, we'd won the last three and we were three-up. For Phil that was a huge confidence boost, beyond our wildest dreams really.

'The eighth was halved and then there was a real incident at the ninth, where you could really tell the match was getting to Phil Mickelson. They were both on the fairway but Mickelson hit a great second, a three-iron or four-iron, to about three feet below the flag. Phil hit a four-iron to about eight feet right of the hole.

'The 9th and 18th, which is close by, are natural arenas and there was a lot going on. Clarke and Duval were coming up 18 and we had a big gallery. Mickelson's caddie went up to the referee, Zorro [one of the European Tour's tournament directors, Spaniard José Maria Zamora], and asked if Mickelson could putt out first. Phil's [Price's] game is not slow but deliberate, not the fastest in the world let's say, so I can only assume the pace we were playing could have been a little off-putting to Mickelson. He wanted to get on with it, so his caddie asked if he could play out of turn – I think they'd had a discussion and Mickelson had asked his caddie to try and speed things up. Of course, Zorro said he couldn't do that in matchplay. Phil was quite entitled to wait for the crowd to calm down before he played. We stood on the ninth green for what seemed like an eternity, while Darren Clarke and David Duval finished their match on 18 before we hit our putt. This, I think, rattled Mickelson as well. Phil was oblivious to this and played at his own speed. Well, Mickelson holed the putt and we missed ours, so we were now only two-up going to the tenth.

'The tenth was another big moment. The wind was very, very awkward around the corner, with the grandstand and the trees affecting things. Mickelson misjudged his tee-shot and ran out of fairway. We took note of this, made sure we played safe and laid up a little further back, to leave us a full shot in. Phil then hit a wedge to no more than 15–18 inches of the hole, a fantastic shot. Mickelson really couldn't match that out of the rough and hit over the back of the green. Phil's putt was conceded and we were back to three-up. To get the hole straight back after losing the ninth showed just how hard Phil Price was focusing and how much he was determined to win.

'The par-three 12th was another key point. We missed the green and Mickelson hit quite close but Phil managed to get up-and-down from quite a difficult lie and Mickelson couldn't better the three. That kept the pressure on.

'They all seem like key points but the 13th was another one. We were in trouble off the tee and Mickelson had hit it very close again in two. I'm sure he felt he'd done enough to win the hole, but Phil hit a magnificent recovery to about eight feet and holed the putt to match Mickelson's birdie.

'It kept the pressure on. "Keep making him play" – that kept running through my mind. At the 14th we were still three-up and they both made par. We again had to chip and putt for par, while Mickelson two-putted.

'Now 15 isn't a great hole for us because Mickelson can easily reach the green in two, and we were struggling. We made a decision that we'd be far better pitching in to the green, rather than taking on a big second shot. So we decided to lay up and give ourselves a chance and at least make Mickelson hole his birdie putt. When Phil did get on for three and missed the putt, though, two putts were good enough for Mickelson to win the hole.

'Even though we're only two-up now, when we talked about things, Phil was still confident he could win the match. On the 16th tee, Phil Price's confidence was sky-high. He reflected that in the swing he made under the severest of pressure. It hadn't been a great hole for us all week. We'd struggled to hit the fairway, which is hard to hit anyway, all week. We hit a three-wood to the middle of the fairway that I thought was one of the best swings he'd made all day. Mickelson matched that. They both hit the green in similar positions.

'Then came the winning putt, fantastic. As Phil told me afterwards, he was trying to roll it down just next to the hole, or at least lag it up and not be silly and take five. Keep the pressure on Mickelson. It went in! It was at least 20 feet.

'It was all a bit surreal as I watched the putt on its way. You know if it goes in we've won, but when it happens you still can't believe it. You think, "Shall I celebrate, what shall I do?" It's not a conscious decision, but you do start celebrating and then you think, "Oh hang on, he's still got a putt for a half." After all the fuss at Brookline, we calmed down very quickly. The emotion Phil showed after that putt went in was about as emotional as he'd been in his career. I don't think he even knows what he said at that moment. It was an unbelievable moment, a release from all the tension. Not just from that week but also from the previous ten weeks. It all came out in that one moment.

'Then, very quickly, I gathered myself and said to Phil: "Look, we could be going down the 17th still," so we started talking about we would do down 17, before Mickelson tried to hole his putt. I tried to bring Phil straight back down, not get carried away with the moment. Mickelson missed. So then we celebrated again. We could properly now.

'All the way round I was looking at the scoreboards and saw how things were going. I knew that ours would be a key match and have a big effect. I wanted Phil's win to go up on the board, the quicker the better, to help the rest of the team still out there.'

Caddie Picking couldn't wait to get to the 18th green to watch the finale, now his player had set Europe on the brink. He arrived breathless at the green at about 4.45 p.m, ten minutes or so after his match finished, having heard a huge roar as he approached which he thought signified the act of victory for Europe. Instead he was greeted with incredulous looks and worried comments from his caddying brethren. Europe had still not sealed their success. Niclas Fasth had been denied at the death. The match was still, at that stage, in a melting pot.

For Fasth and his caddie, Johnstone, it had been yet another sickening blow handed out by Azinger, on whom they were looking to gain revenge:

'The draw couldn't have worked out better. We couldn't have picked ours any better, because Azinger put us out at La Costa in the Accenture World Matchplay early in the season at the 20th hole, the second extra hole, in the third round. It was the first time Azinger was in front for the whole match. We were cruising, in control, but he chipped in a couple of times, holed some long putts. We'd been two-up with four to go, and finished up getting beaten, so we had a score to settle. Niclas was delighted with the draw we got.

'At the first hole, Azinger stiffed it and we've hit a half-decent shot, come up about 15 feet away on the apron. Niclas holed it for the half. That was a great boost to begin the round.

'On the next hole they were both in good position off the tee but I don't know whether Azinger got the wrong yardage or what, but he "airmailed" the green by 20 yards. He's 30 yards past the pin. I thought he'd struggle to get up-and-down and advised Niclas to just get it on the green. But he took a brave line, because I would have played it further right, but he stuck it to six feet and won the hole.

'Then Niclas holed a long putt to win the third as well. So we're already two-up, and then on four we came up in between clubs and went for the longer one. It went long. That left Niclas a really tough up-and-down, he had to throw it all the way there, and the green was all running away from him. He stiffed it to stay two-up.

'On the fifth hole our second shot just caught the downslope and ran to the back edge of the green. Azinger's not even on the golf course. He's missed his tee-shot, way right, in the rough, but he got a free drop on a "line of sight" ruling because of a crane. He's then able to play from the semi-rough on the sixth, hits his approach to about five yards short of the front of the green. When he pitches on, it looks as though his ball's going to sit on the edge of the cup and he turns away in disgust. He walks to the ball and, as he's halfway there, it falls in the hole. He starts dancing around and celebrating. He wins the hole without playing a golf shot really, other than the pitch.

'That was a bit soul-destroying. On the next hole, though, we feel a little better. Azinger's 45 feet away and lags it up six feet short. We've got about a 20-footer and miss. Azinger then misses his six-footer, so we're back to two-up and pretty much in control.

'We halved seven but on eight Azinger's at it again. He snatched the half here, really. Both of them are in the rough. I thought Azinger was too far back to get over the hazard, unless he gets a flyer. I had a look at his ball as I went by, and I didn't think he could get it there. But he opted to go for it. It finished in the hazard, but we don't know it's in. We just know it's not over it. Niclas said: "What do you think? Shall I just pitch out?" I said, "Well, we don't know where his ball is. If you think you can get over, then go for it." He said, "Yes, I can get over, but I don't think I can do much more than that." So I said, "I would go for it because if you can get over it's leaving either a chip or a bunker shot." So he did, hit a good shot, lost it a wee bit right and found the greenside trap. Azinger is in the hazard, drops back, pitches to about ten feet. We hit a decent enough bunker shot to about six feet. Azinger holes his putt, we miss ours. A half in five.

'After another half on nine we did the same thing as we did the day before on the tenth. It was exactly the same shot, exactly the same club, just a smooth wedge – pulled it into the water! Only one-up.

'On 12, Azinger's hit a really good tee-shot to about ten feet, pin-high. We're 20 feet away. Niclas hits a good putt, misses it. I had Azinger down for holing his. I really thought it would be all tied up. He left it short. It was a poor putt, bang on line but short. To me that's criminal in matchplay.

'We got a bit of a let-off there. Then at the 13th, we've hit a good drive and Azinger's right. He gets a flyer out of the rough and goes to the back of the green and we've had an element of luck with the pitch, on to the fringe, but it's popped forward to about eight feet. Azinger misses his and we have this eight-footer to go back to two-up. I'm thinking if we can get this, we're going to be hard-pushed to lose the match from here.

'Now we get some controversy. Azinger and his caddie were standing too close to Niclas, and where the sun was, their shadows were casting on the green – just a yard short of Niclas's ball. With him using a belly putter, he could see the shadows and they were distracting him. So he asked them if they could move. Azinger's caddie was a real nice guy and he apologised, said: "I'm really sorry, Niclas," and stepped back. Azinger didn't budge. Niclas went back to his putt but he had to come up again and he looked over at Azinger. Azinger looked back at him and said: "What?" Niclas said: "Your shadow. I asked you if you could move." Azinger turned away. Now, I don't know whether he realised

where I was, but as he was backing away he said to his caddie: "F***ing prick."
I said to him, "Excuse me?" He said to me: "You heard me." I said – I was
whispering so's not to distract Niclas – "Well, I thought I heard right."

'Anyway, Niclas holed the putt. I said to Azinger: "The man's entitled to do
that." He snapped back: "I wasn't even in his f***ing line." I said: "Whether you
are or not is irrelevant. If he thinks you are, he's entitled to ask." I was making
sure Niclas was out of earshot while this was all going on, so that it wouldn't
have a detrimental effect on Niclas. But Azinger was not going to rattle me. He
marched off. There was a bit of an atmosphere after that, on the way in.

'I don't suppose Azinger was any happier at 15. Niclas played a tremendous
shot there. He missed the tee-shot left into the heavy. He had a one-yard hole
to go for and it had to be hooking, under branches and round the corner, to get
us back over the hazard on the other side and give us a decent chance of
knocking it close. Niclas pulled that shot off superbly and that meant we were
now in line with Azinger, because he couldn't get up on to the green either.
Azinger hit his real close, though. We missed our putt. I could not see Azinger
missing this one as well. It was no more than 3½–4 feet. He did, though. I
thought: "Well, we've had two let-offs now. We cannot lose this." We're two-up
with three to go.

'At 16 Niclas elected to go with an iron off the tee, purely to make it easier to
hit the fairway. It would leave us one club longer, probably, going in. You could
hit three-wood. You couldn't hit driver because driver was going to leave us in
no-man's-land, too close. Three-wood would probably have left us with a
wedge, but with a one-iron off the tee, it would be a nine-iron, eight-iron at the
most. He missed the fairway! That was the cardinal sin with an iron. Azinger hit
a good tee-shot and we couldn't get up to the green, so Niclas could only move
it forward. He hit a poor pitch. We were 40 or 50 metres away and he left it 6–7
metres short. So we duly lost the hole and we're only one-up.

'On 17 we hit an enormous tee-shot and it was cutting, as it needed to, but
not enough. It was probably the wrong club, in hindsight. We should have
probably hit three-wood because Azinger went first – and he was in the left
trap. We knew he would be three shots to the green from where he was. I
thought three-wood would be struggling to make the carry on the bunker on
the right-hand side. Richard Boxall was on-course commentating with Sky and
he told me that Azinger was knackered, under the lip, and he wouldn't be able
to move it much more than 40 yards, he'll not get across the hazard. I thought,
"Well, that's perfect; he's even struggling to get up in three." He's going to have
to hit a quality shot with a long iron or a wood even.

'Niclas asked where he was and I said: "He's played out but it's still him to
play." Azinger hits four-wood, just misses the green, right. It's a good shot for a
four-wood. He's eight, nine yards right of the pin and just off the putting
surface, but he can putt it. We went for just short of the hazard, a decent shot,

just ran out through the fairway in the semi-rough. Fine, pretty much spot-on a nine-iron. We don't have to hit it hard or easy, it's spot-on, and it can't go long, either. He hit a good shot in to about 15 feet. Azinger chips his, left it about 4½–5 feet short.

'All through the tournament and the weeks previous, the way we had been reading putts was, I was looking at them, he was looking at them, and then he would say to me, "I've got such and such," and I would either agree or disagree. Then we would evaluate the putt again, and maybe change his line. On this putt, I looked at both sides and I was convinced, 100 per cent, that I had the line. I used a different protocol. I said to him, "Niclas, I've got this line spot-on if you're interested." He said: "I am. What have you got?" I said: "I've got two balls on the right." He said: "I like it." He hit the putt – but the ball jumped twice. It jumped when it was two feet in its travel and it went up in the air after it had travelled another three feet. His putt came up a ball short. I was convinced it was the right line. Just one more roll and it would have been all over. It was for everything. Now we still have to go down the 18th.

'Azinger hits a great tee-shot, so now the pressure's on us and Niclas backs off his drive a couple of times. He asked Sam if anybody's ball beforehand had run out left of the bunker. He was hesitating because he was wondering if it was three-wood. Sam told him nobody had run out there. I told him, "As long as you're left of the trap, you won't run out. The absolute worst you'll be is the semi-rough." He hit a good tee-shot.

'We get down there and we're to hit first. I said to Niclas: "The only thing you can't do here is come up short because then you've got a 20-metre putt if we don't get on the right level." To me, we've come up with the drive bang-on for a five-iron. With a flag at 191 yards, wind coming in off the right, playing uphill about four or five yards as well. In effect, the shot's playing about 205 yards. Well, we hit a five-iron about 200 yards, so it's a good five-iron for us to get there. I said to him, "You can hit that pretty much solid; it can't go long. You've got to get it up." He hit a great shot under the circumstances, faded it against the wind. I couldn't believe how far up it pitched – six, seven yards past the flag, and just stayed there. I knew we had a tricky putt, but "job done" really. We're one-up, we've greened it and we're on the right tier.

'Azinger is in the bunker. I thought, "The job's not done, but almost done." We get up there. I had a quick squint at Azinger's lie. We're standing there waiting for him to play when I'd cleaned the ball, and I'll never forget this to the day I die, when Niclas said to me: "This isn't over yet. I've got a tough two-putt here."

'It was tough because of the pressure, but to me it was a reasonably easy two-putt really. All you had to do was send it high enough and it was always going to work down to the hole. But it was an impossible one-putt. There was a double-break in it, for a start. As I say, though, I'll never forget it, Niclas then said: "It's a lot of pressure but there's nowhere else I'd like to be right now – two putts to win the Ryder Cup."

'I turned round to him and said: "I just hope you get two putts." He looked at me, and I said: "This'll be close or it'll be in. He's got a decent lie and he's done it before. Just beware here." Sure enough, in it went.

'Even though I'd warned him, I just knew he was devastated. To then try and hole his putt was nigh on impossibile. You could have a hundred goes at this and never hit the hole once. If you were lagging the putt, you were hitting it ten feet outside the hole and just let it wander down. Trying to hole it, you had to take at least six feet of break out of it. You had to hit about four feet above the hole and it had to be at a speed of about six, seven feet past, bang in the middle of the hole. It wouldn't go in any of the sides because it would have been going too hard. We missed.

'Niclas was inconsolable, of course. I can only describe my emotion as "pissed off". Twice we'd given Azinger a lesson on how to play the game and once he's beaten us and now he's halved this match when he was never in our class. Never at any stage was he ever in our class. He would admit that himself, if he was an honest man. It was more dejection for me.

'Niclas was distraught. You have to remember when he's conducting an interview it's his second language as well, so it must have been hard for him to express how he felt to the television interviewers. It must have been hard enough in Swedish!'

There was agonising tension. One of Europe's rookies had had his chance of glory snatched from him. Now another of Torrance's first-timers had been handed a chance to become part of sporting folklore. McGinley, an intense man driven not only by his own will to excel, but by past Irishmen linked with Ryder Cup triumph, was the European professional poised to bring home the golden prize. He would dearly love to follow in the footsteps of Eamonn Darcy in 1987, Christy O'Connor Junior in 1989, and Philip Walton in 1995, and be the next Irishman with his name written indelibly into Ryder Cup history.

McGinley knew, from the reaction up ahead, that there was still another chapter to be written in this year's story. Even before he took to the tee on the last day for his match with Jim Furyk, McGinley somehow had a premonition it might all rest with him, as his caddie Fitzgerald remembers:

'When I met up with Paul on Sunday he told me he had had breakfast with Phillip Price and Pierre Fulke and he had said to them: "One of us could be a hero."

'We went out to practice early. Paul wanted to hit a few balls and then go back and have lunch, relax. He doesn't take much to warm up, so he practised two hours early, then he would have half an hour before we set off.

'Monty was on the range entertaining the crowd. He had the crowd really fired up for the last day. Monty wished Paul luck and then he was off. The final day had begun and I wondered what it had in store for Paul. Things didn't go too well for us at the start and we were two-down by the third. Furyk holed a long putt on the second and we couldn't match his birdie at the third. Paul then hit a great second shot in with a three-iron on the fourth and Furyk missed a five-foot putt for a half after he'd driven into trouble off the tee, so we're back to only one-down. Paul made a great save on the fifth but we ended up disappointed because Furyk birdied and that put us back to two-down.

'On the eighth, though, Furyk made a bad mistake. He over-clubbed from the fairway and hit it through the green into the trees and couldn't recover, so that put us back only one-down again.

'The ninth was a huge point in the match. Paul hit a pretty good drive but it just drifted a little bit. It was hugging the left side and finished a yard off the fairway. Furyk stepped up and hooked his. His ball bounced off the back of the bunker and back into the bunker. We were left with no shot and Furyk had a perfect shot from the fairway bunker. It ended up that Paul had a three-footer for the half, hit it through the break and missed it. That was a real body-blow. Paul had hit a pretty good tee-shot but got unlucky and Furyk had hit a bad tee-shot, but we ended up losing the hole.

'In contrast, though, on the tenth, Furyk drove through the fairway, quite a mistake, and got a very bad lie in the rough. We were fortunate to win the hole with a four. Then on the 11th, Paul holed a 20-foot putt for a half, a huge putt to make.

'It was a case of getting holes back and then giving them away again, and Furyk going two-up and then letting us back in it. There were a few mistakes made by both players from the 7th to the 14th. There was no question, it was tense. It could be a win-or-bust match and both players were aware of that, I'm sure.

'The spotlight has really come on our match now. Paul is one-down going to the 15th. He knew there couldn't be any mistakes at this late stage. Both of them made birdies, so we go to the 16th still one-down. There was a difficult pin-position on 16. Paul was slightly closer but they both two-putted for fours. Still one-down.

'We stepped on to the 17th tee and the noise was just unbelievable. People were listening on their radios to what was going on in the match. The whole match was so close. Paul hit three-wood off the tee. That left us 265 yards to carry the bunker. I said: "It's downwind. You'll have to hit three-wood to take it over the corner." He hit it 290 yards through the fairway, in fact it was closer to 300 yards, all pure adrenalin. He absolutely nailed it. Thankfully we got a good lie in the rough. He was able to get the ball over the burn. He chipped to about 15 foot and Jim was just outside him.

'It took a while before Jim could hit his putt. The crowd were obviously listening on the radio. Niclas Fasth was in front. Everybody thought he was going to win the Ryder Cup for us. Behind us, Phillip Price had beaten Phil Mickelson. Jim's caddie tried to calm the crowd down to give him a chance.

Everyone was getting so excited because it looked like we were just about to win the Ryder Cup. Jim missed the putt. Paul holed his to level our match. It was a great moment.

'Under great pressure, because everything's boiling now, Paul hit a fantastic tee-shot. So did Furyk. We had 203 yards left to the pin. We were only a few yards away from where Christy hit the two-iron. I knew the spot well.

'As we stood on the fairway, up ahead, they were taking an eternity to finish off. Then we heard the roars. It dawned on us that Paul Azinger had holed the bunker shot when we saw him running across the green waving his arms and getting hugged by his caddie. Niclas then missed the putt. He was so unlucky. He was going to be the hero and now he wasn't. Paul said to me: "We need a half to win the Ryder Cup." He knew it was all on him at that stage.

'Furyk was to play first. These were very tough shots. Hearts were beating fast. You admired how they could just make contact with the ball. Jim's ball went into the bunker left. He'd been in there the night before and had got very unlucky in the fourball when it plugged. Paul over-drew his approach and left his ball just left of the green, with quite a difficult pitch shot left. He played the pitch fantastically well. I was surprised it came up short. It was only afterwards when I saw the replay that I saw it landed maybe a foot from where he wanted it to and sort of dug in. It was so difficult, though. If he'd hit it too hard, it would have gone all the way down the slope.

'I nearly jinxed him then after the chip shot, when we were looking at the putt. I said to Paul, "This is a great moment. A putt on the last green to win the Ryder Cup. You've always dreamt of that." Then Jim Furyk nearly holed his bunker shot. It lipped out. I would have looked a right idiot if that had gone in.

'We read the putt. I said to him: "We had this putt two years ago at the Benson and Hedges International." I reminded him it didn't break as much as we thought. He'd hit it left-lip and it had stayed there. I told him I thought this one was only just on the left-lip. He obviously hit this one an awful lot better. I was watching it to the side of him, praying, "Please drop." It did.

'It was such an incredible relief, as well as joy. It would have been so gut-wrenching to have lost the match. The half had done it for Europe. Paul had done it. I really was so happy for him.'

At 4.54 p.m. precisely, the golden prize was Europe's. McGinley's half took the score to 14 ½–11 ½ in the home team's favour.

Billy Foster prepared to put plan 'A' into operation – that of leading the caddies in a wholesale victory dive into the lake. That was scrapped because McGinley was the man to take the first ducking. Furled in an Irish tricolour, Europe's hero of the hour sloshed about in The Belfry's famous finishing hole lake. While McGinley soaked himself in pond water, Torrance, inevitably, soaked himself in tears. His unfancied team had beaten the odds. The man who loved a bet had gambled and won.

Everything was a formality now. Fulke's match with Love was desperately tight, too. It could have all come down to their match, and it could have come down to the 18th hole yet again, that amphitheatre of triumphs and disasters.

They never got that far. Fulke and Love were virtually forced to finish off their match on the final hole fairway, because players and supporters were going wild on the 18th green. It didn't altogether meet with Love's approval as he recalled the accusations levelled at his team in the previous match at Brookline. This time, however, the result was in no doubt. This time there was no one left still to putt to try to save the day. Love refused to accept a full point graciously offered by Fulke, and settled for a half. That took the match position to 15–12.

While Fulke and Love called it a day, Parnevik and Woods played on, neither seeming sure what to do. Unlike the match ahead of them, though, one player was ahead. That was Woods. The way the matches had developed, it could have worked out the way Curtis Strange planned his draw, but in the end his trump card was never used.

Parnevik's caddie Ten Broeck had had a premonition they would be playing the world No. 1. But he didn't know they would be playing him for nothing:

'Somehow I just had a feeling we would be playing Woods. The signs weren't good. Jesper was not feeling great. Now not only is he not playing well, but he's got a fever and he's sick. He starts off horrendously. He's playing pathetically. He's two-down after six holes and should be about four-down. I told him at the seventh, "Right now Tiger's thinking to himself there's no way you can beat him." He said: "Well, you know, I was thinking that, too!" I said, "Come on, hit a few slaps on to the green, make a few putts, and make him think twice about it."

'Jesper got back in the match, won a couple of holes and got it back to even. Then he won the 13th to go one-up, hit a lob wedge to six feet, but he lost the 15th to a par. I was thinking at this stage that it wasn't going to really matter, but I did appreciate what it would mean to Europe's momentum. It did matter if they could be looking at the board and seeing Parnevik was beating Woods, that would be very important.

'Then when we got to the 16th, with our match even, it was quite a weird scenario because no one seemed to be really with us, even though there was a crowd. Jesper made a five-foot putt to halve the hole and just about that time McGinley made the putt. When we were walking to the 17th tee, the crowd was going absolutely wild.

'We drove off 17 and as we walked down the fairway I think Tiger and Jesper, if it was agreeable, wanted to just walk in. Jesper asked the referee of our match if they could just go in and he said, no, they couldn't. I don't know if he was wrong or right but they carried on. During our singles, Woods never made a birdie until the match was all over. The only birdie he made was on the 17th hole. That put him one-up.

'Jesper can hardly concentrate. He's really wanting to celebrate. He still wants to get something out of the match, though, and wants to make sure now he just gets over the lake and finds the green and doesn't embarrass himself. He ends up playing a great third shot and Tiger concedes a five-foot putt for a halved match, the right thing to do under the circumstances. Tiger wanted to make his putt and win the point for his own gratification but it didn't work out. He missed from seven feet and then gave Jesper his. There were so many distractions, it was hardly surprising Tiger missed.

'It was a very enjoyable feeling, even if America had lost. I had no problem with that. We partied. I remember Dave Renwick, Lee Westwood's caddie, saying, "If it was a drinking competition between the caddies the score would have been 24–4 – and Lance would have got the only four points for the Americans!'

European celebrations went on long into the night. McGinley dried out, but not for long. Westwood insisted on the team climbing on to tables to be introduced again and again. "Tell them who I beat," said a euphoric Price. It has become his catchphrase.

Sam Torrance's team had been led to the water and they had, indeed, drunk copiously.

HOW WE RAN AWAY WITH THE RYDER CUP

2004: A RECORD WIN FOR EUROPE

OAKLAND HILLS, MICHIGAN, DETROIT, 17–19 SEPTEMBER
USA 9½ EUROPE 18½

CAPTAINS: Hal Sutton (USA)
Bernhard Langer (Europe)

(European names first)

Fourballs (morning):
C. Montgomerie and P. Harrington (2 and 1) 1, P. Mickelson and T. Woods 0
D. Clarke and M.A. Jiménez (5 and 4) 1, D. Love III and C. Campbell 0
P. McGinley and L. Donald (half) ½ , C. Riley and S. Cink (half) ½
S. García and L. Westwood (5 and 3) 1, D. Toms and J. Furyk 0

Foursomes (afternoon):
M.A. Jiménez and T. Levet 0, C. DiMarco and J. Haas (3 and 2) 1
C. Montgomerie and P. Harrington (4 and 2) 1, D. Love III and F. Funk 0
D. Clarke and L. Westwood (1 hole) 1, P. Mickelson and T. Woods 0
S. García and L. Donald (2 and 1) 1, K. Perry and S. Cink 0

Fourballs (morning):
S. García and L. Westwood (half) ½, J. Haas and C. DiMarco (half) ½
D. Clarke and I. Poulter 0, T. Woods and C. Riley (4 and 3) 1
P. Casey and D. Howell (1 hole) 1, J. Furyk and C. Campbell 0
C. Montgomerie and P. Harrington 0, S. Cink and D. Love III (3 and 2) 1

Foursomes (afternoon):
D. Clarke and L. Westwood (5 and 4) 1, J. Haas and C. DiMarco 0
M.A. Jiménez and T. Levet 0, P. Mickelson and D. Toms (4 and 3) 1
S. García and L. Donald (1 hole) 1, J. Furyk and F. Funk 0
P. Harrington and P. McGinley (4 and 3) 1, D. Love III and T. Woods 0

Singles:
P. Casey 0, T. Woods (3 and 2) 1
S. García (3 and 2) 1, P. Mickelson 0
D. Clarke (half) ½, D. Love III (half) ½
D. Howell 0, J. Furyk (6 and 4) 1
L. Westwood (1 hole) 1, K. Perry 0
C. Montgomerie (1 hole) 1, D. Toms 0
L. Donald 0, C. Campbell (5 and 3) 1
M.A. Jiménez 0, C. DiMarco (1 hole) 1
T. Levet (1 hole) 1, F. Funk 0
I. Poulter (3 and 2) 1, C. Riley 0
P. Harrington (1 hole) 1, J. Haas 0
P. McGinley (3 and 2) 1, S. Cink 0

THE CADDIES

RONAN FLOOD (PADRAIG HARRINGTON 2004, 2006)

Padraig Harrington and his Stackstown, Dublin, clubmate Ronan Flood, a two-handicapper, first met playing amateur golf 18 years before appearing in the Ryder Cup together. Flood took over from the long-serving Dave McNeilly in May 2004, originally as a temporary measure, but then the Irish banker, who had done a short stint previously with Harrington, decided to take time off work to make the partnership more permanent.

GLEN MURRAY (SERGIO GARCÍA 2004, 2006)

South African Murray, who took up caddying soon after national service in the police force, was in his 12th year when he shouldered the bag for Sergio García at Oakland Hills. Murray had a highly successful six years with Retief Goosen before switching to García in 2002. Since then, the pair have won on both sides of the Atlantic.

CHRISTIAN DONALD (LUKE DONALD 2004, 2006)

Luke's elder brother and former golf pro Christian had jokingly suggested he would caddie for Luke if he made his card – and the joke became a reality. A victory in Luke's 2002 US Tour rookie season firmly established the pair in America, but in 2004 the Donalds ducked back across the Pond to try to make the Ryder Cup team.

CRAIG CONNELLY (PAUL CASEY 2004, 2006)

Connelly, a Scot and former Solheim Cup caddie, was with Swede Helen Alfredsson when he got the call from Casey only days before the 2004 Ryder Cup. Connelly opted for the caddying profession soon after leaving school, moving over to the LPGA Tour in 1998, where his most successful bag was that of Rachel Teske.

DARREN REYNOLDS (PAUL McGINLEY 2004, 2006)

Dubliner Reynolds, mascot for his school golf team just like his dad Tony was for Europe at Oakland Hills, gave up his architectural studies to draw clubs, Roger Chapman proving to be his most successful bag. Padraig Harrington, having won the Asian Open during a short stint together, recommended him to McGinley.

MICK DONAGHY (IAN POULTER 2004)

Donaghy, a Scot, began his caddying at the tender age of 10 at the Cowglen club in Glasgow and took 27 years' experience to his first Ryder Cup. As 'Mr' Parnevik's bagman (he mostly uses the formal title), the pair narrowly missed out on the 1994 Open title and a place in the 1995 Ryder Cup. In 2003, he joined Ian Poulter and within a month the extrovert and colourful Englishman won the Wales Open.

OWEN CRAIG (THOMAS LEVET 2004)

Craig, formerly in retail middle-management, was a complete rookie caddie in 1998 when Thomas Levet took a chance on him. The pair have been together ever since and with the Northern Irishman by his side, renowned joker Levet took Ernie Els to an Open playoff in 2002, sealing his Ryder Cup place with a thrilling 2004 Scottish Open victory.

THE ACTION

'Monty stood back, took a breath, made a great putt. The ball goes in. He drops the putter. He's all emotion. I think he knew it was an important putt. Then it suddenly seems to dawn on him just how important.'

American captain Hal Sutton was brimming with confidence going into the 2004 Ryder Cup at Oakland Hills, a tough, traditional layout that had hosted five US Opens and two US PGA Championships. Sutton had double the amount of players in the world's top 20 than Europe, a dominance nearly always the case for Ryder Cups. He had five major winners, one of them 2004 Masters champion Phil Mickelson, and Bernhard Langer had none. Sutton also had Tiger Woods, who was due an outstanding week after a quiet run that had seen him deposed as world number one. The match was being played on a course that historically did not favour Europeans, one that was sure to play similarly to the seven US majors it had hosted. The home crowd would surely be worth a couple of points, although everyone hoped the hysteria and bad behaviour of 1999 at Brookline would not be part of the gallery's weaponry.

However, knowing they were once again the underdogs, Europe pulled together even more and decided this was going to be a week to enjoy not to fear. Langer feared nothing and he had crushed Sutton the last time they were in opposition, in the 2002 singles at The Belfry, just as he had in 1985 at the same venue. Also, none of Europe's players was out of sorts in the build-up to the match, unlike some of the Americans, with the possible exception of Colin Montgomerie. His much-publicised divorce had affected his form, causing him a slip down the world rankings and European order of merit.

Monty was up for the match, however. The players gave him the thumbs-up and Langer handed the 41-year-old Scot one of his two wild-cards, the first time he had needed one in seven consecutive appearances. Luke Donald, who had returned to Europe and subsequently sacrificed a place in the US top 30 by so doing, earned the other Langer pick. After winning twice in seven weeks leading up to the match, and with his experience of matchplay as a former Walker Cup player, Donald's selection, although proving a huge disappointment to his rival Fredrik Jacobson, was fully deserved.

Langer's only ripple of worry came with a sudden dip in form by Padraig

Harrington three weeks before the match. But the Irishman came good at the eleventh hour, winning the German Masters just a day before the team met up to fly out to Detroit. Harrington's victory, and the knowledge they had their talisman in Montgomerie, was a huge fillip.

Langer was 'hands-on', even supervising meals on the flight to America, devising a pie comprising ingredients from Britain, Spain, France and Ireland, followed by his mum's own recipe for Black Forest Gateau. Europe's team was a good mix, too, of experience and rookie enthusiasm. Montgomerie, Harrington, Darren Clarke, Lee Westwood, Sergio García, Paul McGinley and Miguel Angel Jiménez had all been tested in the Ryder Cup cauldron. Donald, Paul Casey, David Howell, Ian Poulter and Thomas Levet could not wait for their first taste of action.

The same could be said of the caddies. Alastair McLean, Billy Foster, John Graham and Mick Doran had Ryder Cup records as long as their carrying arms, experience that would prove vital in the team room and to their younger brethren on the bags. All four seasoned veterans came back into the fold quite late in the Ryder Cup campaign, indeed McLean joining up with Montgomerie – after over two years away – just a fortnight before the match, but happy to get the call:

'We split up in May 2002 and he called me up on the Sunday, the week the Ryder Cup team was to be finalised. We met up at Munich on the Tuesday. I'd had 20 months with Adam Scott, but I had been doing very little for five months. Ten years with Monty had been pretty good, though. I wouldn't have had the lifestyle I'd had if it weren't for him. I owed more or less everything I had to Monty.

'Monty's always been a pretty steady guy. It's just his mindset that needs juggled about a wee bit. So I wasn't fazed by going back on his bag. I don't know how tough it was for him to ask me, but he sounded pretty chirpy afterwards. He played well in the BMW, led with a little while to go.

'A few things had been playing on his mind that year and one of them was worrying about needing a wild-card for the first time. His life had been a bit of a shambles and that was affecting his golf. The golf wasn't working and that was affecting his life. It was a real vicious circle. When he got the nod from Bernhard, it was huge for him. He had a very strong case for being picked. We've always enjoyed the Ryder Cups and that was the main reason for going back to work for him.'

With European captain Bernhard Langer's caddie, American Russ Holden, doing the logistics for the bagmen, his vice-captain Anders Forsbrand and assistants Joakim Haeggman and Thomas Bjørn acting as lieutenants, the practice sessions went ahead. Langer used the old Seve Ballesteros ploy of encouraging the team to play for $100 stakes to sharpen up their will to win. Another ploy, all Langer's own, was to encourage his men to sign autographs and bond with the American crowd, unlike their counterparts, who stayed largely aloof from the gallery. Winning hearts and minds was to pay off handsomely.

Langer was certainly on the ball in other ways, as Montgomerie's caddie McLean reveals:

'The course was set up very fair and it favoured anyone who was accurate. Monty wasn't hitting it too straight going into the week. Bernhard's seen Monty close up for donkey's years and he said to him: "I think this is something you are doing wrong, Monty, and if you wouldn't mind trying this . . ." He just said to Monty that he was moving his hips, rather than leading his swing off with his arms. Monty worked on this a wee bit and it just slipped into place. A few shots later it was perfect. Monty was actually giving it a little slide, a wee cutter again, and he was long. It was unbelievable: Monty of old. That continued for a couple of practice days and when he got going in the games he drove well.'

Europe's captain was counting on Montgomerie and Padraig Harrington's experience to get Europe off to a confident start in match one, fully expecting his rival to try to trump him. When the draw came out on Thursday night, there were whistles and cheers of expectation. Sutton had thrown his top two men into battle first out, Tiger Woods pairing up with Phil Mickelson.

The American captain reasoned that the two highest-ranked players in the world would be the pair to show the way, whip up the crowd and instil confidence in his following players. Woods and Mickelson were not exactly bosom buddies, however. And Mickelson had decided to change his club manufacturer only a couple of weeks before the match. The Masters champion had not spent much time team-bonding either. They might have been the highest-world-ranked players at Oakland Hills, but that did not give Woods and Mickelson any right to victory. Caddie McLean relished the curtain coming up on the 35th Ryder Cup:

'Bernhard sent them out to play an extra nine holes foursomes, so I could tell what was in his mind. They were using a different golf ball and it was to give Colin an opportunity to hit some shots with Harrington's ball and vice-versa.

'Monty said Langer had chosen him for a reason and now he had to do what he was chosen for, and he always wants to play against the best.

'There didn't seem to be so much apprehension being the first to tee off. You wonder how the crowd is going to be, especially after 1999. It was pretty exciting kicking the whole thing off, but I didn't feel the hairs rise up on the back of my head like I did at Oak Hill in 1995.

'Padraig can chat the hind legs off a horse and has an awesome sense of humour. He's a real funny bugger. He was so relaxed and that helped calm things. His caddie Ronan is a lovely guy and the four of us had a lot of laughs. Even though you've been there before, you get not fright but a real buzz of expectation. It's so good to have three guys you can have a joke with in such a pressure-cooker match.

'Woods and Mickelson didn't seem so relaxed, didn't even look as though they were talking. I don't know why Hal Sutton thought he could put these two out and overwhelm anybody. We said, OK, bring 'em on.

'It was a pretty awful start for all four of them. None of them hit the fairway. Tiger hit a tree. Monty was the least bad. He went in the right bunker. All of them could find the green, but only Monty was close. He hit a great seven-iron about 165 yards to 10 or 12 feet and he binned it.'

Europe were off to the best of starts. The American spectators, significantly, were immediately hushed. Their hero Mickelson, shoulders slumped in resignation, had had his opening putt rejected by the green's slope, sending it back behind him. Woods could not work his magic. Montgomerie, the man reviled and abused by the 1999 gallery at Brookline, had struck the first blow for Europe. Destiny already seemed to be calling Monty, and his caddie McLean recognised the old resolute man he knew so well:

'Monty was so determined. I could see it in his eyes. But him and Padraig were great together. They dovetailed so well. Padraig did his bit at the third and they gave themselves a cushion for when Woods and Mickelson came back at them, as you knew they must do at some time. Tiger hit a great approach at the fifth and Phil made his first birdie at the seventh, so we were only one-up at the turn.

'While Monty had got us off to such a fantastic start, Padraig became the steadying influence because he made a lot of birdies. They both putted well, that was the difference. After Monty birdied the 12th, I thought that would be it. Padraig was playing so well and he's such a strong character, I felt that even if Monty didn't come in on another hole, we couldn't get beaten. They were working together so well. We went three-up with four to play and even though Phil holed a big putt to win 16, Monty had just a tap-in on the next to close it down.'

The defeat of Woods and Mickelson was also a dream start for a caddie only four months into his career and making his Ryder Cup debut, Harrington's great friend Ronan Flood:

'I know there was a worry about Padraig's form just before the match, but when his back's to the wall, that's when he's at his best. Funnily enough, where he won the German Masters I'd caddied for him before. For us both, it was a great lift before heading off for America.

'Padraig played well in practice, he'd won the week before, so we weren't that surprised when we saw the draw. It was a different Monty to the one I'd seen on the tour. He was standing on the first tee with a great presence, just didn't believe he could be beaten. It wasn't as noisy as I'd thought it would be. I'd been at The Belfry and the noise when the guys went to the first tee was absolutely deafening. The whole week, it wasn't as noisy as The Belfry. But that was because the Europeans played so well and didn't give the Yanks anything to shout about! There was a great buzz, though. I'd spoken to Billy Foster about what to expect and he'd said it makes all other tournaments look like a pro-am. Billy and the more senior caddies were great to us. Standing on the first tee with Padraig and Monty and having Alastair there as well was definitely a great help. If it was just yourself and your player it would be a lot more nerve-racking, you feel a little bit protected.

'It was all a bit sombre, but when they called out the European pairings, you could hear Tony Reynolds, Paul McGinley's caddie's old man, roar out from the stand, which was just to the left: "You'll never beat the Irish." He's dressed up in all the Irish gear. All the players loved it. He became the team mascot.

'It was a case of us doing our own thing. Monty played well and we enjoyed it. All four of us laughed a lot, but we didn't get involved too much in trying to play each other's shots. Padraig played his game and Monty played his game. We gave each other advice, but there was no dominant partner.

'If I'd been a spectator, I would have been happy to watch Woods and Mickelson together, but there was so much expectation on their shoulders and that was a great position for us to be in. You had to have a certain amount of sympathy for Mickelson. He was out there trying 110 per cent; he wasn't trying to hit bad shots. It just wasn't there for him that week.'

Although the spiking of America's top guns was paramount to Europe's start, it was not the first European point recorded. That was claimed by Darren Clarke and Miguel Angel Jiménez over Davis Love III and Chad Campbell.

Clarke's caddie Billy Foster was the motivator, in the locker-room, at dinner, in the bar when a sing-song was to be organised . . . and at practice. Foster, serving at his eighth Ryder Cup and in his fourth encounter alongside Clarke, had paired back up with the Ulsterman for a third time less than three months before the match, having parted company at the end of 2002. Foster also added to the spectators' amusement:

'I got a call after the British Open at Royal Troon and met Darren in Ireland the week after to discuss the past and the future, and decided to go back again for a third term, maybe third time lucky! The Ryder Cup was unexpected, but it was great to be doing my eighth match. It would have been a straight run of nine, but I fell out with Seve a couple of months before Oak Hill in '95. I felt it was the strongest team we'd had for four or five Ryder Cups. There were no weak links and they were all in form.

'There was a fantastic team spirit, probably the best I've been involved in. There was a great set of caddies. We had so much fun, all week. I gave them a few songs I'd picked up over the years, told a few jokes.

'In one of the practice rounds, we were playing with García, Jiménez and Westwood, and off the 12th tee I decided, in my wisdom, to run forward 50 yards in front of everybody and pinch Thomas Bjørn's buggy. I attempted to drive off down the fairway with the bag on my back, with them all running after me. It was just like *The Benny Hill Show*. Bjørn and Westwood were catching me, so I decided to turn the wheel and accelerate away from them. As I did so, the weight of the bag swung me right off the buggy. I did a triple somersault off the buggy, landed on my head with the bag on top of me. I looked up to see the buggy heading straight towards the crowd. The spectators parted like the Red Sea. The buggy went straight through the crowd, didn't harm anybody, thank goodness, and finished up 20 yards in the trees. I was lucky. We're in America. I could have finished up with 20 lawsuits against me.

'Europe were so much more relaxed. Thomas Levet was going through all his tricks. Our players signed autographs on the practice days, and I don't think the Americans did much of that, half the time they weren't even playing together.'

With Clarke and Jiménez hitting it off in practice, as well as both being aficionados of good cigars, Langer's decision to match up the pair raised few eyebrows. Clarke soon smoked out the opposition, as Foster remembers:

'It was the same as The Belfry in 2002. Darren got off to a really hot start. He made an eagle and a couple of birdies very early on and he was four or five under himself after six holes, playing phenomenal golf. They were three-up early doors and far too sharp to be giving much back. Blue numbers were going up all round and confidence was really high.'

The third match of the morning was Paul McGinley and Luke Donald against Chris Riley and Stewart Cink, and it proved the tightest. McGinley had been the hero of the hour at The Belfry in the previous Ryder Cup and a magnificent run in the weeks before this encounter ensured the Dubliner would again be on duty, delighting his caddie and compatriot Darren Reynolds:

'Paul's efforts to get into the Ryder Cup were a fantastic achievement. We had nine weeks in a row at the end of the campaign when he would never normally go more than three. That showed what it meant to him. Out of those nine weeks he contended in nearly every tournament. He could have won any of them.

'So he could have been pretty tired come the Ryder Cup. Getting there was one thing. Being in good enough shape to play was another. He was shattered. He should never have played in the last event before the match, the German Masters. But a couple of days off and he was raring to go for the Ryder Cup.

'It was all a new experience for me, as it was for quite a few of us. I was there to work and I appreciated the win more when I got home because the working days were very long, seven to seven. When I got home, I read the papers, looked at the video and thought: "Jeez. We won the Ryder Cup!"

'Getting changed in the locker-room and getting fired up with the rest of the boys was great. I come from a Gaelic football background and I'm used to a good team feeling. Week by week normally in golf, it's just you and your player. There, 12 caddies would do anything for each other. It had a snowball effect. In our hotel, I saw one American caddie in the bar all week! I'm not saying there was a lot of drinking, but there was a lot of team talking over a couple of beers. I don't know what the American caddies did with their spare time. We met up religiously and all 12 caddies would eat together, have a beer or two together and then go to bed.

'Practice was great – apart from the clothes. I suffered more than most with the fittings because I'm the skinniest, but I couldn't wait to try everything on.

'We practised with Thomas Levet. The Americans loved him. He was joking, doing trick-shots, generally messing with them. It was important that the Europeans did mix with the American crowd and Bernhard did well to tell the boys to go and sign autographs and be friendly with the spectators. I remember in Cologne the week before, we played with Colin Montgomerie in the first two rounds and he said to me, "Are you looking forward to the Ryder Cup?" and I said I was. He warned me that the crowd might be very boisterous after what had happened at one or two previous Ryder Cups, but I couldn't fault one American fan during the week. And I think it was a lot down to Langer. He won them over.

'The first match was a total surprise because Paul spoke to me on the range on Thursday and we didn't expect to play. He felt he would only get the nod in the foursomes. He went back to his room on Thursday for a sleep, saying he would be back in an hour. I was in the locker-room and Joakim Haeggman came up to me and said: "Where's Paul?" I said: "Back in the hotel room." Joakim said: "He's in tomorrow, playing with Luke Donald." I was totally shocked, not that Paul didn't warrant it. He played lovely in practice. I just didn't think he'd play in the fourball and neither did he. I didn't want to ring him and disturb him. He arrived an hour later and Langer told him he was in. I could see by his reaction he was quite shocked. He was delighted, though, and couldn't wait for tomorrow to get out there.

'He didn't know Luke that well; I didn't know Luke. I knew Chris, his brother and caddie, a bit, but it was probably a bit of a risk playing the two together because they knew absolutely nothing about each other. I remember going down one hole and Luke asking Paul where he lived. That's how much they knew about one another. I thought Paul was great on the first tee, though. He said to Luke: "I've been here before, just play your own game."

'They played great together, Luke was great. They were a little bit unlucky. Chris Riley made an unbelievable up-and-down on the last from the back of the green. He had about a 20-yard lob straight down the green on a downslope and hit it to about four feet and holed a great putt. They got a half, but it could very easily have been a win.'

Donald and his brother Christian provided the second of the non-conventional player–caddie partnerships. A former club pro, Christian, at 32 six years older than Luke, decided to give up his career to carry the bag and had already shared a fine start to his sibling's career in America. In the summer of 2004, Luke heeded the advice of Bernhard Langer and European Tour executive director Ken Schofield to come to Europe and play his mandatory 11 events, so that he would not lose the chance of playing in the Ryder Cup. Even though Luke did not quite make the team by right, a victory in the July Scandinavian Masters tipped the wild-card balance in his favour and he showed captain Langer it was a wise choice by winning the week after getting the nod, in the European Masters in Switzerland.

News of the wild-card came when Luke, Christian and Sergio García and his caddie Glen Murray were flying from Munich, where the European team was decided, in a private plane on the way to Switzerland. Christian recounts: 'He got a text message telling him he was in the team. We were the last to know. He had been very, very anxious. He wanted that wild-card very, very badly.'

Langer had, in a team meeting two weeks before the match, asked his players to put down on slips of paper the men they wanted to pair up with – and the ones they didn't. As Luke and Paul Casey had been such successful Walker Cup partners, it seemed almost a foregone conclusion that Luke would pair up with his former amateur partner, but that was not to be, as caddie Christian found out:

'Paul Casey just wasn't quite firing on all cylinders in the practice rounds and almost seemed a bit uptight, so they decided to put Luke with Paul McGinley. Luke was just happy to play with anyone. He was keen to play with Sergio as well. But he just wanted to get in there and get playing as soon as possible. McGinley was a surprise, kind of a last-minute thing.

'I was expecting to be very nervous on the first tee after what I'd been told, but I didn't feel too bad. Our match against Chris Riley and Stewart Cink was tight, but it wasn't a game with lots and lots of birdies. It was either one-up or all-square. Paul gave Luke a lot of encouragement.

'The most memorable part of the first match was at the last hole. We were talking about club selection for the second shot, 213 yards uphill and into the wind, and Luke asked me: "Do you think three-iron will get me there?" I said: "You can hit three-iron, but you'll then be chipping for birdie." We decided on a two-iron. He could almost hit that as hard as he wanted to. It was perfect, ran back a little to about 20 feet. He putted up pretty stone-dead but Riley holed a nine-footer for the half.'

Donald and McGinley's half with Cink and Riley was the last act of the fourball starter because Sergio García and Lee Westwood had, well before, comfortably disposed of David Toms and Jim Furyk 5 and 3. It meant Europe finished the morning session riding high at 3½ points to half a point.

On Westwood's bag was, by his own admission, a reformed character. John Graham's nickname of 'Scotchie' had been hard-earned. The grizzled Scot had, however, turned over a new leaf to get back the bag of the man he had served with distinction in the past:

'I worked for Lee in 1996–97, so I was very pleased to get another chance after all those years away. He had wanted someone on the bag he could trust, but I liked a good drink in the past. Now I've almost given up the drink, maybe just once a month, once every three months. And because I'd won with him before and got on well with him, I got another chance. He knows I'm always going to be reliable. I joined him again in May 2004. He didn't play all that well at first, but he finished fourth at the Open to make sure of his place and he was playing well all the way to Ryder Cup week.

'I wasn't going to go to the Ryder Cup because the day before we were due to fly out I picked up a virus. I thought it wouldn't be fair on Lee if I went to the Ryder Cup and hit him with it out of the blue, but my girlfriend Caroline Rasmussen is an ex-pro and she urged me to go. She gave me cranberry pills to take, but I still had a fever when I got to America, so I went to the hospital. They gave me more pills and they worked.

'We practised with Sergio and big Darren and the practice went very well. If there had been points for Tuesday, Wednesday and Thursday, Europe would have won that as well. We had the spectators on our side. The way the European players signed autographs and mixed with the crowd, had photographs taken with the spectators, it was really good fun to be there. The whole team had a good laugh together, just being the guys that they are.

'Lee was always going to play with Sergio in the opening match. They'd done well together in the past. They are good for each other. Sergio likes a lot of banter and keeps the chat going, whereas Lee's more the solid type.

'They got off to a great start and were three-up after five holes. Apart from the great team spirit, another big reason for Europe getting off to such a great start was their putting. They were so much better than the Americans over the first day, especially, and Lee definitely had his putting boots on. David Toms and Jim Furyk hardly got a look in.'

With putting being the key, García's caddie Glen Murray was glad his man found his touch:

'Leading up to the Ryder Cup, Sergio hadn't really been putting well, which is always a bit of a worry. He hits it well all the time, he's the best driver in golf, especially after his swing changes the year before, but his putting was letting him down a bit. He'd won twice in America, good tournaments, too: the Buick Classic and the Byron Nelson. To show how good his ball striking was, I don't think many players have won a tournament using 120 putts.

'He putted really well at the Ryder Cup, though. He made loads of putts. That got his putting back on track in his career.

'I didn't feel odd being a South African among the Europeans. You hear about the camaraderie of the Ryder Cup and I was keen to see what it was like.

It's unbelievable how the guys gel together. The banter, maybe it's the different cultures, but it gets everybody going. One guy is out on his own, though. Billy Foster is really inspirational. Even if he's not there working in the future, they really should have him there just for morale's sake.

'Bernhard's a very serious guy. He wasn't going to miss anything out. He got the guys to write down who they didn't want to play with, for instance – not a thing you want out in the open, but the sort of thing the captain needs to know.

'There was a certain relaxed attitude for us that didn't seem to be there for the Americans. Sergio gave out these coloured bracelets, lucky charms I guess, to several of the players. I'll remember the Wednesday practice session forever. On the first tee, they told me to have a go. I gave it a rip!

'With Lee it was a great fourball pairing. We got on top early, so had the others, and I remember thinking: "This place is quiet." And then after we'd finished and we were having a quick lunch I thought: "Jeez. This place is dead." On the first day, the crowd were very quiet. They were kept quiet. Any time Lee or Sergio needed a putt they made it and I remember thinking: "Lee's got steel balls with the putter." Whenever there was a clutch-putt, he made it.'

Europe's tails were up. The home crowd were hushed. Someone had to stir them up. Thomas Levet's caddie Owen Craig remembers the arch-stirrer and he also recalls why a good few home fans in the gallery might have been on his affable French player's side:

'Thomas was highly entertaining in practice. He has this wee trick with sand-irons and the driver, hitting the golf ball on his chin. He just loves the crowd, thrives on the interaction with them.

'Chris DiMarco was working the crowd up right from the start of our match, but we expected that. He needed to. The Americans were on the back foot. Chris really got pumped up on the sixth after he holed a 30-footer to take them two-up. Miguel had missed a short putt on the fifth. Those two holes changed things a wee bit. It was the key point in the match and decided things ultimately. It was pretty close after that, but we weren't able to get back at them. Haas hit to a few inches on the 16th and that finished it.'

If DiMarco had fired up the gallery and given the Oakland Hills faithful some hope, then Colin Montgomerie and Padraig Harrington soon sowed the seeds of doubt as they nullified the first American point with victory over Davis Love and Fred Funk.

Harrington's role as a linchpin for Europe and a successful run of foursomes practice matches had left caddie Ronan Flood in no doubt his same pairing would be out in the afternoon:

'We only had time for a quick sandwich and then it was back to the range for a few quick warm-up shots. I guess it wasn't much more than half an hour, 40 minutes, before we were back out there. All week, Padraig didn't have a chance to put in anywhere near as much practice as he would normally.

'In the afternoon, Love was the mainstay, but Funk just didn't play great at all. Fred did hole a good birdie putt, though, and that produced the first high-five. Then we knew what the crowd could do because the whole place just went mental. It was the first chance the American crowd had to celebrate – and they took it. It was very noisy. But we got two in front just before the turn. On the eighth, Colin had a great chip; and then, on nine, Padraig hit a great nine-iron to about six feet.

'At the 11th, we missed a putt and we stood back thinking we were going to go back to only one-up, but they missed their shorter one and it kind of disheartened the Yanks. Then, at 12, Love hit a monster of a tee-shot. He couldn't have left Funk with much more than a seven-iron, maybe six, but Funk made a complete bollocks of the second shot. After that, the Yanks were gone. They'd thrown away two holes, could have stood on the 13th tee level. When we were given chances, we took them. We beat them on 16 when Funk went into the water.'

Montgomerie's caddie Alastair McLean had his own view of the point where their match turned and when it was sealed:

'Monty's fabulous chip and his foresight at the eighth turned our match. It was an unbelievable shot. Padraig had gone just a wee bit long, and I mean only a wee bit. But because the greens were so slopey, Monty couldn't go at the pin because the ball would have just run away. And the further away you aim from the pin, the more speed the ball would gather off the slope. Although Monty was only maybe 25 feet away from the hole in a straight line, he had to have his back to it, then chip up the hill into the semi, hopefully check it in the semi, to let it dribble down the green. It almost went in the hole. That made sure of the half.

'Love probably drove the furthest and straightest in the world at that stage. At the 12th we found the left rough and had to lay up. Davis has hit his drive so far, something like 470 yards, believe me; well, at least 400, gone forever. He'd caught one of the downslope ripples on the fairway as well. Funk had 170 to the front of the green. It's probably a par-five Fred never gets up on anyway. He put it in the right-hand bunker. Davis came out well, but they missed the putt and lost the hole. From looking like a certain loss, we won it – and that was really the end of it.'

Great friends and stablemates Darren Clarke and Lee Westwood were still battling it out when the second match finished. It had been a torrid start against Tiger Woods and Phil Mickelson, but Europe would not lie down. Westwood's caddie John Graham knew it was by no means a lost cause:

'Darren hit a six-iron at the eighth hole to about an inch and that began a big turnaround from three-down. Then, at the tenth, Darren hit one of the best shots of the week. It even got recognition from the home crowd. Lee only had about a three-footer left and he made it. We were back to all-square. Mickelson then missed a five-footer or so on the 11th and we were in front for the first time.'

Clarke's caddie Billy Foster remembers the fightback well:

'Phil obviously wasn't on the top of his game and he was letting a few wides go, so they just had to be patient and wait for things to happen. At the tenth, we were in between an eight and a nine-iron. We went for the low one and it had to be a solid one. Darren gave it the stare and I knew he'd made a great strike. He turned to me and said: "Well, I can't hit it any better than that." What he meant was if it was short, then I was a tosspot!

'It was then a game we looked like cruising, but all of a sudden we lost 17 after problems in the bunker and it went back to all-square. You're thinking to yourself, you don't really want to lose this now. In hindsight, everybody wondered what Hal Sutton was thinking of, putting Woods and Mickelson together, but they're the top two American golfers. If you beat them, it's a great morale-booster for our team.

'Phil had taken the mickey out of Darren a few times about his shank on the 17th at the PGA Championship. Clarkey had said to him: "You know it'll come back and haunt you somewhere." Sure enough, it haunted him right there on that 18th tee. Phil hit one of the worst tee-shots I've ever seen from a top-class player. It made us reasonably comfortable. It was a pleasant view!'

Westwood's caddie Graham saw it thus: 'Walking off the 17th I said to Darren: "I'm glad Phil Mickelson's hitting this tee-shot." Mickelson hit a horrific three-wood. It's nearly 500 yards and he's miles left, nearly out-of-bounds. Lee hit a great drive, just smoked the middle of the fairway. After seeing Mickelson doing what he did, Lee must have been under extreme pressure. He showed incredible guts. The Americans had to take a penalty-drop near the fence. That was that.'

Right behind the drama being played out on the 18th, Sergio García and Luke Donald were completing a 2 and 1 victory over Kenny Perry and Stewart Cink. Donald's brother Christian saw it this way:

'I'd been expecting us to pair up with Sergio for the foursomes. We drew Cink again, so we were getting to know his game. Him and Kenny Perry got a bit frustrated because they had a couple of lip-outs and there were plenty of groans from the crowd. Luke and Sergio putted well, though. Sergio hit a great shot to about four or five feet on the ninth and that took us two-up at the turn.

'It was fairly tight then for a while but we stayed in control and then on the 16th Luke had about a ten-footer to close the match down. It just tickled the hole, but we were two-up with two to play. Luke then hit a great five-iron at the par-three 17th, to about 15 feet, and that pretty much sealed it. They were absolutely delighted. Sergio loves to celebrate. But we looked the happier pair all the way round. I don't think the Europeans took it all so seriously. To me, the

Americans looked under pressure. I sometimes heard in the crowd, "Come on, guys; it's not good enough," when they missed a putt.'

One day over and Europe were in overwhelming control 6½ points to 1½. The European camp could hardly contain itself. Wise old heads pleaded caution, however, feeling a backlash must come.

Sergio García was again paired with Lee Westwood for the fourball Saturday morning session, this time against veteran Jay Haas and the man who was determined to set the crowd alight, Chris DiMarco. García's caddie Glen Murray noticed a distinct rise in temperature:

'I don't know whether Hal Sutton had got word out to the people, but this day was loud. Although they were down, the crowd had changed. The chanting that was going on was unbelievable. It was negative chanting towards us.

'DiMarco was getting them going. He'd done the same the day before, but it hadn't worked. This time it was working. They were making a hell of a noise. He was pumping his fists and they yelled louder. Any negative comments that came from the gallery towards Lee and Sergio, though, all they would do was look at the people who were doing it, and smile and just raise their caps to them and say "thank you". That kind of confused the crowd a little.

'I remember Sergio having a little word with Chris on the sixth hole: "Look here, keep it friendly." Chris was very good. He said: "Fine, whatever." But the crowd were really up by then and there were loads of comments coming at us. Sergio hit it in the water and they were cheering. But it still didn't upset him or Lee.'

Westwood's caddie Graham pinpoints their key hole:

'On the eighth, Lee was in the right semi; Sergio was in the first left-hand trap and he had 200 yards to the flag. He was going to take a five-iron, but it was uphill so he took a two-iron and hit just an incredible shot to 25 foot. It won the hole for us and proved mighty important later on.'

A tight match inevitably came all the way down to the last hole, which García and Westwood had to win for the match. With red dominating the morning scoreboard, the chants of "USA, USA" punctuated an atmosphere that was becoming more frenzied by the moment. A European point in the first match would be vital for morale; defeat would only lift the crowd further. Caddie Murray witnessed a bizarre finale:

'We birdied the 16th to get it back to all-square and we had a chance to go one-up at the 17th. Sergio hit a wonderful shot to five feet, straight under the hole. He pulled the putt. That was a big disappointment.

'At the 18th, we were in the fairway bunker and we had such a big lip in front of us we couldn't get to the green. We hit an eight-iron third shot just short, left, on a similar line to where Lee was lying in two. The green has a big slope behind the hole. We were trying to chip it up on a line that would help Lee, so he could see where it would roll back to the hole. Where the flag was, Lee knew he couldn't stop it quick enough. Sergio hit the damn thing too hard, so it was no help to Lee. It ran about 50 feet past. Lee hit a pretty good chip, but not quite hard enough. It didn't roll back enough, finished about 10 feet away. Sergio decided he should have a go with his putt. It was impossible to hole it. He made it. Lee hit a pretty good putt, nearly made it. But it was a bit of an unsatisfactory half.

'That putt on 17 should have gone in. That was the putt Sergio needed to make, and he missed.'

As the morning panned out, it was a significant half. Behind García and Westwood, Clarke and Ian Poulter, making his debut, were on the receiving end of a reinvigorated Woods, who had been paired with an old college chum, Chris Riley. Woods' scowl at last turned to a grin as he finally made his point.

A 4 and 3 defeat to Woods and Riley was taken hard by Poulter. The flamboyant Englishman had made the team in dramatic fashion, having been disappointed in 2001 when he missed out, agonisingly, by just one spot in the table. His caddie Mick Donaghy had suffered with him in Munich in a roller-coaster BMW International last round, where arch-rival Swede Fredrik Jacobson put Poulter under pressure on the final qualifying day for the Ryder Cup:

'It was a fantastic effort by Mr Poulter to make the team. He picked himself up when he could have been down and out, and made the team on sheer guts. There was so much pressure on him. At the sixth hole on the final day at Munich, he was in the bunker, decided to attack with a three-iron and went out-of-bounds, ran up a double-bogey. On the ninth, he hit a fantastic shot to about eight feet. I urged him to ignore the leaderboard and concentrate on his eagle chance, but he sneaked a glance, as I thought he would, and he saw Freddy Jacobson had gone birdie, birdie, birdie, birdie to move second. It must have flustered him a bit. He missed the putt. Then he found the bunker off the tenth and made quadruple-bogey.

'I suggested he might take a trip to the portable toilet next to the 11th tee to compose himself. He never missed a shot after that. I've seen a lot of golf under pressure and that was of the highest calibre. He was six-under for the last eight holes, eagled 11 and eagled 18. When he left the course, though, he was devastated, thought he was still going to miss the team. After it was clear he was in, he was proud of his finish. He didn't want to make the team shooting 80. It all gave him a lot of confidence.'

Denied his Union Flag trousers and with his spiky hair less colourful than usual, Poulter buckled down to practice and when his time came could not wait to get at Woods and Riley. That could have been the problem, thinks caddie Donaghy:

'He wasn't worried about not being able to wear his gear. There's enough attention on you, being a rookie in the Ryder Cup. Ian was fired up for his match when his turn came. But that became a disappointment. One of the big problems, I think, was he probably had too much time on the first tee. He got there far too early for his match and had too much time to sit there, wondering. I think he learned from that lesson, so that on Sunday, he spent as little time as possible: just walk on and tee it up.'

Harrington and Montgomerie also wilted to Stewart Cink and Davis Love to further raise the tempo of the home crowd. Montgomerie's bagman Alastair McLean faced disappointment before his man ended a sequence of 30 successive matches in the Ryder Cup:

'Monty hadn't played terribly well and he was ready for the rest. It had all been decided by him and Bernhard. It was a very emotional moment for Colin when he was rested. It was the first match he'd missed since he made his debut in '91. We went to the range for practice, just to fiddle about a bit, but there wasn't much point. We just watched the big screen. Then he went off in his cart and supported the rest of the guys. He probably did as much for the team just by being there as by playing. It's a big European thing. If they're not playing, they make good and sure they are out there supporting. They do that ever so well.'

One of the most significant matches of all time was coming towards its dramatic conclusion. It was a match that proved a triumph for Langer's bravery in throwing two rookies together. If anyone had thought that Paul Casey and David Howell might prove just to be cannon fodder, they were hugely mistaken, as Casey's caddie Craig Connelly, brought in at the last moment, observes:

'I worked for Paul in Munich when he clinched his Ryder Cup place, then I went back to the States to work for Helen Alfredsson. I certainly didn't think I was going to be in the Ryder Cup. Then the Sunday morning before the Ryder Cup, I was in Tulsa when I got a phone call telling me to get myself to Detroit, that I was in. Helen was fantastic, but she pulled my leg. She was due to give me some money, but she said: "I don't have any cheques left." Anyway, Monday morning I'm on a flight to Detroit to meet Paul instead of flying to Portland.

'I'd had experience of the Solheim Cup, and representing your country is a big deal regardless of the circumstances. The Solheim Cup was massive, but to go from caddying on the LPGA Tour to next day being part of the Ryder Cup, having only caddied for Paul once before, was obviously going to be a real test for me. As far as the caddying goes, you're doing the same job, but the Ryder Cup is a huge step up, it's the biggest golfing event in the world.

'There was another great trial for me. I had ten pairs of Ryder Cup trousers to wear during the week, none of which fitted. I had to have two inches taken off the waist and four inches off the leg. Monday wear was a beautiful green shirt with khaki pants. I turn up with black pants, not a very fetching combination. Within a couple of days, though, everything got sorted after I had an appointment with the tailor.

'I think most people thought Paul would have paired up with Luke Donald because of the Walker Cup. Paul was a little bit disappointed not to be playing on the Friday, but he knew it was a team event and he had to accept it.

'Saturday, though, we took part in what I think was the most pivotal moment in the Ryder Cup. David Howell was fantastic all day, so calm, so cool, played great. So was Paul. He's a birdie–bogey man, though, while David's more steady. Bernhard came up to me on the first tee and said: "Stay calm. Just do what you do best." He'd never met me before, so I wondered what that was! Seriously, it was a nice moment for the captain to bother with little old me.

'He'd put out a good pairing. They are good friends, they live near each other, and get on really well. They fed off each other.

'It was tight early on. David hit a great shot in to about nine feet at the sixth to take us one-up. Then Paul made a fantastic birdie on eight. At no time did the Americans look as though they were in charge of the game, but Paul's good putt – it was a 25–30-foot left-to-right swinger – calmed him and David down and got them going.

'There were high-fives all round, but Jim Furyk then went and holed a 15-footer down the hill to get the half. Paul really can putt well, though, and on the tenth he sank a really good 15-footer to take us two-up. After Paul rolled the putt in, he walks over to David and David goes to give him a high-five. As Paul puts his hand out, David gives him the old dropped wrist. "I don't think so, mate!"

'Unfortunately, Jim Furyk then got the bit between his teeth, though, and made four birdies. While Paul and David were both in it most of the time, Chad Campbell hadn't really been doing anything apart from a good putt on the front nine. Then all of a sudden he rolls in a 35-footer from the back edge on 16. Paul and David had putts of 20–25 feet and they didn't make them. So, suddenly, we're one-down with two holes to go.'

Howell's caddie Mick Doran, appearing in his fifth Ryder Cup, had taken over his fellow Englishman's bag less than three months before Oakland Hills. Doran knew his man's inner strength but could hardly believe his physical power when it came to the crucial 17th, where Howell became the first player that week to birdie the perplexing short hole. It was to earn the man they all call 'Howler' the accolade of 'European shot of the year': a sizzling six-iron from 203 yards to five feet on perhaps one of the world's toughest par-threes. A six-iron? Hmm. Doran did not think that would be enough:

'Putting two rookies out together, I thought, was a good idea, because they had nothing to lose. They came out with probably the best drives on the first that there'd been, both hit the middle of the fairway.

'Everything was going so well, it was a surprise to go one-down after the 14th. Now we were on the back foot. Then David hit real close on 15, a nine-iron or wedge, can't remember, but he put it to two foot, it was more or less a gimme, and that took us back to all-square. Then Chad Campbell steps in. I couldn't believe it. I was now thinking if we get a half here in this match it's a good half, and hopefully they do get at least a half or they'll both be deflated, probably thought they should have had it in the bag really.

'So the 17th was going to be a big, big hole. I wanted him to hit one more, to tell the truth, and take a five-iron. I thought he would always be struggling to get a six-iron there. He pulled the six-iron. I thought he absolutely crunched it. He said he didn't think he'd hit it pure, but he must have hit it half-decent because it was a lot of yardage. It was such a tough pin position all week, on the right-hand side all the time and almost impossible to get close to because of a slope moving from right to left on a rock-hard green.

'He hit it to five feet. It was a tough putt to come still, such a pressure putt. There was a bit of break on it and it was going to be like lightning. He knew he had to hole it or it was curtains. He did.'

Back to all-square. Could the Englishmen now change the complexion of the morning? Connelly continues:

'On the 18th, David went first and didn't hit a particularly good shot. Paul's over his tee-shot and has a lot to think about now. Paul thought he hadn't caught his drive that well but still managed to find 300 yards! What Paul thinks he doesn't catch, most people would have been happy to hit it like that. He just busted it down there. He told me after the round, though, that he had a look at the 18th tee as he was approaching it, from behind, and looked where Phil Mickelson had hit it the day before. He'd realised how far left Mickelson had hit it. I questioned him why the hell was he thinking that when he was about to hit probably the most important tee-shot of his life!

'But he hit the middle of the fairway and then he thought he'd hit a great shot in to the green. The pin was middle left on the two-tier green. He wanted to finish just left of the TV tower, which meant starting it on the right edge of the green. He started it right. It just hung there, hung there and hung there. We didn't know, but he'd put it to the same spot as Sergio had not long before, 30 feet down the tier. When we got up to the green Bernhard came up to us. He told Paul exactly what Sergio had done with his putt. Bernhard was fantastic. I thought Sergio had been very, very lucky or very, very good.

'I was attending the flag. Paul hit the putt, and I'm thinking to myself: "That's low, that's low." I'm thinking, "My God, that's too low." As it came over the hill, I thought it was going to break dramatically, but after it got to the top it just came down straight, straight, straight. It finished four or five feet past, longer than people have said since, longer than people gave him credit for. And he had to putt through his shadow. It was a great putt and fair dues for a hard day's work.

'Once we'd come off the green, big Darren Clarke was on his way out. We got the thumbs-up. They'd all been watching on the giant screen on the range.

Darren said afterwards that they played the first already one-up. It was only what Paul and David deserved.'

The European rookies' exhilarating win contributed greatly to an overwhelming victory by Darren Clarke and Lee Westwood over Jay Haas and Chris DiMarco in the opening afternoon foursomes, Clarke's bagman Billy Foster recalls:

'The crowd started to get a bit boisterous but Casey and Howell shut them up. I can't stress the point enough. Darren and I were just off the practice ground and heading for the first tee. We were already 2½–½ down and there was a chance it could be 3½–½, but when we teed off at the first, Casey holed the putt to win the match. There was such an adrenalin rush. "How good is that?" I said to Darren. If it had been Monopoly, it was a 'Get out of Jail Free' card. It was a massive boost for the team.

'Haas and DiMarco had a little bit of fairway bunker trouble. They caught a couple of lips and left the ball in there to gift a couple of holes to Darren and Lee, who were just rock-solid and on top pretty well all the time. It would have needed an exceptional pair to beat them and Haas and DiMarco weren't that. Darren's ironplay was almost immaculate. He hit to just a few inches to put us three-up by the eighth and we stayed that way until the 11th. Then it was Lee's turn. He hit a lovely shot in to less than three feet and that took us to four-up.

'Darren played for a flyer on 14 and didn't get it, came up short of the green. That caused them a bogey and I thought we'd be going down 15. Haas had a putt to keep the game alive on the 14th but he missed a short one. *Adios, Amigos!*'

That opening success was soon cancelled out by Miguel Angel Jiménez and Thomas Levet's 4 and 3 defeat to a Phil Mickelson licking his wounds after being dropped in the morning and partner David Toms. Levet's caddie Owen Craig felt that flattered the Americans:

'It was fairly close. Again, it probably all came down to a couple of short putts missed. Mickelson had hit two or three wayward tee-shots, but they'd got away with it every time, somehow found a way to the green. Then, on the ninth, we missed a shortish one, which was crucial. On ten, we played for a bit of jump from the light rough, but it didn't jump and we came up a bit short. Miguel hit a fantastic pitch and we missed the putt. That changed the match.'

Luke Donald and Sergio García then had to fight hard to swing back the balance. Christian Donald, after a morning off, watched his brother come good:

'We got off to a good start. Luke was hitting fairways and greens, and Sergio's putting was great. We were two-up after nine and three-up after 11, but the Americans wouldn't give up and they clawed their way back. We were only one-up with one to play and a game that had looked in the bag could have slipped away from us. A half would have been very unsatisfactory.

'On 18, Luke hit a great four-iron after Sergio's drive. He was on the wrong side, but he still hit the green, the most important thing. We were about 40 feet, maybe just less, away, with a bit of a ridge to go over for Sergio. Furyk had hit a three-iron, I think it was, to just a little longer, but with a slightly easier putt for Funk. Fred hit his putt ten feet wide but then Sergio hit an amazing putt up and over the rise, to about two feet. We had it, or so I thought. Furyk then went and holed the ten-footer. Luke told me his legs were shaking a little bit on the putt, but he rolled it in and that really was it.'

Well before that tight match ended, Padraig Harrington and Paul McGinley had hammered another nail into the coffin of America's hopes, this time defeating arguably the best pairing the home side could put out, leaving Woods empty-handed again and nullifying the power of Love. No one could beat the fighting Irish, says Harrington's caddie Flood:

'We got the nod we were to play foursomes with Paul, which was great. Padraig and Paul get on real well together and so do Darren [Reynolds] and me. That was one of the most memorable moments of the Ryder Cup – four Irish guys heading off. There was a huge Irish contingent in the crowd, so it was great craic. There were Irish flags everywhere for that match. When we walked onto the ninth green, we counted nine Irish tricolours in the stand alone. There was a great buzz.

'It wasn't a great start. Padraig hit a terrible tee-shot left at the first and we lost that and then we lost the second. Padraig was feeling a little bit tired, but losing the first two seemed to get them going. From the third tee on they played really solid golf and they would have been hard for anybody to beat. We might have been playing two of the best players in the world, but with the two of them so determined and the huge following we had, it was brilliant. When our match finished on 15, the whole place erupted. I remember the Irish crowd bursting onto the green after we'd won and the American police not knowing how to handle it. They didn't understand what was happening. It just doesn't happen in America. The Irish supporters broke out in a chant of 'Olé, Olé, Olé'. It was Darren's old man who actually led the whole thing.'

McGinley's caddie Reynolds was delighted to be taking on Woods, especially knowing he had his own leprechaun in the gallery:

'We were practising on the ninth and I looked on the giant screen showing fixtures for the afternoon. I said to Paul: "That's the best they can come up with. It's exactly who you want to play. On your game, you two can beat anybody."

'When we got on the first tee, the support was unbelievable. It was my first time in Tiger's presence. You couldn't miss my dad Tony in the crowd. He got stuck in with some great Irish guys. But he was very fair and I think the Americans liked him. He had a tricolour wrapped around him and wore a special Irish hat. Monty came up to me and said: "Your dad's great. It's great to have him here." With Harrington and McGinley together and us two Irish caddies, it was great patriotism, but that's how we Irish are.

'But all of a sudden we were two-down and I said to Ronan: "Jeez, we haven't got into the match yet and we're two-down." Ronan said: "We won't panic yet." The two lads felt the same, ground out, hit fairways and greens, made a couple of putts.

'All of a sudden we've got it back to level after nine. On the tenth, I got a bit shaky. I wasn't ever nervous on the first tee, even knowing we were with Tiger. But all of a sudden at the tenth, I'm a bit edgy. Paul drove it into the right rough, drew a very bad lie. Padraig hacked it up the fairway as best he could. Paul had a 60-yard chip and I remember walking forward of him. As soon as he hit it, I could see it was a beautiful shot. It bounced about four feet short, straight in the hole, caught the lip and bounced out the back. It was stiff, it was given. All of a sudden every bit of edginess drained out of my body.

'Then we went a couple up after 12. At the 13th, the par-three, Langer came up to Paul and said: "Keep it short, 20 feet's good here." The pin was back left. We hit the green. Tiger's hit through and we could see he's bunkered. When we walk up to the green, Tiger's ball is plugged, really buried. I can't see us losing the hole. Myself and Ronan dropped the bags. Obviously tension was setting in on Langer. He came over to us after Love hit the shot and told us not to be leaving the bags there. We said, "Why?" and Langer said: "Well, because, if he knifes this next shot and hits the bags, you're going to cost us the hole." So we moved the bags and crouched down so the crowd could see the play and I said to Ronan: "I think he's talking crap. It's only if one of our guys hits our bag that there's a problem." I think that showed how the tension was. I said to Ronan: "We want to check this out," although I was 101 per cent I was right.

'We went three-up and on 14 Padraig hit a great drive and Ronan said he'd go over and speak to Langer now. Langer told Ronan he was sorry and that it had been the heat of the moment. He'd been anxious to get everything right. "We want to win this match. I apologise. It's the Ryder Cup," Bernhard said to Ronan. He'd won two majors and played in a lot of Ryder Cup matches and even he was unsure of the Rules of Golf at that point because of all the pressure of trying to win.

'On 15, we're in the middle of the fairway and the yardage was perfect for a sand-iron. Paul hit it to five feet. When I got up there, I knew Padraig wouldn't miss it. He rolled it in to win the match and that was the biggest kick I got out of the Ryder Cup, when I heard them singing "You'll never beat the Irish" by the side of that green. It made the hair stand up on the back of my neck.'

For the European camp, there were no premature celebrations (many remembered Brookline) but an air of confidence at being 11–5 ahead after day two. Only three points were needed to keep the Ryder Cup, another half point on top for victory. When the singles draw appeared, Hal Sutton had put out his team in the order that they qualified, with the two wild-cards going out in the last two matches. Points on the board early was obviously Sutton's gambit. It was a last throw of the dice.

Woods was, thus, first man out. Who would be taking him on? Paul Casey's caddie Craig Connelly soon found out:

'We were all congregated around the 12th green during the Saturday afternoon foursomes when Thomas Bjørn came up to Paul and said: "Looks like Tiger's going to lead off. Are you up for it?" Paul didn't have to say yes. It was exactly what he wanted. I think it's exactly what anyone would want: teeing off number one and trying to make a point against the opposition's best player. Paul was well up for it.

'When it got to Sunday, though, Paul didn't play particularly well. He wasn't nervous. It just didn't happen. Paul knows if only he'd played half-decent he'd have beaten Tiger.

'For the first eight holes, Woods' driving was the worst I've seen for a player of his calibre, but he got away with it. He hit it so wide that he found bare lies. His short game's the best in the world.

'At the first, Tiger had hit a tee-shot that should have been deep in the trees, but when he got to his ball, there's this fantastic gap between two bunkers and all he has to do is hit the front of the green and it rolls up. If you start thinking "he's lucky, I'm unlucky", you get beaten. Paul never did that. He was more disappointed in his own game, not thinking about where Tiger was and how he was getting away with it.

'We three-putted the first, gave him a hole start. You can't afford to do that with Tiger. We halved the second in fives and at the third Tiger hit in long and right. Paul didn't hit a great shot and we halved it in fours. Then at the fourth Paul found a real nasty lie. Tiger had hit a snap-hook that should have gone in the houses. Gets there, between the trees and the houses, he has a great line in to the green. Paul hits long and right on five, probably a wrong club by the caddie!

'They'd moved the sixth forward. You could drive it. Having said Tiger had hit some of the worst tee-shots I'd ever seen, on six he hit one of the best drives I've ever seen. He was 15 feet from the pin at the back. Paul was in between a driver and three-wood. Obviously he had to get there, so he tried to back off a driver a little bit and hit in the left bunker. He's got a 35-yard bunker shot and he absolutely stiffs it, sits in its pitch mark about two feet away. Tiger gracefully gives him it and then two putts from 15 feet, a half.

'That's how it was. All much of a muchness. We can't seem to get anything going. At the 12th, we miss the fairway so we can't get the green at the par-five. Tiger hits a perfect drive and then a three-iron to about 25 feet. There was the loudest noise I've ever heard in my life at a sporting venue. I've been to Parkhead, Hampden Park, Ibrox, Highbury and I'd never heard anything like this. Tiger gave it the old pumped fist, like when he's winning majors. You could feel the ground move.

'It put Paul behind the eight-ball. After that, he tried his best but nothing would go right for him.'

The Americans were battling back, up in nearly every match. It needed an immediate riposte. There could be no better man in the European team for never-say-die, as Sergio García's caddie Glen Murray knew all too well:

'We stuffed up the very first hole. Phil put it in the trees and he had no shot. He tried to hit out of the trees to the green, hit the tree and bounced down into the rough. He's only 40 yards in front of us, playing three in the rough. We were hitting up the fairway. The pin was back right and with a small landing area. We tried to hit it left of the flag but I don't know if subconsciously he wanted to go for the flag. He pushed it a little and plugged in the right-hand bunker. It gave Phil a chance to hit on the left side of the green and two-putt. We didn't up-and-down it, so we halved that flipping hole.

'So we should be one-up, but we aren't. Then on the second, the par-five, Phil hit three-wood off the tee. It's dog-leg, right-to-left off the tee, he's a left-hander and it's an easy cut with the driver. I don't know where that decision came from. He hit it in the left bunker. But he laid up 80 yards short and still made birdie. We were coming out of the semi-rough and it came out a little soft. We hit it into the front bunker. Again. All Sergio could do was at least make birdie by up-and-downing it to stay one-down.

'The third hole, Sergio hit a six-iron. The pin was tucked close to the left bunker and you can't hurt left there. We found the left bunker to go two-down. Phil's hitting the ball shockingly but he's made a couple of putts. Two-down. It was a bit of a shock to the system.

'I wasn't at Brookline, but you wonder what's going on in Sergio's head. Was he thinking about that? The whole board's bloody red!

'Phil was hitting it really badly. But he was making putts, hitting out of the trees and making putts. You don't want to be playing matchplay against somebody like that.

'As time went on, though, you felt something had to give. But at seven, Sergio hit in the back bunker after getting a bit of a flyer out of the rough. He made an unbelievable up-and-down for a half.

'At the eighth hole, we hit into the rough and he shanked his second shot. We had a bit of a weird lie, a downhill slope, and we went two-down again. Then it all changed.

'It was a five-iron on the ninth to about 18 feet left of the hole that started it and a great putt that turned it. Phil hit a good shot on the green, too, but Sergio made his and Phil didn't, so that left us only one-down.

'Suddenly it was our turn to hole the putts. Sergio holed a really long one on the tenth, must have been 25 to 30 feet, and suddenly we're all-square, but you can't argue with two good birdies like that. If it had been putts that turned it, then Sergio's ironplay was great, too. He hit to pretty much given on 11, must have been less than two feet. Phil had a longish one and finished up needing to hole a four-footer for just par. We were up at last.

'We'd won three holes in a row, all to birdies, on quite a tough stretch. That was huge. Walking down the 12th hole, I felt they were getting flustered. Phil's caddie shouted at a couple of the camera guys, telling them they weren't allowed to walk in front of Phil, they had to stay behind him. You could see Phil was getting a little pissed off.

'At 12, we had a good chance to make it four in a row, but we missed a short putt. The 13th was a big hole, though. Phil hit quite a good shot in, but he just missed the green right. His ball took a bit of a hop and finished in the thick stuff above the green with a downhill chip, pretty much an impossible shot. Sergio hit a good shot, but he caught the slope and his ball rolled about 35 feet down. It was a real 'Wall of Death' putt up the slope. Phil was pretty much dead, no shot, all he could do was hit to about where our tee-shot was. Sergio ran his right up to the cup, given, and Phil missed his par, so suddenly we are two-up.

'The holes to come were not exactly birdie holes, so if we could just make pars I felt we were going to hang in there. That was pretty much what we did. We parred 14 and then on 15 Sergio hit it right off the tee and didn't really have a clear second shot. He hit a kind of low nine-iron from 100 yards and it went just over the green. He had a really fluffy lie, with no green to work with, but he managed to get it six to eight feet. I remember the green was really crusty and it was a quick left-to-right putt and he made it. That was probably the biggest par he made in the match. Two-up, three to go.

'Then Phil made the most bizarre choice with his second shot on 16. Sergio hit it right off the tee and Phil hit into the semi-rough left. We couldn't go for the green because the pin was at the back and if you hit it in the bunker over the green, you cannot get up-and-down. The only place you can get up-and-down and make four is short. You can't hit it at the flag because there's water there. So we hit it left. Phil tried to hit this weird run-up shot, with a hook, around the water. I told myself he was never going to make it. He went into the water. Sergio putted up to five or six feet, and that was that. We were really chuffed. It was a great victory.

'At that stage, it wasn't over, but around the time Sergio was turning it round, a number of guys were doing the same. You can't help thinking your match had played a bit of a part in the turnaround.'

Europe's twelfth point and first of the singles was indeed a great morale-booster. Just two more and the Ryder Cup would go back across the Atlantic. Darren Clarke's caddie Billy Foster knew his man would be in the thick of it. He was, literally, at the end of his match:

'Darren and Davis were sharing a box of cigars. They bring "ammunition" with them for each other, depending on which side of the Pond they are. I felt it would be a big match, but a good-natured one.

'I'm sure Darren would have been up in the best two or three scores of the day, if not the best. Davis played well early doors then Darren had a few chances around the middle.

'By the turn, Davis was one-up, then the 11th and 12th were big holes. We thought we'd won the 11th when Darren holed a great putt from just off the back of the green, up and over the hill. Davis had a 35-footer, with probably a six-foot break on it for a half, and holed it to stay one-up. Then, on 12, Darren hit two great shots on the green and looked like winning that. Davis hit a tree with his second shot and finished up way short of the green, but got it up-and-down for a half again.

'It looked as though Darren might get beaten again. He was two-down with three to play. Davis hit reasonably close on 16, but Darren nearly holed his second shot. It spun across the hole and finished up about three, maybe four, feet away. He holed that to go to 17 only one-down.

'On 17, the short hole, Darren hit a great shot, but we'd been in between clubs and his ball just went through the back of the green into longish stuff. He'd been working very hard on his chipping a month before, with [coach] Pete Cowen. This was the moment to get a chip right! Davis had put too much cut on his and finished up in the deep bunker. He pitched about five feet past. Darren then holed his chip. His hard work in practice paid dividends. We got very excited – high fives and shoulder slaps. It was just about the most emotional I'd ever seen Darren on a golf course, and with good reason. He'd slid under the ball just like playing a bunker shot and it was in from the split-second it pitched onto the green.

'He's so lifted. Now I'm thinking, Darren's going to get his win at last. On 18, he hit two lovely golf shots, ripped a drive straight down the middle and then hit a five-iron in the middle of the green. It was a great shot, but it went just six inches the wrong side of the hog's back. Fair play to Davis. He hit into the left rough near a drain, which he was close to standing on. I know some golfers who would have stretched their foot another three or four inches, said it was interfering and taken a free-drop. He never took a drop and it just goes to show the integrity of Davis and the friendship and respect he and Darren have for each other. He chipped it out, hit on to the green, made his bogey. Darren ran his ball down and had a three-footer to win the match. Unfortunately, he didn't hole it. Obviously we were very disappointed not to get his first singles win. He's halved two and lost two. But somewhere inside his heart, I guess, he felt a half was a very fair result. I wouldn't say he was happy with it, but his disappointment was lessened. It was a compliment to the two guys that their match was played in the right spirit and showed that the Ryder Cup is heading the right way.'

David Howell had already suffered a crushing defeat to Jim Furyk well before Clarke's match came to its pulsating climax. As Howell's caddie Mick Doran observes: 'When David hit a fantastic six-iron to four foot on the fifth and Furyk got inside him, that just about summed up how it went.'

With the way the match behind him was going, Lee Westwood's clash with Kenny Perry looked as though it would be in line for a place in the history books. When Westwood prevailed, and with Colin Montgomerie assured of at least a half, 14 points were guaranteed. The Ryder Cup could not change hands. Caddie John Graham was happy to be part of it all:

'Lee went one-up after winning the second. The wind at the course made it difficult to pull the right clubs all the time and a lot of the guys went over the back with the second shot, because the flag was front left. Everyone had been taking the mickey out of Lee because of his chipping. But after going through, he chipped it to about five feet. It was a fantastic chip.

'Then Perry got into the groove, won the next to pull it back, won the next to go one-up and he was two-up after six. We just kept grinding, grinding, grinding. I felt Lee would get back into it and by the turn we were only one-down.

'At the 12th, Lee then holed a 15-footer and we were back to all-square, match on. That wasn't just our match, either. Things had swung our way all across the board, after quite a worrying first couple of hours.

'I kept saying to him, coming in: "Be patient. Don't try and win it here on 15 or 16 . He had a chance to win it on 17 with a birdie, but I said: "Just roll it up. If it goes in, it goes in, if it doesn't, we're still one-up.

'On the 18th, Lee hit a really good drive, up the left again. Then he hit a seven-iron. I think he came off it a bit and it finished short right. He putted up to four or five feet. Well, that's all I thought it was. Since I've watched the finish on tape it's got longer every time I've watched it! I don't help him line the putts up any more, didn't all week, because he's such a good reader himself. Perry makes a 12-footer for par. It's down to Lee. He kept his head down, hit a great putt. I could hardly look. But next minute I saw his fists in the air and that was it.'

The man who was to leave his indelible mark on the 2004 Ryder Cup was heading for his destiny. And by his side it was fitting that Colin Montgomerie had his most influential caddie of all, Alastair McLean:

'We were a bit wary on Saturday night. A bunch of us had been there and been disappointed. Nobody was taking anything for granted. When we saw the draw, we didn't understand Hal Sutton's reasoning. Whether he had run out of ideas . . . I don't know. Paul Casey didn't lose too much sleep over playing Tiger Woods; García's playing awesome; Clarkey's always up for anything.

'Monty's out as back-up. He's a great team player, but you don't need him to go out first in the singles, especially if they are going to come back at you. I guess we knew they had to put out their best players first. The last time, some of their best players didn't even get going.

'David Toms was going to be a tough guy to beat, a steady player and an awesome putter. Monty got off to a good start with a great wedge right over the pin at the first, birdied it, one-up. They both made birdie on the second and then Toms made birdie on the third, holed a 30- or 40-footer. Then Toms missed a putt inside three feet. It was one of those where you wondered, do you give him it? If he'd walked over to the ball and thrown it back to Toms and said: "Have I done the right thing?" I'd have said: "Yes, that's fine."

'When Toms missed the putt, it was a complete shock. In your mind you'd made a half and gone on to the next tee still square. To go one-up was a terrific boost.

'Monty's golf wasn't that good. I think he only hit three fairways. One was with a three-iron, another was with a three-wood and the other was the driver. But he scrambled great. His was real piss-you-off matchplay golf.

'There weren't many scoreboards, something else that worked in our favour because there wasn't an awful lot of cheering going on. The crowds didn't really know what was happening in the matches, so they weren't really cheering all the American wins. And, at that point, as we went to the seventh green two-up, there were a lot of them. All the matches had started and I think the only match in blue was Monty's game.

'Monty made a great half on eight. He ducks into a bunker, comes out of the bunker as best he can and then hits a wedge out of the rough, 128 yards, stone-dead. Toms has hit a great drive, hit a lovely shot to about 20 feet, missed the putt. Half in par. Then we missed the green on nine, long left, never the place to be, but he stiffed it again.

'Toms then missed a six-footer, a very, very holeable putt for Toms, so Monty got away with it again. It couldn't last. Toms won the 11th with a four-footer, although Monty made him work for it by chipping to four feet from the bunker. You could feel Toms picking up momentum and the crowd was definitely doing the same by now.

'On 12, Toms hit a lovely, lovely shot to six feet. They both hit eight-irons and Monty hit a superb shot as well, only about four feet outside Toms. Monty bolts his in, Toms misses, so we're still one-up.

'Monty had two great putts on the next hole, ran in about a ten-footer second putt, for another half. Then he made a mess of the next, double-bogeyed it. That took it back to square. Although they were square, you felt the momentum was still with Toms. Monty wasn't playing awfully well now. He missed the 16th fairway on the left as well. He had a niceish lie in the rough and a pretty good distance, but I said: "You'd better just hit this a wee bit left." It came out and went straight down the pin. I'm not sure whether it was meant or whether the rough opened up the clubface, but the ball pitched right behind the pin. It released because it was coming out of the rough, finished up 15 feet long. His putt never left the hole. It was in from the minute he hit it. Toms made a solid par, but we were one-up.

'On 17, Monty hit a solid tee-shot but didn't quite make it up on to the green, he was on the fringe. Toms hit a beautiful shot right over the flag, but going for that pin you were never going to stay on the green. His ball pinged off the green. Monty hit a great chip to about four feet – still a bit smelly, but anything as close as that is a good chip. Toms chips down stiff. So Monty has this wee bender. Straight in the hat.

'Most of the matches had come back our way now, the guys had picked up. I said to him: "Monty that was hard work." He said: "It was rather." He didn't know it was all going to depend on him, though, not even on the tee-shot at the last. We asked Langer what was needed; well, I certainly did, but didn't learn anything. Monty and Langer chatted going down 18, but I don't know whether Bernhard said anything. There was a huge cheer on the 18th green. There was a lot of dancing and jumping around going on. I couldn't tell if they were on the green, which wouldn't have been clever. I thought Westwood had made it, that was it. I didn't know, and I don't think Monty knew, that we still needed half a point and that he was going to be the one to make sure we got it.

'Because he hadn't hit many fairways, I was thinking three-wood at 18. Monty hit three-wood and hit it so well. There was a bunker down at 310 yards and I told him we can't reach that, you'll be fine. He stops about a yard short of the bunker. He was pumped up! Toms hit an all right shot just in the left rough and hit his second short, just right of the green. Monty goes for a five-iron. Langer told him to hit the right half of the green and he'd be just fine. He did just that. But the greens have got really solid now. His ball bounced through the green, just into the first cut. He's still putting, but he's on the other side of the big crown that ran through the middle of the green. Toms chipped strong, about 15 feet big.

'We discussed the shot we now had. He said: "The only way I can hit this putt is through the semi-rough." It was about the same sort of borrow as he'd had with that fantastic chip earlier in the week, playing with Padraig. He felt as long as he got his ball over the hill, the momentum should then take it down through the first cut. If he hit it too soft, it was going to break away left far too quickly; too strong and it could run off the green. Monty hit this unbelievable putt, all the way up the fringe, all the way over the top, still going through the fringe, came out the fringe on the other side and pulled up in it, breaking left. It just makes the green and runs all the way down to the hole to four, maybe five, feet. He could have taken another 20 balls and not done that.

'Toms to go. You don't want people to miss putts but I wanted him to miss this one! But he does hole it. The only good thing was that he was on the line Monty's putt was on and Monty asked: "Did that break right-to-left?" The green seemed to be going the other way. Watching Toms let us know it broke the opposite way to what you might have thought.

'Monty stood back, took a breath, made a great putt. The ball goes in. He drops the putter. He's all emotion. I think he knew it was an important putt. Then it suddenly seems to dawn on him just how important it was. Not just to win his match but the significance of it, the next day, the next week, the next year, for ever. Monty went over to Bernhard. He thanked him for choosing him. Langer said he had just seen the reason why he'd chosen him.'

Montgomerie's highly valued singles record was intact and Europe could celebrate. A crushing disappointment for Luke Donald to Chad Campbell had been part of the early home surge. Thomas Levet's caddie Owen Craig was worried on two counts going into the match with Fred Funk. He could hardly believe an in-form Levet was still pointless. And he could hardly believe the scoreboard. In the end, though, he delighted in Levet creating Gallic history:

'I knew Thomas was playing very well. A couple of wee things just hadn't gone our way in both our matches. We both badly wanted to win.

'Fred's a similar character to Thomas, they get on quite well, but I knew we could beat Fred. Thomas had that attitude. When we teed off, everything was red apart from Monty being level. I think our match became a very key one. We got three-up over holes five, six, seven and at that time we were the only ones really in command. Things then started turning. I think it was good for everybody to see how much we were in command, it definitely helped in Europe's fightback.

'Thomas stayed in control until we teed off at 16 and then realised Europe had won. Thomas was very excited, he just wanted to start celebrating, being the person that he is. I had to try to keep his mind on the job. I wanted him to win his match. He didn't seem to be 100 per cent with it! If they'd not been told to play to a finish, I think he might have shaken hands on a half he was so elated we'd won. I probably wanted it more than he did in the end. I had to keep saying to him: "Go on, Thomas, we want to win this." It was majorly important for him to win, so that everyone shared in the victory on the points table. And it was the first time a Frenchman had won a point.'

Ian Poulter was determined to get something out of his Ryder Cup. Poulter was providing back-up out in the country, but could he have sealed Europe's win before Montgomerie? Neither he nor caddie Mick Donaghy knew:

'It was great to be playing Mr Riley. Obviously Mr Poulter wanted his own back after the fourball and he'd already beaten Mr Riley in the Accenture Matchplay in Carlsbad earlier in the year. I'd said to Billy Foster that I thought we were going to whop them, but I also had a feeling they were going to come back. Monty's birdie on the first and then some blue on the board gave us a bit of a buzz. We'd just left the range. It geed up a lot of players who hadn't teed off yet.

'When we did get off, I felt our match was going to be quite important. Some of our guys were going to struggle to get their matches back. The sixth, a driveable par-four because they'd put the tee forward, was a key point. Mr

Poulter played a fantastic bunker shot to 3½–4 feet. Mr Riley followed him in. If we hadn't birdied that, it would have been level-pegging. At that point there seemed to be a lot of cheering going on for the Americans.

'The 11th took us two-up after Mr Poulter hit another great shot and holed a five-footer. Mr Riley couldn't up-and-down. At the 12th, though, Mr Riley birdied, so we went back to only one-up and it stayed that way after they both parred the next.

'On 14, Mr Poulter hit a really good shot from the rough, obviously couldn't stop it because it was coming out like a bullet, straight over the flag. He chipped up to four feet. Mr Riley had a tricky two-putt, but one of the best putters on the planet putted up to five feet and missed. That was huge.

'At the 15th, once we walked off the tee they started cheering. Lee had just made the putt for the tie. We knew that was about it. Some drunken spectator abused Mr Poulter. That was a shame. Considering the Yankees were getting annihilated, I thought the crowd had been fantastic. It was down to how the European team had handled themselves. I'd heard a Yankee radio station say: "These guys are too nice to hate."

'The 15th's a little par-four up the hill and Mr Poulter hit a sand-iron really close, to about four feet, to go three-up with three to play. We wondered if the match had been won or what. On 16, he hit a 140-yard wedge, he was pumped up and the ball was flying well, just past the hole. He two-putted down from about 25 feet, and that was that. Mr Riley's putt lipped out. Bob's your uncle!

'There's still some argument going on as to who holed the winning putt. The bookies gave it to Monty. We didn't know when he had holed his putt on 18. Some people said that Mr Poulter holed the winning putt when he won the 16th. When the handshakes were done, I didn't care. I'd been too busy concentrating just to get it done. The last thing you want to do is lose 16 because 17, 18, anybody can win them. He didn't want a half-point. He didn't want anything less than a point. He's not the quietest kid and he'd built himself up a bit too much to be disappointed.'

Padraig Harrington featured in the penultimate match. He and caddie Ronan Flood finished up the last Europeans out on the course in the encounter against Jay Haas. Even though the overall match was long over, there was still a point to make for a record, recalls Flood:

'On the first tee, Langer was there, things seemed anxious. We really could need this match. I'd felt disappointed going out at the end, because you think you're not going to be in the thick of it, but standing on the first tee, you're thinking it could be a disaster because the Yanks have opened up so well.

'After that, though, we just did our own thing, didn't really look at scoreboards. We played the first hole badly, but he won the second with an eagle – a drive and an eight-iron to about four feet – and from there on in he played well.

'As we went on, you didn't need to see any scoreboards because you could feel from the crowd the momentum was changing to Europe. We were having a good match. Padraig was three-up after 12 holes. On the 13th, Haas holed a good putt then the whole place erupted. We couldn't really hear each other. By the time we got to the 14th tee, it was all over. Monty had holed his putt to win the Ryder Cup. We were told we had to play the match out. When we walked down the 14th fairway, you could hear a pin drop! It was like letting the air out of a balloon. You just pricked it with a pin and it exploded. There was nothing left there. It was tough to finish out and keep focused because you knew it was finished elsewhere. Haas wanted to win because it was probably his last Ryder Cup. Padraig should have finished him off earlier than he did, but I think it was because of the whole thing being over that it took a bit of the momentum out of him.

'It was totally dead until we got to the 17th green and then everybody was there watching us finish off. We didn't realise, but if Padraig won, it would keep the Yanks out of double figures. We went up the last one-up and he hit in the trap right. Haas was short in two but made a great chip from over the back. Padraig pitched it well past in three. He hit this putt as if there was a wall behind the hole. He nearly took the back of the wall out, but he holed the putt to close down the match and then there were people everywhere. It was party time. We must have been on that green for about an hour. I don't drink, but I must confess to a sniff of champagne!'

The final match going out was that between Paul McGinley and Stewart Cink. There was to be no final putt glory for McGinley this time. He and caddie Darren Reynolds still became part of an historical victory, though:

'We weren't panicking, but you thought to yourself if it carried on that way there was a slim chance they could turn it. If I remember rightly, no European was leading when Paul teed off.

'At the first, Cink picked up after five or six shots. Cink was high up in the world rankings, but his game is very much about putting. When we'd played him on Friday, he'd missed quite a few putts, so he wasn't at his sharpest. Paul played it just right, hit fairways and greens, holed a few putts and never gave his man a chance.

'At the 13th, Langer came over and told us we'd won the Ryder Cup. Paul kind of backed off his tee-shot a bit. It was only a little eight-iron, but we lost the hole to take it back to only two-up. The atmosphere with the crowd had gone deflated. We'd won the Ryder Cup. I said to Paul: "This is like a funeral." He said: "I guess this is what happens when you win and you're still out there. We're just excess now." I said: "Yes, but Paul, you can't do what you did on the last. You've killed him all day and just showed him respect on the last with an eight-iron in your hand. Keep doing what you were doing. Go for the pins." He did and closed him out at the 16th. It was a strange feeling, not exactly an anticlimax, but, out on the course, it was a bit flat. When we got in, though, there was quite a party!'

It was some party, as Darren Clarke's caddie Billy Foster remembers. Foster has had many a soaking at the end of matches in the past and this time was no exception. Foster also found bunker trouble:

'I'd rather hoped that the match could have finished at the 16th so we could have got all 12 caddies to give it a running jump into the lake, but I got just as wet as other years. García chased me all round the 18th green until I gave up and lay down and he poured a whole magnum of champagne over me. Then we decided to have a long-jump competition off the 18th green into the front bunker. I got buried.'

The final celebration was a more poignant one, however, and Lee Westwood's gnarled caddie John Graham not only felt utmost emotion but caused some, too:

'The whole team felt it was good that it came down to Monty. When Harrington holed the last putt of the match, Ronan [Flood] put the flag back in. Everybody was celebrating, but I nipped on and took the flag back out. I thought to myself, what am I going to do with it? I thought, if I got all the players to sign it and put a little message on it, I could give it to Monty. That night, they took us by limousine to the players' hotel and I got Bernhard to present it to Monty. He was quite tearful and said he would treasure it for ever.'

HOW WE WON THE O'RYDER CUP

2006: THE RECORD IS EQUALLED

THE K CLUB, COUNTY KILDARE, IRELAND, 22–24 SEPTEMBER
EUROPE 18½ USA 9½

CAPTAINS: Ian Woosnam (Europe)
Tom Lehman (USA)

(European names first)

Fourballs (morning):
C. Montgomerie and P. Harrington 0, T. Woods and J. Furyk (1 hole) 1
P. Casey and R. Karlsson (half) ½, S. Cink and J.J. Henry (half) ½
S. García and J. M. Olazábal (3 and 2) 1, D. Toms and B. Wetterich 0
D. Clarke and L. Westwood (1 hole) 1, P. Mickelson and C. DiMarco 0

Foursomes (afternoon):
P. Harrington and P. McGinley (half) ½, C. Campbell and Z. Johnson (half) ½
D. Howell and H. Stenson (half) ½, S. Cink and D. Toms (half) ½
C. Montgomerie and L. Westwood (half) ½, P. Mickelson and C. DiMarco (half) ½
L. Donald and S. García (2 holes) 1, T. Woods and J. Furyk 0

Fourballs (morning):
P. Casey and R. Karlsson (half) ½, S. Cink and J.J. Henry (half) ½
S. García and J. M. Olazábal (3 and 2) 1, P. Mickelson and C. DiMarco 0
D. Clarke and L. Westwood (3 and 2) 1, T. Woods and J. Furyk 0
H. Stenson and P. Harrington 0, S. Verplank and Z. Johnson (2 and 1) 1

Foursomes (afternoon):
S. García and L. Donald (2 and 1) 1, P. Mickelson and D. Toms 0
C. Montgomerie and L. Westwood (half) ½, C. Campbell and V. Taylor (half) ½
P. Casey and D. Howell (5 and 4) 1, S. Cink and Z. Johnson 0
P. Harrington and P. McGinley 0, T. Woods and J. Furyk (3 and 2) 1

Singles:
C. Montgomerie (1 hole) 1, D. Toms 0
S. García 0, S. Cink (4 and 3) 1
P. Casey (2 and 1) 1, J. Furyk 0
R. Karlsson 0, T. Woods (3 and 2) 1
L. Donald (2 and 1) 1, C. Campbell 0
P. McGinley (half) ½, J.J. Henry (half) ½
D. Clarke (3 and 2) 1, Z. Johnson 0
H. Stenson (4 and 3) 1, V. Taylor 0
D. Howell (5 and 4) 1, B. Wetterich 0
J. M. Olazábal (2 and 1) 1, P. Mickelson 0
L. Westwood (2 holes) 1, C. DiMarco 0
P. Harrington 0, S. Verplank (4 and 3) 1

THE CADDIES

GRANT BERRY (HENRIK STENSON 2006)

Berry, who like Henrik Stenson made his Ryder Cup debut in 2006, has spent most of his adult life caddying. After shouldering his pro's bag at his home Ringway Club near Manchester Airport as a teenager, Berry then took the plunge and decided, at 20, to be a full-time caddie. He first worked on the European Ladies Tour for Beth Boozer but then moved onto the men's tour. While Berry served four years apiece with Gordon Brand Junior and Russell Claydon and had a stint with Howard Clark, he has been on the bag for no less than six Swedes during his career, including two stints with Stenson. His latest began 18 months before their epic week at The K Club.

GARETH LORD (ROBERT KARLSSON 2006)

Lord played in the 1990 England Boys Home Internationals at Hunstanton alongside Lee Westwood and fashioned his game in the same Warwickshire team as Steve Webster. After graduating at the University of Tennessee in Chattanooga, the Coventry man took a teaching pro job in Germany. Taking time off to caddie for his old pal Webster at the 1998 German Open and German Masters, in which they finished second and fourth, persuaded Lord a more lucrative future lay in carrying clubs rather than instructing with them. That subsequently led to a call from Robert Karlsson in 2004, a Ryder Cup debut for them both two years later and life turning full circle, in a way, for Lord and Westwood!

THE ACTION

'It would have been so fantastic for Darren to do it . . . I said to him, "It's going to be your destiny to win this."'

Stung by their overwhelming defeat at Oakland Hills, the United States team was ready to hit back. What better place to do so than Ireland, with its great ties to America? Only an outrageous putt in 1999 had prevented the US suffering a whitewash in 13 years' dominance by Europe. Could Tom Lehman and his men stop the rot? Would Ian Woosnam and his team take Europe to further glory and make it a hat-trick of victories?

Lehman had been part of America's only triumph in five encounters, one of the home team that shaded the result in Boston in 1999. He had apologised for his part in the infamous invasion of the 17th green at Brookline. Now, with the slate clean, Lehman wanted victory but with dignity and good feeling between the protagonists. With Irish eyes smiling down on them, the two teams did show great sportsmanship towards each other. However, friendliness to the visitors could only go so far. Those same Irish eyes and voices played their parts in driving Europe to another overwhelming success.

To try to turn the tables this time, Lehman even flew over his team three weeks beforehand for two days of practice, soaking up – and that was to prove a fitting phrase – the autumn conditions and negotiating the Palmer layout at The K Club. The Americans could not have been better prepared.

While they featured four rookies to Europe's two, the US, as usual, had the upper hand as far as world ranking was concerned. They had the world's top man, of course, in Tiger Woods. Phil Mickelson and Jim Furyk were jockeying for number two and three spots in the world. Going into the match, Mickelson had just overtaken Furyk. Woods was giving off signs he would be living up to his talisman status. He'd taken the four US rookies to dinner to give them a run-down on what to expect. With his partnership with Mickelson from 2004 – not exactly one made in heaven – split, the world's top player was expected to lead from the front this time.

The home side had its own men in the world's top echelons, such as Sergio García, Luke Donald, David Howell, Henrik Stenson and Padraig Harrington. America had Zach Johnson, J.J. Henry, Vaughn Taylor and Brett Wetterich making their debuts, compared to Europe's newcomers Robert Karlsson – a man who might have played in 1999 but for an extraordinary wild-card decision by the then captain Mark James – and fellow-Swede Stenson. While the US had four rookies to two, Europe was the much younger outfit. Pundits reckoned it was going to be a close-run encounter after Europe's team was finalised at the BMW International Open in Munich three weeks before the match.

At that time, there were also murmurs: would Woosnam have the acumen to better Lehman? The little Welshman's shortcomings with his grammar when holding press briefings and his dread of making speeches were hardly serious leadership faults. But some figures in the media, although not many went on the record for fear of upsetting the European apple cart, felt things might go pear-shaped at The K Club. And when Woosnam announced his wild-cards, one player in particular launched an astonishing tirade against the captain. Thomas Bjørn, upset he had not got the nod from Woosnam, was fleetingly, until he saw the error of his ways, the captain's arch-detractor. Bjørn reckoned he was worthier than Lee Westwood for the second of Woosnam's picks. There was no criticism by anybody, however, about the other wild-card, which went to Darren Clarke.

It had been an awful time for the Ulsterman. With his wife Heather suffering from cancer, Clarke had had a fragmented two years, spending as much time at home as he could to be with Heather and their two young sons Tyrone and Conor. When Heather died on 13 August, it was thought that Clarke, who had frequently and understandably said that the Ryder Cup was one of the furthest things from his mind, would not want to play at The K Club. However, Clarke made himself available, knowing Heather would have wanted him there. The only question was, would he be ready? A work-out in the Madrid Open the week before the match showed that his spirit was high and his game in good shape, apart from his putting. With an Irish crowd urging him on, Clarke could be a vital part of Europe's bid to thwart America. And so it turned out. Both of Woosnam's choices proved themselves beyond all doubt.

At the start of the week, as both teams flew in to Dublin, while Irish eyes were smiling the weather certainly wasn't. Heavy rain made the course play heavy and long. Because the visitors were more used to clement conditions, Europe was already in the ascendancy. First high winds, then lashing rain, did not dissuade the crowds from turning up to watch practice. Even when the teams could play no more than nine holes because of the conditions, thousands turned up at the gates. Their numbers swelled even more, despite suffering the trials of tortuous journeys by shuttle buses or ankle-deep mud in car parks, when the greatest sporting event ever to be played on Irish soil began in earnest.

The match started with the fourballs. In 2004 at Oakland Hills, Colin Montgomerie and Padraig Harrington handed Europe a huge psychological advantage by chalking up the first point of the match when they beat Tiger Woods and Phil Mickelson. Woosnam was looking for something similar from Montgomerie and Harrington, who this time faced Woods and Jim Furyk, successful partners from the previous year's Presidents Cup.

Alastair McLean was again on Montgomerie's bag. This time his charge had not needed a wild-card, as he had for the previous encounter, which was a fillip for Monty, as McLean observed:

'Monty had qualified well, well in advance. That kept him chirpy. In the previous one, he was uptight because he hadn't made it, he wasn't playing awfully well and he had to be a pick. That reflected in his golf, because he then often tries too hard. This time he was much, much more relaxed because he'd got in early.

'He'd never won at The K Club, but he'd had a third and a second there. He'd finished second the last time we'd played on the course, so he was happy to be going back. It may not always have the best putting surfaces, but it was only going to have to cater for 24 guys.

'The weather was atrocious. We'd intended to go to the course, just to have a wee scout about, but it didn't work out that way. Monday was spoiled. I can't believe anybody was out there on the course on Monday. We knew the weather was going to be pretty rubbishy. Every forecast was very poor.

'We had to play 18 holes as soon as we could, just in case the weather didn't allow it later. So we practised on the Tuesday, playing with Padraig Harrington. They lost on the last to Henrik Stenson and Paul McGinley. Colin wasn't playing awfully well. The previous two weeks he hadn't played awfully well, either. He had putted quite well. In the World Matchplay, he won a couple of matches, but these could have swung either way. But he'd putted well, and his determination got him through.

'In the first practice round, he played nicely, but he wasn't going to beat the world. The next practice day was pretty similar. Then the last practice day we could see something in his swing that wasn't quite right, so we just changed it a wee bit. We went out after lunch to practice, after a wee talk, and he started hitting the ball quite well. We got a proper turn going on his swing, and he started hitting nicely. He left practice that day feeling comfortable with his swing. That was good. The next day was the match.

'It's almost like Europe expects Monty to go out first. And Woosie's no fool. He knows Monty and Padraig beat the top two players in the world the last time out. You don't have to be a genius to reckon that Woods is going to play with Furyk in the top game. That was always going to be on after the partnership they'd formed in the Presidents Cup the previous year. You could bet your house on who the top four players were going to be.'

When Montgomerie and, particularly, Harrington, from Dublin, walked onto the first, the noise from the crowd above them in the stand and lining the tee and fairway was ear-splitting. It had its effect on everybody, especially the official starter for the European Tour, Ivor Robson. In a few moments he will rather forget, Robson went through his Ryder Cup routine, announcing the match would begin with 'foursomes'.

The players looked bemused. Montgomerie made as if to retire, pretending he would not be wanted on the tee in that case. Woods seemed perplexed, then grinned as he realised Robson's gaffe. Montgomerie's caddie McLean sympathised with the starter:

'Poor Ivor. He was as nervous as anybody else. You can't help but be nervous and excited. Even Tiger's got to be affected. The roar that greeted these guys on the first tee was just unbelievable. Doesn't matter how long you've done it, Ivor was very, very nervous. You could see his papers shaking in his hand.'

Then they were off. Furyk went first, splitting the fairway. Woods then pulled his drive violently, sending his ball into the lake by the clubhouse and giving the eager spectators a close-up view of the world number one as he tried to extricate himself from his opening folly. McLean continues:

'Tiger slams a three-wood left, going left. He finds the lake. This is the best player in the world by not even the length of the country but the length of the world. He's got to have been affected by something. You can only assume it was the crowd.

'Monty hits a good shot. All week I've felt it was a three-wood. And all week he's said he wanted to hit driver. It's got a bigger head, and he was scared he might miss the ball! So he hits driver. Fair enough. Every time he hit driver down there, he hit a really good drive. It was just the same all those years ago when he teed off at Oak Hill [in the 1995 Ryder Cup]. I always thought that was a three-wood as well.'

Harrington had sent his ball into the trees on the right and, like Woods, was out of the hole after Montgomerie found the green. Furyk drew first blood by holing his putt as Montgomerie missed his.

The occasion seemed to be unsettling Woods. After teeing off at the second, he ran for the portable toilet. His caddie Steve Williams was already inside. An anxious Woods waited, on one leg some of the time, buttons undone, until a sheepish Williams emerged from the portaloo and he could dive in. Woods' emergency stop, though, could not halt his poor start. Apart from one hole, it was virtually Furyk versus Montgomerie and Harrington over the first nine holes. But the American pair did dovetail better coming home. There was a reason for a disappointing start for his player and Harrington, McLean says:

'Padraig didn't play that badly, but the trouble with him and Monty was that they just couldn't buy a putt. They played really well at the start, but they were pinned back by the turn. Tiger hit a great shot on eight, and then Furyk holed a great putt – must have been 35 to 40 feet and with four or five feet of bend on it.

'We should have won ten and we didn't. Then Woods and Furyk won 11 and 12. So we lost four holes out of five in the middle section. We were right up against it. And Tiger was beginning to find his game. We went three-down on 13. To be fair to the boys, though, they didn't panic, stayed patient. Monty hit a great tee-shot on 14, holed the putt, got one back – two-down. Then Padraig pulled another back. It made for a very, very exciting finish. At the 17th and 18th holes, anything can happen. But, unfortunately, the putts just wouldn't go in. They were both halved. The Americans got the start they wanted.'

So, first point went to the visitors. However, the matches following looked promising for Europe.

The man in form coming into the Ryder Cup was undoubtedly Paul Casey. At Wentworth the previous week, where Woods and Furyk had surprisingly not survived the first round, he won the World Matchplay Championship in some style. Casey had grown in stature since his 2004 Ryder Cup debut. And so had his caddie Craig Connelly:

'We were a little bit better prepared than 2004. Getting the call at the 11th hour two years ago was nice, but I would say it was only half enjoyable. I enjoyed this one more because I was part of the whole qualifying experience as well. Paul had made the team with some weeks to go. He'd been really consistent, knocking on the door every other week. He went into this Ryder Cup – I guess we both did – full of confidence.

'The World Matchplay Championship was great preparation – gets your eye in, gets your feel for matchplay. You can be a little bit more aggressive and play golf differently. He was really aggressive at Wentworth. He went for a lot of shots. It was almost frightening how focused he was, though, to get to the final and win it.

'We mainly practised with Luke and David, and then on the Thursday we were paired with Robert, playing greensomes [when both players drive off and then choose which ball to play for the second shot]. I felt we'd play with Luke or David in one or both of the formats. Paul has good experience with both of them in World Cup and Seve Trophy matches. I thought we'd play with David in the fourballs, but we ended up playing with Robert against Stewart Cink, who can be a tough customer, and one of their rookies, J.J. Henry.

'It made sense. Both of them are long and both play aggressively; they're both birdie machines. But I don't think it's been documented enough: the 2006

European team was as strong as any team there had ever been. I hear the 1981 US team was a bit tasty, but I think this team rivalled it. We had such quality in depth. And anybody could play with anybody. So you had to expect players would have to sit out. No one would have said at the start of the week we'd have Robert and Paul together. You'd have automatically expected the two Swedes to go out together. But it worked.

'Robert began in fantastic style. Paul was very steady. They complemented each other really well. We were three-up after nine. Then Stewart and J.J. just hit us with a barrage of birdies.

'We found ourselves one-down with three to play. At 16, J.J. has knocked it through the back of the green, over the water, in two. He hit a great shot in, long but only about 15 feet away. Paul kind of missed his tee-shot and then hacked out. The ball squirted out in the heavy rough, and he still had a six-iron in. Robert's in the water. The writing looked on the wall.

'For the record, Paul hit in to about 60 feet – it keeps getting longer and longer! He bins it. That changed the match back in our favour. We could have won it then. Both Paul and Robert had eagle putts of about 30 feet at the last to win the match. But it wasn't to be. It was a great half, though.'

For Karlsson, it was a poignant moment. It had taken seven years for the Swede, the tallest man on the European Tour at six feet five inches, to finally prove his stature as a Ryder Cup player. Karlsson had taken his omission from the 1999 Brookline team, when Andrew Coltart was preferred to him, with great dignity. The present captain's faith in him had been justified.

One of the criticisms levelled at Woosnam was that he didn't keep in touch with his players as much as he should have done. That was patently not the case as far as Karlsson was concerned. The captain contacted him to ask a leading question – even before the Swede was 100 per cent sure of being in the team, as his caddie Gareth Lord reveals:

'When Robert won in Hamburg [Deutsche Bank Open, TPC of Europe] that pretty much meant he was in. It was still mathematically possible he could be caught, though. Then on the Monday lunchtime the week after his win, when we were in Malmo, he got this text from Woosie saying, "Who do you want to play with?" He thought it was somebody winding him up, so he ignored it. We were staying in a big house that week, and a load of tour people came round. One of them was Rowles [Martin Rowley, Woosnam's caddie], and so Robert asked him, "Is this Woosie's number?" Rowles checked his phone and said "Yes, it is." Robert said, "Oh, hell. I thought somebody was taking the p***!" That night, Woosie phoned Robert and said, "Why haven't you replied to my text. Who do you want to play with?" Robert told him it hadn't really sunk in that he was in the team yet. After gathering his thoughts, he said, "Well, Stenson in the fourballs, and Monty in the foursomes." Woosie told him everybody wanted to play with Monty in the foursomes.'

Having given his choices, Karlsson began The K Club encounter – with Casey. Caddie Lord appreciated captain Woosnam's decision making:

'This is where Woosie is to be commended. He got the pairings brilliantly right. Resting Luke Donald twice, Henrik Stenson twice and David Howell twice, you'd have said we'd struggle. And you wouldn't have said Robert would play with Casey. As it happens, they play a similar game, and they did make a good pair – but we hadn't thought of it.

'On the Thursday in practice, Robert and Paul were the second of three fourballs, and you wondered, "Is this going to be the eight that are going to start?" Then, halfway round the nine holes, we found out. Woosie came out on the course and told us. We knew we were playing the next morning. It was about an hour and half before the opening ceremony. It was a bit disconcerting for the third fourball of Donald, Stenson, Howell – numbers nine, 11 and 13 in the world – and McGinley. They knew, pretty much, that they wouldn't be playing. But I think they were also told they were definitely going to play in the afternoon. You thought to yourself, "What if the morning fourballs win 4–0, surely he's not going to split things up?" But Woosie had already decided on his pairings for the first day. We didn't know exactly who we were playing with, but we did know we'd be out in the morning. Everyone was playing well, by all accounts, so it was understandable. But it was some decision by Woosie.'

When the draw came out on Thursday late afternoon, one of Karlsson's opponents was familiar to the Swede, as Lord remembers:

'We stayed on and played in Boston after the US PGA and Akron [World Golf Championship, Bridgestone Invitational], and while a few of the American Ryder Cup players were there, Robert was the only one from the European team, and we ended up playing with J.J. Henry on Thursday and Friday. Of course, we played J.J. in both the fourballs. It was funny, Robert kidded J.J. on Saturday when they were walking around, asking him, "What time do you want to play on Sunday?" They felt it was odds on they were going to get each other again.

'On the Friday morning, Robert played fantastically. He had seven birdies. Casey eagled the fourth, but I think that was the only hole he beat Robert on going out. Paul was always there. Cink and Henry came back in 29, though, so it looks like they [Karlsson and Casey] threw it away, but they didn't. Both teams were eight-under better-ball. Either pair would have won any other match.'

The half for Casey and Karlsson added to a point already in the bag for Europe, placed there by a new and telling partnership from Spain – Sergio García and José Maria Olazábal.

However, before the pair went into battle, an emergency meeting went on behind the scenes between their two caddies. Glen Murray, the South African bagman for García, who was serving at his second Ryder Cup, explains how he and Olazábal's caddie, Phil Wobbly Morbey, had to become diplomats:

'To be honest, we didn't really get a lot of information about what was going to happen and who we were going to be paired with. We played with Ollie twice in the practice rounds, so obviously we were both thinking we would be playing with him. But there was a fair chance Sergio was going to play all five games. All week I kept asking him, "Do you know who you're playing with?" and he said, "No, not really." So, I couldn't take anything for granted. There was a fair chance we could play with Lee [Westwood] in the fourballs again.

'Then, come Thursday afternoon, Woosie laid his cards on the table, as it were. The two front practice groups were the pairings, and the four at the back were to be left out. It came as quite a shock to those last four guys. Leaving out Luke Donald? That was huge.

'So, it was to be Ollie. When it became clear, me and Wobbly decided to have a little chat. I don't know if Woosie took it for granted that because they're Spanish they're great friends. They're good friends, but I wouldn't say they are any closer than that. They play practice rounds together now and then, but I wouldn't say they call each other up all the time.

'Wobbly and I both knew this could go either way. Ollie is such a perfectionist. He can't expect to put his head down and just worry about his game alone, though. Sergio needs encouragement. We talked about it quite a bit, and Wobbly decided the best thing he could do was to have a word with Ollie.

'The key to the partnership, though, was going to be the start they got off to against Toms and Wetterich. If they went down, I think it could have been a catastrophe. As it turned out, they started on fire.

'I think Wetterich was very nervous, and he looked a little out of his league, but that first tee would have intimidated anyone, let alone a first-timer.

'We both hit down the middle at the first. Sergio birdied the first; Ollie birdied the second. Although David Toms followed him in, they birdied the fourth and sixth. They were hot, and as soon as they got their tails up there was no stopping them.

'Even though they haven't played that much together, it turned out really well. Ollie was fantastic to play with. He's so clutch under pressure with his putting.'

Olazábal had been the one to suffer at Brookline with that infamous invasion of the 17th green, but in Madrid the week before the Ryder Cup he urged everyone to move on from 1999 and forget the past. For the former two-times Masters champion, The K Club represented a new era. It was his first Ryder Cup match in seven years. However, he could not be accused of panicking about his place. In fact, it was almost brinkmanship that took Olazábal on a hunting trip the week the team was decided in Munich. The way things worked out, the phlegmatic Spaniard was not knocked out of the team.

For Morbey, it was a poignant moment when Olazábal's place was sealed. He explains exactly what he said to Olazábal:

'When Woosie was named as captain, it was great motivation for José to get in and a massive ambition for me. I'd been seven years away, and I'd always looked forward to the match.

'When I knew we were playing with Sergio, I had a word with José. Sergio is a very, very upbeat player who wears his heart on his sleeve. He's flamboyant, and he's a fantastic golfer. Ollie's a bit different. He can be very hard on himself. A couple of poor shots and his head can go down. So I said, "If you keep Sergio going, you're going to win. If Sergio sees you down, he might get down on himself and make it hard for the team to win." José was very good. He didn't take it the wrong way.

'He was fantastic with Sergio, even though José didn't play that well straight away. He certainly kept his head up. He made a couple of important birdies, but Sergio played magnificently.'

The last match out in the morning drew rapturous applause from the gathering at the first tee, the noise from the spectators reaching a crescendo never heard before in a Ryder Cup as Darren Clarke made his entrance. Clarke was with his fellow wild-card Lee Westwood, ready to play against Phil Mickelson and Chris DiMarco. The crowd willed the Northern Irishman to hit a good drive. He didn't disappoint them. His caddie Billy Foster, featuring in his ninth Ryder Cup, was by his side for a fifth time in the matches. Foster recognised what Darren's appearance meant:

'It had been a tough time for Darren. He'd done well to keep competing to a certain level. I have to take my hat off to the fellow. To keep going like he did was an incredible achievement. He fully deserved his wild-card. Woosie had played with Darren the day he shot 60 at The K Club and won there. The world of golf knows he's one of the best strikers of the ball in the business, and on his day he's a match for anybody. So, as long as Woosie thought he was mentally strong enough to cope with it, he had to be a pick.'

Foster is not just a great asset because of his experience, he is the arch spirit-lifter. If there is an escapade to be had or a ducking to be given, the Yorkshireman is not far away from the action. However, because of having to change flights after a week at the Madrid Open, where Clarke tuned up after an eight-week layoff, Foster arrived too late on Monday to help Europe in a first victory over America, as he explains:

'The caddies had just finished the "Bucket Challenge" between the European caddies and American caddies, which, unfortunately, I missed. They chip from 15 yards away, first one to chip in wins it for the team. Harrington's caddie Ronan Flood holed his first chip to win the crystal trophy for Europe, which got the week off to a great start for us.'

Clarke had had putting problems in Madrid, but any worries he had disappeared in practice, as Foster observed:

'Some guys struggle before the Ryder Cup, but when it comes to the match, from nowhere, they seem to raise their games. Darren raised his putting game that week.

'Practice was all about just getting used to the conditions. The weather was poor, so it meant nine holes Wednesday, nine holes Thursday, which was perfect. Our lads know the course well. They just needed to gauge the flight of the ball, things like that. Normally, it's three days of hard slog, and by the time the match starts, you can feel worn out.'

When their match began, Foster, despite all his previous experiences, was floored by the reception on the first tee:

'The K Club will go down in history as something special for all those involved in it – starting with the fantastic crowd. You'll never get the atmosphere again like we had there. It was like being at a football match. But while the crowd was boisterous, they were also fair. It was something very special that we'll remember for the rest of our lives.'

Beginning the week with old friends made all the difference, too, says Foster:

'Lee was the perfect partner, not just because he'd won twice round The K Club, but because he's such a great team man. He'd won 4½ points out of 5 at Oakland Hills, so he was well worth his wild-card. And he's obviously a natural partner for Darren. He was a bit of an unsung hero, 4 points out of 5 this time, never lost a match, fantastic.

'You looked at the team on paper, and Lee and Darren had the two toughest games you could get – Woods and Furyk and Mickelson and DiMarco.

'I thought the opening morning was always going to be very traumatic for Darren. I know he'd thought about that first tee-shot for a couple of weeks. And his reception was absolutely scary, like walking into the ring in a world-championship boxing match with thousands of people shouting and stamping their feet. I had tears in my eyes. I knew what Darren was going through. I thought, "He's going to break down." Fair play to him, he stood up like a man – took it all – and bombed his tee-shot 300 yards straight down the middle. The best shot he hit all week. If it had been me, I'd have hit three foot behind and the divot would have knocked the ball off the tee. What strength of character.

'He then hit a wedge into the green, pitched it ten feet past the hole. It spun back, he nearly holed it, it finished up about 12 feet away, and he sank the putt.

'From there, it was a bit nip and tuck, but Darren and Lee always looked in control. They came to the last hole. Darren had a real good yardage – a perfect five-wood yardage for him – and he hit a great shot, a little bit right, but he just flew the bunker. He had an eagle chance from just off, about 20 feet. Mickelson hit a great shot, but he flew it too far and went over the green. You're never going to rule Mickelson out of chipping in, but once he missed, Darren just hit up stiff. That was it, a good scalp.'

It was the start of a glorious Ryder Cup for Woosnam's wild-cards and an indifferent week for Mickelson and DiMarco, who only picked up one point between them. As it had been at the three previous Ryder Cups, the opening morning belonged to Europe, this time by 2½–1½.

During the morning, just as in years past when Ireland had its great run in the football World Cup under Jack Charlton, there came a chant that the Irish have commandeered from the Spanish: "*Olé, olé, olé, olé*". It was to be a joyous theme tune – a song for Europe.

It was now time for the second part of the strategy devised by Woosnam on the Wednesday, no doubt in collusion with his two vice-captains Peter Baker and Des Smyth. Woosnam had decided all 12 of his team would play on the opening day, come what may. The men sitting out for Europe were Casey, Karlsson, Olazábal and Clarke, while Woosnam put out Howell and Stenson together, reformed the 2004 pairings of Donald and García and Harrington and McGinley, and then caused something of a surprise by teaming up Montgomerie and Westwood.

It proved to be a close-run thing in the afternoon, with all the matches going right to the 18th. Crucial halves were made by both sides at the last hole, before García and Donald made the only full point of the afternoon in the final match.

Harrington and McGinley set the afternoon in motion, the two Dubliners drawing a huge wall of noise from the home fans. Their match against Chad Campbell and Zach Johnson provided Harrington, astonishingly for such a solid Ryder Cup performer, with his only half point of the week.

McGinley's caddie for a second successive Ryder Cup, Darren Reynolds, had this to say about the match:

'Paul took not playing in the morning on the chin. By their reactions, some of them weren't too happy. Paul had practised really well, and we were expecting a run in the afternoon.

'They played really well together, Paul and Padraig, and the only reason they didn't get a full point was that Campbell and Johnson birdied the last three holes. I was glad Paul got something out of it. His form had dipped quite a bit going into the Ryder Cup.'

After the popular Irish duo, the new pairing of Howell and Stenson took on two of America's stalwarts, Cink and Toms. Stenson's caddie Grant Berry had rejoined the Swede right at the start of the Ryder Cup campaign and watched his man achieve a goal. Then when the matches started, Berry understood what a Ryder Cup in Ireland was going to be all about:

'When I started with him, he told me he wanted to get into the Ryder Cup. He played well enough to do that with a couple of seconds and a third at the end of 2005, but the start of 2006 – second, first, seventh – was a revelation. The job was done. A third in the TPC just rubber-stamped it, and he wasn't one of the players who had to sweat over a place.

'Obviously, it was my debut too, but I wasn't really nervous until I went down to the first tee on the first morning. Woosie got the players and caddies to go down. It was the noisiest cauldron I've ever been in. Tiger was trembling. I think they were all trembling. I thought, "Wow! How am I going to do this later on?" But then, after watching the next group go off, you get a bit used to the noise. The initial group in the morning all looked terrified! But 10,000 people around a little tee is going to intimidate anyone – certainly the Americans.

'At first, Henrik thought he might only be playing two matches when he was told on the Thursday he wasn't in the morning fourballs, because he didn't think he'd be wanted for foursomes. He was delighted when he knew he'd be playing Friday afternoon. And he played his best golf, by far, that day. David [Howell] was struggling a bit, but he putted really solidly, and it was almost like Henrik didn't have to putt anything. Henrik was getting us in the right position, and Howler was putting up close. They combined very well.

'It was close. Henrik hit a brilliant drive down 16 to leave Howler with a five-iron in. Howler had blocked his three previous shots, so he pulled this one. Cink had stiffed his bunker shot. Henrik then hit a fantastic chip from a bad lie close enough for us to halve the hole. That proved crucial. We halved the last two holes.'

The third match, Montgomerie and Westwood versus Mickelson and DiMarco, certainly surprised Montgomerie's caddie Alastair McLean:

'Monty and Westwood! That was out of the blue. We're not sure where that came from. We certainly didn't practice with Lee as a partner. Woosie obviously had it worked out. It turned out to be one of his master strokes.

'Mickelson wasn't playing awfully well. But DiMarco . . . he's so tough, that guy. Even if he's not got his best game with him, he makes things happen with sheer will-power. But it's alternate shots, and if Phil's not at the races, you've always got a chance.

'Since that final practice, you could see Monty's game actually clicking, and he was hitting the ball great. In the previous two or three weeks, he'd been putting nicely. That kind of deserted him on the first morning, but his game had come back. Then, with Lee, he started to putt quite nicely again and play well, so it was not far away from being the complete package. Monty's beginning to drive well, putt well; Lee's driving unbelievably well, long and straight. So there was nothing to fear. It was tight all the way, though. I guess the half was a fair result.'

Luke Donald and Sergio García rounded off the afternoon matches against America's top pairing, Woods and Furyk. It was a perplexed Donald who took to the course, as his brother and caddie Christian observed:

'It had never entered his mind that he wouldn't be starting the match off. He was really shocked when he was told.

'I think Luke was a little nervous at the start, understandably after sitting out the morning. It can take a little while to get going, and you don't have much room for error in foursomes. He hit his first drive quite wide. But I remember Sergio putting his arm round him and saying, "Perfect, partner." That sort of thing is very big for a partnership. It helped Luke to settle down. Sergio was very supportive, especially at the start of their match. Sergio's a great partner for Luke, and they trust each other.'

García's caddie Murray, equally baffled at Donald being left out, takes up the story:

'Number nine in the world. The only thing I can think is that Woosie maybe thought he was a short hitter, but it's hard to leave out a player like that.

'At the first hole, Furyk hit Tiger into the trees, and I don't think they had a shot. It was a double for them. We hit way right of the trees, but we were conceded a four. So we went up early, but it was a bit of a shaky start. We bogeyed the third, and then Luke made two huge putts. He made a 15-footer on four just in front of Furyk, and then Furyk missed. Then on five he sank a hallelujah over the hill, left-to-right. It must have been over 45 feet. That took us two-up. Then we stuffed the next hole up.

'We won ten with a par, and then at the 11th Sergio pushed the second shot right of the green, and we were dead. At 12, Luke made another big putt. At 13, Jim made a putt, and then on the 14th Tiger hit a three or four-iron to four feet. At the 15th, how Jim's tee-shot stayed out of the water, I'll never know. He must have plugged on the bank. Luke rifled one straight down the middle, but we both made pars. The finish was brilliant. I don't think Tiger had the right line on 16, and he hit through the fairway, but we were both forced to lay up. Sergio then hit a sand-wedge to about a foot. Jim's 12 to15-footer, though, just snuck in.

'At 17, Luke's shot finished in the semi, but Sergio hit an unbelievable shot, again to a foot, and we were given it. At 18, Sergio found the fairway, but Tiger hit a great drive. Luke played a rescue club. He started it just right of the flag, but it was drifting towards the water a little. It just stayed out. Furyk was next, and he hit the most unorthodox shot you'll ever see. It was in the water from the start. That was it.'

The absorbing afternoon session again produced a 2½–1½ result in Europe's favour, giving the home side a 5–3 advantage. The chants of '*Olé, olé, olé, olé*' in the tented village got even louder.

Woosnam said that night, when he announced his eight for the Saturday fourballs, that if things went according to his plan, he would again give everyone a game.

When the draw was announced, it showed Karlsson and Casey again taking on Cink and Henry. Karlsson and his caddie Gareth Lord had had an interesting little interlude the previous day. But they weren't on a spying mission, insists Lord:

'We went out and supported the team in the afternoon. But I had six friends over from American college, two of them pros, and they were in the [US] PGA tent. Robert and I went over to them for about half an hour. It was quite bizarre. Obviously the pros knew who Robert was. We were sitting there with a load of Americans . . . we got some strange looks. "What are these two guys doing with them?" Some people found it quite worrying. But we were only there for a chat with my friends, not for any ulterior motives.

'Our Saturday match was pretty similar to Friday's, to be honest. The noise walking to the first tee was incredible. I'll never forget it as long as I live.

'This time Casey was the more dominant partner, he was fantastic. Robert played well, just didn't hole as many putts, that's all.

'Henry looked as though he could win it for them. He finished three, three, five. Robert and Paul did their best. They were one-up, and Casey made a four on 16. Robert had a chance of a four. But Henry hit a fantastic rescue club to ten to 12 feet and holed it. Then, on 17, he stiffed it. We were one-down.

'Then Robert just missed the fairway on 18. Casey hit the fairway and then hit a three-wood into the green. It was a lot of club, but he had to make sure he got there. He just cut it in – an awesome shot. Henry hit the green, but long, about 60 feet away. The pin was at the front, severely downhill. Henry rolled it about 12 to 15 feet past. Casey rolled his about four feet past. Henry then misses. Casey holes out. You could see from their faces, it was another wound for the Americans.'

Casey's caddie Connelly says he saw similarities in the match to 2004, when his man and Howell crucially turned the match at Oakland Hills:

'Paul had had to sit out Friday afternoon, but all credit to Woosie for giving everyone a game on the first day. Everyone then had a point.

'It was Paul who saved us losing on Saturday. On 18, he hit in a beautifully flighted three-wood. He had too much club, and he had to cut it back into the wind. It finished pin-high, 18 feet. It was a smelly putt – slick, downhill, massive swing right-to-left. It just slid past the hole. But he made that clutch-putt, just like he'd done in 2004.

'That was huge, because it took the momentum away from America. Just as they were thinking of making the first point of the day – and, actually, only their second full point of the week – and getting back at us, they'd had it snatched from them. Maybe it wasn't quite as important as Oakland Hills, but it did stop the Americans in their tracks.'

Olazábal and García then extended Phil Mickelson and Chris DiMarco's forgettable Ryder Cup without much trouble, says García's caddie Murray:

'You never have an easy match, but this was our easiest. DiMarco wasn't playing great. I'm sure Phil is a hard guy to play with under those circumstances, but they didn't gel all that well.

'Not much happened early on, but come the eighth hole, Ollie made an unbelievable putt for birdie to take us two-up. Then Sergio hit an amazing six-iron to the ninth hole and sank a 12-footer. Three-up. On ten, Ollie made a putt in front of DiMarco, which is the name of the game in match play. That's what Ollie and Sergio kept on doing to the guys.

'At the 14th, Phil made a two, but DiMarco's body language walking down the 12th, 13th and 14th made me think we'd already won the match. On the 16th, Sergio hit a five-wood into the left-hand bunker and hit it out to a foot.'

Olazábal's caddie Phil Morbey had had another chat:

'It was a bit like Seve and José of old. I thought they'd be good in fourballs, but I talked to Woosie and said, "I don't think you can possibly play José in the foursomes. He could play well for 16 holes and then hit two destructive shots and lose the match." He said, "Yeah. No problem."'

That was another of America's much-vaunted Presidents Cup duos overcome again. Darren Clarke and Lee Westwood then paired up once more to try to outdo the top twosome: Woods and Furyk. Defeat again for Woods would surely have a telling effect on the visitors. Clarke's caddie Foster had to tell his caddying teammate John Scotchie Graham not to get carried away:

'It's never over against Woods and Furyk. Lee had just holed a good putt on the 14th to put us four-up, and as we were walking off the tee, Scotchie, Lee's caddie, turns to me and says, "Eh, Billy man. That's a greeat scalp for us todee." I said, "John, Sod off! All right, we're four-up with four to play, but there's nothing won here yet, pal. There's a lot of hard work to go yet. Shut it!"

'Of course, Furyk hit a four-iron on 15 to about 12 feet and holed it for birdie. Then, at the next hole, Furyk and Woods have both hit to eight feet in three. Darren's got 121 yards to the flag; he hits a little wedge, just off the back of the green. I'm thinking, "That's us going down 17." I'm looking over at Scotchie, wanting to strangle him, saying, "You big mouth, Scotchie!"

'Then, Darren chips in.

'It was quite a nice lie, but it was absolutely lashing it down. We'd been working hard to stop him chipping with a lob-wedge all the time. He'd started chipping with a sand-wedge more. This time he left the lob-wedge in the bag and picked out the sand-wedge. I thought it was going to stick on the edge of the hole, but it just dropped in – for a famous victory.'

The fourth match featured Stenson and Harrington. While the crowd were almost willing local man Harrington to chalk up his first point, it didn't happen, although it provided plenty of excitement. One of the American rookies proved to be a thorn in Europe's side, as Stenson's caddie Berry reports:

'Every time we looked like getting a hole back, Zach Johnson followed us in. But it was really the one game that excited me, because I always thought we were going to pull it back. Harrington chipped in on 15, but then Johnson followed him in. Then we birdied 16, and on 17 we were in a reasonable position, so you thought it could still be saved. Then Zach chipped in. It was all over.

'Johnson was phenomenal, especially as it was his first Ryder Cup. I think he made seven birdies. Every time he was asked a question, he answered it. He was brilliant. It stands in my mind most, because it seemed to have more atmosphere and more excitement than the other games, even though we lost.'

Europe's tails were well up, though, and, remarkably, they again won the session 2½–1½, to move 7½–4½ points ahead.

García and Donald, the latter even more perplexed at missing another game, were first out in the afternoon. They were drawn against Mickelson again, but the then world number two had a new partner in Toms. The switch made the match more difficult for Europe, says García's caddie Murray:

'This was a tough match. Not much happened early on, but then Phil and David hit in the water off the seventh tee to give us an advantage. Toms, though, then hit a good putt on 12, and we messed up 13.

'Luke rifled it down the fairway at 15 – a huge tee-shot under pressure. The opponents went in the water again. That levelled it up. It needed something special to separate them. Sergio came up with it.

'At 16, Sergio hit it right off the tee, and it wasn't the easiest of lay-ups for Luke. He hit into the wood chip and mud. You never know how the ball's going to come out from a lie like that. It took two of us to put the divot back! It was a magnificent shot by Sergio, pitched about pin-high and spun five metres short. Luke made the putt. What a putt that was.

'The best part of the 16th was that you had to walk past the crowd to get to the green, and the noise when we walked past was deafening, but when Luke made that putt the hairs on my arms stood up.

'The 17th is such a tough tee-shot. Luke once again rifled it straight down the middle. It was just an eight-iron on for Sergio. That was it again.'

At lunch on Saturday, a certain large Scotsman had been champing at the bit. However, Colin Montgomerie was soon striding to the first tee, again partnering Lee Westwood for the foursomes. This time Chad Campbell and Vaughn Taylor were the opposition, which presented only half a mystery to Montgomerie's caddie McLean:

'We weren't expecting to be rested for the morning fourballs. We got up there and watched the team tee off at 8 o'clock. Monty was disappointed. I think he wanted to play all five. Not one of our guys wants to be told he's rested. They are all up for it now, but the way Woosie's got it organised, he's got to pull out somebody. Everybody played twice on the first two days, and that was a momentous decision by Woosie. Everything was working in his favour. Not one of our guys was really playing badly. If somebody was mistiming it a bit, they had a partner who was playing really well. They all got pulled through.

'We didn't know much about Vaughn Taylor, but we knew Chad Campbell was a very steady player. He's a down-the-fairway man – a good distance. He's an on-the-green man and a good putter. Just what you need for foursomes. It was Vaughn Taylor who played really well, though, and he putted very well. I was thinking, he might be the sort of guy you don't want to draw in the singles.

'Lee and Monty fed off each other. They were joking with the crowds. You could almost imagine you weren't at a Ryder Cup. It could have been a practice round somewhere. They always seemed to be up, which obviously helps. But it was a such strange partnership. Lee had never played with Monty before Friday, but it worked.

'The whole side was finding momentum, and we were one-up with two to go. Then we hit a clumsy chip on 17, and Lee just missed the putt. That was all-square.

'They were really focused on 18. Lee hit an incredible drive, then Monty hit a three-wood. It was 255 yards to the pin, and Monty carried 250, leaving a left-to-righter for Lee and the eagle chance. It was an awesome shot in by Monty, one of the best of the week. The opposition are on as well but a long, long way away, maybe 100 feet. Lee's sitting about 12 to 15 feet away. I thought we had two chances to win the match. They could three-putt and Lee and Monty two-putt, or they could two-putt and Lee hole his. Blow me, though, if Chad Campbell doesn't hit an unbelievably good putt; it almost goes in the hole. The putt's conceded. Now Lee still has a chance to win it. Lee hits a good putt, but it just stays up on the left side, doesn't break like the pair of them have read it. So it's a halved match. A good half.'

One of the defining moments of the 2006 Ryder Cup happened in the next match, Casey and Howell versus Cink and Johnson. It happened at the 14th, where Casey celebrated an historic hole in one. Before that, though, Casey's caddie Connelly found that the first tee was pretty special, too:

'When we were going to the first tee, Micky Doran, Howler's caddie, said to me, "Let's see if we can get a reaction." We walked onto the tee – the reaction was almost frightening. We were just carrying the bags onto the tee, and it was like being on the centre-spot of a 60,000-seater stadium.

'There was plenty more noise to come, though. At the 14th, it was pretty deafening. What a fantastic occasion – a hole in one at a Ryder Cup? A hole in one is always a bit special, but in the Ryder Cup!

'I think Mr Howell clubbed him. It was a perfect four-iron for him, but he wanted to verify it was exactly right. I don't recall what Ian said, but for us, the numbers added up to a perfect four-iron. We were not trying to carry it up to the flagstick, just trying to put it onto the green somewhere. Being five-up, you don't want to do anything silly.

'He hit it with a little draw. It looks good. It hits the green and rolls on. Absolutely deadweight, it drops in.'

It was the fifth hole in one in Ryder Cups, the fifth by a European. The first was in 1973 at Muirfield by Peter Butler. The others are documented in this book – Nick Faldo in 1993, and Howard Clark and Costantino Rocca in 1995.

This one was special, though. It was the first ace to finish a match. On another historical note, there was also the first technical hole in one as the players agreed on a half, thus ending proceedings.

Connelly celebrated, then pulled himself together, remembering his duty:

'I lost it. I went for Paul, but David was embracing him. I turned to Micky, and we hugged each other, jumping around like madmen.

'David offered them the half! They took it, of course. Hole halved in one. Game finished.

'Someone mentioned, "What about the ball?" I looked up and suddenly realised it was 223 yards away. So I sprinted down there, over the bridge, with the crowd getting noisier and noisier as it all sank in. I didn't have a tee-peg on me, so I went over to one of the match officials and got one. I fixed the pitch-mark, tapped it down. I took the ball out of the hole, said "Thank you very much" to it, kissed it and put it in my pocket. That was my moment. Paul's got the ball now, though. I got a thank you for retrieving it. That was my reward.

'Up to the 14th, though, David and Paul gelled so well. David will gell with anybody; he's such a lovely guy. And there was such a calmness about Paul – the whole week, but especially when he was playing with David.'

If that was a spectacular end for one section of the crowd, then behind there was to be more disappointment for a large bulk of spectators naturally following Harrington and McGinley. Their match ended on the 16th, with Woods and Furyk finally getting back into their stride, as McGinley's caddie Reynolds recounts:

'Tiger had played poorly in the morning with Furyk. He wasn't going to play badly again. We got to within only one-down at 15, but then Jim holed a raker across the green; Paul missed a 15-footer for birdie. That was pretty much the end of the game.'

In a quite extraordinary feat, not only in playing but in statistics, Europe had again won the session 2½–1½. That took them into the singles draw on Saturday night 10–6 ahead. That was exactly the same lead as Europe had had at Brookline. Woosnam was quick to point out, 'No mistakes now, boys. Remember how good the Americans are at singles.'

Now came the guessing, and the second-guessing, and the third-, fourth and fifth-guessing by the captains. Lehman had to get back level very quickly if his team were not to founder. Like Ben Crenshaw in 1999 at Brookline, Lehman said he had 'a feeling' that it was not all over. But it was.

First out was to be Montgomerie. No surprise. He was looking to maintain his unbeaten record in singles. His caddie McLean reveals, though, that his man had a slight fear that record might be under threat if Lehman did as everyone expected him to:

'Woosie reckons Monty is a good leader, so he puts him out first. Whoever's going out first, you've got to think they'll be playing Tiger. So Monty was thinking there's his record on one hand and on the other there's Tiger! When the draw comes out, it's David Toms who we've drawn. David's a great player, a nice lad, but Monty's beaten him before. It's going to be tough. But it's almost a sigh of relief when you know you're not playing Tiger – I don't care who you are.'

A tumultuous reception greeted Montgomerie at the first tee, and he responded, walking over to the stand to thank the spectators for their support. Then, as McLean says, the only thing on Monty's mind was winning:

'It was pouring with rain, but Monty got an unbelievable welcome on the first tee. He said that really, really settled him down. He was so relieved it was time to get on with it. I had no fears. Every round he played, he got better and better. He was driving well, putting well. You know David Toms is going to give you a match whether he's playing good, bad or indifferent, he's such a steady player. That's just the way it turned out.

'Monty got straight into his stride. He birdied the third and fourth. Then there were hiccups by them both. The conditions were not great, though.

'We get to the 18th, and it's still not decided. Monty's one-up. We have a 240-yard carry. You don't want to plop it in the water and just give it away. So I told him to maybe keep it out on the right. He just flushes it. He carries it 255 yards. It's easily on the green, but because I'd said keep it a wee bit on the right, he did, and he found the sand.

'He had such an awkward bunker shot – around 35 yards, heading towards the water. He hit such an unbelievable bunker shot. He knocks it just a wee bit left, maybe seven or eight feet. But it has a bit of bend in it. It's not far off the same distance as Oakland Hills, but with seven or eight inches of borrow on it.

'David's on and hits a good putt up to four feet. But he's got maybe even more bend on his – certainly not a given.

'It's all down to Monty's putt, though. He hits such a great stroke: "Thanks, David." He then said to me, "Thank goodness that's all over! We did well again. Thanks." It was an emotional drain. It all flooded out of him.

'It was so important to get that first point on the board. But, to be honest, the guys behind us were performing beautifully. It was all blue. That had given Monty confidence at the top. He can feel that even if something goes wrong with his game, the guys behind are all performing.'

Before Montgomerie had added his point, however, the first one of the singles went to America. Sergio García, with a 100 per cent record from four matches, was looking to be the first European to go nap. With Stewart Cink seemingly able to do no wrong, though, García was to be disappointed, as his caddie Murray explains:

'Sergio didn't really play too badly, apart from messing up the sixth and seventh holes. Cink started birdie-birdie. He parred the third and then went birdie-birdie again, making putts from everywhere. He's aptly named!

'We made a silly bogey on six from just left of the green. He missed a pretty straightforward putt, the sort of putt he hadn't been missing all week. Then, on seven, he tried to get a little bit clever with a front pin, and he hit it too soft, into the water. That put us five-down – tough to get back.

'Stewart was in the water at eight. Woosie came to speak to Sergio at the eighth green. It wasn't that Sergio wasn't trying, it was more for support.

'Ten I was a little bit shocked about. Stewart hooked his tee-shot up against the out-of-bounds fence. As far as I've ever known, you don't get relief from it. But when we asked the referee, he said, "It's a local rule." He got a free drop. I couldn't believe it. Cink managed to make a par, which was big at that stage. We didn't get a hole back.

'Sergio was pretty rattled. But he had been for a time. Cink played so slowly. The referee was really pushing us to go along, but Sergio was not the culprit. I think that irritated Sergio a little bit.

'He came back with a great birdie on 11 to go only three-down, but 12, the par-three, was a real killer. Sergio hit his to five metres or so, a good tee-shot with the pin up against the water. Stewart hits down the hill from way right – the ball's going like a train. It's going three, four, yards past. But it hits the back of the hole and goes in! We're four-down again.

'The next hole was pretty much the same again. Stewart makes it from the front edge, another 25-footer. Sergio follows him in to stay four-down. He just didn't seem to be able to do anything about it. I mean, Sergio chips in on 14 and Stewart makes a bomb on top of it.

'That was it. Losing the sixth and seventh was crucial, though. There's a huge difference when you've got momentum on your side.'

After Montgomerie cancelled out America's point, Casey then enhanced Europe's position. Everyone was counting down. The board was blue. So were the Americans. Casey just added to the ecstatic chants of "*Olé, olé, olé, olé*" now ringing all around The K Club. Casey's caddie Connelly knew his man would shoulder his responsibility against one of America's deadliest, Jim Furyk:

'Everybody was saying the Americans had to go top-heavy if they were going to get anything out of the match. But Woosie had such strength in depth he could put anybody anywhere.

'Paul pretty much knew he was going to go somewhere near the top. We drew Furyk – and what a match they offered up.

'Jim didn't get off to the best of starts. Paul played really solidly, holed a few putts early on but gave Jim a hole with a three-putt on the fourth, which he wasn't too happy about. But then he got it back by holing a lovely 15-footer on five, to go three-up.

'You can never underestimate Jim Furyk, but from then on Paul played just so solidly – he didn't make any mistakes. We were four-up, then Jim got it back to three on 11. We get to 14 again. It's a four-iron again, of course. He hit a good tee-shot and then holed a 25-footer. At that time you're thinking, "Maybe we've got him." Jim then rolls in on top of him.

'At 15, the two of them hit fantastic shots, but they both missed their putts and only made pars. Paul has a 12-footer for birdie on the 16th and thinks if Jim misses his eagle chance then he closes out the game. Jim holes his eagle putt, so we're now only two-up.

'At the 17th, Paul thinks, "Nothing silly." He hits a three-wood, then a sand-iron to about 20 feet. He rolled it in. That was it. A highly competitive round of golf by both of them. Jim had had three birdies and an eagle on the back nine. But it was over.

'Paul was on fire the whole week. He'd carried his confidence and his game over from the week before. He had everything under control. All I had to do, really, was carry the bag. In the two years I've worked for him, I've never seen him so much in control of his game.

'I walked up to the 16th to see the matches finish. The sound there was just unbelievable. The crowd was definitely our 13th man.'

Connelly was just in time to see Woods overcome Karlsson. It had not been an easy passage for the world number one. As his caddie Lord, says, it was vital it should not be a formality. But losing was furthest from Karlsson's mind when he found out who he would be playing:

'I knew Robert would be three to seven [in the singles matches]. Nobody told me this, but you get a feeling. They're not going to leave a rookie down the bottom, just in case it all goes wrong, and he's not going to be first or second. But he was playing so well, I could see him going in at number three, something like that.

'Of course, he's number four. Then you get the pairings sheet, and T. Woods is number four! I spoke to Robert on the phone. The players had had a team meeting. He said, "Have you seen who we've got?" I said, "Yes," wondering what his reaction was going to be. He said, "You know, I can't wait." You almost got the feeling that if you were going to play Tiger, it was a good time to play him. And even if you're going to get beaten, you could give it your best shot.

'Whatever happens, you don't just want to give a point away early. It was important to have blue on the board, of course, but if there was going to be red on there, not matches that were a lost cause. Monty and Harrington had said it was important to be shown to be fighting for the point. That was certainly so in Robert's case. Tiger's point was never guaranteed until the end.

'Robert won the first but was basically one-down virtually all the day. They were trading birdies here and there, but he never seemed to be able to get any better than one-down.'

After an extraordinary gaffe by Woods' caddie Steve Williams at the seventh, though, there was just a sniff of a chance for Karlsson – if Woods was going to rely heavily on his nine-iron. With shades of 1987, when Ben Crenshaw had to play a good deal of his match against Eamonn Darcy without a putter, Woods was without one of his favourite weapons. Williams had dropped it into the water at the seventh. Mind you, a putter is a putter and absolutely vital, whereas Woods can fashion pitch shots with almost anything, as Lord explains:

'We didn't know! We saw Steve just trying to dip the towel in the lake. But apparently he supported himself, while he was crouching down, with the nine-iron, slipped and dropped it in.

'As we went from the seventh to the eighth, I heard Steve say to the rules official, "No, seriously, I have just dropped the nine-iron in the water. Can you get the guy with the rake to try to rake it out?"

'Robert was unaware, though. Halfway down eight I said, "He has actually dropped his nine-iron in the water." Robert said, "You're joking." I said, "No, I promise you, it's gone." So he went and had a look in Woods' bag. Sure enough, there was no nine-iron. We had a good laugh about it. I said to Robert, "You'll have to think about that when you're telling me off for getting a club wrong. At least I've never lost one!" He said, "You're right. And it's not as if it's not an important event." Woods just seemed to be laughing about it, though. He didn't seem in the slightest bit flustered. There was just one shot when he would have needed it. That was on 13. He just went down the grip of an eight-iron – and hit that close. So no harm done. If he had lost and needed it more, it might not have been quite so funny to Tiger, though.

'Robert was one-down after 13, one-down after 14, so it could have gone either way. On those finishing holes at The K Club, anything can happen.

'At the 16th, we were in perfect position but two-down. Woods was in the left rough, which was very wet. I thought he would lay up. I was mistaken. He took an almighty swipe at his ball, hooked it 20 yards around a tree and over water – right into the middle of the green. I was 20 yards away from him and couldn't see the ball at all. From the loft of his club, I thought he must be laying up, and I said so to Robert. But then you could see it wasn't a lay-up swing. We hit a five-iron from five or six yards in front of him. We had 213 yards, something like that. He must have had about 220. He hit an awesome shot, simple as that. He hit a six-iron! To 15 to 20 feet.

'That meant we were right up against it. Robert didn't have to stiff it, but we knew we had to get a three at least to carry on. Robert hit a poor shot into the water, pushed it a touch. That was the end.

'All right, Woods won – but it certainly didn't feel like failure, being beaten 3 and 2, because there was nothing in it. I don't think many people expected Robert to beat Tiger. But it was important not to give it away, and he definitely didn't do that.'

While Karlsson was trying to stall Woods, Howell was producing a spectacular run behind. Four birdies in quick succession from the 11th – a chip-in, two 25-footers and a 12-footer – closed the door shut on Wetterich. That decided when and where the Ryder Cup was first to be retained and then won.

Luke Donald was the player who made sure Europe could not lose by sinking the five-footer that won him his match against Chad Campbell at the 17th.

This match was a repeat of Oakland Hills but not a repeat as far as the result went. Donald got his own back on Campbell, as his brother Christian recalls:

'We had to have a chuckle when we saw the draw. Luke was after revenge. I suppose you shouldn't call it revenge, but he really wanted to make up for being beaten in singles the last time, when he didn't play well.

'At first everything was very even, but I just felt Luke was in total charge, and I was just waiting for him to get in front. Sure enough, he was three-up after 13. But you know it's still not over. Luke's a good one for keeping his feet on the ground.

'He had a great up and down from the bunker at 14 and played some great shots to keep in front. Even then, at 17, when Campbell had gone in the water, he said to me, "I've got to stay focused because he might pitch in."

'Of course, he didn't, and it was a great moment for us when Luke holed out to close down the match.'

Donald could actually claim to have won it for Europe, because behind him Stenson could not lose and a half was guaranteed. There were other cast-iron points on the way for Europe. In theory, that would have taken Europe over the winning line. However, as players can get disqualified in Ryder Cups, theory does not count. Because Stenson's match was still just alive when Donald's putt went in for the 14th point, that has to stand as the retention of the Cup and not victory.

As Christian Donald says:

'There are different ways of looking at it. There were people that were dormie when Luke won his match. I think it comes down to the way TV show it. It's fine if they stick to the same rules all the time.'

That victory, which ensured 14 points for Europe were already in the bag, happened at 1545 hours. Within a minute, the Cup was won by Stenson on the 15th. Over to his caddie Berry:

'When the draw came out, I thought we might be in a decisive position. You had to think that [matches] six, seven, eight or nine, if things went to plan, would probably win the Ryder Cup. Guys like Harrington said, "Try not to look at the board. Just focus on your own job."

'The moment I saw the draw, I felt he could win. The course is set up for long-hitters. I presume Henrik was brimming with confidence when he saw the draw, just because of knowing the way the course was set up. Vaughn Taylor on somewhere like Valderrama, a tougher course where long-hitting isn't so much of a premium, would probably be a fair match.

'Henrik did hit big, as well. At the first, he flew the trap straight into the hazard. He hit 310 yards in the air, obviously fairly pumped up. That was with a three-wood!

'Vaughn birdied the first and hung on until the sixth, where he was in the water in two, and Henrik knocked it to 12 feet. At the next, Henrik hit right off the tee but found the green with a nine-iron and holed the putt to go one-up.

'Vaughn then three-putted nine, and Henrik got up and down from the trap on ten. On 11, a severe dog-leg, Henrik pulled it a bit. When we got down there, his ball was sitting on the crossing point, only 85 metres from the flag. He had a sand-iron in his hand. Vaughn's having to hit driver then seven-iron.

'On the 12th, Henrik hit a decent shot to 25 feet, and Vaughn three-putted from 50 feet. On the 13th, another dog-leg, Henrik did the trick again, pulling it round the corner. I think Vaughn was hitting a six or a seven-iron in, and Henrik had 78 metres to the flag. Henrik's advantage was massive.

'Henrik was four-up on 15. He hit past the hole, but then luckily holed a five-footer. I say luckily because he felt his game was creaking a bit. He told me, "I'm glad I didn't have to go up 16." I don't think he was creaking that much, though.'

'Olé, olé, olé, olé' greeted a bemused Stenson's act by thousands of fans who knew exactly what the state of the match was. The Swede reverted to being – a Swede. Even as it dawned on him what he had done, he took it pragmatically, as Berry says:

'To be honest, Henrik was just in the zone, trying to get the game over with and win. We'd kind of figured something was going to happen around there. They said that was the putt that had won the Ryder Cup. But he felt it was a big team effort, and he'd just done his job.

'I think if it had been a closer finish in the whole match, like with McGinley [in 2002], it would have been an incredible feeling, but Henrik had just gone out there to get his job done. He'd done it in a professional manner, being 100 per cent focused.

'Peter Baker said, "Get on the buggy," and he drove us up to 16. As we were approaching, he said, "Get your ears ready for this one." The crowd were going ballistic. The atmosphere was electric. When you see the older players break down in tears, it dawns on you how big an event it is. When Henrik saw how it affected other people, he realised, after he'd done his job, how big a deal it was.'

Ten minutes after Stenson put the rubber-stamp on another European victory, at 1556, Clarke sealed his win against Johnson on the 16th. The crowd hardly cared that the script had been ruined by Howell and Stenson. Their hero had come up trumps again. Clarke, who admitted afterwards that he could hardly keep his eye off the scoreboard as he hoped against hope he could seal the winning point – without doubt, for Heather – received an ovation unprecedented in a week in which the clapometer had disappeared off the scale.

Caddie Foster was relaxed about how things were going generally but could not drop his guard, dearly hoping it would be his great friend who provided the finishing touch:

'In my eight previous Ryder Cups, it's always been tense after nine holes on a Sunday. You're always looking at the board, thinking, "Do this, do that." In this Ryder Cup, I could go down the back nine and enjoy it, knowing we were going to win it.

'But when Darren holed a putt on 12 from 80 feet, or whatever it was, it was a case of trying to keep the emotions in check. You had to stop seeing the victory line. That's when you can go wrong. You have to stay focused on what you're doing.'

A putt that crucially just brushed the hole on the 15th and failed to do the honourable thing ended Clarke's chance of getting in before Stenson. However, neither he nor Foster knew how important that miss was. From what Foster says, it was a miracle that Clarke got the ball anywhere near the cup:

'People won't realise, but Darren was struggling with his emotions over the last three or four holes. That's what really impressed me about him. When he holed the 80-footer on 12, I tried to get him to take a minute on the 13th tee to really try and regroup and focus on what he was doing. He blocked it right in the rough and made bogey. Then he hit a great three-iron on 14 to about 12 feet but missed the putt. On 15, he hit a great drive – a decent shot on the green. The putt nearly went in.

'I said to Darren on the 16th tee that it could be down to him. Going down 16, he mentioned to me he was really struggling with his emotions. I tried to wrestle with him to keep focused on what he was doing.

'At about that time, unbeknown to us, Howler had holed three or four tramliners to win his match. All I knew was that Donald was probably going to win his match, in front of us, and Stenson, behind, was just about home. But it still looked like Darren was going to retain it or win it.

'It was, well, not unfortunate, because you want to get it in the bag as quick as you can, but it would have been so fantastic for Darren to do it. There was a big cheer when he was playing his third shot on the 16th, though, and he said, "We've won it, haven't we?" I said, "Well, not necessarily. We might have only retained it." I said to him, "It's going to be your destiny to win this."

'As it happened, it all went bang, bang, bang. We had three points in about two minutes.

'I think Darren would be the first to say "It's a team game", and you just want to win it. Holing the winning putt at the Ryder Cup, maybe because it was Ireland and maybe because of his circumstances, would have been poetic justice. But, at the end of the day, it didn't matter.

'It was very emotional when he finished, though. He did brilliantly, absolutely brilliantly, under the circumstances. He has my utmost respect for what he did.'

Captain Woosnam hugged Clarke; the *olés* rang out. However, matches still had to be finished off.

Another of The K Club's favourites, McGinley, went on to the 18th with Henry. The finale to the match proved to be a debacle, with a streaker defying the security cordon to run on to the green before the match was over. McGinley had already decided what he was going to do, though. He made the magnanimous gesture that could have saved Lehman's men suffering America's greatest defeat, 19–9.

McGinley's caddie Darren Reynolds, saw it this way:

'Paul always had his nose in front, and on the last he had a 35-feet putt for eagle. Henry had hit a great drive but just caught the lip of the bunker. He chipped out sideways and then had at least 22 feet for birdie. It was downhill with a bit of break – a tricky putt.

'I felt we'd won it. I was standing at the back of the green. As soon as Paul had hit his putt, I thought it was going to come up way short, but he had obviously read the green well. He left it stiff. Henry gave him the putt.

'I remember taking my bib off and putting something in the bag, ready to watch J.J. take his putt to try to halve the match. I thought he only had a thin chance of making it. And, anyway, I thought Paul deserved to win the game the way he'd played. Then, all hell let loose.

'I turned around, and from the back of me a streaker's run across the green. Paul had started walking towards J.J. He gave him the putt. The game was halved.

'At the time, I don't think Paul knew it could have been a record win. He got caught up in it all. It doesn't matter. A few people were upset because they might have had bets on scores. But I think Paul will be remembered for it. The game was so close all along, maybe the half was a fair result. It was a lovely sporting touch.'

Soon after, Harrington's disappointing week ended with defeat to Verplank. Wild-card Verplank, though, did rewrite the Ryder Cup records. He became the first American to officially hole in one in a Ryder Cup, getting the ball in the cup at the 14th and repeating Casey's feat of the previous day. Now we'd had a hole in one on paper by Cink and a hole in one on turf by Verplank.

Not long after Harrington's defeat, Olazábal's cup ranneth over as he marked his return to the Ryder Cup ranks by overcoming the hapless Mickelson. The Spaniard's victory was a significant act for his caddie Morbey:

'We were on the 14th when Europe did it. But I never won a singles match with Woosie. We had three halves. So I was up for beating Mickelson.

'On 14, Mickelson missed the green but chipped down to about four feet. José's stiff. He says to me, "Shall I give him the putt?" I said, "No chance." He said, "Well, he gave me one a similar length." I said, "No it wasn't, it was a bit shorter than that. And you know I haven't won a Ryder Cup singles. Don't give him it." He said, "I don't know." I said, "It's up to you." He gave him it.

'So now I'm thinking, "I hope we win this match," because if we only get a half, I'm going to be pig sick. But it worked out, and I must admit to being really emotional about it. I had a bit of a cry on his shoulder on the 17th green. It meant a lot to me.'

It was left to Mickelson's equally ineffectual pairs partner DiMarco to close the proceedings as he went into the water twice at 18 to concede to Westwood, who made it a remarkable 8½ points out of 10 in the last two Ryder Cups.

Then it was time for everyone to celebrate. Woosnam, downing a Guinness in one go and smothered in champagne, took his bows. His closing ceremony speech, which had caused him more sleepless nights than any of his pairings, may not have been exactly Churchillian – 'This has been the greatest week in history' – but his team and his decisions had been poetry in motion.

Foster, the most experienced European Ryder Cup caddie of them all, sums up Woosnam's leadership:

'Woosie was very unfairly criticised in the press. The lads couldn't understand it. They really wanted to go out there and do it for him.'

The celebrations, as one would expect in Ireland, went on until the late hours of the morning. There was one rather unexpected moment during the riot of delight, as Stenson's caddie Berry reveals:

'Mick Doran, Howler's caddie, had the brainwave of going over to the tented village. We were in team colours. Everybody in the tented village was clapping us . . . trays of beers appeared. We had a singsong with the crowd. There was an Abba cover band.

'They told us, "Bring some players down," so we went back. Howler said he'd go and so did Padraig. When they arrived, they were actually mobbed – it was almost dangerous. They were then bodysurfing over the crowd. Harrington got up on the stage. He'd lost a shoe.

'Ronan Keating got on the pool table and sang a couple of songs. Then Phil Mickelson appeared from nowhere. He jumped on the table and said, "This tune has been going through my head for the last few days. I wonder if you can help me with it? *Olé, olé, olé, olé* . . ."'